ANIMAL METROPOLIS

Canadian History and Environment Series

Alan MacEachern, Series Editor

ISSN 1925-3702 (Print) ISSN 1925-3710 (Online)

The Canadian History & Environment series brings together scholars from across the academy and beyond to explore the relationships between people and nature in Canada's past.

ALAN MACEACHERN, FOUNDING DIRECTOR
NiCHE: Network in Canadian History & Environment
Nouvelle initiative canadienne en histoire de l'environnement
http://niche-canada.org

UNIVERSITY OF CALGARY
Press

EDITED BY

Joanna Dean, Darcy Ingram, and Christabelle Sethna

ANIMAL METROPOLIS

HISTORIES OF HUMAN-ANIMAL RELATIONS IN URBAN CANADA

Canadian History and Environment Series

ISSN 1925-3702 (Print) ISSN 1925-3710 (Online)

University of Calgary Press
2500 University Drive NW
Calgary, Alberta
Canada T2N 1N4
press.ucalgary.ca

LIBRARY AND ARCHIVES CANADA CATALOGUING IN PUBLICATION

Animal metropolis : histories of human-animal relations in urban Canada
/ edited by Joanna Dean, Darcy Ingram, and Christabelle Sethna.

(Canadian history and environment series ; 8)
Includes index.
Issued in print and electronic formats.
ISBN 978-1-55238-864-8 (softcover).—ISBN 978-1-55238-865-5 (open access PDF).—
ISBN 978-1-55238-866-2 (PDF).—ISBN 978-1-55238-867-9 (EPUB).—
ISBN 978-1-55238-868-6 (Kindle)

1. Human-animal relationships—Canada. 2. Human-animal relationships—
Canada--History. 3. Urban animals—Canada. 4. Urban animals—Canada—
History. 5. Animals and civilization—Canada. 6. Animals and civilization—
Canada—History. 7. Urban ecology (Sociology)—Canada. 8. Urban ecology
(Sociology)—Canada—History. 9. Urban wildlife management—Canada.
10. Urban wildlife management—Canada—History. I. Dean, Joanna, editor
II. Ingram, Darcy, editor III. Sethna, Christabelle Laura, 1961-, editor
IV. Series: Canadian history and environment series ; 8

QL85.A546 2017   304.2'70971   C2017-900231-7
                                             C2017-900232-5

The University of Calgary Press acknowledges the support of the Government of Alberta through the Alberta Media Fund for our publications. We acknowledge the financial support of the Government of Canada. We acknowledge the financial support of the Canada Council for the Arts for our publishing program.

This book has been published with the help of a grant from the Canadian Federation for the Humanities and Social Sciences, through the Awards to Scholarly Publications Program, using funds provided by the Social Sciences and Humanities Research Council of Canada.

Alberta Government   Canada   Canada Council for the Arts / Conseil des Arts du Canada   NICHE

Front cover art: "Sovereign" by Mary Anne Barkhouse
Copyediting by Peter Enman
Cover design, page design, and typesetting by Melina Cusano

Table of Contents

Illustrations

Tables

Acknowledgments

This collection evolved from a series of discussions between the editors that stretch back to 2012 and to a growing network of scholars in the Ottawa area who share an interest in that broad and increasingly complex trend known as "the animal turn." As we reflect on the collection five years later, we find ourselves indebted to many animals, both human and non-human. For the focus on urban animals as the collection's unifying theme we are grateful to Heather Hillsburg, then a doctoral student in the Institute of Feminist and Gender Studies at the University of Ottawa. For making the project possible, we thank the contributors, each of whom worked hard to make the collection come together. Sean Kheraj kindly agreed to write the epilogue. At the University of Calgary Press, series editor Alan MacEachern received us enthusiastically, and Peter Enman, our first contact at UCalgary Press, did everything possible to expedite the volume through the evaluation process, and later shepherded us through the final stages of copy editing. Melina Cusano did a marvelous job of reproducing the image we selected for the cover. Feedback from two external evaluators strengthened the collection along the way. At Carleton University, the opportunity to organize the 2014 Annual Shannon Lectures in History on Beastly Histories enabled us to develop further our knowledge of the field and to benefit from the ideas and advice of many scholars. In addition to the Shannon Lectures, we have honed our ideas for the collection over the years through discussions at various conferences including the Canadian Historical Association's annual conference and the Quelques arpents de neige environmental history workshop.

Joanna would like to thank her student, Amanda Sauermann, whose enthusiasm for the topic of animals inspired the development of a course in animal history in 2009; Carleton's History Department for supporting the course; and the many curious students in that course's various iterations. Thanks also to many human friends who taught her to see the horse differently and to Wyatt, Paddy, and Ruby for reinforcing those lessons. She also thanks her co-editors for their generosity at times when family demands diminished her availability for this project.

Darcy would like to thank Kathleen again and again for living through another project; their children Raine and Liam for their refreshing insights into animals and their occasional insistence that living through another project wasn't what they wanted to do that day; and Piper, their Jack Russell Terrier, who tries with enormous enthusiasm to translate her nineteenth-century foxhunting skills into a viable career opportunity in various corners of twenty-first-century Canada and who insists on reminding them that holes are for digging, cars are for chasing, and a rancid bag of garbage is *irresistible*.

Christabelle thanks her mother, Gloria Sethna, and her aunts for nurturing a love of animals from early childhood onward. Alongside the encouragement of Darcy and Joanna, Stephen Brown, Vicki Burke, Fatima Correia, June Larkin, Marina Morrow, Isabelle Perreault, and Brian Ray were very supportive of her foray into this area of study. She is grateful to Saucy, Cinderella, Friday, and Beauregard, who showed her that loving a pet is an honourable endeavour.

The process of working together on this project has given to it a level of richness and diversity that none of the editors could have accomplished alone. Working consensually, each took part in a long list of tasks: contacting authors; maintaining records of correspondence; arranging meetings; communicating with the press; writing proposals; responding to the external reviewers; compiling manuscript materials; fielding chapters and assisting authors with revisions; preparing the index; designing the cover; and developing an increasingly nuanced understanding of human-non-human animal relations in Canada that we have attempted to deliver. This division of labour ebbed, flowed, and overlapped over time, and the editors are listed in alphabetical order to respect the individual and collective labour behind the project.

Introduction: *Canamalia Urbanis*

DARCY INGRAM, CHRISTABELLE SETHNA,
AND JOANNA DEAN

Beaver. Moose. Caribou. Think "animal" in Canada, and these and other iconic creatures of the Canadian wilderness are sure to come first to mind. Yet Canada has become increasingly urban since Confederation, to the extent that more than 80 per cent of the population today is considered to live in an urban setting.[1] That urban identity has shaped profoundly the material and cultural contexts of human/nonhuman animal relations. Emblematic megafauna aside, urban Canadians are far more likely to encounter in their daily lives anything from dogs and cats to deer, squirrels, raccoons, sparrows, foxes, rabbits, skunks, pigeons, mice, cockroaches, crows, and coyotes, not to mention the many species encountered primarily in the form of consumer goods. It is to that dimension of the urban experience, in all its barking, mooing, neighing, chirping, chewing, digging, foraging, performing, and more perfunctory forms, that we turn.

The essays in this collection explore the intersection of a variety of human and nonhuman animals as they negotiate their way in Canada's urban spaces. They bring together a diverse range of perspectives, including but not limited to insights derived from animal, environmental, cultural, critical animal, posthumanist, and species studies; social analyses of class, race, and gender; and the colonial and imperial contexts of human–animal relations. Balancing this diversity is their common appreciation of the temporal dimensions of that relationship. In its own way, each essay contributes to the topic a sense of historical contingency derived from a wide range of methodological innovations, empirical sources, and ethical considerations. In doing so, they collectively push forward from a historiography that features nonhuman animals largely as objects within human-centred inquiries to one that considers at various levels of complexity their eclectic contacts, exchanges, and cohabitation with human animals. In the process, the essays underscore the blurry nature of the spatial boundaries – urban, rural, wilderness – so often employed as interpretive frameworks for human–animal interaction. In short, they indicate clearly the impact of Canada's urban identity on how Canadians think about and experience their nonhuman counterparts, and in turn on the many animals that live in, move through, or otherwise encounter urban Canada.

One might still be inclined to ask: Do we need a collection on the history of human–animal relations devoted specifically to *urban* Canada? It is a good question, and one that is best answered with its counterpart in mind: Given Canada's longstanding urban identity and the degree to which the question of the urban animal looms large in so many other contexts, why don't we already have one? We will respond by concentrating on three interrelated topics: the evolution of what is now referred to as the "animal turn" in the humanities and social sciences; the peculiar trajectory of Canadian historiography relative to nonhuman animals; and finally the support that Canadian history offers with regard to the evolving human–animal nexus – in other words, why the history of urban animals in Canada matters.

Taking Stock of the Animal Turn

In many ways, the animal turn is something of a *return*. Indeed, phrases such as taking "stock" (a word long linked to domesticated animals or "livestock"), or for that matter a term so central as "capital" (also long associated with agricultural animals including cattle, forms of mobile property or "chattel" that were traded on the "stock exchange") in the world today are among the many animal metaphors that fill our daily lives. The ghostly animal presence that lingers in so much of our language is but one indication that, as Claude Levi-Strauss observed, nonhuman animals have long been central to how we human animals think about ourselves and the world around us.[2] Urbanization, industrialization, the rise of science and technology, human population growth, and other developments associated with the course of modernity over the past few centuries have by no means severed those links. But that package has changed the ways in which human animals think about and treat nonhuman animals. In 1977, John Berger wrote a foundational essay entitled "Why Look at Animals?" in which he argues that the past two centuries witnessed a process "by which every tradition which has previously mediated between man [*sic*] and nature was broken." The nonhuman animal, whose life had run parallel to that of the human, had disappeared in the nineteenth century only to be replaced by a proliferation of empty simulacra: animal imagery, animal toys, dependent pets, and, most tellingly, the zoo. Berger mourned: "Everywhere animals disappear. In zoos they constitute the living monument to their own disappearance." Most significantly, nonhuman animals no longer return our gaze: "the look between animal and man . . . has been extinguished."[3] Berger's essay spoke to a generation's alienation from capitalist modernity. His sense of despair at the loss of profound human–animal connections has resonated in the decades since, reaching a wide public audience and providing inspiration for a divergent literature. In one echo of those sentiments, Akira Lippit describes technological representation as a "vast mausoleum for animal being."[4] Support for Berger's argument can be found in the underlying emptiness of representations of nonhuman animals that have appeared in many major urban settings, from street art such as the sculptures of cows in Calgary and the moose of Toronto to Louise Bourgeois's magnificent egg-filled spider "Maman" that towers over tourists in all its high art Freudian glory at the National Gallery of Canada in Ottawa.[5] The explosion in animal representations is even embodied in totemic fashion by one particular species of human animal – the urban hipster – whose earrings, t-shirts, sweatshirts, stockings, bags, and brooches routinely feature animal imagery.

But Berger's nostalgia for a pre-industrial past has come under criticism on a number of grounds. Historians have demonstrated that the nineteenth-century city was, in fact, teeming with animal life. As Hilda Kean points out, rather than disappearing from the everyday, "animals continued to play significant roles in the domestic life of city dwellers both as objects of affection and as the mainstay of the transportation system."[6] We might be better to accept, as does Scott Miltenberger referring to nineteenth-century New York, that cities are "anthrozootic" because they are "defined and made by interspecies relationships."[7] Many of these urban animals were not holdovers from a traditional past; they were creatures remade for industrial capitalism. The heavy draft horse was a "living machine." Harnessed to the efficiencies of the streetcar and the inflexible might of the iron horse, its muscular animal body was shaped by the human need for power.[8] Jason Hribal identifies these animals as members of the industrial working class, simultaneously powering the capitalist machine while resisting its oppression.[9] The urban equine population peaked in the late nineteenth century, with horses urbanizing even faster than humans did. Contra Berger, nonhuman animals did not disappear with modernity. Rather, they played a key role in shaping the city in the nineteenth century, and many animals remained in the city well into the twentieth century.

Nor was the animal image always an empty simulacrum. In a critical reading of Berger's essay, film historian Jonathan Burt points out that although the real animal continues to live and suffer in modernity, the animal image has been transformational in moving humans to mitigate that suffering.[10] Writing shortly after Berger, historians James Turner and Keith Thomas interpreted the radical shift in our relations with the natural and animal worlds at the beginning of the nineteenth century very differently. They observed growing emotional engagement with the nonhuman animal and the rise of animal welfare movements. Soon after, Coral Lansbury and Kathleen Kete fleshed out the class and gender dimensions of this transition with their histories of antivivisection movements in London and Paris.[11] And in her important work, *The Animal Estate: The English and Other Creatures in the Victorian Age*, Harriet Ritvo allowed for the central place of animals in the British imaginary.[12] These historians demonstrated that not only were nonhuman animals continuing to live in the city but they also continued to live in meaningful ways in the minds of humans.[13]

Since then, a growing literature on the animal turn has begun to chart the place of animals in modernity. In fields ranging from law, geography, philosophy, science, environmental studies, anthropology, and bioethics to linguistics, literary criticism, ecofeminism, postcolonialism, and cultural studies, and in areas of animal studies devoted specifically to the subject, we see ongoing efforts to grapple with the complexities of human–animal relations. Journals like *Anthrozoos, Society and Animals, Journal for Critical Animal Studies*, the listserv H-Animal, and book series such as Harriet Ritvo's "Animals, History, Culture," and Nigel Rothfels's "Animalibus: Of Animals and Cultures," have provided a multidisciplinary forum for scholars. Among the Canadian scholars to participate in these developments, Robert Preece, in *Animals and Nature: Cultural Myths, Cultural Realities*, debunks the notion that Western approaches to nonhuman animals are pejorative, claiming that they are complex and wide-ranging historically. Janice Fiamengo's important collection, *Other Selves: Animals in the Canadian Literary Imagination*, delves into themes such as the barrier between humans and animals, animals as metaphors, and the ethical treatment of animals. Nicole Shukin provides a sharp critique of global capitalism by insisting that "the discourses and technologies of biopower hinge on the species divide," which she observes in the "rendering" of animals, in the double meaning of their representation and their slaughter. The provocative *Queer Ecologies: Sex, Nature, Politics, Desire*, edited by Catriona Mortimer-Sandilands and Bruce Erickson, encourages us to interrogate the many gendered, raced, classed, and sexualized meanings of "nature" in order to queer natural environments and their human and nonhuman animal populations and communities.[14] From this perspective, some scholars have moved to challenge transphobic and heteronormative narratives, as in Myra Hird and Christabelle Sethna's work on transspecies organisms and sex education pedagogies, respectively.[15] To follow the pertinent observations of Julie Livingston and Jasbir K. Puar, "studies of mutually constituted, co-emergent, cohabitative interspecies encounters, riddled with hierarchies of power and the complexity of incommensurate ontologies," are "all the rage."[16]

Animal studies can be conceived in terms of two intersecting strands. One strand of thought converges on the cultural power of the visual or symbolic animal and probes the boundaries between human and nonhuman species, destabilizing notions of human exceptionalism. Here, scholars of various perspectives have turned to contemplate the complexities of human identity, the paradoxes of modernity, and questions of power relations. Donna Haraway highlights the breakdown and inchoate merger by the late twentieth century of formerly assured categories human/animal/technology and the political implications that lie therein.[17] This posthumanist approach points toward an acceptance of multiplicity, liminality, ambiguity, and hybridity. Cary Wolfe observes that posthumanism represents not so much anti-humanism as an opportunity "to rethink our taken-for-granted modes of human experience, including the normal perceptual modes and affective states of *Homo sapiens* itself, by recontextualizing them in terms of the entire sensorium of other living beings."[18] Rosi Braidotti's contribution is the "bioegalitarian turn," which advocates that we relate to animals as animals ourselves, a practice that "spells the end of the familiar, asymmetrical relation to animals, which was saturated with fantasies, emotions, and desires and framed by power relations."[19] The venerable Jacques Derrida has also intervened, asking perplexing questions about his human self-identity when gazed upon by his cat.[20] As Kari Weil summarizes: "It has become clear that the idea of 'the animal' – instinctive beings with presumably no access to language, texts, or abstract thinking – has functioned as an unexamined foundation on which the idea of the human and hence the humanities have been built. It has also become clear, primarily through advances in a range of scientific studies of animal language, culture, and morality, that this exclusion has taken place on false grounds."[21]

A second strand emphasizes the sentient animal, with its susceptibility to pain, and raises ethical and political concerns about the human treatment of nonhuman animals. Drawing on the work of philosophers Peter Singer and Tom Regan, this strand encourages a political response to animal suffering. Published in 1975, Singer's *Animal Liberation* embedded ethics regarding nonhuman animals in the language and politics of the late 1960s and the 1970s via its discussion of speciesism. Regan's *The Case for Animal Rights* further advanced that movement's philosophical framework in both intellectual and activist circles, giving it a critical and in some cases radical edge with regard to the challenges it posed to mainstream attitudes and practices.[22] Later, Martha Nussbaum suggested that a "capabilities approach" is an appropriate basis for animal rights, a position with which Singer disagrees.[23] One wing of activist academics, loosely gathered under the name Critical Animal Studies, has taken aim at the intellectual abstractions of animal studies scholars who, in their eyes, further exploit the nonhuman. John Sorenson's recent collection *Critical Animal Studies: Thinking the Unthinkable* calls for a more politically engaged response to animal suffering. Particularly interesting here is the chapter by David Nibert, which links, in the tradition of Upton Sinclair's 1906 novel *The Jungle*, today's urban slaughterhouses to the abuse of animals, women, and poor immigrants.[24] In the same volume, Carol J. Adams decries the war on compassion. Like other ecofeminists who support vegetarianism or veganism, she proposes that the suffering of nonhuman animals reflects the androcentric domination of nature and is related to men's sexual oppression of women. She calls elsewhere for a feminist tradition of care, rather than a rights-based position on animal cruelty.[25]

These developments have been informed by parallel shifts in the sciences, most obviously with regard to the study of animals, but also in response to the ethical questions raised by humans' growing technological capacities. Well-entrenched beliefs about what it means to be human have likewise been disturbed, and considerable effort has gone into undermining the status of the individual white, adult, male human as the yardstick by which the living world is measured – a unit that has long been central to the humanist ethos. Biologists in particular have brought through their studies of nonhuman animals – initially primates, then cetaceans and elephants – a growing recognition that boundaries separating human and nonhuman animals were artificial constructions. At the same time, developments in areas ranging from medicine to artificial intelligence have challenged what it means to be human, and indeed what it means to be an animal of any sort. Convinced by initiatives including those of Peter Singer, Paola Cavalieri, and the Great Ape Project, various governments have even moved in the direction of conferring basic legal rights on nonhuman hominids because of their many similarities to humans (of course, privileging those animals bearing the closest resemblance to humans is perhaps simply an extension of humanism).[26]

Some of the most interesting endeavours in animal studies go beyond the recognition of the almost-human, rational, agentic, and sentient animal to a consideration of formations, networks, and assemblages. Bruno Latour's Actor Network Theory (ANT), especially in the hands of geographers Chris Philo and Chris Wilbert, provides a way of understanding action to be agential, networked, and inclusive of nonhuman animals.[27] ANT, however, grants agency not only to fully sentient beings but also to less sentient beings such as bacteria as well as to objects such as microscopes. In David Gary Shaw's application of ANT to cavalry, the stirrup and the bit are as much a part of the network as the horse, or the rider.[28] Gilles Deleuze and Felix Guatarri destabilize liberal notions of human agency and subjecthood, but their approach offers the more richly metaphorical concepts of assemblage, entanglement and becoming-animal.[29]

Historians have been slow to join this discussion, but they are well positioned to further it within animal studies, especially with regard to the critical question of agency in nonhuman animals.[30] Contributors to the 2013 animal issue of *History and Theory* found agency to be a unifying thread; Vinciane Despret draws mainly upon Deleuzian assemblage, or as she prefers, *agencement*, to move that individuals (animals, humans, and even plants) become companion-agents, just as Chris Pearson describes militarized dogs as agents working in alliance with humans.[31] Their work gives historical substance to Donna Haraway's notion of intra active becoming.[32] In fact, the extension of agency to other species, and the inclusion of a much more diverse set of actors, may have repercussions for the practice of history, as when humans move from centre stage when whales shape our actions, or when wolves and lions consume us, rather than we them.[33] Observing change over time also provides evidence for agential action, and historical records provide evidence for the transmission of something we might call culture within communities and across generations of nonhuman animals. In the same issue, Mahesh Rangarajan suggests that the history of India's Gir Forest lions is evidence of cultural memory because their behaviour around humans suggests lessons learned and passed on from one generation of lions to the next. Jon Coleman makes a similar case for North American wolves, and Ryan Tucker Jones contends that whales in the North Pacific have been co-crafters of human history.[34] Historians have also contributed to discussions of the agency of individual animals, especially working animals: Eric Baratay's horses, Jason Hribal's circus animals, and Erica Fudge's dairy cows resist, and through their resistance they demonstrate their own subjectivity, will, and interests.[35]

Urban Animals and the Development of Canadian Historiography

In the last decade or so there has been a veritable flood of international literature on the urban history of the nonhuman animal. Scholars such as Nigel Rothfels, Louise Robbins, Susan Nance, Takashi Ito, and Katherine C. Grier consider animal as spectacle in urban zoos and circuses, and in so doing have tracked the sale and display of animals considered exotic along circuits of imperial power in which cities figured as hubs of transnational exchanges.[36] Peter Atkins's collection *Animal Cities: Beastly Urban Histories* puts forward contributions on cities including London, Paris, Edinburgh, and Melbourne. Philip Howells similarly deals with dog stealing in London, and Hannah Velten re-animalizes the same city in her *Beastly London: A History of Animals in the City*. Catherine McNeur asks readers to tour nineteenth-century New York, a city teeming with horse manure, livestock waste, offal, and garbage, all of which delighted the roaming pigs, which lower-class Irish and German immigrants and African Americans treasured as a food source. There, attempts to sweep pigs off the street in a misguided attempt to corral a cholera epidemic led to battles between city police and poor women responsible for pig keeping. Andrea Gaynor studies the regulation of chickens in Australian suburbia, while Alice Hovorka reminds us that chickens continue to outnumber people in African cities like Gaborone.[37] Some of the most intriguing investigations are of nonhuman animals that inhabit urban spaces via their own agency, among them a wide variety of birds and mammals, along with larger species that routinely roam the urban periphery, including deer, coyotes, and in some cases bears and cougars. Karen Brown's research on rabies in southern Africa reminds us of the intimacies of human and canine bodies in impoverished urban settings. Etienne Benson tracks the urbanization of the gray squirrel in North America.[38] Dawn Biehler's *Pests in the City* describes the urban ecologies that supported the proliferation of flies, bedbugs, cockroaches, and rats, and a 2015 special issue of *Environment and History* presents a similar focus on "creepy crawlies." In yet another instance, a collection on "trash species" edited by Kelsi Nagy and Phillip David Johnson II explores why humans designate certain nonhuman animals as offensive, useless, or unworthy urban co-habitants.[39]

By contrast, nonhuman animals, urban or otherwise, have not received the kind of critical attention in Canadian historical circles that they have in other contexts since the 1970s. This omission is startling because at the most elementary level animals have played a considerable role in determining the location of many settlements of both Indigenous and European origin. "Ottawa," Canada's capital, is derived from an Algonquin term associated with the fur trade, while "Toronto" is most likely a Mohawk reference to weirs used to catch fish.[40] In similar fashion, nonhuman animal names are stamped on towns and cities across the country, from Moose Jaw to Whitehorse to Rivière-du-Loup. Conversely,

Winnie the Pooh, A.A. Milne's much-loved children's storybook bear, was inspired by First World War Canadian Lt. Harry Colebourn's purchase of a cub he named after his hometown of Winnipeg.[41] Even Canadian urban history itself has yet to consider seriously the nonhuman animal as urban resident. This field tends more toward the inert entities of landscape and water, and to corresponding movements for planning and sanitation.[42] Yet a majority of households in the country now shelter a pet that serves many familial roles, including as a facilitator of human-to-human relationships in urban spaces like dog parks. Moreover, evidence of a burgeoning "pet economy" fuelled by the commodification of "dominance-affection-love" relations between humans and their companion animals is everywhere in cities, from pet clothing boutiques to grooming services to veterinary clinics to no-kill shelters.[43]

Ironically, the relative scarcity of animals in Canadian historical analyses of the past four decades is perhaps best understood as a response to a curious historiography in which animals were for a long time abundant. Consider, for example, the basics – the kind of stuff that makes it into introductory textbooks on Canadian history. Be it in the context of furs, fish, or farms, the relationship of nonhuman animals to Indigenous peoples and European colonizers has long been central to Canada's national metanarrative – so much so that when Harold Innis set out in the 1930s to write his now-classic economic analysis *The Fur Trade in Canada*, he decided to devote his first chapter to the beaver. "It is impossible," he insisted in that book's first paragraph, "to understand the characteristic developments of the trade or of Canadian history without some knowledge of its life and habits."[44] That text soon joined other economic analyses of Canadian staples, many of which also happened to be animals, whether the species that comprise the nation's fisheries, the cattle and other livestock that underpinned economic growth in the continent's interior, or the bison that were pushed to the point of extinction. Popular history too was replete with animals. From wolves to bears to mosquitoes, wildlife figured frequently in often-romanticized historical narratives of life, war, travel, and adventure in colonial North America. Underlying this narrative was the *terra nullius* ideology of white settlers that set the stage for the physical, biological, and cultural genocide of Indigenous peoples and paved the way for the development of Euro-North American colonial cities with their racialized spatial configurations, reducing the Indigenous to the status of the savage and the animal.[45]

Within academic circles, economic history gave way to political history during the 1950s, but the two perspectives overlapped considerably, and it was not until the 1960s, and really the 1970s, that there appeared some profound challenges to this trajectory. Informed by the rise of movements for social justice manifest in social, labour, women's, and urban history, the subsequent generation of Canadian historians began to diverge considerably from their predecessors. In their efforts to address Canada's past in ways that brought forward marginalized voices while emphasizing agency and contingency, they levelled many important challenges. At the same time, however, they abandoned many seemingly cliché topics from the past – one of which was animals, which had for so long been connected in academic circles to economic history and to what was now being labelled scathingly as geographical determinism. In this way, the process of politicizing history from below went only so far. The accompanying geographical shift away from the rural and frontier world in favour of urban and industrial analyses that fitted so well with contemporary historical analysis in the United States and Europe pushed animals even further outside the scope of Canadian historiography. As a result, animals were left behind as nationalist, historical, literary, and emblematic clichés.

The first concerted efforts to bring animals back into Canadian history came from environmental historians. Ironically, for a nation in which the environment figures so prominently, environmental history itself took a long time to develop, hampered as it was by the same reluctance to engage critically in a topic that was so heavily associated with prominent figures like Harold Innis, Arthur Lower, and Donald Creighton, and that fitted so poorly with the theories and frameworks of a discipline that had in other respects become increasingly diverse in its efforts to tackle everything from race, ethnicity, and gender to culture, postcolonialism, and power. That began to change in the 1990s with the publication of a growing number of environment-oriented studies that dealt wholly or in part with animals. Inspired by a well-developed environmental historiography in the United States, Canadian historiography caught up quickly, and wildlife in particular now figures prominently in the work of environmental historians including Bill Parenteau, Tina Loo, John Sandlos, George Colpitts, Darin Kinsey, Darcy Ingram, and Neil S. Forkey.[46] In the process, environmental historians established links to anthropologists, with whom they and other Canadian historians already shared common interest in the experiences of Aboriginal peoples. A focus on Indigenous scientific knowledge has charted alternative ways of understanding the natural world, with the potential to destabilize more dominant assumptions about animal agency and sentience.[47] They also found common ground with historical geographers, many of whom have long been attuned to the kind of spatial issues with which environmental historians were grappling. Mindful to varying degrees of the urban, most of this work nevertheless takes as its immediate focus issues associated more closely with the bread and butter of environmental history, for which Canada offers no end of opportunities – namely wildlife, wilderness, parks, conservation, preservation, and resource development and management. Discussions of animal sentience, subjectivity, or agency are seldom addressed, and concepts such as animal network theory, assemblage, or posthumanism are even more rare. In this way, environmental history too has only just begun to address the animal turn and with it the place of urban animals in Canadian history.[48]

Why the History of Urban Animals in Canada Matters

The laggard pace at which this kind of scholarship moves in Canada is at odds with the voracious appetite for tales about urban nonhuman animals as evidenced in traditional and social media. The *Toronto Star* marked the end of 2015 with a year's worth of "quirky animal stories" that ranged from the opening of the city's first cat café to the birth of panda cubs at the zoo to a runaway peacock called Henley. Each story contained embedded links to photos and footage that came primarily from ordinary individuals who are able increasingly to capture urban wildlife in action with pocket-sized audiovisual technology and post their observations rapidly to the internet.[49] This high level of interest may or may not support the thesis that we experience "nature deficit disorder," meaning human alienation from direct contact with natural world.[50] Direct contact has its joys and sorrows. A feel-good newspaper article about the sighting of an Arctic snowy owl perched on a neighbour's roof in the city of Niagara Falls, a live camera feed of hibernating grizzly bears in Vancouver's Grouse Mountain, or a special hashtag for a photo of a red fox napping inside an

Ottawa public bus that circulates in the twittersphere, are often trumped by deadly outcomes for both animals and humans.[51] At one end of the spectrum, a Toronto man is convicted for bashing three baby raccoons with a shovel because they were apparently destroying his garden. At the other, a woman is sentenced to jail for stopping her car on a busy highway south of Montreal to assist a family of ducklings, resulting in the death of two people who crashed into her vehicle.[52]

These examples point to the complexities of urban interspecies coexistence and to the difficulties of distinguishing the urban from the suburban, the rural, and the wild in the context of sprawling cities, reforestation, and wildlife protection. Clearly, as Annabelle Sabloff's important ethnographic study of animal–human encounters in Toronto reminds us, cities do not stand apart from nature. In fact, the city and its environs "teem with animal and vegetable presence" in parks, conservation areas, hiking trails, ravines, gardens, petting zoos, pet cemeteries, animal sanctuaries, and game farms.[53] Herein the nonhuman may have a clear advantage over the human. A host of studies have shown that various creatures living in urban and periurban areas have "colonized" these spaces in large numbers and in great concentrations by modifying or adapting their behaviours. Thanks to this process of "synurbanization," some species become nocturnal hunters, some breed earlier, and some vocalize at louder pitches.[54]

In acknowledgement of what the city and nature can offer each other, the Museum of Vancouver held an exhibit in 2014 entitled "Re-Wilding the City." The exhibit reinforced the notion that while defining nature is an impossible task, demarcating the urban in a Canadian context is not a simple matter either. From 1971 to 2011 Statistics Canada identified an urban area as having a population of at least 1,000 and a density of 400 or more people per square kilometre. Anything outside that was considered rural.[55] This definition excludes a northern centre as important as Churchill, Manitoba. Moreover, small centres can be urban in their consequences for animal–human relations. The 1960s relocation of Indigenous people in the north into settlements is a case in point. The relocation disrupted long-established relationships between the Inuit and sled dogs. Dogs had been essential draft animals and companions to Inuit hunters for 800 years, but with the appearance of the snowmobile, dogs were no longer essential, and in the close quarters of the settlements, unchained dogs became a menace to children. The Royal Canadian Mounted Police killed hundreds of these dogs. The experience came to stand for all that the Inuit had lost in modernity.[56] The relationship of dog and Inuit in the consolidated settlements was an urban one, in which the dog became a leashed dependent rather than a partner in the hunt.

For the purposes of this collection, the urban may be defined broadly to encompass the ways human and nonhuman animals coexist in industrial modernity, rather than simply in terms of human population density and spatial geographical boundaries. Significantly, cultural geographers have insisted over the last two decades upon a "transspecies urban theory" in order to account for the impact of cities on the natural environment, the interaction of human and nonhuman animals, and wildlife ecology.[57] In ways that echo many of Berger's sentiments, Jennifer Wolch calls for a "Zoöpolis" that is predicated upon our ability "to renaturalize cities and invite the animals back in – and in the process re-enchant the city."[58] In similar fashion, Chris Philo proposes that the nonhuman animal has been subjected to "human chauvinism." He suggests that "animals should be seen as enmeshed in complex power relations with human communities, and in the process enduring geographies which are imposed upon them 'from without' but which they may also inadvertently influence 'from within.'"[59] Finally, one can glean much in this regard from William Cronon's lauded *Nature's Metropolis: Chicago and the Great West*, which reminds us that the city is embedded in the country, and functions by virtue of its connections with the natural world around it. Arguing that "a rural landscape which omits the city and an urban landscape which omits the country are radically incomplete as portraits of their shared world," Cronon brings the smells and noise of pigs into the heart of Chicago.[60]

A considerable amount of Canadian urban historiography has long been concerned with metropolitanism in ways comparable to that of Cronon, most notably in the metropole-hinterland approach associated with historians such as Harold Innis and given further purchase through J.M.S. Careless.[61] Through such perspectives Canadian urban history is, unsurprisingly, one of nodes, networks, and communication lines flung across vast distances, connecting metropolitan centres in patterns that only sometimes responded to the lay of the land. Animals were pulled along these lines, as beaver, cod, and later beef and hogs, were shipped to the metropole, in turn shaping cities in their passage. During the 1970s and 1980s, social historians contributed new perspectives on animals as they scrutinized the fabric of the everyday urban and industrial life. In "Pigs, Cows and Boarders: Non-Wage Forms of Survival Among Montreal Families, 1861–91," Bettina Bradbury notes the economic importance of domesticated animals to working-class families in that city and the impacts of an evolving regulatory context that saw such animals pushed out of the city for reasons including health, sanitation, public order, aesthetics, and propriety. Margaret Heap similarly underscores the centrality of horses in Montreal in her review of the impact of the carter's strike of 1864, while Peter DeLottinville's account of Montreal's Charles Mc-Kiernan, better known as "Joe Beef," highlights among other things the nineteenth-century tavern keeper's menagerie featuring monkeys, parrots, various wild cats, bears, and at one point a buffalo. Approaching the urban from a history of medicine perspective, J.T.H. Connor examines vivisection in Canadian cities in the context of biomedical research during the nineteenth century.[62]

More recently, a number of Canadian historians have acknowledged the importance of nonhuman animals in the urban environment in ways that speak to current trends within the animal turn. We have already mentioned the ways in which Canadian environmental historians have brought animals back into focus. In Stéphane Castonguay and Michèle Dagenais's edited collection on the environmental history of Montreal (which draws heavily on the metropolitan-hinterland framework), Darcy Ingram describes the foxes, horses, and hounds that formed the fox hunt on the periphery of that city. At other points he deals with the rise of the animal welfare movement in urban Canada in response to the abuse of horses and other animals. Sean Kheraj has examined animals in Stanley Park, Vancouver's beloved public green space, and described nineteenth-century Toronto and Winnipeg as "multi-species" cities teeming with dogs, cows, horses, sheep, pigs, and chickens. Reflecting yet another approach, Lianne McTavish and Jingjing Zheng have highlighted the successful campaign in the 1950s to rid rural and urban Alberta of rats, and Richard Mackie observes similar efforts with regard to cougars on Vancouver Island in British Columbia.[63] An overlooked arena is Canadian food studies, in which animals and animal products are literally consumed. Ester Reiter has shown that histories of urbanization, precarious labour, and fast food restaurants serving cheap meat-filled hamburgers are mutually constitutive, while meat and dairy figure prominently in Ian

Mosby's account of food rationing and its relationship to gender and urban economies during the Second World War.[64]

At the microscopic level, bacteria and other biota fit into histories of pestilence in humans and animals, notably those involved in the decimation of Indigenous populations after contact with white settlers, cholera outbreaks in the nineteenth century, influenza in the twentieth, and, more currently, a range of deadly flu strains, many of which are noteworthy for their ability to cross species boundaries. Several of these pandemics, which flourish in the compact living conditions that make up the urban environment, are still associated with racialized migrants of the human and nonhuman kind.[65] Canadian historians have made some significant contributions to this literature, as evidenced by Cole Harris and Paul Hackett on First Nations' experiences of smallpox and other diseases, Magda Fahrni and Esyllt W. Jones on influenza in Montreal and Winnipeg, Liza Piper on polio in Chesterfield Inlet, and Geoffrey Bilson's oeuvre on cholera, which has much to say about Canadian cities as vectors for the spread of this bacteria-based illness.[66] Still, the focus moves typically from these tiny life forms directly to humans, with relatively little consideration of the place of animals in these and other outbreaks. Here, Patricia Thornton and Sherry Olson's work on the interconnection of horses and flies as vectors for the spread of bacteria and an explanation for shifting rates of infant mortality in Montreal provides a striking illustration of the potential such a perspective offers.[67]

Animal Metropolis at a Glance

Much more remains to be done as if we are to consider the possibilities in Canada of histories that de-centre the human animal. Given Canada's status as a nation on the front lines of modernity, occupying half a continent on which the many and diverse inhabitants of urban, rural, and wild alternately collide and cohabit in ways few other countries can imagine, the possibilities to do so are endless. *Animal Metropolis* gestures in this direction.

The ten essays that comprise this collection are organized in roughly chronological order. They didn't have to be. Each chapter stands alone, and complementary themes invite various groupings. Readers interested in an analysis of animals as spectacle, for example, might begin with

Christabelle Sethna's discussion of the racialized journey of Jumbo, which links the zoo and circus elephant who was killed in St. Thomas, Ontario, to histories of slavery and freakery. From there, they would find it valuable to proceed to William Knight's analysis of the fish on display at the Dominion Fisheries Museum in Ottawa, Ontario; to Kristoffer Archibald's assessment of polar bear tourism in Churchill, Manitoba; and finally to Jason Colby's exploration of orca captivity in Vancouver, British Columbia. In doing so, they would discover through Sethna and Archibald a sense of the ways in which inhabitants of cities in economic decline have turned to nonhuman animals to revive their fortunes via tourism – in Sethna's case through the memory of Jumbo, in Archibald's through a complex web of interests reflected in Churchill's Indigenous and non-Indigenous populations. They would also find links between Colby's treatment of live, captive, captivating whales for entertainment purposes and Knight's consideration of live and dead fish culture exhibits held supposedly in the name of science.

Other readers might wish to begin by considering the place of nonhuman animal labour in the city. A photo essay by Rachel Poliquin on the history of beavers in Stanley Park honours this iconic species as the ultimate hard-working comeback animal. In spite of a fur trade that virtually wiped out the creature, the beaver surfaces again and again, labouring diligently in its own interests in ways that defy human management of the built environment. Sherry Olson's coverage of horses in industrializing Montreal redirects our focus away from humans and toward the horse as key not only to the labour demands of the nineteenth-century city but also to its spatial layout. As Olson notes, the draft horse had a profound impact on urban design, the traces of which reveal a city built much closer to human and animal scale than it would be following the advent of electric passenger cars and the automobile. From a strikingly different angle, Joanna Dean demonstrates the unforeseen consequences of animal labour through the circulation of tetanus bacilli from horse to human. From here, she describes a new form of animal labour in which horses' living bodies were used in the production of tetanus antitoxin. Carla Hustak's investigation of dairy cows echoes some of these concerns in the connection of milk production to issues of sanitation, municipal regulation, and urban reform at the turn of the century, the implications of which stretch far beyond her specific example of Hamilton, Ontario. Yet another approach can be found in Darcy Ingram's interest in the care of labouring animals in the nineteenth-century city vis-à-vis the evolution of Canada's animal welfare movement. In following this route through the text, readers will also meet via Ingram and Hustak some careful consideration of the intersection of animals and gender; in Ingram's case it concerns the marginalization of women in Canada's animal welfare movement while in Hustak's account it emerges with regard to the intersection of cows, infants, and motherhood. They will also no doubt find that the question of animal labour underpins both Sethna's and Colby's explorations of animal spectacle and performance.

An equally profitable approach would be to consider those chapters that speak to the history of medicine and public health. Hustak's inquiry on sanitation and Dean's discussion of tetanus carry us to George Colpitts' research on efforts to eliminate the spread of rabies to human and human animals in and around Banff, Alberta, during the 1950s. As a unique and compelling deconstruction of multiple binaries, be it wild versus domestic nonhuman animals; the city versus the periphery; or urban versus wilderness space, Colpitts' chapter manages in one way or another to complement much of what takes shape in *Animal Metropolis*. Perhaps most importantly, it invites us to consider the degree to which the environment and environmental history perspectives figure in these chapters, be it in Olson's careful attention to the built environment of Montreal, Archibald and Colby's awareness of the intersection of urban and wilderness identities in Vancouver and Churchill, or Ingram's attention to the impact of agricultural and industrial economics on an animal welfare movement that drew much of its energy from the urban world.

We hope this edited collection functions as a stepping stone for Canadian scholars to participate in the animal turn, and that readers will come away with a sense of the vitality that characterizes this area of inquiry. No one discipline or field of study, whether environmental or social history; ecofeminism, postcolonialism, or posthumanism; or cultural or urban geography, has a lock on research into nonhuman animals or their encounters with humans. Overall, *Animal Metropolis* is rooted in the discipline of history, some of it environmental and some not. However, we are convinced that Canadian scholars from various disciplines will offer their theories, methods, and epistemologies to the animal turn, providing the grounds for the fruitful exchanges. In this way, we stand to gain a new and valuable multidisciplinary scholarship.

Notes

1   Statistics Canada, 2011 Census of Population, Population, urban and rural, by province and territory (Canada), http://www.statcan.gc.ca/tables-tableaux/sum-som/l01/cst01/demo62a-eng.htm.

2   Claude Lévi-Strauss's comment about totemic animals, "Les animaux sont bons à penser," has become a touchstone in animal studies, to the point that it is often mistranslated (most frequently as "animals are good to think with") and misinterpreted. See *Le Totémisme Aujourd'hui* (Paris: Presses Universitaires de France, 1962).

3   John Berger, "Why Look at Animals?," in *About Looking* (London: Writers and Readers, 1980), 1–26; quotations on pp. 24, 26. The essay was first published in three parts in 1977, and in Penguin Books Great Ideas series as *Why Look at Animals?* (2009).

4   Akira Mizuta Lippit, *Electric Animal: Toward a Rhetoric of Wildlife* (Minneapolis: University of Minnesota Press, 2000), 187. Film historians who have developed Berger's declensionist narrative include Gregg Mitman, *Reel Nature: America's Romance with Wildlife on Film* (Cambridge, MA: Harvard University Press, 1999), and Derek Bouse, *Wildlife Films* (Philadelphia: University of Pennsylvania Press, 2000). See also Randy Malamud, *Reading Zoos: Representations of Animals and Captivity* (New York: New York University Press, 1998).

5   "'Udderley Art' Public Art Exhibit: Where Did All the Cows Go?" *The Examiner*, 22 February 2010, http://www.examiner.com/article/udderly-art-public-art-exhibit-where-did-all-the-cows-go (accessed 19 December 2014); "Moose in the City," http://www1.toronto.ca/wps/portal/contentonly?vgnextoid=1b-9833d602943410VgnVCM10000071d60f89RCRD&vgnextchannel=4284ba2ae8b1e310VgnVCM10000071d60f89RCRD (accessed 19 December 2014); and "National Gallery of Canada: Collections." https://www.gallery.ca/en/see/collections/artwork.php?mkey=101000 (accessed 19 December 2014).

6   Hilda Kean, *Animal Rights: Political and Social Change in Britain since 1800* (London: Reaktion Books 1998), 44. See also her "Traces and Representations: Animal Pasts in London's Present," *The London Journal* 36, no. 1 (2011): 54–71.

7   Scott Miltenberger, "Viewing an Anthrozootic City: Humans, Domesticated Animals, and the Making of Nineteenth-Century New York," in Susan Nance, ed., *The Historical Animal* (Syracuse, NY: Syracuse University Press, 2015), 261–71.

8   Clay McShane and Joel A. Tarr, *The Horse in the City: Living Machines*

in the Nineteenth Century (Balti-more: Johns Hopkins University Press, 2007); Ann Norton Greene, *Horses at Work: Harnessing Power in Industrial America* (Cambridge, MA: Harvard University Press, 2008); Margaret Derry, *Horses in Society: A Story of Animal Breeding and Marketing Culture, 1800–1920* (Toronto: University of Toronto Press, 2006); Leah M. Grandy, "The Era of the Urban Horse: Saint John, New Brunswick, 1871–1901" (MA thesis, University of New Bruns-wick, 2004). See also Joanna Dean and Lucas Wilson, "Horse Power in the Modern City," in *Powering Up: A Social History of the Fuels and Energy that Created Modern Can-ada*, ed. Ruth Sandwell (Montreal: McGill-Queen's University Press, 2015).

9   Jason Hribal, "Animals Are Part of the Working Class: A Challenge to Labor History," *Labor History* 44, no. 4 (2003): 435–54, and "Animals Are Part of the Working Class, Reviewed," *borderlands* 11, no. 2 (2012): 1–34.

10   Jonathan Burt, "John Berger's 'Why Look at Animals?': A Close Reading," *Worldviews: Global Religions, Culture, Ecology* 9, no. 2 (2005): 203–18. For his arguments on the impact of the visual animal on animal welfare movements, see Burt, *Animals in Film* (London: Reaktion Books, 2002).

11   James Turner, *Reckoning with the Beast: Animals, Pain and Humanity in the Victorian Mind* (Baltimore: Johns Hopkins University Press, 1980); Keith Thomas, *Man and the Natural World: A History of the Modern Sensibility* (London: Allen Lane, 1983); Coral Lansbury, *The Old Brown Dog: Women, Workers,*

and Vivisection in Edwardian England (Madison: University of Wisconsin Press, 1985); Kathleen Kete, *The Beast in the Boudoir: Petkeeping in Nineteenth-Century Paris* (Berkeley: University of Cali-fornia Press, 1994).

12   Harriet Ritvo, *The Animal Estate: The English and Other Creatures in the Victorian Age* (Cambridge, MA: Harvard University Press, 1987)

13   Matthew Brower submits that Berger's elegy is itself a compensa-tory fantasy. Like Jonathon Burt, Matthew Brower calls for us to understand image making (in his case, wildlife photography) as a historical process that structures our relation with animals. Matthew Brower, *Developing Animals: Wild-life and Early American Photogra-phy* (Minneapolis: University of Minnesota Press, 2012), xv.

14   Robert Preece, *Animals and Nature: Cultural Myths, Cultural Realities* (Vancouver: University of British Columbia Press, 1999); Janice Fiamengo, ed., *Other Selves: Animals in the Canadian Literary Imagination* (Ottawa: University of Ottawa Press, 2007); Nicole Shukin, *Animal Capital: Rendering Life in Biopolitical Times* (Minne-apolis: University of Minnesota Press 2009), 11; Catriona Mortim-er-Sandilands and Bruce Erickson, eds., *Queer Ecologies: Sex, Nature, Politics, Desire* (Bloomington and Indianapolis: Indiana University Press, 2010).

15   See Myra J. Hird, "Animal Transex," *Australian Feminist Studies* 21, no. 49 (2006): 35–50, and Christabelle Sethna, "Animal Sex: Purity Educa-tion and the Naturalization of the

Abstinence Agenda," *Sex Education* 10, no. 3 (2010): 267–79.

16   Julie Livingston and Jasbir K. Puar, "Interspecies," *Social Text* 29, no. 1 106 (Spring 2011): 3.

17   Donna Haraway, "A Cyborg Manifesto: Science, Technology, and Socialist-Feminism in the Late Twentieth Century," *Simians, Cyborgs and Women: The Reinvention of Nature* (New York: Routledge, 1991), 149–81. See also her *Primate Visions: Gender, Race, and Nature in the World of Modern Science* (New York: Routledge, 1989).

18   Cary Wolfe, *What is Posthumanism?* (Minneapolis: University of Minnesota Press, 2009).

19   Rosi Braidotti, "Animals, Anomalies, and Inorganic Others," *PMLA* 124, no. 2 (2009): 526. See also Maneesha Deckha, "Toward a Postcolonial, Posthumanist Feminist Theory: Centralizing Race and Culture in Feminist Work on Nonhuman Animals," *Hypatia* 27, no. 3 (Summer 2012): 527–45.

20   Jacques Derrida, "The Animal that Therefore I Am," trans. David Wills, *Critical Inquiry* 28, no. 4 (2002): 369–418. Gerald L. Bruns, "Derrida's Cat (Who Am I?)," *Research in Phenomenology* 38 (2008): 404–23. For another insightful critique of animal rights see Matthew Calarco, *Thinking Through Animals* (Stanford, CA: Stanford University Press, 2015).

21   Kari Weil, "A Report on the Animal Turn," *differences: A Journal of Feminist Cultural Studies* 21, no. 2 (2010): 1–23, esp. 19.

22   Peter Singer, *Animal Liberation* (New York: New York Review, 1975). Tom Regan, *The Case for Animal Rights* (Berkeley: University of California Press, 1983).

23   Peter Singer, "A Response to Martha Nussbaum," 2002, http://www.utilitarian.net/singer/by/20021113.htm, (accessed 9 January 2016).

24   David Nibert, "Animals, Immigrants, and Profits: Slaughterhouses and the Political Economy of Oppression," in *Critical Animal Studies: Thinking the Unthinkable*, ed. John Sorenson (Toronto: Canadian Scholars Press, 2014), 3–17. See also Upton Sinclair, *The Jungle* (Tucson, AZ: Sharp Press, 2003 [1906]).

25   Carol J. Adams, "The War on Compassion," in Sorenson, *Critical Animal Studies*, 18–28. See also Josephine Donovan and Carol J. Adams, eds., *The Feminist Care Tradition in Animal Ethics: A Reader* (New York: Columbia University Press, 2007); Carol J. Adams, "Ecofeminism and the Eating of Animals," *Hypatia* 6, no. 1 (Spring 1991): 125–45; and *The Sexual Politics of Meat: A Feminist-Vegetarian Critical Theory* (New York: Continuum, 1990).

26   See Paola Cavalieri and Peter Singer, eds., *The Great Ape Project: Equality Beyond Humanity* (New York: St. Martin's Press, 1993); Paolo Cavalieri, "The Meaning of the Great Ape Project," *Politics and Animals*, 1, no. 1 (Fall 2015): 16–34. See also "Ireland May Be the Next Country to Free Animals as 'Non-Human' Persons," http://www.projetogap.org.br/en/noticia/ireland-may-next-country-free-animals-non-human-persons/ (accessed 26 January 2015).

27   Bruno Latour, *We Have Never Been Modern*, trans. Catherine Porter

(Cambridge, MA: Harvard University Press, 2001 [1991]); Chris Philo and Chris Wilbert, *Introduction to Animal Spaces, Beastly Places: New Geographies of Human-Animal Relations*, ed. Chris Philo and Chris Wilbert (London: Routledge, 2000), 1–35.

28 David Gary Shaw, "A Way with Animals," in *History and Theory* 52, no. 4, Special Issue: Does History Need Animals? (December 2013): 1–12, and " Horses and Actor-Networks: Manufacturing Travel in Later Medieval England," in *The Historical Animal*, ed. Susan Nance (Syracuse, NY: Syracuse University Press, 2015).

29 See J. Macgregor Wise, "Assemblage," in *Gilles Deleuze: Key Concepts*, 2nd ed. (Durham, UK: Acumen, 2013), 91–102, and Vinciane Despret, "From Secret Agents to Interagency," *History and Theory* 52, no. 4 (December 2013): 29–44.

30 For example, see Susan J. Pearson and Mary Weismantel, "Does the 'Animal' Exist? Toward a Theory of Social Life of Animals," in *Beastly Natures: Animals, Humans and the Study of History*, ed. Dorothee Brantz (Charlottesville: University of Virginia Press, 2010), 17–37.

31 Despret, "From Secret Agents to Interagency," ibid., 29–44; Chris Pearson, "Dogs, History and Agency," ibid., 128–45.

32 Haraway describes the co-evolution of and intimate working relationships of canine and human in *When Species Meet* (Minneapolis: University of Minnesota Press, 2007), and *The Companion Species Manifesto: Dogs, People, and Significant Otherness* (Chicago: Prickly Paradigm Press, 2003).

33 Jennifer Adams Martin argues that we might usefully move humans off stage altogether. In "When Sharks (Don't) Attack," she suggests we turn from the familiar and human-centred stories of shark attacks to consider the larger history of shark communities. Jennifer Adams Martin, "When Sharks (Don't) Attack: Wild Animal Agency in Historical Narratives," *Environmental History* 16, no. 3 (July 2011): 451–55. See also Linda Nash, "The Agency of Nature or the Nature of Agency?" *Environmental History* 10, no. 1 (January 2005): 67–69. Animal history also forces the historian to recognize the human as an embodied and material being engaged in messy and complicated ways with other such beings. As Val Plumwood observed of her own violent and intimate encounter with a crocodile, "Crocodile predation on human threatens the dualistic vision of human mastery of the planet in which we are predators but can never ourselves be prey. We may daily consume other animals in their billions, but we ourselves cannot be food for worms and certainly not meat for crocodiles." Cited in Brett L. Walker, "Animals and the Intimacy of History," *History and Theory*, 52, no. 4 (December 2013): 45–67.

34 Mahesh Rangarajan, "Animals with Rich Histories: The Case of the Lions of Gir Forest, Gujarat, India," 52, no. 4 (December 2013): 109–27. See also Jon Coleman, *Vicious: Wolves and Men in America* (New Haven, CT: Yale University Press, 2004), and Ryan Tucker Jones, "Running into Whales: The History of the North Pacific from below the Waves," *American Historical Review* 118, no. 2 (April 2013): 377.

35   Eric Baratay, *Le point de vue animal: Une autre version de l'histoire* (Paris: Seuil, 2012); Jason Hribal, *Fear of the Animal Planet: The Hidden History of Animal Resistance* (Oakland, CA: AK Press, 2013); and Erica Fudge, "Milking Other Men's Beasts," *History and Theory*, 52, no. 4 (December 2013): 13–28. Vinciane Despret presses historians to pay attention to subtler signs. She notes that we tend not to notice the agency of the working animal who actively, and willingly, collaborates: "When animals do what they know is expected of them, everything begins to look like a machine that is functioning, and their obedience looks "mechanical," a word that conveys its meaning very well." Despret, "From Secret Agents to Interagency," 43.

36   Susan Nance, *Entertaining Elephants: Animal Agency and the Business of the American Circus* (Baltimore: Johns Hopkins University Press, 2013); Nigel Rothfels, *Savages and Beasts: The Birth of the Modern Zoo* (Baltimore: Johns Hopkins University Press, 2008); Louise E. Robbins, *Elephant Slaves and Pampered Parrots: Exotic Animals in Eighteenth-Century Paris* (Baltimore: Johns Hopkins University Press, 2002); Takashi Ito, *London Zoo and the Victorians, 1828–1859* (Woodbridge, UK: Boydell and Brewer, 2014); and Katherine C. Grier, *Pets in America: A History* (Chapel Hill: University of North Carolina Press, 2006).

37   Peter Atkins, ed., *Animal Cities: Beastly Urban Histories* (Burlington, VT: Ashgate, 2012); Philip Howells, "Flush and Banditti: Dog-Stealing in Victorian London," in *Animal Spaces, Beastly Places: New Geographies of Human-Animal Relations*, ed. Chris Philo and Chris Wilbert (London: Routledge, 2000): 350–55; Hannah Velten, *Beastly London: A History of Animals in the City* (London: Reaktion Books, 2013); Catherine McNeur, *Taming Manhattan: Environmental Battles in the Antebellum City* (Cambridge, MA: Harvard University Press, 2014); "The 'Swinish Multitude': Controversies over Hogs in Antebellum New York City," *Journal of Urban History* 37, no. 5 (September 2011): 639–60; Andrea Gaynor, "Animal Agendas: Conflict over Productive Animals in Twentieth-Century Australian Cities," *Society and Animals* 15 (2007): 29–42; Alice Hovorka, "Transspecies Urban Theory: Chickens in an African city," *Cultural Geographies* 15 (2008): 119–41.

38   Etienne Benson, "The Urbanization of the Eastern Gray Squirrel," *Journal of American History* 100, no. 3 (2013): 691–710.

39   Karen Brown, *Mad Dogs and Meerkats: A History of Resurgent Rabies in Southern Africa* (Athens: Ohio University Press, 2013); Dawn Biehler, *Pests in the City: Flies, Bedbugs, Cockroaches and Rats* (Seattle: University of Washington Press, 2014); *Environment and History* 21, no. 4 (November 2015); and Kelsi Nagy and Phillip David Johnson II, eds., *Trash Animals: How We Live With Nature's Filthy, Feral, Invasive and Unwanted Species* (Minneapolis: University of Minnesota Press, 2013).

40   Alan Rayburn, *Naming Canada: Stories about Canadian Place Names* (Toronto: University of Toronto Press, 2001 [1994]), 229–37.

41   Alex Tesar, "Finding Winnie: Everyone's Favourite Bear Goes to War," *The Walrus*, November 2015, p. 25. "Winnipeg" is a Cree term for "muddy water."

42   Except for one full article on houseflies, with a paragraph on horses, the abstracts in *Urban History Review* make only very occasional reference to nonhuman animals. See Valerie Minnett and Mary-Anne Poutanen, "Swatting Flies for Health: Children and Tuberculosis in Early Twenti- eth- Century Montreal," *Urban History Review* 36, no. 1 (2007): 32. Several articles consider disease in the Spring 2008 issue, although the role of the microbe is largely offstage.

43   Taryn M. Graham and Troy D. Glover, "On the Fence: Dog Parks in the (Un)Leashing of Community and Social Capital," *Leisure Sciences: An Interdisciplinary Journal* 36, no. 3 (2014): 217–34, and Heidi J. Nast, "Loving . . . Whatever: Alienation, Neoliberalism and Pet-Love in the Twenty-First Century," *ACME: An International E-Journal for Critical Geographies* 5, no. 2 (2006): 300–327.

44   Harold Innis, *The Fur Trade in Canada: An Introduction to Canadian Economic History* (Toronto: University of Toronto Press, 1930).

45   For example see: Sherene H. Razack, *Dying From Improvement: Inquests and Inquiries into Indigenous Deaths in Custody* (Toronto: University of Toronto Press, 2015), 166–71; Olive P. Dickason, *The Myth of the Savage and the Beginnings of French Colonialism in the Americas* (Edmonton: University of Alberta Press, 1997 [1984]), 61–84;

and Truth and Reconciliation Commission of Canada, *Honouring the Truth, Reconciling the Future: Summary of the Final Report* (Ottawa: Library and Archives of Canada, 2015), http://nctr.ca/assets/reports/Final%20Reports/Executive_Summary_English_Web.pdf (accessed 9 January 2016).

46   Bill Parenteau, "'Care, Control and Supervision': Native People in the Canadian Atlantic Salmon Fishery, 1867–1900," *Canadian Historical Review* 79, no. 1 (1998): 1–35; Bill Parenteau, "A 'Very Determined Opposition to the Law': Conservation, Angling Leases, and Social Conflict in the Canadian Atlantic Salmon Fishery, 1867–1914," *Environmental History* 9, no. 3 (2004): 436–63; Tina Loo, *States of Nature: Conserving Canada's Wildlife in the Twentieth Century* (Vancouver: University of British Columbia Press, 2006); Tina Loo, "Making a Modern Wilderness: Conserving Wildlife in Twentieth-Century Canada," *Canadian Historical Review* 82, no. 1 (2001): 92–121; Tina Loo, "Of Moose and Men: Hunting For Masculinities in British Columbia, 1880–1939," *Western Historical Quarterly* 32 (2001): 296–319; John Sandlos, *Hunters at the Margin: Native People and Wildlife Conservation in the Northwest Territories* (Vancouver: University of British Columbia Press, 2007); George Colpitts, *Game in the Garden: A Human History of Wildlife in Western Canada to 1940* (Vancouver and Toronto: University of British Columbia Press, 2002); Darin Kinsey, "Fashioning a Freshwater Eden: Elite Anglers, Fish Culture, and State Development of Québec's 'Sport' Fishery" (PhD thesis, l'Université

du Québec à Trois-Rivières, 2008); Darcy Ingram, *Wildlife, Conservation and Conflict in Quebec, 1840–1914* (Vancouver: University of British Columbia Press, 2013); Neil S. Forkey, "Anglers, Fishers and the St. Croix River: Conflict in a Canadian-American Borderland, 1867–1900," *Forest and Conservation History* 37, no. 4 (1993): 160–66.

47   See, for example, Paul Nadasdy, "The Gift in the Animal: The Ontology of Hunting and Human-Animal Sociality," *American Ethnologist* 34, no. 1 (February 2007): 25–43. Harvey A. Feit, "Hunting and the Quest for Power, the James Bay Cree and Whitemen in the Twentieth Century," in *Native Peoples: The Canadian Experience*, 2nd ed., ed. R.B. Morrison and C.R. Wilson (Toronto: McClelland & Stewart, 1994), 181–223.

48   For an intervention in Canadian rural history see Royden Loewern, " 'Come Watch This Spider': Animals, Mennonites, and Indices of Modernity," *Canadian Historical Review* 96, no. 1 (2015): 61–90.

49   "From Henley to the High Park Peacock, Toronto's Animal Tales from 2015," *Toronto Star*, 27 December 2015, http://www.thestar.com/news/gta/2015/12/27/unbelievable-cute-quirky-animal-stories-of-2015.html (accessed 8 January 2016).

50   Richard Louv, *Last Child in the Woods: Saving Our Children from Nature-Deficit Disorder* (Chapel Hill, NC: Algonquin Books, 2005).

51   Corey Laroque, "Rare Sighting: Snowy Owl Spotted in the City," *Niagara Falls Review*, 6 November 2008, http://www.

niagarafallsreview.ca/2008/11/06/rare-sighting-snowy-owl-spotted-in-city (accessed 26 January 2015); Grouse Mountain Bear Cam, https://www.grousemountain.com/wildlife-refuge/bear-cam (accessed 26 January 2015); "Fox Takes Nap in an Unlikely Place and #busfox Is Born," *CBC NEWS*, 23 July 2014, http://www.cbc.ca/news/canada/ottawa/fox-takes-nap-in-an-unlikely-place-and-busfox-is-born-1.2715625 (accessed 29 January 2015).

52   See Alex Consiglio, "Man Who Attacked Raccoons With Shovel Pleads Guilty," *Toronto Star*, 12 March 2013. http://www.thestar.com/news/crime/2013/03/12/man_who_attacked_raccoons_with_shovel_pleads_guilty_to_animal_cruelty.html (accessed 17 December 2014); and "Emma Czornobaj Gets 90 Days in Jail for Duck-Stopping Deaths, *CBCNews*, 18 December 2014. http://www.cbc.ca/news/canada/montreal/emma-czornobaj-gets-90-days-in-jail-for-duck-stopping-deaths-1.2877437 (accessed 18 December 2014).

53   Annabelle Sabloff, *Re-ordering the Natural World: Humans and Animals in the City* (Toronto: University of Toronto Press, 2001), 5.

54   Maciej Luniak, "Synurbanization-Adaption of Animal Wildlife to Urban Development," in *Proceedings of the 4th International Symposium on Urban Wildlife Conservation, 1–5 May, 1999*, ed. William W. Shaw, Lisa K. Harris, and Larry Vandruff (Tucson, Arizona: 2004); Stephen S. Ditchkoff, Sarah T. Saalfeld and Charles J. Gibson, "Animal Behavior in Urban Ecosystems: Modifications Due to Human-Induced Stress,"

Urban Ecosystems 9 (2006): 5–12; and Jim Sterba, *Nature Wars: The Incredible Story of How Wildlife Comebacks Turned Backyards into Battlegrounds* (New York: Broadway Books, 2012).

55 This changed in 2011, to reflect the variation between small population areas of 1,000 to 29,999, large centres with over 100,000, and medium centres between. See http://www.statcan.gc.ca/subjects-sujets/standard-norme/sgc-cgt/notice-avis/sgc-cgt-06-eng.htm.

56 See the *Qikigtani Truth Commission: Thematic Reports and Special Studies* (2013); Frank James Tester, "Mad Dogs and (Mostly) Englishmen: Colonial Relations, Commodities and the Fate of Inuit sled dogs," *Creative Technologies* 34, no. 2 (2010): 129–47; and "Can the Sled Dog Sleep? Postcolonialism, Cultural Transformation and the Consumption of Inuit Culture," in *New Proposals: Journal of Marxism and Interdisciplinary Inquiry* 3, no. 3 (June 2010): 7–19; and *Qimmit: A Clash of Two Truths* (National Film Board: 2010). Animals continue to figure in the modern northern imaginary. A 2014 video game, *Never Alone*, tellingly focuses on the relationship between an Inupiat girl and a mystical fox.

57 Jennifer R. Wolch, Kathleen West, and Thomas E. Gaines, "Transspecies Urban Theory," *Environment and Planning D: Society and Space* 13, no. 6 (1995): 735–60.

58 Jennifer Wolch, "Zoöpolis," *Capitalism Nature Socialism* 7, no. 2 (1996): 29.

59 Chris Philo, "Animals, Geography, and the City: Notes on Inclusions and Exclusions," *Environment and Planning D: Society and Space* 13, no. 6 (1995): 655–81. See also Jody Emel, Chris Wilbert, and Jennifer Wolch, "Animal Geographies," *Society and Animals* 10, no. 4 (2002): 407–12.

60 William Cronon, *Nature's Metropolis: Chicago and the Great West* (New York: W.W. Norton, 1991), 51.

61 J.M.S. Careless, *Frontier and Metropolis: Regions, Cities, and Identities in Canada Before 1914* (Toronto: University of Toronto Press, 1989).

62 Bettina Bradbury, "Pigs, Cows and Boarders: Non-Wage Forms of Survival Among Montreal Families, 1861–91," *Labour/Le Travail* 14 (1984): 9–46; see also Bettina Bradbury, *Working Families: Age, Gender, and Daily Survival in Industrializing Montreal* (Toronto: University of Toronto Press, 2007); Margaret Heap, "La grève des charretiers à Montréal, 1864," *Revue d'histoire de l'Amérique française* 31, no. 3 (1977): 371–95; Peter deLottinville, "Joe Beef of Montreal: Working-Class Culture and the Tavern," *Labour/Le Travailleur* 8/9 (1981/82): 9–40, esp. 14–15; J.T.H. Connor, "Cruel Knives? Vivisection and Biomedical Research in Victorian Canada," *CBMH/BCHM* 14 (1997): 37–64.

63 Sean Kheraj, "Demonstration Wildlife: Negotiating the Animal Landscape of Vancouver's Stanley Park, 1888–1996," *Environment and History* 18, no. 4 (2012): 497–527; Darcy Ingram, "Horses, Hedges and Hegemony: Foxhunting in the Montreal Countryside," in *Metropolitan Natures: Urban Environmental Histories of Montreal*, ed. Stéphane Castonguay

and Michèle Dagenais (Pittsburgh: University of Pittsburgh Press, 2011), 211–27; Darcy Ingram, "Beastly Measures: Animal Welfare, Civil Society, and State Policy in Victorian Canada," *Journal of Canadian Studies / Revue d'études canadiennes* 47, no. 1 (2013): 221–52; Sean Kheraj, "Living and Working with Domestic Animals in Nineteenth-Century Toronto," in *Urban Explorations: Environmental Histories of the Toronto Region*, ed. L. Anders Sandberg, Stephen Bocking, Colin Coates, and Ken Cruikshank (Hamilton, ON: L.R. Wilson Institute for Canadian History, 2013), 120–40; and "Animals and Urban Environments: Managing Domestic Animals in Nineteenth-Century Winnipeg," in *Eco-Cultural Networks and the British Empire: New Views on Environmental History*, ed. James Beattie, Edward Melillo, and Emily O'Gorman (Bloomsbury, 2015); Lianne McTavish and Jingjing Zheng, "Rats in Alberta: Looking at Pest-Control Posters from the 1950s," *Canadian Historical Review* 92, no. 3 (2011): 515–46; Richard Mackie, "Cougars, Colonists, and the Rural Settlement of Vancouver Island," in *Beyond the City Limits: Rural History in British Columbia*, ed. Ruth Sandwell (Vancouver: University of British Columbia Press, 1999): 120–41. See also Jodi Giesbrecht, "Killing the Beast: Animal Death in Canadian Literature, Hunting, Photography, Taxidermy, and Slaughterhouses, 1865–1920" (PhD diss., University of Toronto, 2012).

64 Ester Reiter, *Making Fast Food: From the Frying into the Fryer* (Montreal and Kingston: McGill-Queen's University Press,

1991); and Ian Mosby, *Food Will Win the War: The Politics, Culture and Science of Food on Canada's Home Front* (Vancouver: University of British Columbia Press, 2014).

65 Alfred W. Crosby, "Ecological Imperialism: The Overseas Migration of Western Europeans as a Biological Phenomenon," in *The Ends of the Earth: Perspectives on Modern Environmental History*, ed. Donald Worster (Cambridge, UK: Cambridge University Press, 1989), 103–17; Myron Echenberg, *Africa in the Time of Cholera: A History of Pandemics from 1817 to the Present* (Cambridge, UK: Cambridge University Press, 2011); Esyllt Jones, "'Co-operation in All Human Endeavor': Quarantine and Immigrant Disease Vectors in the 1918–1919 Influenza Pandemic in Winnipeg," *CBMH/BCHM* 22, no. 1 (2005): 57–82; Ho-fung Hung, "The Politics of SARS: Containing the Perils of Globalization by More Globalization," *Asian Perspective* 28, no. 1 (2004): 19–44.

66 Cole Harris, "Voices of Smallpox around the Strait of Georgia," *The Resettlement of British Columbia: Essays on Colonialism and Geographical Change* (Vancouver: University of British Columbia Press, 1997), 3–30; Paul Hackett, "Averting Disaster: The Hudson's Bay Company and Smallpox in Western Canada During the Late Eighteenth and Early Nineteenth Centuries," *Bulletin of the History of Medicine* 78, no. 3 (2004): 575–609; Magda Fahrni and Esyllt W. Jones, eds., *Epidemic Encounters: Influenza, Society, and Culture in Canada, 1918–20* (Vancouver: University of British Columbia Press, 2013); Esyllt W. Jones,

Influenza 1918: Disease, Death and Struggle in Winnipeg (Toronto: University of Toronto Press, 2007); Liza Piper, "Chesterfield Inlet, 1949 and the Ecology of Epidemic Polio," *Environmental History* 20 (2015): 67–98; Geoffrey Bilson, *A Darkened House: Cholera in Nineteenth-Century Canada* (Toronto: University of Toronto Press, 1980). For an application of Alfred Crosby's ideas to Canada, see Liza Piper and John Sandlos, "A Broken Frontier: Ecological Imperialism in the Canadian North," *Environmental History* 12, no. 4 (October 2007): 759–95.

67   Patricia Thornton and Sherry Olson, "Mortality in Late Nineteenth-Century Montreal: Geographic Pathways of Contagion," *Population Studies* 65, no. 2 (2011): 157–81.

The Memory of an Elephant: Savagery, Civilization, and Spectacle

Christabelle Sethna

Oversized roadside attractions marking small urban centres are a familiar feature across Canada. Perhaps the most curious among these is an enormous statue of an elephant positioned at the west entrance to the city of St. Thomas, Ontario. Elephants are not, of course, native to this part of the world. They originate in Africa and Asia and are unsuited to cold climes. However, elephants have long journeyed to rural and urban Canada as zoo exhibits and circus acts. Notably, the storied African elephant Jumbo, the main attraction of Barnum and Bailey's profitable travelling railway circus, was killed unexpectedly by a freight train on 15 September 1885 in St. Thomas, where his likeness was memorialized in concrete a century later.

This chapter represents a contribution toward "species studies," which arises out of animal rights activism and parallels racial justice movements. But more recently, species studies has been implicated in consolidating "links between species, race, and transnational power structures that underlie the production of culture."[1] Species studies scholars suggest that studying the "circulation of nonhuman species as both figures and materialized bodies within the circuits of imperial biopower" can yield rich information about colonial encounters.[2] Perhaps because "the ultimate subaltern" is said to be the nonhuman animal, "animalization" is a recurring aspect of those circuits.[3] In this chapter animalization refers to the ways in which human animals are othered by "discourses of animality" and rendered abject. Although animalization can provide compelling insight into the ways human animals are racialized under colonialism, the comparable experiences of nonhuman animals caught up in the very same regime are often obscured.[4] I suggest that because animalization and racialization are mutually constitutive, the collision between the Grand Trunk Railway's iron horse and "the world's first international animal superstar"[5] should not be treated as mere historical curiosity. Rather, Jumbo's life, death, and afterlife can be understood as a violence-filled colonial journey that followed a well-worn track common to captive nonhuman and human animal bodies alike, particularly in the business of slavery and freakery. The international urban dimensions of their commodification were striking.

Bodies on Display

For centuries blacks, primarily from central, southern, and western Africa, were abducted and transported in chains across the Atlantic in a dreaded journey known as the "Middle Passage."[6] Survivors were sold into slavery to white owners in Europe and the Americas. African human animal bodies were also put on public display in cities as exotic specimens to be examined by natural historians or to serve as entertaining curiosities. In the cases of slavery and freakery, both individual oddities and racial peculiarities were read simultaneously as the monstrous signifiers of the inherent animality of savage Africans and the racial superiority of civilized Europeans.[7] Out of these racialized human-animal hybrids arose the spectacle of the abject subhuman that could be consumed, literally and symbolically, in life, death, and afterlife. Nonhuman animals fared no better. As the trade in human slaves from Africa wound down in the 1860s, and the scramble for Africa wound up, the demands of European and American zoos and circuses for exotic big game increased. Killing large nonhuman animals for sport and displaying their body parts as trophies have long been associated with imperial power. Large elephant tusks were prized because ivory was the "white gold" of empires, used to fund commercial expansion and to make items such as pianos, combs, and handles for flatware. Capturing large "charismatic megafauna" alive and exhibiting them in colonial metropoles until their upkeep became too problematic also served as an imperial status symbol.[8]

Jumbo was one of many creatures netted for this lucrative transnational enterprise.[9] He was born circa 1860 in what is now the Sudan near the border with Eritrea. The region was remote, serviced neither by roads nor railways.[10] Elephant hunters from the Hamran tribe who made a living selling tusks and bones killed the elephant calf's mother two years later in order to capture him alive for European animal traders. The traders surmised correctly that Europeans accustomed to Asian elephants (*Elephas maximus*) in zoos would be keen to view the larger African species (*Loxodonta africana*), considered more exotic because of its fan-like ears. Assumptions about Asian and African elephants sometimes mirrored beliefs about Asian and African peoples; Asian elephants were said to be smaller and more docile in comparison to their larger and fiercer African cousins.[11]

The elephant hunters delivered Jumbo, along with another captive elephant calf, a rhinoceros, giraffes, ostriches, antelopes, porcupines, and birds of prey to a Bavarian trader who handed them off to an Italian. The latter took the creatures on an arduous desert trek followed by an ocean voyage to the port of Suez, a railway journey to the port of Alexandria, a boat to Trieste, and yet another train to Dresden. Many died en route, including the second elephant calf. A Prussian purchased the remaining lot and toured his newly acquired "Grand Menagerie" from town to town to entertain the local populace. Zoos across Europe soon made individual purchases from the Grand Menagerie, with Jumbo going to the Jardin des Plantes in Paris. This urban landmark housed plants, animals, and the Muséum national d'histoire naturelle. Notable natural historians such as Georges-Louis Leclerc, Comte de Buffon, as well as Jean-Baptiste Lamarck and Georges Cuvier, trained here.

These Enlightenment figures' ideas about racial degeneration contributed to the spread of scientific racism. In the early nineteenth century Cuvier, author of *The Animal Kingdom* (1817), would go on to examine Saartjie Baartman from the Khoikhoi tribe of South Africa when she was exhibited in Paris by her keeper on account of her large buttocks and genitalia. After his examination he pronounced: "her movements had something of brusqueness and capriciousness which recalled those of a monkey."[12] After Baartman died in 1815, possibly from alcoholism or syphilis, she remained a figure on display. Cuvier made a plaster cast of her body and preserved her skeleton and genitalia separately. These were exhibited at the Musée de l'homme in Paris in Case no. 33 until 1974. France agreed to repatriate Baartman's remains to South Africa in 2002 but officials could not confirm that they belonged to Baartman. Two centuries later, she continues to embody the fractured postcolonial and multicultural relations between Europe and Africa.[13]

Jumbo remained at the Jardin des Plantes until overcrowding – thanks to the purchase of two more African elephant calves as well as oxen, monkeys, tortoises, birds, and stags – led his owners to trade him to the Zoological Society in London. Society members founded the London Zoo to support scientific and educational endeavours, but the Society succumbed to the lure of displaying creatures that appeared exotic in Britain.[14] Matthew Scott, a junior keeper assigned to Jumbo, noted his small stature and poor condition before transporting him to his new home by train and boat. Scott nursed Jumbo to health, but the elephant would have occasional rages, smashing the doors and windows of his enclosure and eventually damaging his tusks and shortening their length greatly.

The possibility that Jumbo may have been exercising some agency, possibly acting wilfully out of anger or loneliness at being held captive, did not occur to Abraham Bartlett, a former taxidermist and by then Superintendent at the London Zoo. Rather, he diagnosed the elephant's behaviour as "fits of temporary insanity."[15] Consequently, Bartlett and Scott beat Jumbo into submission, with Bartlett recalling: "He [Jumbo] quickly recognized that he was mastered by lying down and uttering a cry of submission. We coaxed him and fed him with a few tempting morsels, and after this time he appeared to recognize that we were his best friends, and he continued on best terms with both of us."[16] The diagnosis and treatment of Jumbo's behaviour paralleled the medicalization of black slaves' resistance to slavery. Slaves who tried to escape were depicted as wilful runaway savages and were said to suffer from "Drapetomania" or "Dysthesis Ethiopica," mental health afflictions that could be remedied by enforcing the runaway's submission to his or her master.[17]

Over the next two decades Jumbo grew to the impressive proportions of 11 feet in height and 7 tons in weight, achieving international renown as the world's largest land animal in captivity. As a resident of the city at the heart of the vast British Empire, he became a fixture at the London Zoo. Visitors fed him buns, and even the royal family was said to be a fan of the pachyderm. Trained by Scott to give children rides on his back, Jumbo was fitted with a *howdah*, a canopy seat in which Indian maharajahs and British sahibs participated in tiger hunts and ceremonial processions in India.[18] Despite his African origins and his Indian trappings, Jumbo evolved into a quintessential British icon, reinforcing colonial tropes about the positive value of white civilizing missions that tamed beastly human and nonhuman animal life from the tropics.[19]

Yet Jumbo was hardly docile; his ongoing nightly destruction of his quarters encouraged Bartlett's belief that African elephants were too savage to be domesticated. A more sympathetic Scott called Jumbo "the most intelligent animal the world has ever seen," and acknowledged that "like all other creatures, [he] prefers his liberty."[20] He attempted to calm Jumbo by plying him with beer and whisky, but Jumbo's acting out increased as he became sexually mature at approximately age twenty. During the period known as "musth," bull elephants, possibly because of heightened levels of testosterone, become extremely aggressive, posing a grave danger to other human and nonhuman animals. Rampaging elephants and the forceful steps taken to quell them have been used as literary vehicles by authors such as George Orwell to express the power and the powerlessness of imperial rule.[21] Elephants are not, however, empty metaphors. When fractious behaviour was observed in Chuny, an Indian elephant exhibited on the London stage, he was executed in 1826 – shot with volley upon volley of bullets then stabbed to death with a sword. Members of the public paid to see him dissected.[22]

Jumbo's hormone-fuelled conduct ensured his disposability: morphing from an avuncular noble savage beloved by children into an uncontrollable priapic beast that was the stuff of colonial nightmares about restless natives and dark-skinned rapists. Anticipating that he would have to shoot the elephant, Bartlett welcomed the timely offer P.T. Barnum made to purchase Jumbo for £2,000 and ship him to the United States.[23] Barnum was a well-known American showman who made a career and a fortune out of dime museums, often exhibiting individuals who were, as Rosemarie Garland-Thomson puts it, "physically disabled" or "exotic ethnics."[24] Early success emerged in the form of Joice Heth, an old, blind African-American woman he advertised as the 161-year-old nursemaid to George Washington and later as a ventriloquist's dummy. William Henry Jackson, a young African-American with microcephaly, proved to be another crowd pleaser. Nicknamed Zip or "What's It?," Jackson played the role of a monkey-like simpleton. It is speculated that Heth and Jackson drew large audiences because of white "nostalgia for degrading images of blacks" in popular literature, plays, and blackface minstrel shows, and because of the belief that Africa was a mysterious continent "inhabited by savages and wild men, creatures only marginally human."[25]

In the 1870s Barnum entered the circus business, soon turning a handsome profit. The circus has its origins in the travelling equestrian and acrobatic performances of Englishman John B. Ricketts. He and his American assistant, John Durang, came to Montreal and Quebec City in the late eighteenth century. They presented a variety of acts that included a pantomime featuring Captain James Cook and Hawaiian natives. In the nineteenth century, visits from members of the British Royal Family, replete with Aboriginals performing sports and dances for the overseas guests, were popular occasions for spectacle. So too was the circus, along with other forms of entertainment, such as melodrama, burlesque, and animal menageries.[26]

Elephants, newspapers, and railways were crucial to the success of the American circus in its "golden age" (1870–1920).[27] Elephants were a critical source of circus labour. Some were also conditioned to perform tricks for audiences with a growing appetite for variety, novelty, and mastery over the natural world. Trainers used an elephant hook – a pointed baton intended to prick sensitive spots on the elephant's body – as well as a system of commands and rewards to generate the learned memory responses they required in these nonhuman animals. Newspapers published circus stories, articles, announcements, images, and schedules that circulated widely, and journalists were often invited to attend circus performances. Railways, which were built primarily by nonwhite immigrants, fashioned cities out of wilderness, a process indicative of both industrialization and modernity. Rail transport brought human and nonhuman animal circus labourers and performers, and elaborate equipment and costumes to rural and urban locations. By the time Barnum made his offer to purchase Jumbo, the elephant had distinguished itself as the "quintessential entertainment industry animal," even serving as the advertisement for travelling circuses.[28]

Public outcry in London over the sale of Jumbo and a lawsuit attempting to block his release delayed his shipment to New York. So too did Jumbo's fierce refusals to enter the crate in which he would cross the Atlantic Ocean. The news resulted in an uptick in zoo visitors and a slate of sympathetic correspondence from adults and children addressed to the elephant.[29] A patriotic public interpreted Jumbo's resistance as his disapproval of the United States, a vulgar nation tainted by its history of slavery, while a more sympathetic crowd attributed it to Jumbo's affection for the African cow elephant, Alice, routinely cast as his "wife."[30] Narratives that anthropomorphized nonhuman animals as monogamous and heteronormative were standard fodder for adults and children; even James Joyce wrote famously: "Love loves to love . . . Jumbo, the elephant, loves Alice, the elephant."[31] However, Scott racialized the pair as slave siblings, possibly to enhance the pathos of Jumbo's departure for public consumption or to empathize with the elephant's distress. Recounting Jumbo's parting from Alice, Scott positioned himself as the heartbroken slave father and the elephants as his slave offspring sold to two different masters.[32]

From Zoo to Circus Elephant

Elephant and keeper arrived finally in New York City on 8 April 1882 after crossing the ocean on a ship filled with other migrants. The next day a team of eight horses and two elephants pulled and pushed Jumbo's crate in a parade followed by gawking crowds along Broadway Avenue to the Madison Square Garden circus grounds.[33] Alluding to imperial victory – this time of the New World over the Old – Barnum crowed that Queen Victoria, along with "every child in Great Britain," was mourning the loss of "the colossus of elephant."[34] The origin of Jumbo's name remains unclear. But thanks to the sensational publicity surrounding Barnum's purchase, the word "jumbo" came to refer to an object of gargantuan dimensions, and "Jumbomania" inspired advertisements, songs, toys, plates, poems, cartoons, cards, and jewellery.[35] Even Charles Edenshaw (1839–1920), a respected Haida artist from the remote settlement of Masset in Haida Gwaii (then the Queen Charlotte Islands), was influenced enough by Jumbomania to carve the elephant's likeness into a walking stick.[36]

Barnum's approach to circus entertainment combined elements of dime museums and freak shows with human and nonhuman animal acts Orientalized as exotic.[37] Jumbo, who joined thirty other performing elephants in the Barnum and Bailey circus, was also represented in freakish terms. One circus worker compared him to Nelse Seymour, a tall blackface minstrel performer.[38] Another broadcast: "his trunk is the size of an adult crocodile, his tail is as big as a cow's leg, and he made footprints in the sands of time resembling an indentation as if a very fat man had fallen off a very high building."[39] At other points, he was portrayed as a gentle giant. Barnum averred that Jumbo was "perfectly lamb-like."[40] Scott also insisted that Jumbo had never hurt him except by accident and once had even saved his life.[41] Yet his American elephant trainers used an elephant hook on his ears, chains to secure his feet, and whips to lash his hide in order to mould Jumbo from zoo pet to travelling circus figurehead.[42] When circus elephants resisted such conditioning they were punished severely. Pilot, a large Asian bull elephant in the same circus as Jumbo, was isolated, chained, and immobilized after injuring circus workers. One of Jumbo's trainers, Col. George Arstingstall, then shot the "ferocious monster" to death. Pilot's carcass was used to make glue and buttons and his tusks were fashioned into billiard balls.[43]

A few months after Jumbo's arrival in New York City, Barnum sent a letter to American consulates asking for their assistance in preparing a new circus spectacle. He wished to locate "not only <u>human beings of different races</u>, but also where practicable, those who possess extraordinary peculiarities such as giants, dwarfs, singular disfigurements of the person, dexterity in the use of weapons, dancing, singing, juggling, unusual feats of strength or agility etc. [emphasis in original]." Barnum requested that the respondent provide descriptions and photographs of as many as these "specimens" as possible.[44] A decade earlier, Barnum had concocted a "Congress of Nations," composed mainly of working-class whites of Irish descent who played sumptuously costumed potentates, kings, and queens from Eastern and Western civilizations. In contrast to this "racial masquerade," his new "Ethnological Congress" was based squarely upon the precepts of scientific racism, entertaining primarily white audiences with displays of yellow, brown, and black performers from around the world and reflecting the notion of American exceptionalism.[45] Some "professional savages" performing in the Ethnological Congress were itinerant African-American workers who were the most easily exploited because they stood at the bottom of the circus labour hierarchy. Black men were more likely to be assigned dangerous work like feeding and grooming elephants and cleaning their quarters. As performers, they were expected to display their blackness as the phylogenetic "missing link" between human and nonhuman animals under the big top.[46] Some of these performers came from as far away as Australia. One of Barnum's recruiters, Robert A.

Cunningham, born in Godmanchester, Quebec, even abducted and transported two groups of Queensland aborigines to the circus. Tambo, one of the young aborigine boys in the first group, took sick and died in the winter of 1883. His remains were exhibited in a Cleveland, Ohio, dime museum, only to be rediscovered in a funeral home in that city in the 1990s.[47]

Audiences attending the Ethnological Congress circus performance thrilled to an introductory pageant of horses and riders dressed in gold and purple, accompanied by drums, cymbals, and horns. After the pageant left the ring, a journalist recorded:

> Jumbo came forth in all his modern magnificence, with a troop of children on his back. At his heels was the baby elephant and at his side a trainer in full evening dress. Following was a band of Sioux Indians and cowboys from the plains. Then came the curiosities from the museum. There were the giant and bearded lady, the long-haired wonder, and the fat boy, and the female white Moor and the tattooed man, and bringing up the rear was the Hindu serpent sorceress with a necklace of snakes.[48]

Barnum was able to transport this parade of racialized human and non-human animal oddities to border communities in the United States and Canada by virtue of the Grand Trunk Railway (GTR). During the 1860s, lines operated by the GTR linked together Toronto, Montreal, Sarnia, and Kingston, as well as Portland, Maine, and Port Huron, Michigan. Several railway lines, including the GTR, were built in southern Ontario, with St. Thomas serving as their hub. St. Thomas, incorporated as a city in 1881, came to be known as "Railway City," boasting one of the largest and most impressive railway stations in the province. As a result of rail traffic, the population increased to over eight thousand in the early 1880s.[49] St. Thomas was also notable as one of the border settlements for thousands of bonded and free blacks using the Underground Railroad to flee slavery in the United States. When the Civil War south of the border ended, many of these black settlers went back to the United States. Others put down roots in the area. With the expansion of transcontinental railway routes, black men from Canada, the United States, and from overseas found employment as track sleeping car porters and dining room attendants, albeit experiencing serious racism on the job.[50]

Each year Barnum's circus journeyed thousands of miles by rail, decamping in New York, Pennsylvania, New England, New Brunswick, Quebec, and Ontario.[51] When he visited the city of Hamilton, Ontario, in the summer of 1883, the streets were packed with adults and children eager for a glimpse of a creature described in hyperbolic terms as "the Pride of the British Heart. The biggest Elephant, or Mastodon, or whatever he is, in or out of captivity. His uplifted trunk reaches upward of 26 feet. His weight is near ten tons. His height is beyond belief. His giant stride is over one rod!"[52] Scott claimed that Jumbo did not like travelling by train because the noise and movement kept him in a "constant ferment of nervous excitement."[53] Nevertheless, Jumbo persevered in his specially built railway Palace Car, winning many fans along the way. Two weeks before his death, Jumbo and the Ethnological Congress captivated audiences in Quebec City; five thousand people eager to see "many strange people, animals and birds" were turned away from the full house.[54]

He arrived in Chatham, Ontario, on 14 September 1885 to announcements trumpeting the "Ethnological Congress of Savage Tribes," "JUMBO, THE WONDER, AND CHILDREN'S GIANT PET," "JO-JO, the Marvellous Dog-Faced Boy," "NALA DAMAJANTI, The Heroic Hindu Snake Charmer," "TRAINED ANIMALS, Horses, Dogs, Pigs, Ponies, Bears, Lions, Tigers, Hyenas, Goats etc.," as well as a street parade and excursion rates on all railways.[55] The next evening, circus workers including Scott tore down a fence, creating a shortcut over train tracks to herd the animals to their tents. An unscheduled freight train bore down the track just as the elephants Tom Thumb and Jumbo were crossing the rails. Unable to stop in time, the train hurtled into the procession, tossing Tom Thumb into a ditch with a broken leg and smashing into Jumbo, driving one of his tusks into his brain. The *New York Times* reported on his demise:

> There were deep gashes in his flank, his feet were torn, and the blood ran out of his mouth, but Jumbo looked more majestic than ever before. The great beast gave one groan after being struck. Then he assumed an attitude of determination, which he maintained until the sands of his life ran out. Long after his life was extinct his keeper [Matthew Scott], who brought him from the Zoological Gardens in London, laid on his body and wept.[56]

"JUMBO"—Killed in St. Thomas, September 15, 1885   COMPLIMENTS OF ANDERSONS LIMITED, ST. THOMAS, ONT.

1.1 Photographer T. H. Scott's iconic 1885 photo of Jumbo's dead body circulated as a postcard for a local St. Thomas business. Courtesy of Elgin County Archives.

The Circus of the Afterlife

It is estimated that the amount Barnum paid the London Zoo for Jumbo was multiplied many times over in circus revenues during the elephant's short three-year tenure in the United States.[57] A remunerative circus attraction in life, Jumbo remained so in death and beyond. In Jumbo's afterlife, his dead body was rendered into a posthumous spectacle for consumption. After learning of the collision, Barnum supplied stories to a hungry press about Jumbo's heroism, claiming that the elephant tried to save Tom Thumb but was killed in doing so. Those at the scene in St. Thomas would later deny this version of events.[58] Barnum also requested local photographer T.H. Scott (no relation to Jumbo's keeper) to capture the corpse on film. In Scott's iconic photograph, the elephant's enormous bulk rests at the centre of the frame, surrounded by a semicircle of white men and boys. Only one woman is discernible at the far left edge of the crowd. Jumbo's keeper stands near his massive head; a railway official leans against the lifeless elephant, his left arm resting proprietarily on Jumbo's hide.[59] A locomotive, which the photographer asked to be positioned in the background for pictorial interest, looms above the carcass.

The photographer's son later divulged, "some wiseacre in New York copyrighted the picture and made a fortune," turning it into a souvenir postcard for public distribution.[60]

The souvenir postcard's Gulliveresque image replicates several other staged visual representations of large African animals shot dead; a hunter, most often male and white, posing triumphantly atop or beside a dead animal-turned-trophy yet dwarfed by the size of the fresh kill.[61] Many such animals were taxidermied for private or public display, and Jumbo was no exception. His death occurred in the same year in which rival European powers concluded the Berlin Conference. Although they agreed to suppress the slave trade, they severed Africa arbitrarily amongst themselves, scrambling for a share in the continent's natural resources. Notable was the trade in ivory, leading to the slaughter of thousands of elephants and the exploitation of villagers.[62] Jumbo's African body was also partitioned into a number of fetish objects. Out of self-interest or a desire for respectability, Barnum had donated both money and animal specimens to American natural history institutions. Boston's Tufts University was a recipient of his largesse, even building a museum named in his honour on campus. Suspecting that Jumbo might be ill, Barnum had pre-arranged the donation of Jumbo's hide to the university and his skeleton to the Smithsonian Museum, and hired Henry Ward, a leading American natural historian and taxidermist, to dismember Jumbo and stuff him.[63]

Across the Atlantic, the *London Daily News* opined upon the news of Jumbo's death: "Shall England have no relic of an elephant over whose parting from far shores so many English boys and girls, and elderly men and women for that matter, were understood to have shed tears?"[64] On the scene, St. Thomas residents were quick to seize their own spoils. While waiting for Ward and nearby butchers to arrive, throngs were charged an admission fee to view the body. A few enterprising citizens hacked off their own souvenirs – a sliver of an ear, a clipping from the trunk, a bristle from the tail, a slice of a tusk. One individual, moved by the "delicious aroma" that arose as Jumbo's remnants were burned, reportedly ate a slice of his roasted flank. A paste made out of his fat was sold in local apothecaries, purportedly as a remedy for men's erectile difficulties.[65] Small items like a screw, a button, and a matchstick holder found in his stomach were preserved for posterity. Similar game hunting behaviour was also observable among white mobs attending the lynching of African-Americans. They

The articles in this frame were found in the stomach of Jumbo after his death in St. Thomas on September 15, 1885.
Donor: Mr. B. Summer

The small ivory elephant was carved from a piece of Jumbo's tusk. It was purchased by Mr. Arthur Caskey who was a boy at the time of Jumbo's death.
Donor: Miss Phyllis Matthews

1.2 Some of the contents of Jumbo's stomach remain on display at the Elgin County Museum. Courtesy of Elgin County Museum.

seized body parts from the victims and photographed dead bodies to create fetish souvenir objects and postcards, marking the lynching as a "performance spectacle."[66]

In contrast to the feeding frenzy surrounding Jumbo, the local press was respectful, even reverential, but it also attempted to cash in on the elephant's passing. For five cents, mourners could purchase from the *St. Thomas Weekly Times* a printed memorial tablet honouring "THE PET OF THOUSANDS AND FRIEND OF ALL." The tablet bore a solemn verse:

> If the tomb's secrets may not
>   be confessed,
>
> The nature of thy private
>   life unfold.

A heart has throbbed 'neath
    that leathern breast,

And tears adown that dusky cheek
    have rolled;

Have children climbed upon
    that back, and kissed
    that face?

What was thy name, and
    station, age and race?[67]

This curious verse belonged to a well-known poem, "Address to the Mummy at Belzoni's Exhibition," by Horace Smith. Smith penned the poem after attending an exhibit on Egyptian antiquities that Giovanni Battista Belzoni held in London in 1821. A one-time circus performer and amateur archaeologist, Belzoni plundered tombs in Egypt and sold their contents to collectors. His exploits galvanized widespread interest in Egyptology and in mummies in particular. The use of a verse about a dusky Egyptian mummy to memorialize a dead pachyderm reinforced the notion that Orientalized creatures remained spectacles for consumption long after their deaths.[68]

The newspaper additionally proposed building a local monument to the elephant,[69] but Barnum, who had benefited years earlier from "mummy fever," exhibiting mummies and sarcophagi in the 1830s, had other ideas. He breathed new life into Jumbo's remains, adding them to his travelling show.[70] He toured the preserved hide and skeleton internationally, sometimes positioning them alongside the newly purchased Alice, now anthropomorphized as Jumbo's grieving "widow."[71] Barnum eventually donated Jumbo's heart to Cornell University, his skeleton to New York's Museum of Natural History, and his hide, which had been padded and stuffed to increase its dimensions as per Barnum's instructions, went to Tufts University. Jumbo, taxidermied as a natural history specimen and a wonder of nature, devolved into a popular mascot for the university's sports teams. In 1975 a fire destroyed the Barnum Museum and, with it, Jumbo's hide. A university employee scooped up the hide's ashes and

1.3 Ringling Brothers Circus Parade in St. Thomas, 1895. Courtesy of Elgin County Archives.

stored them in a peanut butter jar. The jar continues to be used "to inspire the college athletic teams that bear his name."[72]

St. Thomas residents likewise prided themselves on a fetishistic connection – however remote – to a piece of the elephant – however small – because his death "had brought a measure of fame" to their city, vaulting it most unexpectedly onto the international stage.[73] E.H. Flach, at the time a young boy who witnessed the collision, found one of Jumbo's toenails on the tracks and exhibited it in the window of his family business for decades.[74] Other residents who were present at the spot where Jumbo died later recounted their interpretation of events and had their photos taken "for posterity."[75] One resident penned a children's storybook about Jumbo.[76] Various plastic, cardboard, and papier maché versions of Jumbo appeared in the city's parade floats, school assignments, and annual shivarees. These bore a suspicious resemblance to the large-eared "Dumbo" and

"Elmer," two cartoon elephants that were popular entertainment and educational figures for children in the postwar period.[77] A local dry cleaning business took Jumbo's name as its own.[78] And when Hollywood produced a musical about a circus elephant called *Jumbo*, starring Doris Day and Stephen Boyd as the star-crossed singing sweethearts, the manager of the local Capitol cinema lobbied, albeit unsuccessfully, to host the Canadian premiere in St. Thomas.[79]

Remembering Jumbo

In 1977, a simple plaque commemorating Jumbo was installed near the site of the collision that killed him. However, as the centenary of his death approached, the city swung into action to capitalize on the occasion with the spectacle of a holus-bolus resurrection of the elephant, sparking another round of Jumbomania. By the early 1980s, St. Thomas had lost its status as a major railway hub. The automobile, which was introduced for the first time in Germany the year Jumbo was killed, rapidly supplanted flesh-and-blood and then iron horses as *the* modern means of ground transportation, ushering in an era of "automobility" that changed drastically both lives and landscapes.[80] Ontario had the largest number of registered passenger vehicles in the country; in 1904 that number topped off at 535, but by 1930 it had jumped to 490,906.[81] Automobile manufacturing sprang up in the cities of Windsor and Oshawa. The provincial government pumped money into a road network that included a superhighway inspired by the German *autobahn*. It was inaugurated in 1939 as the "Queen Elizabeth Way" (QEW). The QEW and the province's rapidly growing network of highways, which extended south into the United States, contributed to urban growth and automobile tourism.[82] During the Second World War, the volume of railway traffic through St. Thomas spiked temporarily but declined thereafter. Passenger rail and freight service to the city ended in 1957 and 1965, respectively, and railway workers began working for nearby manufacturing plants connected to the Ford Motor Company.[83]

A Jumbo Centennial Committee (JCC) was struck after Mayor Doug Tarry floated the idea of building a larger than life-sized statue of Jumbo. Tarry was well aware of oversized roadside attractions marking small towns and cities in the province. Such monuments have been interpreted as "a system of totemic representation" signalling the vitality of a community and a distinctive sense of place in order to put a town or city "on the map."[84] Tarry noted that a Canada goose (27 ft., 150,000 lbs.) represented Wawa; Dryden was branded by Max the Moose (18 ft., 4,000 lbs.) and Kenora by Huskie the Muskie (40 ft., 2.5 tonnes). "Every town wants its own thing," Tarry told a television reporter, "this [statue of Jumbo] is our thing."[85] The choice of an African elephant killed in a freak accident was far more incongruous a totem for a small southern Ontario city than indigenous creatures such as a Canada goose, a moose, and a muskie. However, the image of a large elephant, whether Asian or African, had by now metamorphosed into a generic communication device advertising abundance, greatness, and affluence.[86]

The JCC certainly had Jumbo-sized ambitions. Members hoped that a grandiose statue of Jumbo would become a recognizable tourist attraction, boost a local economy battered by the recession of the early 1980s, and draw international attention once again to a city that lay within easy driving distance of the United States.[87] In effect, the JCC would invoke the spectacle of Jumbo to brand St. Thomas as a still-spectacular city. Some St. Thomas residents were unconvinced of the benefits of associating themselves with Jumbo's tragic death; one voiced her opposition to the scheme only when she realized that the proposed statue was not an April Fool's joke.[88] Yet others were convinced that it would work wonders. A St. Thomas lawyer told the city council that if "a big rock" (Ayer's Rock) in Australia could attract international tourists so too would Jumbo's statue with a wallop of "promotion, promotion, promotion. That's what does it. Jumbo ice-cream, Jumbo hot dogs, Jumbo this, Jumbo that. Everyone in every language knows what Jumbo is. Jumbo means big."[89]

Still, opposition erupted over the Jumbo-sized cost of the statue. Winston Bronnum,[90] the New Brunswick artist who had already dotted Maritime Canada with large roadside attractions such as a moose, an old racehorse, and a potato, was selected to sculpt Jumbo's likeness. Estimates of the cost ballooned quickly from $50,000 to $75,000.[91] Robert Stollery, JCC chair and owner of a Ford Motor Company dealership, headed the fundraising campaign with the help of the Kiwanis Club. Courted by big city media seeking interviews, Stollery remarked cheerfully: "We think the exposure St. Thomas will get all over North America will make the worry, the blood, sweat and tears all worthwhile."[92] Residents pitched in to raise the money, selling Jumbo-related paraphernalia such as gold and silver

1.4 A Jumbo Days bumper sticker, 1985. Courtesy of Elgin County Archives.

commemorative coins as well as mugs, plates, posters, bumper stickers, hats, T-shirts, bags, buttons, and children's colouring books emblazoned with his image. Safari-style hats for men and women were a pricier item. These were modelled after the fedora worn by "Indiana Jones," the lead character in a popular action-adventure Hollywood film, *Raiders of the Lost Ark* (1981). Significantly, the fictional Jones was based on the real life Belzoni.[93] In this cinematic account of Belzoni's adventures, actor Harrison Ford portrays Jones, a white American archaeologist who uses brains and brawn to triumph over rough-and-tumble savage tribes, murderous Arabs, and thuggish Nazis in Egypt. His facility with fists, pistols, and whips remains a staple of popular narratives of white male heroics in colonial lands. Local newspaper advertisements capitalized on this Orientalized plotline; advertising copy flaunted "Indiana Jones and the JUMBO HATS," depicting Jones "crashing through the forest with a trail of wild savages behind"[94] in a desperate quest for a fedora.

Just where to erect the statue also emerged as a cause for concern. The actual site of Jumbo's death was not an option. With the construction of new manufacturing plants to the east of the city, the downtown core had become destabilized despite attempts at its revitalization. Tarry and the JCC made a case for the west entrance of the city, proposing that a concrete Jumbo could anchor an urban complex of appealing art shops, tea houses, cafés, an artist's gallery, and a museum spotlighting the city's automotive, railway, and natural histories.[95] Further controversy erupted over the direction the statue should face. Stollery opted for an eastward-facing Jumbo because passing motorists would be able to see "an exciting profile of the beast" for over a mile. However, local administrator Bob Barrett was sensitive to the fact that the statue would be located on public land

1.5 Crowds celebrating Jumbo Days surround the unveiled statue of Jumbo, 1985. Courtesy of Elgin County Archives.

adjacent to a residential street, admonishing that homeowners driving up Talbot St. would be exposed to "an obscene view" of the elephant's enormous rear end.[96] One homeowner complained to the City Council that the statue would stand directly opposite her private residence, while an engineer worried that a full frontal vision of a massive pachyderm might distract motorists on Highway 3.[97]

Despite objections to cost and location, a spectacle planned for the elephant's "HOMECOMING WEEKEND" during "JUMBO DAYS" proceeded apace. In early June, after a three-day journey from Bronnum's Maritime studio, the concrete rendition of Jumbo rolled into St. Thomas in several pieces chained to a flatbed truck.[98] Security guards hired to protect the statue from potential vandals led a pleased Stollery to remark cheerfully, "This one of the first of many ways Jumbo is helping fight unemployment in St. Thomas."[99] The timing of the spectacle – 27 June to 1 July 1985 – had no relation to the date of Jumbo's death. The dates coincided with the annual Canada Day holiday weekend that celebrates the anniversary of the enactment of the British North American Act, virtually guaranteeing the attendance of large crowds. The local newspaper did its bit, recycling an interview with the late George Robbins, a resident who had witnessed Jumbo's death in his youth. Robbins proposed that the elephant had committed suicide and recalled that his keeper had moaned in anguish over dead Jumbo's body.[100] These touching details were sandwiched between fun-filled advertisements and announcements. The local mall took advantage of JUMBO DAYS with an advertisement for a "JUMBO SAFARI SIDEWALK SALE" and a "JUMBO DOLLAR PROMOTION" on aluminum foil, toilet tissue, tropical fish, cat food, and flea collars. Announcements for the HOMECOMING WEEKEND betrayed hints of the city's decline, calling upon residents to "write to your loved ones who have left St. Thomas and invite them home for this historic occasion" with the promise not of employment but of an antique car parade, a musical band, a 100-gun firecracker salute and, last but not least, performing elephants from the Canada's Super Circus International.[101]

JUMBO DAYS publicity turned out to be so spectacularly compelling that a decision was made to reveal the reconstituted statue prematurely. On 28 June, 106-year-old Ruby Copeman, a local luminary who was a young girl at the time of Jumbo's death, unveiled the monument in front of a crowd estimated at 800 persons. The artist had sculpted Jumbo's trunk curled back upon his forehead in a friendly salute. But he also endowed his creation with freakishly long and pointed tusks, a feature the elephant did not possess in life because he had worn them down in captivity. A dairy farmer gazing at the monument noted that in contrast to other roadside attractions in Ontario, Jumbo was not an indigenous but an "international" symbol for St. Thomas.[102] A few days later, two circus elephants identified as Sahib and Judy were photographed flanking the statue, each raising a foreleg in honour of Jumbo.[103] It was estimated that in the month following the unveiling 30,000 visitors came to see the statue from all the Canadian provinces and some American states, with other visitors dropping in from Australia and New Zealand. In contrast only 15–20 individuals attended the actual centennial anniversary of Jumbo's death at the plaque erected near the location of the collision, with Mayor Tarry commenting: "Nothing else has put St. Thomas on the map like Jumbo's death and it is still doing so today, although not quite like it did 100 years ago."[104]

Conclusion

Tarry's statement was nothing if not poignant. The statue of a friendly but powerfully tusked bull elephant resurrected from the dead a century after Jumbo's ill-fated encounter with the Grand Trunk Railway's iron horse mirrored the well-meaning, albeit exaggerated hopes of politicians and residents to jolt St. Thomas back to economic life. Yet Jumbo was hardly the vehicle to turn this small city into an international automobile tourist destination. Today, the statue remains at the west end of St. Thomas with a reproduction of a small locomotive and a decorative flowerbed for company. The automobile industry and manufacturing sector are in tatters, storefronts on the main streets are boarded up, and unemployment runs high, but a local craft brewery has produced a Railway City Dead Elephant Pale Ale in a cheeky nod to Jumbo's memory and the city's history.[105]

Jumbo's metamorphosis from African captive to British icon to American celebrity to Canadian roadside attraction masks a colonial journey from a putative state of savagery to civilization to spectacle. This journey was punctuated by the violence of abduction, captivity, and commodification, and not by the joyful abundance, greatness, and affluence that generic images of large elephants have come to communicate. Jumbo's fate was common not just to other charismatic megafauna transported to zoos and circuses in cities in Europe and the New World but also to many human animals designated slaves and freaks, establishing how closely racialization and animalization are intertwined. Still, had Jumbo eluded his original abductors he may not have fared any better given the partition of Africa by colonial powers and the rapacious trade in ivory. Similarly, with or without Jumbo as its roadside attraction, St. Thomas would surely have experienced the same economic blight that has only intensified its grip on small urban centres in southern Ontario with the advent of globalization, often said to be a modern-day manifestation of colonialism.

Notes

1   Neel Ahuja, "Postcolonial Critique in a Multispecies World," *PMLA* 124, no. 2 (2009): 556–63. For their background research I thank my research assistants Sarah Mackenzie, Cathrine Chambers, Simone Parniak and Emma Burgess. I am also grateful to Donna Hanson, St. Thomas Public Library; Archivists Gina Coady and Stephen Francom and assistant Meineke Kulasinghe, Elgin County Archives; Michael Baker, Elgin County Railway Museum; and my colleagues William Jenkins, Louis Patrick Leroux, Andrew McClellan and Amani Whitfield. Joanna Dean, Cameron Glennon, Darcy Ingram, Nigel Rothfels, and Christine Waechter were encouraging from the start.

2   Ahuja, "Postcolonial Critique," 556.

3   Shefali Rajamannar, *Reading the Animal in the Literature of the British Raj* (New York: Palgrave Macmillan, 2012), 6; and Ajuha, "Postcolonial Critique," 55–59.

4   Kay Anderson, "'The Beast Within': Race, Humanity, and Animality," *Environment and Planning D: Society and Space* 18 (2000): 301–20. See also Colleen Glenney Boggs, "American Bestiality: Sex, Animals, and the Construction of Subjectivity," *Cultural Critique* 26 (Fall 2010): 98–125, and Nicole Shukin, *Animal Capital: Rendering Life in Biopolitical Times* (Minneapolis and London: University of Minnesota Press, 2009).

5   Paul Chambers, *Jumbo: This Being the True Story of* The Greatest Elephant *in the World* (Hanover, NH: Steerforth Press, 2008), 7. This is just one of several popular books recounting the details of Jumbo's story.

6   David Eltis, *The Rise of African Slavery in the Americas* (New York: Cambridge University Press, 2000).

7   Robert Miles and Malcolm Brown, "Representations of the Other," in *Identity and Belonging: Rethinking Race and Ethnicity in Canadian Society*, ed. Sean P. Hier and B. Singh Bolaria (Toronto: Canadian Scholars' Press, 2006), 19–30; and Rosemarie Garland Thomson "Introduction," in *Freakery: Cultural Spectacles of the Extraordinary Body*, ed. Rosemarie Garland Thomson (New York and London: New York University Press, 1996), 1–19.

8   Nigel Rothfels, "Trophies and Taxidermy," in *Gorgeous Beasts: Animal Bodies in Historical Perspective*, ed. Joan B. Landes, Paula Young Lee, and Paul Youngquist (University Park: Pennsylvania State University Press, 2012), 117–36; Nigel Rothfels, *Savages and Beasts: The Birth of the Modern Zoo* (Baltimore: John Hopkins University Press, 2002); Harriet Ritvo, *The Animal Estate: The English and Other Creatures in the Victorian Age* (Cambridge, MA and London: Harvard University Press, 1987); John M. Mackenzie, *The Empire of Nature: Hunting, Conservation and British Imperialism* (Manchester: Manchester University Press, 1988); and Ian Jared Miller, *The Nature of the Beasts: Empire and Exhibition at the Tokyo Imperial Zoo* (Berkeley: University of California Press, 2013).

9   For a sense of the enormity of this enterprise, see Nigel Rothfels, "Catching Animals," in *Animals in Human Histories: The Mirror of Nature and Culture*, ed. Mary J.

Henninger-Voss (Rochester, NY: University of Rochester Press, 2002), 182–230.

10   Chambers, *Jumbo*, 10.

11   A. D. Bartlett, *Wild Animals in Captivity* (London and Bungay: Richard Clay and Sons, 1899), 61–62.

12   Georges Cuvier, quoted in Bernth Lindfors, "Circus Africans," *Journal of American Culture* 6, no. 2 (Summer 1983): 10.

13   Bernth Lindfors, "Ethnological Show Business: Footlighting the Dark Continent," in Thomson, *Freakery*, 210; and Lydie Moudileno, "Returning Remains: Saartjie Baartman, or the 'Hottentot Venus' as Transnational Postcolonial Icon," *Forum for Modern Language Studies* 45, no. 2 (2009): 200–212.

14   Robert W. Jones, "'The Sight of Creatures Strange to our Clime': London Zoo and the consumption of the exotic," *Journal of Victorian Culture* 2, no. 1 (1997): 1–26.

15   Bartlett, *Wild Animals in Captivity*, 47. On animal resistance, agency and injury, see Jason Hribal, *Fear of an Animal Planet: The Hidden History of Animal Resistance* (Petrolia, CA: CounterPunch and AK Press, 2010).

16   Abraham Bartlett, quoted in Chambers, *Jumbo*, 68. The original quotation appears in Bartlett, *Wild Animals in Captivity*, 46.

17   Ariela Gross, "Pandora's Box: Slave Character on Trial in the Antebellum Deep South," *Yale Journal of Law and the Humanities* 7 (1997): 267–316. For a brilliant treatise on willful bodies and objects, see Sara Ahmed, *Willful Subjects* (Durham, NC, and London: Duke University Press, 2014).

18   Sujit Sivasundaram, "Trading Knowledge: The East India Company's Elephants in India and Britain," *The Historical Journal* 48, no. 1 (2005): 27–63.

19   These tropes were also apparent in British picture books for children. See Alix Heintzman, "E is for Elephant: Jungle Animals in Late Nineteenth-Century British Picture Books," *Environmental History* 19, no. 3 (July 2014): 553–63.

20   Matthew Scott, *Autobiography of Matthew Scott, Jumbo's Keeper and Jumbo's Biography* (Bridgeport, CT: Trow's, 1885), 79 and 75.

21   George Orwell, *Shooting an Elephant and Other Essays* (London: Secker and Warburg, 1950 [1936]), http://www.orwell.ru/library/articles/elephant/english/e_eleph. (accessed 19 July 2016).

22   Sivasundaram, "Trading Knowledge," 55–60.

23   Bartlett, *Wild Animals in Captivity*, 48–49.

24   Thomson, "Introduction," in Thomson, *Freakery*, 5.

25   Benjamin Reiss, "P. T. Barnum, Joice Heth and Antebellum Spectacles of Race," *American Quarterly* 51, no. 1 (March 1999): 87; and Bernth Lindfors, "P. T. Barnum and Africa," *Studies in Popular Culture* 7 (1984): 20.

26   Ian Radforth, *Royal Spectacle: The 1860 Visit of the Prince of Wales to Canada and the United States* (Toronto: University of Toronto Press, 2004), 206–41, and James S. Moy, "The First Circus in Eastern Canada," *Theatre Research in Canada*

/ *Recherches théâtrales au Canada* (January 1980), http://journals.hil. unb.ca/index.php/TRIC/article/ view/7538/8597 (accessed 10 August 2014). See also Louis Patrick Leroux, "Reinventing Tradition, Building a Field: Quebec Circus and its Scholarship," in *Cirque Global: Quebec's Expanding Circus Boundaries*, ed. Louis Patrick Leroux and Charles Batson (Montreal and Kingston: McGill-Queen's University Press, 2016), 3–21.

27 Janet M. Davis, *The Circus Age: Culture and Society Under the American Big Top* (Chapel Hill and London: University of North Carolina Press, 2002).

28 Susan Nance, *Entertaining Elephants: Animal Agency and the Business of the American Circus* (Baltimore: Johns Hopkins University Press, 2013). See also Susan Nance, "Elephants and the American Circus," in *The American Circus*, ed. Susan Weber, Kenneth L. Ames, and Matthew Whitmann (New York, New Haven, CT, and London: Bard Graduate Centre and Yale University Press, 2012), 233–49.

29 A. H. Saxon, *P. T. Barnum: The Legend and the Man* (New York: Columbia University Press, 1989), 292–93.

30 Susan Nance, "Jumbo: A Capitalist Creation Story," *Antennae* 23 (Winter 2013): 86; and Chambers, *Jumbo*, 94.

31 James Joyce, *Ulysses: A Reproduction of the 1922 First Edition* (Mineola, NY: Dover, 2002), 319. See also Christabelle Sethna, "Animal Sex: Purity Education and the Naturalization of the Abstinence Agenda," *Sex Education: Sexuality,* *Society and Learning* 10, no. 3 (2010): 267–79.

32 Scott, *Autobiography*, 68.

33 "Jumbo Landed in Safety," *New York Times*, 10 April 1882.

34 "Jumbo," *New York Times*, 11 April 1882.

35 Saxon, *P. T. Barnum*, 293; and Philip B. Kunhardt, Jr., Philip B. Kunhardt III, and Peter W. Kunhardt, *P. T. Barnum: America's Greatest Showman* (New York: Alfred A. Knopf, 1995), 281.

36 Charles Edenshaw, Exposition at the National Gallery of Canada, 7 March 7–25 May 2014, http://blogs. ottawacitizen.com/2014/03/07/ charles-edenshaw-a-giant-of-haida-art-now-at-the-national-gallery-of-canada/ (accessed 21 March 2014). My thanks to Joanna Dean for this information.

37 Janet Davis, "Spectacles of South Asia at the American circus, 1890–1940," *Visual Anthropology* 6, no. 2 (1993): 121–38.

38 "Jumbo in his Quarters," *New York Times*, 11 April 1882.

39 "The Great and Only Jumbo," *New York Times*, 22 March 1883.

40 "Jumbo Landed in Safety."

41 Scott, *Autobiography*, 81–86.

42 "Jumbo in his Quarters," *New York Times*, 11 April 1882.

43 "Subdued Only By Death," *New York Times*, 6 April 1883. See also Nance, *Entertaining Elephants*, 105–37.

44 Letter from P. T. Barnum, dated 9 August 1882, reprinted in Roslyn Poignant, *Professional Savages: Captive Lives and Western Spectacle*

(New Haven, CT, and London: Yale University Press, 2004), 58.

45 Bluford Adams, "'A Stupendous Mirror of Departed Empires': The Barnum Hippodromes and Circuses, 1874–1891," *American Literary History* 8, no. 1 (Spring 1996): 34–56; Davis, "Spectacles of South Asia," 121-138.

46 Carolyn Strange and Tina Loo, "Spectacular Justice: The Circus on Trial, and the Trial as Circus, Picton, 1903," *Canadian Historical Review* 77 (June 1996): 159–84.

47 Poignant, *Professional Savages.*

48 "At Barnum's Circus," *New York Times*, 27 March 1883. A similar quotation also appears in Chambers, *Jumbo*, 176.

49 Ron Brown, *In Search of the Grand Trunk: Ghost Rail Lines in Ontario* (Toronto: Dundurn Press, 2011).

50 See Heike Paul, "Out of Chatham: Abolitionism on the Canadian Frontier," *Atlantis* 8, no. 2 (June 2011): 165–88; and Sarah-Jane Mathieu, *North of the Color Line: Migration and Black Resistance in Canada 1870-1955* (Chapel Hill: University of North Carolina Press, 2003), 61–99.

51 Les Harding, *Elephant Story; Jumbo and P. T. Barnum Under the Big Top* (Jefferson, NC: McFarland and Co., 2000), 3.

52 Elgin County Archives (hereafter ECA), ECVF box 50, file 28, Brian Henley, "When the circus – and Jumbo – came to town" *Hamilton Spectator*, 16 July 1994.

53 Scott, *Autobiography*, 76.

54 "Barnum and Jumbo in Quebec," *Quebec Daily Telegraph*, 1 September 1885.

55 ECA, ECVF box 50, file 28, "Jumbo's Last Visit: Barnum Returns No More," *Hamilton Daily Spectator*, 18 September 1885.

56 "The Great Jumbo Killed," *New York Times*, 17 September 1885.

57 Phineas T. Barnum, *The Life of P. T. Barnum, Written By Himself* (Buffalo, NY: Courier Company, 1888), 333.

58 ECA, ECVF, box 68, file 25, Letter to the Editor by E. H. Flach, "E. H. Flach, an Eye-Witness, Tells Story of Jumbo's Death," *St. Thomas Daily Times*, 9 April 1907.

59 Elgin County Archivist Stephen Francom identified Jumbo's keeper and the railway official.

60 ECA, ECVF, box 68, file 25, Letter to George [George M. Dingman] from "Nipper" [N. B. Scott] 30 November 1978. Confusion reigns over the identities of the men in the foreground of this famous photo. I have adopted the identification provided by Stephen Francom.

61 Donna Haraway, "Teddy Bear Patriarchy: Taxidermy in the Garden of Eden, New York City, 1908-1936," *Social Text* 11 (Winter 1984–85): 20–64.

62 Adam Hochschild, *King Leopold's Ghost: A Story of Greed, Terror, and Heroism in Colonial Africa* (New York: Houghton Mifflin, 1998).

63 Andrew McClellan, "P. T. Barnum, Jumbo the Elephant, and the Barnum Museum of Natural History at Tufts University," *Journal of the History of Collections* 24, no. 1 (2012): 45–62.

64 *London Daily News*, 18 September 1885.

65 ECA, ECVF box 50, file 28, "Jumbo," *St. Thomas Weekly Times*, 24 September 1885. See also John Sutherland, *Jumbo: The Unauthorised Biography of a Victorian Sensation* (London: Aurum Press, 2014), 136.

66 Harvey Young, "The Black Body as Souvenir in American Lynching," *Theatre Journal* 57 (2005): 639–57.

67 ECA, ECVF, box 50, file 28, "Jumbo," *St. Thomas Weekly Times*, 24 September, 1885. See also Wayne Paddon, George Thorman, Don Cosens, and Brian Sim, *St. Thomas: 100 Years a City 1881–1981* (St. Thomas, ON: St. Thomas Centennial Committee, 1981), 124.

68 Scott Trafton, *Egypt Land: Race and Nineteenth-Century American Egyptomania* (Durham, NC: Duke University Press, 2004). See also Carley Henderson, "The Face of the Mummy" (2008). *Undergraduate Research Awards*. Paper 1, http://scholarworks.gsu. edu/univ_lib_ura/1. (accessed 19 July 2016). Museums large and small have acquired several mummies; Canada's Niagara Falls Museum unknowingly housed the mummified body of the Pharoah Rameses I until it was sold to an Atlanta museum, where it was positively identified and subsequently returned to Luxor, Egypt. See Laura Ranieri, "Niagara's most famous mummy," *stcatherinesstandard.ca*, 20 April 2012, http://www.stcatharinesstandard. ca/2012/04/20/niagaras-most-famous-mummy. (accessed 19 July 2016). Several museums in Canada still showcase mummies in their collection of Egyptian antiquities. The Redpath Museum in Montreal, in collaboration with artists and anthropologists, has even attempted to model and display the mummies' reconstructed facial features. See Redpath Museum: Third floor. http://www.mcgill.ca/ redpath/exhibits. (accessed 19 July 2016).

69 ECA, ECVF box 50, file 28, "Jumbo," *St. Thomas Weekly Times*, 24 September 1885.

70 McClellan, "P. T. Barnum," 52.

71 *New York Times*, 18 April 1886.

72 McClellan, "P. T. Barnum," 58. See also Rachel Poliquin, *The Breathless Zoo: Taxidermy and the Cultures of Longing* (University Park: Pennsylvania State University Press, 2012), 6.

73 W.L.F. Edwards, *The Story of Jumbo* (St. Thomas: Sutherland Press, 1935), 14.

74 ECA, ECVF, box 68, file 25, letter to the Editor by E. H. Flach.

75 ECA, EVCF Hundredth Anniversary of Jumbo, box 1, file 30, *Official Souvenir Program, JUMBO 1885–1985*, 12.

76 Edwards, *The Story of Jumbo*.

77 Charlie Thorson is credited with creating "Elmer the Safety Elephant" for the Toronto police department's traffic safety program. He modelled Elmer after the Disney Studio's Dumbo. See Gene Walz, "Charlie Thorson: Bugs Bunny's Winnipeg Connection," *Take One* (Summer 1997): 30–33.

78 Information extracted after viewing a series of photos related to Jumbo that are on deposit at the ECA.

79 ECA, Scrapbook, "Jumbo's Ghost Unlocks Trunk Full of Memories,"

St. Thomas Times Journal, 28 June 1985.

80 Peter Merriman, "Automobility and the Geographies of the Car," *Geography Compass* 3, no. 2 (2009): 586–99.

81 Stephen Davies, "'Reckless Walking Must Be Discouraged': The Automobile Revolution and the Shaping of Modern Urban Canada," *Urban History Review/ Revue d'histoire urbaine* 18, no. 2 (October 1989): 124.

82 See Edwin. C. Guillet, *The Story of Canadian Roads* (Toronto: University of Toronto Press, 1967), 166–68; John C. Best, *Thomas Baker McQuesten: Public Works, Politics, and Imagination* (Hamilton, ON: Corinth Press, 1991), 147; and John Sewell, *The Shape of the Suburbs: Understanding Toronto's Sprawl* (Toronto: University of Toronto Press, 2009), 49–74.

83 Paddon, Thorman, Cosens, and Sim, *St. Thomas*, 15, 143–45; and Don Cousens, personal communication, Elgin County Archives, 30 May 2014.

84 David Stymeist, "The Totemic Art of Small-Town Canada," *Journal of Canadian Studies/Revue d'études canadiennes* 46, no. 1 (Winter 2012): 5–27. For an updated list of Canadian roadside attractions see: http://www.roadsideattractions. ca/ontario.htm. (accessed 19 July 2016).

85 "St. Thomas' Jumbo the Elephant," CBC Digital Archives, 1985. http://www.cbc.ca/archives/ categories/lifestyle/travel/super-sized-sights-of-canada/st-thomas-jumbo-the-elephant.html (accessed 26 August 2014). See also:

"Big Things in Ontario," http:// www.bigthings.ca/bigon.html (accessed 26 August 2014).

86 Nance, "Jumbo," 89–93.

87 Richard John Auckland, "Urban Symbols: A Case Study of Jumbo the Elephant and St. Thomas, Ontario" (Senior Honours Essay, Department of Geography, Faculty of Environmental Studies, University of Waterloo, 1986).

88 Ibid., 22–26. See also ECA, ECVF, box 90, file 5, St. Thomas History–Jumbo, "Not everybody climbing on Jumbo's bandwagon," *London Free Press*, 8 May 1984.

89 ECA, R9 S5 Sh6, box 3, file 6. Jumbo Statue Project, 1983–1987, "Kiwanis Club tells council . . . No Jumbo statue if people don't want it," *St. Thomas Times-Journal*, n.d.

90 http://www.bigthings.ca/artists/ bronnum.html. (accessed 19 July 2016).

91 ECA, ECVF, box, 90, file 5, St. Thomas History–Jumbo, "Jumbo's statue's cost keeps pace with fame," *London Free Press*, 26 March 1985.

92 ECA, Scrapbook, Tim Gallagher, "San Francisco Here I Come! Jumbo Stirs Interest in U.S.," *St. Thomas Times-Journal*, n. d.

93 Barbara J. Black, *On Exhibit: Victorians and Their Museums* (Charlottesville: University of Virginia Press), 151. For more on the relationship of Orientalism to Hollywood films see Ella Shohat, "Gender and Culture of Empire: Toward a Feminist Ethnography of the Cinema," in *Film and Theory: An Anthology*, ed. Robert Stam and Tony Miller (Oxford: Blackwell, 2000), 669–96.

94 ECA, R9 S5 Sh6, box 3, file 6, Jumbo Statue Project, 1983–1987, "Indiana Jones and the JUMBO HATS," *St. Thomas Times-Journal*, n. d.

95 ECA R9 S5 Sh6, box 3, file 6, Jumbo Statue Project, 1983–1987, Clyde Warrington, "Statue of Jumbo could revitalize west end: Stollery," *St. Thomas Times-Journal*, n. d. See also Paddon, Thorman, Cosens, and Sim, *St. Thomas*, 148–49.

96 ECA R9 S5 Sh6, box 3, file 6, Jumbo Statue Project, 1983–1987, Clyde Warrington, "Which is best? East or West for Jumbo Statue," *St. Thomas Times-Journal*, n. d.

97 ECA, ECVF, box 90, file 5, St. Thomas History–Jumbo "Council ignores late complaints about Jumbo," *London Free Press*, 6 March 1985.

98 ECA, Scrapbook, "JUMBO – Finally Here," *St. Thomas Times-Journal*, 6 June 1985 [?].

99 ECA, Scrapbook, "Mammoth Security for Jumbo Statue," *St. Thomas Times-Journal*, 11 June 1985.

100 ECA, Scrapbook, Commemorative foldout from the *St. Thomas Times-Journal*, June 28, 1985.

101 ECA, Jumbo Elda Mae Patterson Fonds R6 S6 SH5, box 1, file 25, newspaper advertisement foldout and Scrapbook, "The Great Jumbo" pamphlet.

102 ECA, Scrapbook, Alex Horkay, "Our Jumbo home at last!" *St. Thomas Times-Journal*, 29 June 1985 [?]. See also Auckland, "Urban Symbols," 20.

103 ECA, Scrapbook, clipping of newspaper photo dated 2 July 1985.

104 ECA, Scrapbook, "Moment of silence Sunday in city pays tribute to Jumbo anniversary," *St. Thomas Times-Journal*, 18 September 1985.

105 Greg Keenan, "How the Economic Storm Battered St. Thomas, Ont.'s Factories," *Globe and Mail*, 9 July 2011. In 2015 a second life-sized statue of Jumbo was unveiled, this time at Tufts University. Depicted comparably to the St. Thomas version, but this time with Jumbo's true-to-life shortened tusks, Tufts' bronze mascot commemorates the 125th anniversary of the taxidermied elephant's arrival on campus. Big things are still expected of Jumbo, with one of the donors remarking that "a new Jumbo [will] lead to enhanced enthusiasm for Tufts and thus over the years to more involvement and contributions to the university." See Gail Bambrick, "Big Man on Campus," *TuftsNow*, 21 April 2015, http://now.tufts.edu/articles/big-man-campus (accessed 12 November 2015). An art exhibit featuring materials from Canada and the United States preceded the statue's unveiling. See also Andrew McClellan, *Jumbo: Marvel, Myth, and Mascot* (Woburn, MA: Hannaford and Dumas, 2015)

The Urban Horse and the Shaping of Montreal, 1840–1914

SHERRY OLSON

And when did you last meet a horse on the streets of Montreal? In Mount Royal Park, next to the antenna at the summit, a small modern stable houses the eight black horses the police use to patrol the park; and close to the St Lawrence riverfront, an old wooden "horse palace" shelters several of the horses who drive tourists along the cobbled streets of the old centre. In the core of the city today, however, between the mountain and the river, horses are scarce, despite the fact that from 1840, when the city was incorporated, to the First World War, the city depended on several thousand horses.

Dependence on horses, I shall argue, shaped the urban landscape and our interpretation of city living. The phantom thousands still cast their shadows on the layout of the town, and our sensitivity to plans for to-morrow's habitats will benefit from an appreciation of that long and intense collaboration of humans and horses. First, to get acquainted with the phantom population, let us consider their numbers and their various roles in building the city and making it work. That will lead to a second set of questions, about the design of the city: How did the city accommodate its horses? In what parts of town were their homes and workplaces? In the third section, from diaries and contracts of the horse-dependent decades I extract clues to the behaviours of horses and people as close neighbours. The fourth section considers their interdependence as a factor in the emergence of modern medicine.

The Horse at Work in the City

Painters and novelists have glamorized the warhorse; agricultural economists have interrogated the plowhorse; specialized farmers and gamblers continue to compile elaborate breeding records for racehorses; but in the historiography of cities the heavy-duty draft horse is given short shrift. Daniel Roche and his students have compiled rich sources on the "culture" of horsemanship in France as a model for elite upbringing over centuries. Francis M.L. Thompson has shown that toward the end of the nineteenth century the numbers of horses in British cities were constrained by the demands they made on space and feed.[1] Essays on the omnibus and horse railway report limited ridership and a persistent exploitation of the labour of both horses and humans.[2] For US cities, Clay McShane and Joel Tarr have explored mechanical applications of horsepower and environmental aspects,[3] and Ann Norton Greene expands their perspective by asserting "historical agency" for the horse, through production of power that shaped material and social arrangements.[4]

Trends were similar in all the big cities of eastern North America, with rapid substitution after 1890 of the "horsepowers" of electric and gasoline engines. The Canadian story is nuanced by the rigours of climate, and Montreal in particular by its metropolitan scale of demand for equine services and its mix of cultural preferences in the breeding and management of its horses.[5]

Despite the perennial efforts of cities to discipline drivers and regulate the weights and wheel widths of vehicles, historians have despaired of counting, and precise estimates of the numbers of horses in Montreal are open to question. The coachman or hackman was usually an individual entrepreneur with just one horse, while livery stables might maintain a dozen to provide carriages for business, pleasure trips, and special occasions. The doctor, the pharmacist, and the priest required a horse and carriage (Figure 1); and most of the city's nineteenth-century butchers, bakers, grocers, and milkmen had their own horse and cart. "Carters," whose full-time business was hauling, usually had two horses or three, and operated family enterprises in which sons and nephews were associated, not specified in the records. In the 1840s and '50s, horse-and-cart had to be able to access every dwelling in town, in order to perform vital services: emptying the pit privies, and delivering water from the river and firewood from rafts at the riverside.

2.1 Public carriage, Montreal, ca. 1875. Courtesy of McCord Museum, VIEW-1063.1.

If we estimate from the household heads registered and taxed for horses (Table 2.1), from the 1860s their numbers rose more slowly than total households, much more slowly than metal workers or railway personnel; and their median rent did not rise as much, remaining just a little higher

Table 2.1 Economic status in the horsey trades

NUMBER OF HOUSEHOLDS HEADS

	1848	1861	1881	1901
Carters	287	716	1075	1429
Drivers	10	34	580	874
Labourers	563	2046	5174	9221
All households	5320	12330	33350	65434
Machinists	46	49	372	1243

MEDIAN HOUSEHOLD RENT ($/YEAR)

	1848	1861	1881	1901
Carters	40	48	50	70
Drivers	-	48	40	70
Labourers	40	36	40	60
All households	64	48	50	80
Machinists	62	48	60	80

PER CENT WHO OWN HOUSE

	1848	1861	1881
Carters	31	24	21
Drivers	30	9	6
Labourers	17	6	4
All households	31	19	14
Machinists	20	10	12

Source: Ville de Montréal, Rental taxrolls, City and suburbs

Table 2.2 Horsedrawn equipment registered, Montreal, 1865-1895

FOUR-WHEELED VEHICLES

	1 horse	2 horses	Total	% 2 horses
	(a)	(b)	(a+b)	(b)/(a+b)
1865	738	44	826	5.3
1870	1531	210	1741	12.1
1875				
1880	1634	227	1861	12.2
1885	2168	378	2546	14.8
1890	2964	612	3576	17.1
1895	3225	733	3958	18.5

Source: Ville de Montréal, Annual Reports of Police Chief

than the base-level "labourers." The numbers of "master carters" were declining, that is, the independent entrepreneurs who owned their own animals and equipment. By 1880, about one third of the tradesmen are reported as mere "drivers," that is, waged employees of a livery stable or street railway. By 1901 the wage-earning share amounted to more than half, and their wages were low, a dollar a day.[6]

Can we count the vehicles? To operate year round, even the loner with a single horse needed a variety of equipment: a wheeled vehicle for seven or eight months, a vehicle on runners for four or five, a spare set of wheels in his yard, and harness and housing for animal and gear. Records compiled in Table 2.2 show a trend toward vehicles built for heavier loads, drawn by two-horse teams, and the trend accelerated in the 1890s.

Horses were still delivering all building materials: stone, gravel, and sand from the quarries, brick by the thousands from the brickyards, lumber from the planing mills. The handsome four-horse teams of the breweries attracted attention, as did impressive rigs such as the forty two-horse sleighs that conveyed a trainload of Mexican hemp from the Canadian

Pacific Railway station in the east end (at Dalhousie Square) to the rope and plaster mills at Point St. Charles. "On top of each sleigh were lads with horns from which they blew blasts at frequent intervals."[7] Horses drew the firefighters' steam pumps, and their exertion was doubled by the urgent pace. Exceptional manoeuvres are described much earlier, such as the slow and risky transport of the seven-ton "monster bell" in 1843 from the docks to Notre-Dame Church four blocks away.[8] The bell had to be raised to the top of the 213-foot tower, and this kind of work, too, relied on the muscle-power of horses.

In addition to the resident animals, horses towed the first generation of canal boats, and powered the passenger coaches that fanned out from the city and the farm wagons that supplied the public markets. From the south shore, much of the farm produce crossed the St. Lawrence at Longueuil. From 1819, when primitive steamboats were already plying the St. Lawrence between Montreal and Quebec City, the wagons crossed on a horse boat, that is, a ferry powered by pairs of horses who turned the paddle wheels by walking a treadmill on the deck.[9] The horse boats were replaced by steam ferries in the 1840s, but all the boats were laid up for winter, November through March, and the horses, dependable in all seasons, followed a track laid out on the ice, closely monitored and marked by fir trees (Figure 2.2). In spring and fall, during the two- or three-week spells when the ice was perilous, Montrealers felt the shortages of butter and eggs and poultry, and the horses themselves felt the shortages of feed and clean bedding.

The horse-drawn City Passenger Railway, operating between 1861 and 1893, used three different types of vehicles, for three seasons: open-air summer cars on the rails, closed cars on runners for winter, and wheeled vehicles (the omnibus) for the shoulder seasons when mud and ruts demanded the most strenuous efforts from the horses. The service opened with eight vehicles and six miles of track; by 1889 it was operating thirty miles of line with 150 cars, 104 sleighs, 49 omnibuses, and a thousand horses. The eight million rides a year produced an attractive profit but in fact satisfied only a small share of the daily back-and-forth of the working population. The luxury nature of the service is apparent in the description of a new closed car purchased in 1886 for the line on Saint Catherine Street, with its seven windows on each side, "seats of perforated wood, backs covered with handsome and removable crimson carpet." It featured

2.2 Drawing hay to market across the St. Lawrence River, 1903. Courtesy of McCord Museum, VIEW-3618, Wm. Notman & Son.

three lamps, brass fittings, and a guardrail at each end "to prevent going over a horse if one stumbles."[10]

Although one might suspect steam power of supplanting muscle power (Figure 2.3), all the evidence suggests that the horse and the steam engine were complementary. Horsepower delivered coal from the docks to the industrial boiler plants, and horses drew the logs out of the snowed-in forest to the steam sawmills. "High-tech" construction for the Victoria Bridge (1853–60) employed steam engines for dredge, crane, and pumps but nevertheless employed 144 horses throughout the project for skidding timber, hauling stone, and some of the pile driving. The post office created a railway mail service and in the summer season used steamboats for the heavy-traffic axis of the St. Lawrence River, but the filigree of postal services to every hamlet depended on contracts by stagecoach or horseback, "with a good and sufficient bearskin or oil cloth covering for the mail

2.3 Horse and rider at railway crossing, "Look out for the Engine," drawing by John Henry Walker. Courtesy of McCord Museum, M991X.5727. The railway crossing at grade still tempts the reckless driver. Nineteenth-century Montrealers amused themselves at considerable risk to their horses as well as themselves. Carrying their prejudices with them, British editors criticized the spirited *Canadien* rider and his spirited horse (pictured here), while the *Canadiens* protested the "fast driving" of the offspring of Scottish and English wealth as they showed off their sleighs on a Sunday afternoon; and the older generation of Irish Catholics tolerated the determination of their young people to beg, borrow, or steal a horse for the St Patrick's Day parade.

pouch."[11] At all the transfer points for freight and passengers, the horse ensured the intermodal link: between railway stations in the city, between opposite banks of the river, between the docks and the depot, or the mill and the freight station.

Hydraulics and steam, by concentration of mechanical power, fostered larger enterprises, apparent in Montreal in the 1850s for working iron, building locomotives, and making nails (Figure 2.4),[12] and horse-powered

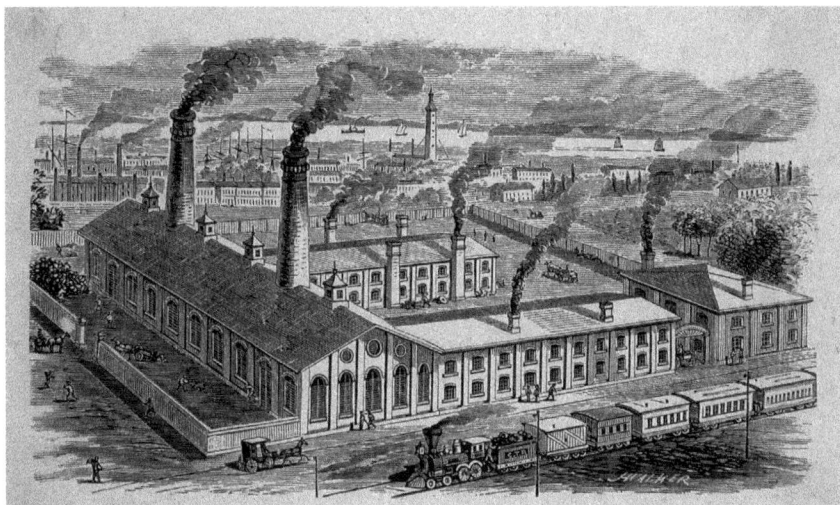

2.4 W. M. Mooney & Co., Horse Shoe Nail Works, Montreal. Wood engraving by John Henry Walker. Courtesy of McCord Museum, M930.50.3.249. Mooney utilized hydraulic power at a canal lock close to the port. At least two larger nail works were already using steam power. The artist points out the presence of horse-drawn traffic and steam carriage through the same streets, sail and steam vessels in the harbour, and coal smoke as the powerful image of industrialization.

enterprises expanded in parallel. The Commissariat, for example, the logistic arm of the British army, awarded a single contract each year to cover all their hauling needs in the Montreal region; they practised competitive bidding but chose always an entrepreneur of relatively large scale and financial worth.[13] In passenger transport, omnibus and rail companies branched out to burgeoning suburbs as independent lines but subsequently regrouped in successive bids for control of the market, reinforced by political alliances.

Concentration of express cartage was generated in 1864 when the Grand Trunk Railway made John Shedden its sole agent for transfer of goods from the point of shipment to the station in Montreal, and from the station to the point of delivery. Inclusion of the wagon express trip in the railway freight rate gave Shedden a unique advantage. At that moment he had 64 horses (the largest stable in town), by the end of the century 400, and expansion continued in 1903 when the firm bought a $100,000 property for development of new stables close to the union stockyards for handling transfer of cattle between railway platforms, steamships, and slaughterhouses.[14]

The horsepower oligopolists, like Shedden and City Passenger Railway, possessed an overwhelming bargaining position relative to their drivers. Shedden's agreement in 1864 provoked a major crisis of labour when the carters resisted the Grand Trunk imposition of a monopoly. All tactics failed - the carters' week-long strike, intervention of the Board of Trade, an appeal to the mayor and city council, and a lawsuit. The result, as Margaret Heap has argued, was proletarianization of the horsey trades.[15] The next year City Passenger Railway reduced wages of its conductors and stifled a strike of conductors and stablemen. (Conveniently for the company, their former manager had become the city's chief of police.) The lagging wages of carters and drivers, the larger proportion of waged drivers, and the decline in their rate of home ownership (as shown in Table 2.1) are all indications of what is now known as "de-skilling": small-scale artisans or entrepreneurs with a degree of independence were being replaced by wage workers with little control over their working conditions.[16]

The shift away from the "walking city" – people and horses – began in earnest with electrification of the street railway in 1892, and by the First World War motorized trucks were replacing the teams of horses. The pressures were complex, and a decisive squeeze came from the rising value of urban land. Thanks to the traffic and trade handled by horses, Montreal had grown in radius to four kilometres along the lines of horsecars, and in height to eight-storey buildings at the centre. Horse traffic was taking up more and more of the ground floor of the city, with a peak of 400 horses per hour on Craig street. Congestion was becoming intolerable. More horses required more calories, more storage capacity for feed and hay, more horses to deliver it, and a longer supply line. For their rations of hay and oats, the horses of Montreal were competing with the horses of New York City.

Horsepower metabolism generated waste products in due proportion, demanding more ground for short-term storage and more steady labour of horses to haul it away. A horse produced on the order of 22 pounds per day of manure, or eleven times the solid waste of a full-grown human male. What value did it command? In the 1840s innkeeper Bartholomew O'Brien was keeping a horse and a cow in the very centre of town, and about once a month Charles Bowman's coachman picked up a cartload of manure from O'Brien's stable and delivered it to Bowman's elegant greenhouse in Côte Saint-Antoine on the slope of Mount Royal. Both parties benefited, but no money changed hands. In the 1850s, gardener Joseph Beauchamp, preparing to sell his two-acre garden on the same sunny slope, contracted with his buyer to share the hauling of 150 cartloads of manure, a critical annual input for forcing their roses and lilies and salads for the early spring market. They probably paid nothing for the manure itself. By the 1880s, however, as the town was producing more manure and the market gardens had moved farther out of town (Beauchamp to Sault-au-Récollet), such mutual arrangements no longer covered the cost of transport, and the municipal government was faced with problems of disposal of the mix of manure, ashes, snow, and refuse they referred to as "street dirt." In 1891 the health inspector reported that there were still 3,000 horse stables in the city, "in general a nuisance, not drained or ventilated, and . . . almost always too close to houses."[17]

In other words, convenience was accompanied by nuisance, and the urban horses, long before they were evicted, were perceived as obsolete. Both Tarr and Greene argue that the nuisance was exaggerated, and the more important factor was an enthusiasm for "progress," which tended to demote the horse and, by 1911, to idealize a "horseless city."[18] The appearance of the "horseless carriage" on the streets of Montreal in 1899 inspired optimism, but as late as the 1940s, farms in the region relied on horses, and Montreal still had 3,000 in service for home delivery of ice, bread, and milk. Both horses and drivers were increasingly marginalized, and their disappearance is now so complete that to discover the impact of the horses on urban design, we shall have to contend with their ghosts.

The Shadow of the Horse on the Design of the city

So long as the city depended on horses, it had to accommodate them. What parts of the city did they occupy? To identify equine habitat, a good indicator is the presence of cartways or passages through a row of houses such as shown in Figure 2.5. Emergence of this feature is evidence of the rise in value of urban land. In the 1840s the horse could use narrow lanes between buildings to reach the yards in the interior of the block, but in the building boom of 1871–72 it was worthwhile for a property owner to build

2.5 Cart entrance under a terrace of houses built ca 1871 on Mountain Street near Wellington. Courtesy of Jason Gilliland.

rooms over any such passage. Plates of Goad's Atlas show 1,100 covered passages in 1881, 2,800 in 1912, most of them 8 to 10 feet wide, adequate for a team of two horses with wagon or carriage. In many cases the owners of adjoining lots had signed an agreement to share and maintain the passage, and the legal servitude itself is a key to the persistence of demand for horsepower and the residential choices of its suppliers.

In Figure 2.6, the extent of covered cartways and of rail yards is further evidence of the complementarity of steam power and horsepower. The two types of transport reached their peak about this time (1912), and every industrial enterprise now needed its rail spur for the boxcar, just as every home half a century earlier had depended on the lane for the horse-drawn cartload of wood or water. The city had grown in great surges, urban population had doubled and doubled again (recall Table 2.1). As new neighbourhoods developed, many workers moved farther from the docks: roofers and painters followed the building frontier, railway employees followed the tracks and locomotive shops, quarriers and stonecutters moved closer to new quarries in Mile End. But the carters and drivers, as late as 1912, were still concentrated in neighbourhoods they had occupied in the 1840s.

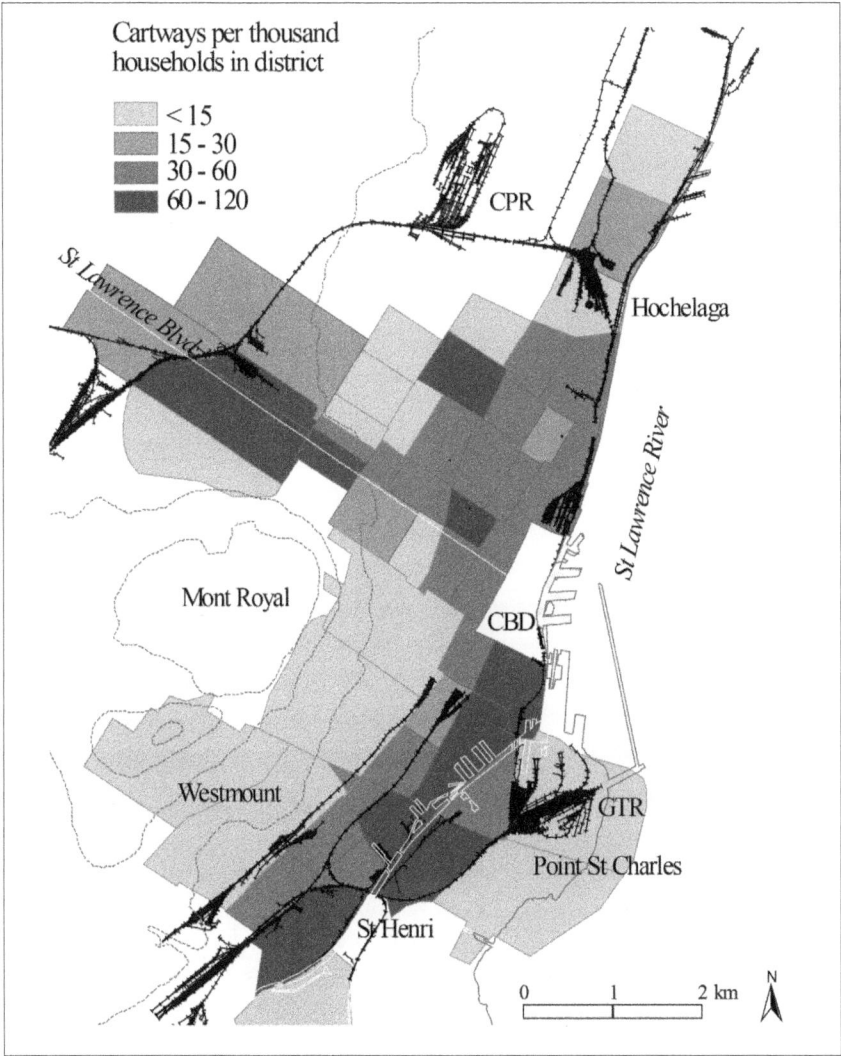

2.6 Cartways per thousand households by district, Montreal, 1912. Re-created in MAP layers after Atlas of C.E. Goad 1912 and Census of 1901 population estimates. Map by Sherry Olson.

The map suggests several classic elements of explanation: topography, centrality, and land values. The topographic constraints can be observed in many other cities, founded on a waterfront, and extending gradually onto higher ground. As businesses demanded cartage of larger volumes and heavier goods, the uphill run was a severe limitation, especially under winter conditions and for the fast travel of firefighters. The carters therefore stayed on the flats nearest river and canal, to take advantage of traffic-generating docks, railway stations, and public markets. A block from the peak traffic intersection (Craig and St. Lawrence streets), the street railway company built its stable for 400 horses. Most carters, however, could not afford high-value land; they did not stable their horses in high-status residential areas, nor in the high-rent business streets near the docks, where they produced daytime congestion stressful to the horses with its stop-and-go demands.[19]

The rise in land values affected also the sizes and shapes of the lots. The oldest blocks, where carters were numerous, were a tinderbox of small houses and smaller stables, sheds and privies, all walled in wood plank, floored with timber, roofed with wood shingle, stuffed with flammables like hay, and separated by board fences 5 to 10 feet high. After the conflagration of July 1852, which destroyed one fifth of the city's housing stock, the all-wood buildings were made illegal for human occupancy, but they were still used for housing horses and carpenter shops. The more resistant brick-clad rows of 1871, two or three storeys high, with their covered passageways into wide, deep lots, would survive longer, but layouts of the 1880s and 1890s featured smaller lots whose narrow frontage and shallow depth eliminated the option for a row of stables at the back of the lot.[20]

The older deep lots were sometimes trimmed. In 1891, when capital was being raised for the electric street railway, city council proposed to accommodate it by widening major arteries like St. Lawrence Main and Notre-Dame East. To shave off a 30-foot (10-metre) strip of frontage from all the lots on one side required tearing everything down and rebuilding on the shortened lots. Compensation hearings record conflicting opinions about the values built into the old horsey layout of yards and "dependencies" convenient for horse-drawn vehicles. The owner of one lot was explicit about the importance of the turning radius of the cart, 16 to 18 feet. The most substantial grocer, resident since the 1830s, argued that his large yard (60 by 47 feet), allowed him to offer parking to south-shore farmers who crossed by the steam ferry and took this route to the downtown markets. "I've often seen 30 or even 40 vehicles in his yard," his agent testified, "It's essential." Mr. Chivé the pharmacist demanded, "With no room for a stable, where will I put my delivery horse?" and the exasperated city lawyer replied, "Let him put it where he wants . . . He can rent a stall in a livery stable for $1.50 a month." At that rate, the cost of housing a horse was approaching the cost of a room in the family dwelling, or the average rent per person citywide.[21]

Horses and people living together

The high-density mix of homes and stables is enough to spark the imagination: at night the sounds of the horses chewing and moving in their stalls, in the morning the jingle and rattle and stomp as the horses were led out, and the scents of hay and leather and piss and manure. Requiring at least minimal care twenty-four hours a day, the horse was part of the household. Horses had names, of course, and faces and personalities. Like those eight black police horses, chosen from the "Canadian" breed, trained to endure brass bands and shouting, and specially shod for traction on ice, each horse was accustomed to a particular person.

Journals and contracts provide further clues to the intimacy between horses and people. Bartholomew O'Brien, the innkeeper, refers to his animals: In May 1843, "Put the colt on grass at 10 shillings a month"; in August, "Got the stable cleansed"; in September, "Brought the horse from grass." "Bought a cow; she calved; saw the calf"; in February, "Horse evacuated white worm 6 inches long." That spring O'Brien sold his horse, gig, and harness, and after that for a Sunday drive he borrowed horse and carriage from his butcher neighbour McShane. But notations in the journal show a continued dependence on hired horsepower: "Took away 7 loads snow." Two days later, "Nine loads." His wife's purchases for operating the small inn (six guestrooms) included a barrel of hops, in the fall eleven cords of birch and maple firewood, two pigs ready for salting, a barrel of apples, a barrel of mineral water, a barrel of oysters . . . [22] Each transaction involved a few shillings for delivery and, in the case of the grain dealer's regular driver, a glass of warmth.

Tracing particular families suggests that over the first half of the nineteenth century, some carters were climbing a recognized ladder of social status, but the strike of 1864 was indeed a turning point, and their contracts confirm a narrowing of opportunities in the following decade. The five children of Pierre and Thérèse Beauchamp came into Montreal in the wake of the great fire of 1852, when reconstruction generated enormous demands for hauling brick and lime and timber. The four sons were carters, and the daughter married another. Each of the five couples was equipped with a kit of horse, harness, cab, and water barrel. Léon, for example, in 1862 rented out his red horse, full harness, three-seat sleigh (brown with red runners), buffalo robes and pillows stuffed in grey cashmere, a large cart, and the feed, all for $5 a month. Each of the five couples managed to obtain a building lot in the same street, built a small wood double-duplex, and improved it with fire-resistant brick cladding. The family occupied a ground floor unit and rented out the twin dwelling and the two little apartments in the attic storey to smaller households (two or three persons), newcomers to the city. The Beauchamp families were financially a little more secure than average, thanks to the houses they had acquired, but they had reached a limit: the spaces they occupied were below the city-wide median in floor area and value. In 1872 Léon's brother Joseph sold his four-wheeled Rockaway of local manufacture, with harness, for $412, about one third less than what he had paid for the house; and when Léon died (about the same time), all the furnishings of the house and stable amounted to $100, just enough to cover legal costs and funeral. His widow Mathilde's inventory encapsuled their modest lifestyle: she noted "a bucket for the house and a bucket for the horse."[23]

Irish-born Arthur Ryan and his wife, after the strike of 1864, ran a little hotel on Wellington street for a few years. In 1871 he sold it to a saloon keeper, but kept his harness and carriage gear and partnered with his father-in-law, John Mulhern, to buy and sell cattle. Ryan had a lease on two one-storey houses with yard, shed, and stables near the St. Antoine market, but a fire on an adjoining lumberyard destroyed everything (19 July 1873), and the landlord's delay in rebuilding, he complained, was forcing him to keep his horses at a livery stable and buy them hay by the bundle instead of by the cartload. When Ryan died (1889), his mother-in-law Mrs. Mulhern, now a widow, managed to pay off the building society; the house was "under order to be pulled down as a danger," and the list of people present at the after-death inventory makes it clear that their social network was still centred on horses. Arthur's brother and eldest son were horse dealers; a son-in-law was a driver, another a grocer, and two witnesses, friends of the family, were horseshoers.

2.7 Mr. Wray's horse and sleigh, Montreal, 1870. Courtesy of McCord Museum, I-44209.1, William Notman.

As the options narrowed, some carters concentrated their activities as wood or coal dealers, and some succeeded in niche markets with specialty vehicles. Charles Dumaine, from the moment of the 1864 strike, used his political connections to develop a business as undertaker: his location was convenient for carting bodies fished from the river and making them available for coroner's inquest. Joseph Wray, who appears in Figure 2.7, obtained in 1883 the contract to operate the new horse-drawn ambulance for the Montreal General Hospital. Wray and Dumaine were among the first to take advantage of the telephone. A few years later Dumaine was questioned about a lucrative racket in funeral ornaments, with associates in Ontario and the United States, and in 1903 he still held his municipal privilege of transporting unclaimed bodies. A reporter described how the horses drawing a flower-strewn wedding carriage, the white-ribboned vehicle for a baptism, the crepe-decked hearse, and the hideous morgue wagon all found their way home to the same stable door, "where they're grooming the horses and talking politics."[24]

In such close everyday proximity, horses and their masters – the "dominant animal" – shared their moments of ill temper, the horseflies, and the fleas; and the families dependent on the horse shared their anxiety about the health of the animal. How serious was the limp, the drooping head, the dripping nose, or the refusal of food?

Pathology and Progress

The great concentrations of hospital patients in nineteenth-century cities made possible new clinical observations in medicine, a new conception of clinical teaching, and integration of laboratory work with scalpel and microscope. Lost sometimes from sight is the intense interaction between observations of humans and of other species – interactions that historians of veterinary medicine argue contributed to the spectacular breakthroughs of the late nineteenth century in the use of antiseptics, surgical techniques, identification of disease vectors, and development of vaccines.[25] Horses in particular, so heavily concentrated in cities, were perceived as valuable enough to merit medical care and scientific research, so that veterinary science emerged as an urban profession. Important centres of innovation in comparative anatomy, comparative physiology, and comparative pathology were Berlin, Paris (Alfort), Vienna, Edinburgh, and Brussels, where the stables of omnibus and horsecar lines provided clinical and experimental opportunities on a scale comparable to the urban lying-in hospitals and institutions of *l'Assistance publique*. In this context, Montreal, with its fast growth, its crossroads location in the transport network of the continent, and its bilingual access to transatlantic networks of science, was large enough to attract in the 1870s a red-hot cluster of young scientists who paid attention to both human and equine disease.

Duncan McEachran and William Osler resettled in Montreal at about the same time (1870) and became close friends and collaborators. McEachran had trained in Edinburgh, started practice in Toronto, and founded a veterinary college in Montreal. He arranged to have his students attend lectures with the medical students at McGill University, and take the same examinations, while the medical students took their classes in pathology and anatomy at the veterinary college. Osler, meanwhile, had done undergraduate work in Toronto and graduate work in medicine at McGill. In his postgraduate work in Berlin, he was deeply impressed with Rudolph

Virchow's comparative method and demonstrations of delicate techniques of dissection that made autopsy the prime tool for research into parasites, malformations, and the body's chemical and cellular responses to infection and injury. In his years in Montreal (1870–72 and 1874–84), Osler mentored students of both institutions and involved them in the one thousand (human) autopsies he directed at the Montreal General Hospital. Taking the same interest in post-mortem examination of other species, Osler published reports on parasites (trichinosis) in the pork supply of the markets, made an examination of the lungs of a horse that died of pneumonia in the flu epidemic, and, with the help of the veterinary students, investigated a bronchitis of dogs at the Montreal Hunt Club; the autopsies showed that a worm was the cause of the fatal "epidemic cough."

The students of the veterinary college obtained clinical experience by daily rounds, visiting 400 horses every morning, patients in their own "horse hospital" and in the stables of Shedden, the street railway, the ice company, and the omnibus company – clients who paid a monthly fee for routine care and diagnostics. Since horses amounted to a large share of their working capital, stable owners recognized the economic value of keeping them healthy. Horses were usually about five years old and fully trained, when they were purchased for urban service, and might work five to ten years before they were sold off to marginal farmers. The street railway drivers (easier to replace than the animals), worked a 12-hour schedule, handling two relays of horses to cover the morning, noon, and evening rush hours, with additional crews of stablemen to handle the feeding and grooming.[26]

Companies dependent on horsepower were interested also in getting the greatest return from that biochemical engine. The applied scientists in Europe provided evidence that the efficiency of the horse as a "living motor" was far greater than the efficiency of the steam engine. A rapid digestion allows the animal to increase oxygen consumption in a spectacular way, and enables heavy work for 4 to 6 hours, on condition of alternate days of rest, adequate fodder (hay), and an appropriate ration of fuels higher in protein, usually oats.[27] The Paris omnibus company, proprietor of ten thousand horses, weighed them regularly to verify that nutrition was keeping pace with energy expended.[28] By the 1870s, agricultural chemists were proposing new combinations of feed; carriage makers were competing to re-engineer harnesses and springs; cities were experimenting with new paving materials to improve traction and reduce the noise of horses' hooves. In Europe, military applications (for supply trains as well as cavalry) justified the creation of national research stables where collaborations occurred similar to that between McEachran and Osler. At Alfort, for example, Étienne-Jules Marey, in connection with his analyses of circulation of blood, created instruments for recording the pulse and heartbeat of the horse, and photographing the shadow of his movements at a walk, a trot, a canter, or a gallop.

Having learned that the trot required twice the energy of the walking pace, and that the limitations were rates of digestion, feeding, and thickness of muscle, research establishments began "tailoring" the horse, by breeding trotters for the hacks and cabs, and heavyweights for hauling at a walk.[29] "Improvement" strategies stimulated international trade in stallions. Meanwhile, the enormous demand for horses during the Civil War in the United States had depleted the Canadian market and come close to ending the tradition of the "all-purpose" Canadian breed descended from the gifts of Louis XIV and appreciated for its combination of docility and spirit. Reconstruction and renewal of the breed, with debate over ideal size and weight, justified the creation of breeding societies, stud books, a research station, and a herd of government mares. Among the enthusiastic horse breeders in Montreal in the 1880s were the veterinarian McEachran, five or six of the city's millionaires, and Osborn Morton, a "fearless jockey" born a slave in Kentucky.[30]

Settlement of the prairies of Canada and the United States demanded import of thousands of horses from Britain, France, and Belgium, while Britain was importing horses from Belgium, France, and Germany for its urban omnibus fleet, and the breeding ventures produced further cross-currents, making Montreal a centre for syndicates for the international market (some more trustworthy than others). At the time of the Boer War (1899–1901) several thousand horses were selected in western Canada and shipped through Montreal to South Africa, thousands more for the First World War.[31] All of these movements – by steamboat and railway, or by a trot across the border – spread diseases, and outbreaks were aggravated by collection of army horses in dense herds, under stressful conditions.

The increase of international traffic in horses therefore required a new level of regulation for testing, quarantine, and disposal of dead animals. Students of the Montreal Veterinary College (MVC) – few but highly selected – founded a suite of veterinary schools in Montreal, both English and French. Joseph-Alphonse Couture became the first inspector at the animal quarantine at Lévis, and organized breeding records for both the *cheval canadien* and the *vache canadienne*. MVC graduates organized provincial and federal laboratories for production of drugs and vaccines, and they spearheaded efforts to obtain inspection of horses for export from Canada (1896), inclusion of horses in the federal Animal Contagious Diseases Act, and the testing of imported horses (1908).[32] All maintained the philosophy of comparative medicine articulated by Osler in a public lecture to the veterinary college in 1876: he used skeletons of a horse, a fish, a goat, and a man to demonstrate the similarity of structure and to impress upon his audience "that similarity in animal structure is accompanied by a community of disease, and that the 'ills which flesh is heir to' are not wholly monopolized by the 'lords of creation.'"[33]

There are, of course, additional reasons why horses and human beings shared their ills. Because of the intimacy among domestic animals (as described earlier), horses suffered from tuberculosis (bovine or human), rabies, and the various tapeworms, roundworms, and pinworms that stunted the growth of human children in nineteenth-century Montreal. Because humans and horses shared the same messy, high-density urban environment, they were subject also to traffic accidents, tetanus (lockjaw), heat exhaustion, slips on the ice, drowning, septicemia, and stress-induced nervous and compulsive behaviours. Despite customary law, municipal bylaws, and sentences as severe as six months in jail, animals were subject to abuse – pranks, beatings, and hard driving. When "Murphy turned out a horse to die" on an unfenced vacant lot, it attracted "vicious boys who pelted the poor animal."[34]

But the vulnerability of the horse to such ills as heart disease, anemia, cirrhosis of the liver, tumours, tooth decay, and sexually transmitted diseases arose in large measure from the commonality of structure Osler and McEachran emphasized. Horses and humans have similar vulnerabilities because they share the fundamental genetic building blocks conserved in a long process of mammalian evolution. Some of the intersections of economic pressures and scientific advance can be glimpsed from two diseases in which horses were centrally involved: an inconvenient epidemic of "horse flu" and the recurrent outbreaks of a more deadly disease known as glanders.

The week-long carters' strike in 1864 had made Montrealers acutely aware of their dependence on horses, and they were further sensitized by a two-week siege of a "catarrh of horses" in October 1872. First observed near Toronto (in Markham and York townships), the disease moved rapidly along rail lines, westward to Chicago, St. Louis, and Omaha; eastward to Montreal (15 October), from there to Halifax and south to New York City and Charleston. By early December the malady reached Santa Fe and Havana. In each city, within two or three days virtually every animal in a stable developed the hacking cough and running nose and eyes. On 18 October all the cab horses in Montreal were reported sick, and at the races at Côte Sainte-Catherine, several contestants (reduced in numbers) were taken with such fits of sneezing that they couldn't run. A week later thirty-nine horses had died. Like flu epidemics among humans, epizootic outbreaks (among animals) had occurred for centuries. Referred to as "the zooty," the disease was rarely fatal, but life-threatening complications like pneumonia would set in if the animals were not allowed to rest. As a result, city health officers ordered the passenger railway and express services to stop running. Until 2 November, human beings had to pull wagons, walk when they preferred to ride, and postpone their weddings. The stablemen, meanwhile, burned sulphur and tar, and dosed the sick horses with patent cough medicines and beer. As caricatured in Figure 2.8, "The stables presented the appearance of hospitals, in each compartment was an equine patient on his bed of straw, while up and down went the hostlers with lights, medicines, and blankets."[35]

Recent concern about influenza in human populations has led to rediscovery of the 1872 horse flu and recognition of the simultaneous appearance of a "chicky flu" that decimated flocks along precisely the same routes.[36] The "avian flu" is just one cluster in a vast array of viral infections, bacteria, and parasites exchanged among people and animals. When transmission occurs between species, it affects each in a different way, and is sometimes accompanied by modifications of the virus which make it more virulent or more easily transmitted among humans. Despite the rarity of transmission between species, the mobility of urban horses made them a high-risk vector. Most were raised on farms and were accompanied by dogs; they transported forest products with all their insect pests, and they were themselves exposed to all seasons and habitats.[37] As we have seen, horses ensured the critical links between other modes of transport,

2.8 "The Doctor's Visit" is drawn from a set of four titled "Les chevaux malades," reporting an outbreak of equine flu, but it points to the importance of clinical experience with urban horses in the development of veterinary medicine. Originally published in *L'Opinion publique*, 7 November 1872. Courtesy of McCord Museum, M985.230.5073.2.

between small towns and large, between rural and urban populations, and across international borders.

Glanders, also a disease known since ancient times, was far more devastating than the flu. No vaccine or cure was known, and a painful death was near-certain. Much like the flu, the infection was transmitted among horses by mucous and respiratory secretions, when horses shared troughs, nuzzled, groomed, and snorted. (Since they do not breathe through their mouths, horses snort to clear nasal passages.) When this "loathsome and fatal" infection was occasionally transmitted to humans (often stablemen or farriers), it caused them also great pain, with lesions of the lymph, "breakdown and liquefaction" in many organs. Obstacles to control were the variability of symptoms and incubation times. Infection might go undetected for months, even years, before symptoms were recognized. In 1889, for example, a court ordered Montreal street railways to compensate a farmer for the pair he had purchased from their pool of "cast-off horses."

The horses looked healthy when he closed the deal but were obviously ill when they arrived at the Compton railway station two days later.[38] A sufficiently specific diagnostic test was developed in Europe in 1890 (a skin patch like the tuberculin test). Canada pioneered systematic testing and in 1902 adopted the strategy of destroying every animal that tested positive. To ensure reporting, the federal government provided some compensation to the owner. By such drastic means, control of glanders was achieved in Canada, Britain, and the United States in the 1930s.[39]

As a vector of disease, the horse is no longer seen as an everyday threat. The masses of urban horses no longer exist; the racehorses are pampered; riding stables and breeders are able to vaccinate their horses against glanders, tetanus, rabies, and anthrax; and some horses are raised for their contribution to vaccines for human diseases. The experience of a century ago is nevertheless pertinent to the growing populations of pets in cities today and the commensals – the mice and rats and pigeons that share our stores and leftovers. Veterinary medicine has again become an urban profession, and scientists have applied new tools to affirm the extent to which humans and other mammals share their genome (about 98 per cent) and therefore their vulnerabilities. As a modern heart specialist argues, "Why *don't* we human doctors routinely cooperate with animal experts?"[40] This has renewed interest in the practice of comparative medicine and comparative pathology, the recognition of a concept of "One Medicine," and the exchange of ideas that McEachran, Osler, and Couture introduced in Montreal in the 1870s.

Conclusion

Our tour of Montreal, between Mount Royal and the St Lawrence River, has pointed out features of urban design that reflect the presence of the horse in the past: the overall layout of the city into streets, blocks, and lots, the surfacing of yards and docks. Spaces were adapted to the gait of a horse, the grades and loads and turns a horse could handle. Surviving lanes and passageways retain the dimensions that satisfied horse and driver, those two large animals that together constituted a formidable instrument for remaking landscapes. Today, in the absence of the horse, there may be good reason for holding fast to the scale of the beast, so close to the scale of the human being; for conserving habitats organized with front-and-back, upstairs-and-downstairs; and for preserving a ground-level city at the scale and pace of the 1890s.

As the city grew, servicing the horses demanded more space and energy. The squeeze experienced by the horses 1900–1920 sheds some light on what happened to the railways half a century later – the land was coveted and converted. The same squeeze is now affecting the automobile, since motor vehicles occupy over one third of the city's ground floor and compete for high-rise and underground spaces as well. Their requirements for smooth paving and compaction of land, by reducing the percolation of water, have aggravated flooding, and their massive waste disposal into the atmosphere is a local health hazard as well as a sizable component of global climate change. The century-old question reappears: What degree of congestion will we tolerate?

Exploring the lives of Montreal's once-upon-a-time horses leaves us with yet larger questions that go deeper into the past: questions about the evolution of species, about our own animal nature and our life-and-death intimacy with other animals. For the city dweller today, any encounter with a horse is an excursion into the past. So next time you meet a horse on the street, you may find yourself face to face with questions the young Charles Darwin, expert in dissection and horsemanship, was asking himself in 1837:

> If we choose to let conjecture run wild then animals our fellow brethren in pain, disease death & suffering & famine; our slaves in the most laborious work, our companion in our amusements. They may partake, from our origin in one common ancestor we may all be netted together.[41]

Notes

Acknowledgment: Jean-Claude Robert shared a first exploration of the topic a decade ago and compiled the statistics of rolling stock. In addition to his *Atlas* and book chapter cited below, he has contributed to the history of streets of Montreal on the website of the municipal archives: http://ville.montreal.qc.ca/portal/page?_page-id=5677,32261565&_dad=por-tal&_schema=PORTAL "Grandes rues de Montréal," in collaboration with the Laboratoire d'histoire et de patrimoine de l'Université du Québec à Montréal.

1 Francis M.L. Thompson, *Victorian England: The Horse-Drawn Society: An Inaugural Lecture* (London: Bedford College, 1970); Francis M.L. Thompson, ed., *Horses in European Economic History: A Preliminary Canter* (British Agricultural History Society, 1983); Ralph Turvey, "Horse Traction in Victorian London," *Journal of Transport History* 26, no. 2 (2005): 38–59; Daniel Roche, *La culture équestre occidentale, XVIe–XIXe siècle: l'ombre du cheval* (Paris: Fayard, 2008), and the sequel, *La gloire et la puissance*, 2011.

2 Norman Beattie, "Cab Trade in Winnipeg, 1871–1910," *Urban History Review* 27, no. 1 (1998): 36–52.

3 Clay McShane, "Transforming the Use of Urban Space: A Look at the Revolution in Street Pavements, 1880–1924," *Journal of Urban History* 5 (1979): 279–307; Clay McShane and Joel A. Tarr, *The Horse in the City: Living Machines in the Nineteenth Century* (Baltimore: Johns Hopkins University Press, 2007).

4 Ann Norton Greene, *Horses at Work: Harnessing Power in Industrial America.* (Cambridge, MA: Harvard University Press, 2009), 58 and xi.

5 Useful for the Canadian historiography are Leah M. Grandy, "The Era of the Urban Horse: Saint John, New Brunswick, 1871–1901" (Master's thesis, University of New Brunswick, 2004); Norman Beattie, "Cab Trade in Winnipeg, 1871–1910," *Urban History Review* 27, no. 1 (1998): 36–52; Darcy Ingram, "Horses, Hedges, and Hegemony," in *Metropolitan Natures, Environmental Histories of Montreal*, ed. Stéphane Castonguay and Michèle Dagenais (Pittsburgh, PA: University of Pittsburgh Press, 2011), 211–27; on urban design and streeting in Montreal, Jean-Claude Robert, *Atlas historique de Montréal* (Montréal: Art global, 1994); Jean-Claude Robert, "Réseau routier et développement urbain dans l'île de Montréal au XIXe siècle," in *Barcelona-Montréal, Développement urbain comparé*, ed. Horacio Capel et Paul-André Linteau (Barcelona: Universitat de Barcelona, 1998), 99–116.

6 The dollar-a-day labourer with a family reported to the Census of 1901 the year's income at $300, and the city's tax assessor estimated his four-room flat at a rental of $60 or $70 a year, excluding heat and the tax for water.

7 *Montreal Star*, 7 February 1885.

8 Cast by Mears & Co. in England, a first bell arrived 21 October 1843; underweight, it failed, and a second bell, heavier still, comparable to that of Notre-Dame of Paris, arrived 19 September 1847. For a drawing, see *Illustrated London News* of 19 August 1843; for details, Louis Adolphe Huguet-Latour, *Annuaire de Ville-Marie* (Montréal, 1872), 410–16.

9 Kevin J. Crisman and Arthur B. Cohn, *When Horses Walked on Water: Horse-powered Ferries in Nineteenth-Century America* (Washington, DC: Smithsonian Institution Press, 1998); local contracts, BAnQ, Notarial archives, Acts of T.-B. Doucet, 21 June and 16 December 1820, 3 November 1827.

10 *Montreal Star*, 27 May 1886.

11   BAnQ, Act of Griffin, 11 December 1829, between Emery Cushing and Andrew Porteous, Post Master at Montreal.

12   Larry McNally, "Technical Advance and Stagnation: The Case of Nail Production in Nineteenth-Century Montreal," *Material History Review* 36 (Fall 1992): 38–48.

13   For example, BAnQ, Act of Gibb, 29 April 1857.

14   *La Patrie*, 8 October 1903, a site bounded by Notre Dame, Richmond, and William streets in St Ann's ward. Shedden's railway privileges extended to numerous other cities, notably in Ontario. Similar shifts toward oligopolistic practice are documented for Paris and London in Nicholas Papayanis, "Un secteur des transports parisiens: Le Fiacre, de la libre entreprise au monopole (1790–1855)," *Histoire, économie et société* (1986): 55–72; Nicholas Papayanis, "The Development of the Paris Cab Trade, 1855–1914," *Journal of Transport History* 8, no. 1 (1987): 52–65.

15   Margaret Heap, "La grève des charretiers à Montréal, 1864," *Revue d'histoire de l'Amérique française* 31, no. 3 (December 1977): 371–95

16   See also Christopher Armstrong and H.V. Nelles, *Monopoly's Moment: The Organization and Regulation of Canadian Utilities, 1830–1930* (Philadelphia: Temple University Press, 1986), and http://stm.info/fr/a_propos/decouvrez_la_STM_et_son_histoire/histoire.

17   City of Montreal, *Annual Report of the Health Department for 1899.*

18   Greene, *Horses at Work*; Clay McShane and Joel A. Tarr, "The Decline of the Urban Horse in American Cities," *Journal of Transport History* 24 (2003): 177–99; Joel A. Tarr, "The Horse: Polluter of the City," in *The Search for the Ultimate Sink: Urban Pollution in Historical Perspective*, ed. Joel A. Tarr (Akron, OH: University of Akron Press, 1996), 323–34.

19   At the core (what we now call "Old Montreal"), 200 cartways remained in 1880, 100 in 1912, but in those blocks there were few private homes, no resident carters, and no stables. The old courtyards had been rebuilt four to eight storeys high, and vestigial "public lanes" functioned as narrow loading docks, accessible only through privately owned passages under buildings.

20   A regulation of 1865, conceived also as a firefighting measure, called for a bearing wall at intervals no greater than 25 feet, and this rule crystallized the practice of laying out building lots 25 feet wide, rather than the 40-foot frontages common in earlier times. On the transition which displaced the load from walls at front and back to the side walls, see Jules Auger, *Mémoire de bâtisseurs, Répertoire illustré des systèmes de construction du 18e siècle à nos jours* (Montréal: Méridien, 1998); on rear dwellings and lot sizes, Luc Carey, "Le déclin de la maison de fond de cour à Montréal, 1880–1920," *Urban History Review* 31, no. 1 (2002): 19–36; on the increase in floor area of working-class dwellings, Jason Gilliland and Sherry Olson, "Claims on Housing Space in Nineteenth-Century Montreal," *Urban*

History Review 26, no. 2 (March 1993): 3–16.

21 BAnQ, Superior Court, Expropriations, dossier 184, Notre-Dame Street East.

22 McCord Museum, Papers of Bartholomew O'Brien, Day Book.

23 Along with many other carters and carpenters, they bought from the Logan estate, at Dorchester and Durham, today Plessis and René-Lévesque boulevard, just north of RadioCanada. The smallest lot was 36 by 75 feet, the largest 40 by 85, typical of the older layouts carters preferred. For details of this family see Sherry Olson and Patricia A. Thornton, *Peopling the North American City, Montréal 1840–1900* (Montreal: McGill-Queen's University Press, 2011); possessions of other carters, Olson, "Feathering Her Nest in Nineteenth-Century Montreal," *Social History / Histoire sociale* 33, no. 65 (May 2000): 1–35.

24 Canada, Royal Commission on Capital and Labor (Ottawa: Government Printer, 1889), vol. 5 Quebec Testimony, witnesses Halpin, Girard, and Murphy. "Voitures de mariage fleuries . . ." *La Patrie*, 5, 9, and 21 October 1903, 10 July 1905, and 26 October 1908.

25 Thomas W. Dukes, "That Other Branch of Medicine: An Historiography of Veterinary Medicine from a Canadian Perspective," *CBMH (Canadian Bulletin of Medical History)* 17 (2000): 229–43; Leon Z. Saunders, "From Osler to Olafson: The Evolution of Veterinary Pathology in North America," *Canadian Journal of Veterinary Research* 51 (1987): 1–26; P.M. Teigen, "Nineteenth-Century Veterinary Medicine as an Urban Profession,"

Veterinary Heritage 23 (2000): 1–5; P.M. Teigen, "William Osler and Comparative Medicine," *Canadian Veterinary Journal* 25 (1984): 400–405.

26 It is likely that the workhorse population of the city was renewed every three years; smaller marginal enterprises like those of Léon Beauchamp and Arthur Ryan were especially vulnerable, seasonally undernourished, and overworked. Rest and nourishment were the prescription for many injuries and ailments, but the workhorses, like their human partners and owners, couldn't afford to rest; cf. Mary Ann Poutanen et al., "Tuberculosis in Town: Mobility of Patients in Montreal, 1925–1950," *Social History / Histoire sociale* 42, no. 83 (May 2009): 69–106.

27 During the War of 1812, Montreal's "Government Horses" were provided with 16 pounds of timothy hay per day, oats (undetermined), and 6 pounds of clean straw weekly. During the Civil War, the Union Army ordered daily rations for wagon trains at 14 pounds of hay and 12 pounds of grain per animal; in terms of the load they could pull under optimal conditions, the team consumed about 6 per cent per day and was underfed (Greene, *Horses at Work*, ch. 4). To complete the European antecedents to Greene's discussion of the "animal motor," see André Sanson, *Traité de Zootechnie* (Orléans: Pigelet, 1901), vol. 3, 295–360. The Paris omnibus company recommended 8 kg of oats per day and had to ensure access to 30 to 50 litres of water.

28 A. Sanson, "Moteurs animés," 304–71, in H. Bouley, J.J. Reynal et al., *Nouveau dictionnaire de*

médecine, de chirurgie et d'hygiène vétérinaires, vol. 13 (Paris: Asselin & Houzzet, 1885); H. Bouley, J.J. Reynal, et al., "Ration," vol. 18, 545–83; "Relations nutritives," vol. 19, 189–94. See also Ghislaine Bouchet, "La traction hippomobile dans les transports publics parisiens (1855–1914)," *Revue historique* 271, no. 549 (January–March 1984): 125–34.

29   In Montreal, McEachran took a special interest in raising Clydesdales from England; Louis Beaubien purchased Percheron stock from France, and Couture focused on improving the smaller Canadian breed, about 1,100 pounds. Paul Bernier, *Le cheval Canadien* (Sillery, QC: Éditions du Septentrion, 1992). For a broader view of trends in animal breeding and international trade, see Margaret E. Derry, *Horses in Society: A Story of Animal Breeding and Marketing Culture, 1800–1920* (Toronto: University of Toronto Press, 2006).

30   After being sold together with a fine horse to a man in St. Louis, Morton escaped to Canada. Employed initially as a servant by members of the wealthy Stephens and Allan families in Montreal, he travelled as a steward on Allan Line ships, managed John Shedden's horse breeding farm in the suburb of Lachine, and developed his own breeding operation at Bluebonnets. At the time of his death – thrown and trampled in a race at the hackmen's summer picnic – he was reported the owner of "the finest thoroughbred stallion in the country" (*Montreal Star* and *La Patrie*, 5 and 6 August 1887).

31   A Canadian regiment, 500 strong, was astonished at the losses in transit despite care in selection and transport: see *Strathcona's Horse: South Africa, 1900–1901* (Edmonton, AB: Lord Strathcona's Horse Regimental Society, 2000); R.J. Moore-Colyer, "Aspects of the Trade in British Pedigree Draught Horses with the United States and Canada c. 1850–1920," *Agricultural History Review* 48, no. 1 (2000): 42–59; and James Robert Johnston, *Riding into War: The Memoir of a Horse Transport Driver, 1916–1919* (Fredericton, NB: Goose Lane Editions, 2004)

32   While programs of veterinary education have since been relocated in agricultural colleges, the suite of three small, pioneering institutions in Montreal left a major imprint on the profession. For details, see Marcel Pépin, *Histoire et petites histoires des vétérinaires du Québec* (Montreal: F. Lubrina, 1986); the online *Dictionary of Canadian Biography*, www.biographi.ca, for the founders: Joseph-Alphone Couture, by Denis Goulet and Frédéric Jean; William Osler, by Charles G. Roland; Duncan McEachran, by Goulet and Jean; Wyatt Galt Johnston, by Denis Goulet and Othmar Keel; Orphyr Bruneau; Victor-Théodule Daubigny, by Louis-Philippe Phaneuf; the classic Harvey Cushing, *The Life of Sir William Osler* (Oxford: Clarendon Press, 1925); and, at the international level, Louis Pasteur.

33   William Osler, "The Relations of Animals to Man," Inaugural Lecture to the Montreal Veterinary College 4 October 1876, *Veterinary Journal and Annals of Comparative Pathology*, December 1876, 465–66.

34   *Montreal Pilot*, 25 August 1859. See also the *Montreal Witness* of

5 March 1873 on cruel practices of the passenger railway; and the *Witness* of 6 August 1887; numerous early incidents in BAnQ, TL36, S37, procès-verbaux des juges des sessions de la paix, Montréal, 1833–1842, such as "maltraité à outrance un cheval attelé" (February 1833).

35   *Montreal Witness*, 17 October 1872.

36   David M. Morens and Jeffery K. Taubenberger, "An Avian Outbreak Associated with Panzootic Equine Influenza in 1872," *Influenza and Other Respiratory Viruses* 4, no. 6 (2010): 373–77; and by the same authors in the same journal issue, "Historical Thoughts on Influenza Viral Ecosystems," 327–37. The origin in Ontario has never been explained, but the events coincide with unique refugee movements from rural Alsace and Lorraine, as reported in Montreal (*La Minerve*, 19 September, 2 and 3 October 1872).

37   United States Department of Agriculture, *Special Report on Diseases of the Horse* (Washington, DC: US Govt. Printing Office, 1942); Nigel Morgan, "Infant Mortality, Flies and Horses in Later-Nineteenth-Century Towns: A Case Study of Preston," *Continuity and Change* 17, no. 1 (2002): 97–130; Denis Goulet and André Paradis, *Trois siècles d'histoire médicale au Québec* (Montréal: vlb éditeur, 1992).

38   Montreal Street Railway Co (appellants) & Percival K. Lindsay (respondent), *The Montreal Law Reports: Court of Queen's Bench*, vol. 6, ed. James Kirby, 125–30.

39   The terms *farcy* and *la morve* refer to the same disease. J. Brian Derbyshire, "The Eradication of Glanders in Canada," *Canadian Veterinary Journal* 43 (2002): 722–26; Lise Wilkinson, "Glanders: Medicine and Veterinary Medicine in Common Pursuit of a Contagious Disease," *Medical History* 25 (1981): 363–84; George Dougal Robins, "A Study of Chronic Glanders in Man," *Studies in the Royal Victoria Hospital Montreal* 2, no. 1 (1906): 1–98. In the 1940s eight workers in a US military laboratory were accidentally infected, and concern resurfaced with respect to its potential for biological warfare. Bridget Carr Gregory and David M. Waag, "Glanders," in *Medical Aspects of Biological Warfare*, ed. Zygmunt F. Dembek (Washington DC: Government Printing Office, 2007), 121–46.

40   Barbara Natterson-Horowitz and Kathryn Bowers, *Zoobiquity: What Animals Can Teach Us About Health and the Science of Healing* (New York: Alfred A. Knopf, 2012), 7, 18; see also Lise Wilkinson, *Animals and Disease: An Introduction to the History of Comparative Medicine* (Cambridge, UK: Cambridge University Press, 1992). On the continuing shared evolution of bacterial and viral infections among humans and their domestic animals, see Ellen K. Silbergeld, *Chickenizing Farms and Food* (Baltimore: Johns Hopkins University Press, 2016).

41   Charles Darwin, Notebook B, p. 232, as cited by A. Desmond & J. Moore, *Darwin, The Life of a Tormented Evolutionist* (New York: W.W. Norton), 238ff.

Wild Things: Taming Canada's Animal Welfare Movement

Darcy Ingram

Introduction

This chapter brings ecofeminist perspectives to bear on perceptions of gender, animals, and ethics in the rapidly urbanizing and industrializing world of Victorian Canada. Its objective is to make sense of the absence of upper- and middle-class women in Canada from a movement that was in other parts of the world so thoroughly associated with them. Their absence, I argue, had little to do with a lack of interest on their part. Rather, it speaks to a process of marginalization that took shape in animal welfare organizations across the country. The many reasons for their marginalization will be articulated below, but the overall rationale was fairly straightforward. In England, where the animal welfare movement developed during the early decades of nineteenth century, observers soon perceived a tendency toward more radical views on the part of the movement's female participants. The American experience quickly confirmed this tendency, so that when Canada's animal welfare movement took shape, the link between women, animal welfare, and radicalism was well established.[1] Augmented by tensions associated with first wave feminism, including demands for greater education, the entry of women into professional circles, and the development of the moral reform, social gospel, and suffrage movements, that link resulted in a paradox when it came to their

3.1 Images such as this from the Toronto Humane Society's *Aims and Objects of the Toronto Humane Society* (1888) captured the widespread understanding of the link between women and animal welfare. Originally published in J. George Hodgins, ed., *Aims and Objects of the Toronto Humane Society*, Toronto: W. Briggs, 1888.

involvement in animal welfare. On the one hand, women were proving throughout the Anglo-American world to be a vital part of the movement to address the ethical dimensions of human–nonhuman animal relations. On the other hand, their vision of animal welfare was often too far-reaching for a society that relied heavily on the exploitation of animals. For many among the mainly white, upper- and middle-class men in Canada who dominated not only the political and economic arenas but also the animal welfare NGOs that developed in urban centres across Canada during the latter decades of the century, this paradox was particularly troubling because of the degree to which their material interests and the Canadian economy were so thoroughly dependent on animals.[2] The result was the widespread perception among both the movement's opponents as well as its movers and shakers that women were simply too radical to be permitted to participate. As a result, their desire to do so had to be directed toward marginal roles. Ironically, one of the key means of accomplishing this was to emphasize the well-established view of women that informed their connection to the movement in the first place – that of the irrational, domestic, nurturing, closer-to-nature, and less-civilized counterpart to the rational, public, cultured, and civilized Victorian middle-class male. In other words, at precisely the time when women were becoming active public sphere participants in the context of first wave feminism and other endeavours, the effort to elevate the status of animals in Victorian Canada was matched by a simultaneous effort to contain, if not lower, that of women. In addition to marginalizing women's participation in the animal welfare movement, such efforts helped to ensure that the movement in Canada remained far more conservative than in England or the United States.

Rethinking Human–Animal Relations in an Urban/Industrial Society

Ecofeminist theory has long grappled with the status of women within the human–animal binary, and some of ecofeminism's central arguments – that the domination of women and the domination of nature (including animals) by men are connected, that the liberation of women and the liberation of nature from such domination are equally linked, and that embracing rather than severing the longstanding historical and cultural connections between women and nature forms a key strategy in that process – speak directly to the politics of animal welfare and rights. As such, the status of women as representatives of an "interconnected" ethical vision based on care and responsibilities (as opposed to a rights-based ethic more commonly ascribed to men) has long positioned them as obvious supporters of animal welfare and rights.[3] That connection seems straightforward until one considers the many implications of the animal welfare movement and the place of women in it during the nineteenth century. In broad terms, those implications comprised sweeping political, economic, social, and cultural changes, including the participation of women in the public sphere and ultimately in the shaping of politics and state policy. Thus while many of the values emphasized in ecofeminism overlap in tangible ways with commonplace perceptions of women and the ideals of first-wave / maternal feminism in the nineteenth century, the place of women in the animal welfare movement was by no means as simple as it may appear.

All of these issues were caught up in the maelstrom of change that characterized this period. Between Darwin's rethinking of the relationship of humans to animals, developments in the medical sciences, and the transformations brought by urbanization and industrialization to established attitudes and practices, Victorians had a lot to contend with when it came to ethics and animals. On the one hand, processes at work were resulting in separation of the humans and animals, inasmuch as urban and industrial life broke longstanding links between them. That break is most notable in the shift from a rural world in which humans and animals were constantly together to an increasingly interdependent society in which the bulk of the human population no longer lived or worked in close quarters with animals. As testament to this separation, one of the most common objectives of municipalities during the nineteenth century was to push animals out of the city as a means of addressing issues including health, sanitation, noise, aesthetics, and social order. On the other hand, were we to magically transport ourselves to a nineteenth-century urban milieu, whether in Montreal, Halifax, Toronto, or any other Canadian city, one of the first things to catch our attention would be the animals. From livestock and labouring horses to dogs and cats both feral and domestic, and finally to the many wild creatures that were adapting in their own ways to the opportunities and challenges of modernity, they were everywhere. In fact, given the demands of the industrial world and the density of the urban spaces in which they moved, they were in some ways becoming even more a part of daily life.[4]

The animal welfare movement was a direct response to these changes. As in the United States, animal welfare NGOs first appeared in Canada in the 1860s, with the establishment of the Canadian Society for the Prevention of Cruelty to Animals (CSPCA) in Montreal in 1869. Attempts to establish SPCA chapters in other Canadian cities were common during the 1870s, but the movement did not really take hold in Canada until the 1880s, alongside urbanization, industrialization, and growing interest in social purity and moral reform. At this point, upper- and middle-class urbanites began to form SPCAs and Humane Societies in cities across the country, so that by the turn of the century there was hardly a city of significant size without one.[5] Tapped into a growing international network, these organizations routinely exchanged materials, and because their cut-and-paste approach to these materials knew no bounds it was entirely normal for animal welfare proponents from Halifax to Victoria to be reading, publishing, and distributing the same information, much of which was coming out of Britain and the United States.

By the 1880s, supporters in Canada were able to draw on a well-developed repertoire that represented animals in sympathetic and at times strikingly human terms. They stocked their libraries with materials including the London SPCA's monthly journal *Animal World*, the Boston-based Massachusetts SPCA's journal *Our Dumb Animals*, and a variety of books, pamphlets, brochures, poems, sermons, society reports, magic lantern slides, and newspapers. Through these materials, supporters presented their subjects in ways that emphasized species' human-like qualities, in part via their capacity to suffer pain but also with regard to their intelligence and their social capacities. In this way, they picked up on the radical challenge that Darwin's evolutionary theory posed to the line that separated humans from nonhuman animals. They drew little inspiration, however, from its survival-of-the-fittest vision or the competitive, cut-and-thrust world of nineteenth-century industrial capitalism that inspired it. Instead, they tended to emphasize cooperation, communication, and community among animals via examples of intelligence, reason, empathy, love, trust, loyalty, and mutual respect. Though the comparison can be easily drawn, this was by no means an edenic or prelapsarian retreat from modernity, but rather a critique of past and present practices and a vision of the direction animal welfare proponents believed civilized society should be headed.

Some of the clearest expressions of these values in Canada are contained in the two books put together by the Toronto Humane Society (THS), *Aims and Objects of the Toronto Humane Society* (1888) and *Work Accomplished by the Toronto Humane Society* (1892).[6] At 232 and 112 pages respectively, these were weighty volumes, and the THS saw that they were distributed throughout the city and to animal welfare NGOs across the country. Both comprised materials from Canada, the United States, Britain, and elsewhere. They presented a variety of narratives common to the movement. Among the most common tropes were dogs rescuing their human companions; birds caring for their young; and horses demonstrating high levels of intelligence. Brought forward in chapters such as "Bird Life," "Kind Treatment of Horses," "Devotion of the Dog," and "Interesting Natural History Facts," these narratives bridged the gulf that separated humans from their nonhuman animal counterparts. In much the same way that Christabelle Sethna argues social purity proponents did with regard to human sexual behaviour, proponents of animal welfare selected from the natural world patterns that appeared to best exemplify the kind of social order they wished to bring forward among humans, made narratives of them, and circulated them as widely as possible.[7]

Equally important to the movement was the depiction of relations between animals and their human counterparts. Through countless examples of human–animal interaction, supporters emphasized not only how humans should treat animals but also how humans should treat each other – all of which speaks to how animal welfare served as a means of establishing behavioural norms for humans. Unlike the examples above, these narratives were not always so positive. Most striking in them was the attention given to violence and brutality directed by humans – almost always men – at animals: the carter who beats his horse mercilessly, boys who shoot songbirds for fun; and countless bizarre instances of cruelty inflicted on dogs, cats, rats, livestock, and other creatures. Often these stories involve animals beset by industrialization in its worst forms, from the treatment of livestock during shipping to the overworking of horses. In this regard, they spoke to the movement's ongoing struggle to come to terms with modernity. Overall, the common theme among this set of narratives entails a reversal that depicts demonstrably uncivilized humans abusing sentient, intelligent, and highly sociable animals.

By contrast, narratives depicting positive relations between humans and animals typically involved women and children. This was fuelled in part by the movement's focus on children's education. Voiced most directly via the movement's Bands of Mercy (children's groups pledged to promote kindness to animals) and its kindness to animals campaigns, such narratives offered young minds carefully selected examples of animal behaviour on which children could model their own actions. In doing so, these materials confirmed those characteristics of care and responsibility commonly associated with women, the family, and the private sphere that fitted neatly into an idealized domestic world, and that offered shelter from the competitive urban industrial world of the nineteenth century. The fact that these three groups – women, children, and animals – were during the nineteenth century linked by their common inability to "speak for themselves," to the point that some NGOs aimed to address all three, underscores their shared identity as defenceless subjects in need of protection.[8] That women often made this link themselves points to the ethics of care and responsibility, but also to a sense of solidarity. As many studies now document, women were drawn to the animal welfare movement in part because the status of animals in society reflected directly on their own marginalization. Buttressed by domestic materials ranging from novels such as Canadian author Margaret Marshall Saunders's *Beautiful Joe*, a dog story which like its equine counterpart *Black Beauty* literally gave a voice to its animal narrator, to the Montreal Veterinary College Society of Comparative Psychology's discussions of animal intelligence, these materials at once elevated the status of animals and challenged that of humans.[9]

Organizing Women: The Parameters of NGO Participation

So how did women fit into this picture? The CSPCA's Ladies' Humane Education Committee offers a good starting point. Established in 1873, it was modelled after the Baroness Angela Burdett-Coutts's organization of the same name in London. Its specific target was children's education – "a sphere of action," it argued, "in which women's influence can be advantageously exercised, as they have opportunities for awakening and training the sympathies of the young, in families, schools, and charitable institutions.[10] The committee worked with teachers and religious leaders to develop humane education programs; organized essay contests on the subject of kindness to animals; distributed materials to families and institutions throughout the city; and set out on a series of fundraising initiatives for the parent society. Popular from the start, it drew forty-five members during its first year of operations. All were from prominent and mostly Protestant Montreal families well connected to the city's growing philanthropic networks.

That the Ladies' Humane Education Committee focused on the wealthy female philanthropist Angela Burdett-Coutts is telling. While women were prominent in the animal welfare movement in England, the more radical female supporters who emerged there and in the United States from the 1870s on did not always endear themselves to upper- and middle-class women seeking to emulate models of respectable female philanthropy.[11]

LADIES' HUMANE EDUCATION
COMMITTEE.

President :

MRS. ANDREW ALLAN.

Vice-President,

MRS. G. W, SIMPSON.

Secretary-Treasurer.

MISS A. McCORD.

Committee.

ALEXANDER, Mrs.	LA ROCQUE, Mrs.
ARCHBALD, Mrs.	LUNN, Miss
BALDWIN, Mrs.	LINDSAY, Mrs. W. B.
BAYNES, Mrs.	LYMAN, Mrs. H.
BIGELOW, Mrs. J. T.	MAJOR, Mrs.
BILLINGS, Mrs.	MACKENZIE, Mrs.
BROWN, Mrs. T. S.	McINTOSH, Mrs.
BRYDGES, Mrs.	MOLSON, Mrs. JOHN
COURSOL, Madame	MUIR, Mrs. R.
CUVILLIER, Miss	MURPHY, Mrs. EDWARD
DAWSON, Mrs.	OXENDEN, Mrs.
DOUGALL, Miss	PAPINEAU, Madame
DRUMMOND, Mrs.	REDPATH, Mrs.
FREER, Mrs.	ROSE, Mrs, W.
MOLSON, Mrs. J. H. R.	RYAN, Mrs.
GIBB, Mrs. J. J.	STUART, Miss
HUTTON, Mrs.	TAYLOR, Mrs. HUGH
JOSEPH, Mrs.	THOMAS, Mrs. F. W.
KERR, Mrs. W. A.	WEAVER, Miss
LEVESQUE, Madame	WHEELER, Mrs.
LANG, Mrs. GAVIN.	WHITNEY, Mrs. N. S.

(For list of Executive Committee see next page.)

3.2 The key players in the Canadian SPCA's Ladies' Humane Education Committee upon its establishment in 1873. Source: Canadian SPCA. *Fourth Annual Report.* Montreal: Protestant Institution for Deaf-Mutes, 1873.

This was particularly true of antivivisectionists who, exemplary though they may have been with regard to their active lives in the public sphere, presented identities that would have been difficult to maintain in the relatively small circles in which this segment of Montreal society moved – all the more so given that many of these women's husbands and sons were prominent and typically more moderate supporters of the parent society. In this sense, Burdett-Coutts's status as 'the richest heiress in all England," a key figure within London's thoroughly respectable Royal SPCA, and a prominent antivivisectionist offered the women of the Ladies' Humane Education Committee a wide range of positions through which they could identify their own activities.[12] Indeed, it is likely that expectations within the group varied considerably, for there seems from its inception to have been something wrong within the committee. Society documents do not explain the issue, and speak in brief but glowing terms of the committee's objectives. Nevertheless, the committee fell apart in 1876 as a result of "insuperable obstacles."[13] Just what those obstacles were is difficult to know, but it is hard to imagine that tensions over its scope, direction, and relationship to the parent society did not loom large. From that point on, the CSPCA's children's education program continued with the assistance of participating teachers and religious leaders, and for the next two decades women all but disappeared from the organization's reports.

What makes the brief lifespan of the CSPCA's Ladies' Humane Education Committee particularly striking, though, is the fact that its members were among the most politically active women in Montreal, and indeed in Canada. Well positioned, often as the relatives of men prominent in their city and nation's political, economic, and social circles, they expressed themselves through participation and leadership in a wide range of religious, philanthropic, and other organizations.[14] Many were active in the just-formed Montreal Ladies' Educational Association, through which they sought to open higher education opportunities to women.[15] As such, the failure of the Ladies' Humane Education Committee demonstrates how the circles in which its participants moved could countenance the growing public role of upper- and middle-class women in organizations aimed at children, the elderly, the unemployed, poor, and even women's rights, but drew the line at animals.

A closer look at the CSPCA helps us to understand why this was the case. In the works since the early 1860s, the CSPCA held a prominent role in the animal welfare movement and was influential in the establishment of like-minded organizations across the country. As the leadership of its well-respected humanitarian president and future city mayor William Workman attests, the society represented well that city's upper- and middle-class English Protestant milieu. It would be a mistake, however, to view the organization as the voice of strident Protestant reformers aiming to curtail cruelty in society. In fact, the CSPCA brought together a wide range of interests connected to animals, including those of foxhunters, sportsmen, conservationists, medical and veterinary professionals, and industrial capitalists engaged in activities involving horses and livestock. While the society's early annual reports note a few female subscribers, the CSPCA was from the start a society comprised of men. At its founding, all of the society's executive members were men, as were all of its medical and legal advisors and all but 2 of its 148 subscribers. That it remained so throughout the century reflected an ongoing effort common within Canada's animal welfare NGOs to exclude women from the society's formal levels of power. This was done not because they were seen to be ineffective, or because they were altogether unwelcome in the public sphere, but precisely because of the considerable impact the movement's more moderate, instrumentally minded male supporters believed they would have on the organization and on the movement in general. As such, the men who ran the CSPCA recognized the skills, the energy, and the connections that women could bring to the movement, and in order to take advantage of this they initially encouraged them to participate in the society's work. But they also recognized that women were connected less directly to economic and recreational activities involving animals, and more directly to the ethics of care and responsibility that informed their work in so many other public sphere arenas. Because of this, Montreal's upper- and middle-class women were seen by many among the CSPCA's founders to be less rational and overly sympathetic to the plight of animals. As such, they threatened to take the movement in directions that posed too great a challenge to the status quo.

The relegation of women to the margins of the CSPCA soon became a pattern in Canada's animal welfare NGOs. During the 1870s, animal welfare proponents in Quebec, Halifax, Ottawa, and Toronto struggled and for the most part failed to establish stable organizations. Problems included the economic climate of the 1870s and the perceived but costly need to employ officers to enforce anti-cruelty legislation. But documents also speak to the failure to effectively integrate women, who were well known for their organizational, fundraising, and other skills, into these fledgling institutions.[16] Though their importance to the movement was recognized widely, the movement's leaders preferred overwhelmingly the establishment of ladies' auxiliaries rather than direct participation, and only the short-lived Woodstock branch of the Toronto-based Ontario SPCA integrated women directly into its operations. This pattern continued when the movement re-emerged in the 1880s with reorganized societies in Montreal and in Halifax, and new organizations in cities including Toronto, Quebec City, Ottawa, Saint John, Winnipeg, and Victoria.[17]

Thus while it is tempting to explain the reticence to incorporate women more fully into the animal welfare movement in terms of conservative gender norms or the parameters of first wave feminism in Canada, There was something else at work here too.[18] Carried too far, the animal welfare movement had the potential to move in directions that were untenable to its committed but more moderate supporters – notably the many upper- and middle-class men who shared a wide range of economic and recreational interests in which animals figured prominently. And by the 1880s, women in England and the United States had established reputations for taking the movement in exactly such directions. Of particular concern were the radical antivivisection societies in which women played prominent roles, and that helped to establish an unflattering view of the relationship between women and animal welfare. Given that it was becoming more common for upper- and middle-class women to participate in the public sphere via institutions including suffrage associations, the YWCA, the WCTU, the National Council of Women and its local counterparts, and various philanthropic and charitable organizations, the persistence of the ladies' auxiliary model was no accident, but rather the product of a relatively moderate movement whose more conservative supporters wished it to remain so.[19] Indeed, it was no coincidence that the Montreal-based CSPCA – at once the most prominent and the most conservative of Canada's animal welfare societies – operated for more than two decades without a ladies' auxiliary despite the tremendous appeal that the movement had among upper- and middle-class women in that city and their participation in many other philanthropic endeavours. Despite expanding its operations in 1882 to include women and children, the Halifax-based Nova Scotia Society for the Prevention of Cruelty (SPC) was not much different in this regard. In 1879, it began to put together a "Ladies' Royal Auxiliary Society" with branches in cities across the province – all but one of which saw men fill the key roles of branch president and secretary.[20] Once established, the Nova Scotia SPC's Ladies' Auxiliary began work in areas of education, and succeeded in establishing Canada's first Bands of Mercy. But it too struggled and fell apart, only to be revived in the late 1880s. When auxiliary members attempted during the 1890s to merge their organization with the parent society, they met with resistance. Following lengthy discussions, the Nova Scotia SPC executive concluded in 1898 that "the ladies were doing good work now and it would not be desirable to alter the present mode of working this Society."[21] Given their status as the oldest animal welfare institutions in the country, the CSPCA and the Nova Scotia SPC had considerable influence, and their advice, along with copies of annual reports, constitutions, and other materials to fledgling societies, helped to establish this pattern of participation elsewhere across the country. Consider, for example, the Nova Scotia SPC's response to the newly established New Brunswick SPCA (based in Saint John) when it sought advice in 1881 on how best to establish its own Ladies' Auxiliary. "We got a lady of good social position" explained SPC secretary John Naylor, "– a leader of fashion if possible – to call upon her lady friends and get them to sign the membership role of the proposed Association. When that was done they and the others were individually invited to attend a meeting when officers were elected . . . after the objects being explained by some of the committee of the Parent Society [sic]."[22] Established in 1885, the NBSPCA's Ladies' Humane Educational Auxiliary fitted neatly into this model, and it soon gravitated toward women's and children's issues, to the point that it became better known for its work in these areas than it was for its work on animal welfare.[23]

The few notable exceptions to this pattern that took shape during the 1880s and 1890s speak in their own ways to the tensions surrounding women's participation in animal welfare circles. By this time, the moral reform and social purity movements were creating greater precedents for women to participate directly in the public sphere, and arguments for women's suffrage were likewise making their way into public discourse. Such participation was most likely to be found in Ontario, where many animal welfare proponents opted to establish Humane Societies rather than SPCAs. Popular in the United States, this model tended to be more open to women's formal participation as both members and officers. It also extended its focus beyond animals to encompass the protection of children and sometimes women. As a result, there are notable differences between the more direct participation of women in some of Ontario's animal welfare NGOs and the persistence of the ladies' auxiliary model in other parts of Canada.

The most influential of these was the Toronto Humane Society (THS). Though established later than its counterparts in Montreal and Halifax, it immediately shared centre stage with them. Arguably the most engaged voice in Canada's animal welfare movement, it drew much of its support from that city's growing moral reform and social purity networks and the many women active in them. In part this stemmed from the society's mandate to address cruelty to children as well as animals, which connected it directly to numerous NGOs already established in the city. But women were also key to the THS's more extreme position on a range of animal welfare issues. From its start, the THS made a concerted effort to include women. Organizers encouraged women to attend the society's inaugural meeting, and its constitution demanded that its council be comprised of a minimum of fifteen men and ten women.[24] Of the women who filled these positions, most were already active in similar institutions. Among them were Mrs. S. Brett, president of the Girls' Industrial Institute; Mrs. John Harvie, president of the Young Women's Christian Guild and the Haven and Prison Gate Mission; Miss Dupont, principal of the Young Ladies School; and Miss Matilda Elliott, who taught at the Mercer Reformatory.[25] During the 1890s many participated in Toronto's Local Council of Women, with which the Toronto Humane Society affiliated, and the National Council of Women.[26] Such dynamics speak directly to the connections these supporters made between animals, women, children, education, and sexual and social reproduction. By this time, the relationship of cruelty to animals on the part of children to violence in adulthood was well established in the minds of animal welfare advocates, and fitted neatly into broader concerns. In an era in which everything from childhood identity to prison reform was being negotiated, educating children to be kind to animals became a central tenet of moral reform, and women active in the animal welfare movement in Toronto assumed considerable responsibility in this arena. They also clearly identified animal welfare as one of the growing number of options for entry into the public sphere. Though still conservative when compared to the range of opinions that existed in England and the United States, the THS adopted a relatively advanced position within the movement's Canadian context, and was willing on occasion to confront controversial issues, including vivisection.

But the THS was exceptional. Outside Toronto, few animal welfare NGOs saw women participate to such a degree. Among the closest to the THS in this regard was the Hamilton SPCA, established in 1887. Headed by federal MP and grocer Adam Brown, its committee included three women, it counted as many as a dozen women among the society's 300 members, and documents indicate that it had many sympathizers among women in the community.[27] In similar fashion, the board of the Winnipeg Humane Society (est. 1895) comprised ten men and five women, and the BCSPCA saw some women participate at this level by the turn of the century.[28] Ottawa presented yet another precedent. Among the many attempts to establish an animal protection society in the 1870s and 1880s, there emerged in that city in 1888 the Women's Humane Society of Ottawa. Founded and established entirely by local women, it addressed both children and animals, but in practical terms it focused mainly on children while supporting the local SPCA in its sphere of operations. During the early 1890s, it helped form the local Children's Aid Society along with its own Children's Aid Committee. Its members were also active in the formation of the National Council of Women and its local branch, to the extent that the Humane Society's president, Lady Sarah Ritchie, and its vice-president, Julia Gwynne, occupied the same positions in the latter organization.[29] But the society struggled with funding and membership numbers, and in 1894 it merged its operations with those of the Ottawa SPCA, dropped "women's" from its title, opened its membership to men, and became the Ottawa Humane Society. Upon doing so, it took up the SPCA's enforcement work and devoted itself more directly to the animals portion of its mandate. Women continued into the twentieth century to be central to the newly reconstituted society, but this move nevertheless resulted in a significant change as men entered, first as general, management, and executive committee members, and before long within the society's directorship. In 1912 the Ottawa Humane Society elected its first male president, and that position would not be claimed by a woman again until 1967.[30]

And these, again, were the exceptions. During travels to promote Ontario's Children's Aid Society in 1895, THS founder and vice-president John Kelso expressed surprise upon discovering among the groups he visited that "all the officers of the Humane Societies were men."[31] And even Kelso's organization had to contend with the likes of Goldwin Smith, a co-founder of the THS who was known for both his strong stance against vivisection and his strident opposition to women's suffrage.[32] As for the Montreal-based CSPCA, women remained outside that organization until 1898, at which point the society saw the formation of yet another women's branch, tasked with the same fundraising and educational objectives of the 1870s. Further testament to this pattern appears in the 1900 compilation *Women in Canada: Their Life and Work*. Aimed at summarizing the contribution of women to public life in the nation for the International World's Fair held in Paris that year, it outlines the work of hundreds of non-governmental organizations in which women played prominent, often leading roles. With regard to animal welfare, however, the compilation mentions only six organizations. Set alongside the text's broader overview of the work of women in Canada, its presentation of these organizations confirms in striking terms the peripheral, auxiliary-based presence they held within the movement.[33] Thus while at the end of the century, the THS could be found coordinating its meetings to coincide with those of the Local and the National Council of Women in order that its members could move easily from one to the other, women of similar political persuasion in many other cities in the country found themselves on the margins when it came to animal welfare.

Women, Animals, and Politics: Public Perceptions and Criticism

So successful was this process of marginalization that Canada presented relatively little home-grown criticism of female animal welfare supporters during the nineteenth century. Indeed, with no antivivisection societies, breakaway institutions, or outspoken women within the movement in Canada, there was not much to criticize. Given the absence of this more radical edge, the importance and genuine appreciation of the work done by women who *were* active in the movement, and the close familial and social links between them and the men who funded and participated in the nation's SPCAs and Humane Societies, it comes as no surprise that NGO records seldom speak of female animal welfare advocates in disparaging terms.

That said, criticism of women in the movement circulated widely in the Anglo-American world, and clearly shaped views in Canada. While it was difficult for anyone to attack animal welfare proponents' most basic premises regarding the cessation of deliberate, wanton, unnecessary cruelty to animals, the movement nevertheless had its share of vociferous critics. For them, the stereotypical image of the overly emotional, radical female animal welfare proponent, in particular that of the antivivisectionist movement, provided considerable fodder. Combined with negative views of first wave feminism and the women's suffrage movement, that image prompted some to dismiss the animal welfare movement altogether. As such, criticism levelled at the THS in 1891 that depicted its "fanatical members" as a group of "zealots," "cat worshippers," and "idealiz[ers of] the brute creation" underscores how casting the movement's more radical supporters in less-than-civilized terms had become a common rhetorical strategy.[34]

Among the best venues for critics was the House of Commons. There, heated debates took place over the direction and policy of the federal government, the key institution with regard to anti-cruelty legislation in Canada during the nineteenth century. When, for example, Conservative MP and Hamilton SPCA president Adam Brown took the lead during the 1880s in a decades-long debate over the prohibition of trap shooting, critics were quick to focus on gender as a means of dismissing his arguments.[35] During the latter decades of the century, the animal welfare movement's most intractable opponent in the House was fellow Conservative MP David Tisdale, a lawyer and former Lieutenant-Colonel in the 39th Norfolk Battalion of Rifles from Simcoe, Ontario, who had little patience for anyone who promoted animal welfare.[36] Describing Brown's efforts as "mawkish sentimental[ism]," Tisdale and his supporters worked throughout the 1880s and 1890s to derail all attempts to amend the Cruelty to Animals Act.[37]

Among the tensions to emerge in the lengthy political debates over animal welfare was the status of women in the public sphere. Given Prime Minister John A. Macdonald's repeated efforts during the early 1880s to expand the federal franchise in ways that would include women, parliamentarians were well primed for such debates.[38] In this context, opponents cast as unimaginable the notion that women should have influence in the political realm. Because women sympathized widely with animal welfare, they contended, the movement had little substance behind it, and they argued this readily. "It must be observed that a great majority of those who signed the petition are ladies," Tisdale noted at one point in reference to public support for Brown, "and I should like to ask if the ladies are to legislate or the members of this House?"[39] Far from new, this argument echoed widespread perceptions of animal welfare as the concern of sentimental, irrational women, and of the illegitimacy of their voice in political discourse.[40] For many of such persuasion, the animal welfare movement served as an excellent means to illustrate these views, given that it drew extensively on those qualities that were employed to argue against women's participation in the public sphere in general. Tisdale summarized this view precisely in his dismissal of Brown's supporters. "We all admire, I am sure, the tender-heartedness of the ladies . . . But when it comes to a matter of sympathy, then good-bye their judgment."[41]

As Tisdale's remarks indicate, the conflation of women and animal welfare meant that the status of the movement came often to rest on the status of the women who supported it. In response, proponents found themselves defending not only the animal welfare movement but also the legitimacy of female opinion. As Brown was quick to remind his detractors, the movement had at least one trump to play in this regard: "When my hon. friend makes satirical remarks on the influence of the ladies, he must remember that he has to begin with the Queen of England," who was by far the movement's most prominent patron.[42] Others presented similar arguments. Among them was Assiniboia West MP Nicholas Flood Davin, who in addition to his interest in animal welfare was one of the most articulate supporters of women's suffrage in the House of Commons during the 1890s.[43] With regard to animal welfare, Davin's counter to opponents rested in part on defending the views of women, which he argued "are nearly always instinctively on the side of what is right and good; and I confess that I have always felt myself that they are much better than we are – that they are in advance of us in their moral feelings."[44] Yet while arguments such as these clearly championed women as defenders of animals, they were almost always focused on instinct and emotion – qualities easily associated both with 'primitive" humans and with animals, and the same ones that Tisdale employed to undermine women's status within the movement.

Among the many issues discussed, some opponents took up contemporary trends in women's fashion as a means to demonstrate women's lack of judgment. Toward the end of the century the fashion industry came under considerable scrutiny for its use of bird feathers and body parts to adorn women's clothing, all of which fuelled a highly destructive millinery industry.[45] Animal welfare proponents mounted a successful campaign during the late nineteenth and early twentieth centuries against this trend, but the irony that the women who wore such clothes were of the same segment of society that supported the animal welfare movement was not lost on critics. In this regard, the trend among upper- and middle-class women to effectively dress themselves both *with* and by extension *as* animals provided a striking contradiction. In effect, it linked upper- and middle-class women to an animal-like identity that critics readily exploited. In 1894, Vancouver MP Andrew Haslam employed the issue to derail yet another series of amendments concerning trap shooting. "The Bill," he argued, "might seem more consistent if there were greater consistency on the part of those who promote it. But the ladies who are the strongest advocates of this Bill, are those for whose pleasure of adornment so many beautiful birds are slaughtered."[46] That this argument undermined the movement's female supporters was only part of its purpose. As important was the fact that such observations encouraged animal welfare advocates to become embroiled in an extended, introspective campaign that consumed considerable energy. In this way, questions regarding women's fashion became a means by which the movement's opponents diverted animal welfare supporters from issues that posed more significant challenges.

In order to trivialize the movement further still, critics in the House of Commons also presented hypothetical examples of women considerably further down the social ladder from the upper- and middle-class "ladies" who consorted with Brown. Tisdale, for example, compared cruelty associated with trap shooting to that of "market women who take domestic fowls to market. They put them in coops and keep them all day without food, and then if they sell them they wring their necks. If the hon. gentleman had ever seen them wring their necks he would bring in a Bill to prevent market women doing so, and we would have to eat our chickens alive."[47]

Liberal MP James Frederick Lister made a similar argument with regard to longstanding provisions against driving animals in a cruel manner:

> An old woman driving her geese home at night might be prosecuted under the provisions of this Act by some neighbor who thought she was driving them too fast. Imagine my hon. friend driving home one of his chickens, and that one of his friends, who might be politically opposed to him, should consider that he had committed a violation of this Act and prosecute him.[48]

That women were rarely if ever prosecuted for cruelty to animals underscores the deliberately absurd terms employed by opponents here to dismiss the movement. But that was only the start. In presenting figures well outside the urban, industrial world that underpinned the animal welfare movement, such rhetoric inversely implied a level of respect for rural women who knew well their place and that of animals in the social order, as compared to upper- and middle-class urban women who did not.

That said, women's active participation in Canada's animal welfare movement was stifled to such a degree that the movement's male leadership often made a better target. In the debates with Brown over trap shooting, critics routinely played on gender to cast the movement in derogatory terms. Tisdale, for example, referred specifically to Adam Brown's efforts as the work of a "tender hearted," urban, and effeminate SPCA president and his "ladies."[49] In an effort to amuse the House as much as to attack Brown, he at one point quipped that the signatures collected in support of Brown's bill came down to the MP's predatory charm over this trusting, loyal, naive segment of society: "I want to confess honestly that I believe that, if I were a woman, and the hon. gentleman should approach me with his genial manners and beaming smile, I would certainly surrender at discretion."[50]

Such tactics took shape outside the walls of Parliament, too. Kelso, for example, was ripe for this kind of critique, given his social activism and his status as one of the most prominent figures in Canada's animal welfare movement. That critique came within a year of the THS's formation, when the society's secretary was the subject of a vociferous personal attack in the Toronto media. "Let the long haired men and short haired women meet and resolute and petition and mix themselves up with other people's business all they have a mind to. It pleases them and doesn't hurt me or anyone else that I am aware of," its author began:

> But there is a class of young men who want severely suppressing. It is the young man of very juvenile appearance, undeveloped faculties, expressionless features and with an appetite for the society of old ladies, bread and butter young women, Y. M. C. A. young men and the goody goody class generally . . . When a young man of this description gets a hobby he is an unmitigated nuisance. Very often they keep within moderate bounds, but every once and a while one of the genus flops over and metaphorically spills himself. When he does, Toronto is hardly large enough to hold him.

Such, the author contended, was Kelso, the "secretary of the Humane Society, the General Reformation Society, the Interfere with Everybody's Business Society, etc., etc., etc."[51] In the lengthy tirade that ensued, Kelso was presented as an effeminate and unreliable leader who received his mandate from women, and whose judgment was no more reliable than theirs.

With that was another telling metaphor, couched in the author's suggestion that he might "warble a little horse sense" to a simultaneously feminized and now animalized Kelso. That Kelso himself would later resign from his post as THS secretary, due to the "constant interference of Mrs. Grassett" and others who promoted a more radical agenda than his own (he later returned as its vice-president) speaks all the more to the struggles both within and outside the movement to grapple with the conflation of women and radicalism.[52]

Conclusion

In sum, there is at work in the context of Victorian Canada's animal welfare movement a discourse that, at its most basic level, presented animals as human, men as women, and women as animals, or at the very least a few rungs down the evolutionary ladder as it applied to the civilized order of things. What is to be made of this?

At first glance, it seems straightforward that women would be prominent in the animal welfare movement in Canada as they were elsewhere during the latter decades of the nineteenth century. That they were not raises a number of issues. From the formation of Canada's first animal welfare NGOs in the 1860s, women were caught in a paradox. On the one hand, their passion, commitment, and skills in areas of fundraising, organization, networking, and children's education made them ideal and in many cases vital participants. On the other hand, the stereotypes and opinions associated with them were seen by many of the movement's more moderate male participants and by opponents of the movement to pose too great a challenge when it came to human–animal relations. As a result, women's participation in animal welfare was from the start a problem. Overall, those societies in which women participated directly – most notably the Toronto Humane Society – were the more radical of Canada's animal welfare NGOs. These, however, were the exception. More often, women's participation was restricted, if not altogether, to the level of auxiliary institutions through which they were able to contribute to the cause but not to shape their parent institutions' scope or mandate. Such marginalization was further encouraged by the movement's opponents, who relied on gender-based arguments to present its supporters as irrational and overly emotional. In short, the qualities associated with women that spoke to so many of the movement's ideals – emotional sensitivity, virtue, kindness, loyalty, instinct, the care of children – ended up speaking against the seriousness with which they might be treated within the movement itself. That these qualities were also employed by the animal welfare movement to elevate animals to quasi-human status is perhaps the greatest irony at hand, inasmuch as they conflated women and the movement's non-human subjects. In effect, their presumably irrational, radical, inconsistent views meant that women were simply too "wild" to be considered full participants in the movement.

In turn, the range and scope of women's participation permits us to draw some conclusions about their real and potential impact within the movement. The irony that promoting maternal feminism led many upper- and middle-class women to become active in the public sphere has often been noted.[53] In the context of animal welfare, however, the ethics of care and responsibility that were so central to first wave feminism, social purity, and moral reform posed a threat considerable enough that there emerged across the nation a pattern of marginalization that limited the capacity of women to extend their views to animals. For the most part, this involved relegating women to the movement's educational sphere of activity, to auxiliary institutions, and to fundraising in order to prevent them from setting the movement's agenda or participating in efforts to deal with enforcement and to shape state legislation and policy – both areas more typically associated with men. The fact that animal welfare NGOs in which women *did* participate tended toward more extreme views suggests that the Canadian movement would have been more radical had women been able to participate in it more fully. Instead, the pattern that unfolded helped pave the way for a remarkably conservative approach to animal welfare in Canada. Given the degree to which contemporary animal welfare legislation at the federal level can be traced directly to its Victorian contexts, that pattern arguably reverberates today.

As part of their emphasis on the links between women and animals, ecofeminists have long argued that their shared experience of marginalization has contributed as much to women's identification with animal protection as have the ethics of care and responsibility with which women are so often associated. If the combination of widespread interest and institutional marginalization observed here and in a number of other studies is any indication, these dynamics have long informed the politics of animal welfare and rights. Future studies that explore personal documents such as diaries and letters, that pursue in greater detail discussions in other non-governmental organizations, that look carefully at the authorship of literary and popular texts dealing with animals, or that consider more closely family, education, and community networks, may reveal women to have played a broader role in Canada's animal welfare movement than presented here. If so, they will underscore further the process of marginalization at work within the movement's formal organizational networks. And that process speaks in turn to what is perhaps the greatest irony at hand. Despite its position as a nexus that contributed to the development of some of the most important women's organizations in the nation, the animal welfare movement in nineteenth-century Canada did not provide much of a forum through which women could speak for themselves or for animals.

Notes

1 The best examples of this are in the context of antivivisection organizations. See Mary Ann Elston, "Women and Anti-Vivisection in Victorian England, 1870–1900," *Vivisection in Historical Perspective*, ed. Nicolaas A. Rupke (London: Routledge, 1990), 259–94; Susan E. Lederer, "The Controversy over Animal Experimentation in America, 1880–1914," in Rupke, *Vivisection in Historical Perspective*, 236–58; Coral Lansbury, *The Old Brown Dog: Women, Workers, and Vivisection in Edwardian England* (Madison: University of Wisconsin Press, 1985). For other works dealing specifically with antivivisection see Anita Guerrini, *Experimenting with Humans and Animals: From Galen to Animal Rights* (Baltimore: Johns Hopkins University Press, 2003), 87; Hilda Kean, "'The Smooth, Cool Men of Science': The Feminist and Socialist Response to Vivisection," *History Workshop Journal* 40 (1995): 16–38; Richard D. French, *Antivivisection and Medical Science in Victorian Society* (Princeton, NJ: Princeton University Press, 1975). On Canada see J.T.H. Connor, "Cruel Knives? Vivisection and Biomedical Research in Victorian English Canada," *Canadian Bulletin of Medical History* 14, no. 1 (1997): 37–64. On the history of the animal welfare movement in Britain and the United States during the nineteenth century see James Turner, *Reckoning with the Beast: Animals, Pain, and Humanity in the Victorian Mind* (Baltimore: Johns Hopkins University Press, 1980); Brian Harrison, "Animals and the State in Nineteenth-century England,"

in *Peaceable Kingdom: Stability and Change in Modern Britain* (Oxford: Clarendon Press, 1982), 82–122; Harriet Ritvo, *The Animal Estate: The English and Other Creatures in the Victorian Age* (Cambridge, MA: Harvard University Press, 1987); Hilda Kean, *Animal Rights: Political and Social Change in Britain since 1800* (London: Reaktion Books, 1998); Diane L. Beers, *For the Prevention of Cruelty: The History and Legacy of Animal Rights Activism in the United States* (Athens, OH: Swallow Press/Ohio University Press, 2006); Susan J. Pearson, *The Rights of the Defenseless: Protecting Animals and Children in Gilded Age America* (Chicago: University of Chicago Press, 2011); Bernard Oreste Unti, "The Quality of Mercy: Organized Animal Protection in the United States, 1866–1930" (PhD diss., American University, 2002).

2 Darcy Ingram, "Beastly Measures: Animal Welfare, Civil Society, and State Policy in Victorian Canada," *Journal of Canadian Studies / Revue d'études canadiennes* 47, no. 1 (2013): 221–52.

3 A useful summary of these issues is found in Greta Gaard, "Living Interconnections with Animals and Nature," in *Ecofeminism: Women, Animals, Nature*, ed. Greta Gaard (Philadelphia: Temple University Press, 1993), 1–12. Carole Gilligan, *In a Different Voice: Psychological Theory and Women's Development* (Cambridge, MA: Harvard University Press, 1982), was key to the development of these ideas. Particularly helpful in establishing the historical framework for these

views is Carolyn Merchant, *The Death of Nature: Women, Ecology and the Scientific Revolution* (San Francisco: Harper Collins, 1990). In addition to Gaard's collection, see Carol J. Adams and Josephine Donovan, eds., *Animals and Women: Feminist Theoretical Explorations* (Durham, NC, and London: Duke University Press, 1995). See also the recent collection by Carol J. Adams and Lori Gruen, eds., *Ecofeminism: Feminist Intersections with Other Animals and the Earth* (London: Bloomsbury Academic, 2014).

4   For a powerful argument regarding the separation of humans and animals during this period see John Berger, "Why Look at Animals?," in *About Looking* (New York: Pantheon Books, 1980), 1–26. For a challenge to this view see Hilda Kean, "Traces and Representations: Animal Pasts in London's Present, *The London Journal* 36, no. 1 (2011): 54–71; and Kean, *Animal Rights*. On the ubiquity of animals in nineteenth-century Canadian cities see Sean Kheraj, "Living and Working with Domestic Animals in Nineteenth-Century Toronto," in *Urban Explorations: Environmental Histories of the Toronto Region*, ed. L. Anders Sandberg, Stephen Bocking, Colin Coates, and Ken Cruikshank (Hamilton, ON: L.R. Wilson Institute for Canadian History, 2013), 120–40; Sean Kheraj, "Demonstration Wildlife: Negotiating the Animal Landscape of Vancouver's Stanley Park, 1888–1996," *Environment and History* 18, no. 4 (2012): 497–527; Turner, *Reckoning with the Beast*; Harrison, "Animals and the State"; Ritvo, *The Animal Estate*; Beers, *For the Prevention of*

Cruelty; Pearson, *The Rights of the Defenseless*; and Unti, "The Quality of Mercy."

5   Ingram, "Beastly Measures," 232–34.

6   J. George Hodgins, ed., *Aims and Objects of the Toronto Humane Society* (Toronto: W. Briggs, 1888); J. George Hodgins, *Work Accomplished by the Toronto Humane Society* (Toronto: Massey Press, 1892).

7   Christabelle Sethna, "Animal Sex: Purity Education and the Naturalization of the Abstinence Agenda," *Sex Education* 10, no. 3 (2010): 267–79. See also J. Keri Cronin, "'Can't you talk?' Voice and Visual Culture in Early Animal Welfare Campaigns," *Early Popular Visual Culture* 9, no. 3 (2011): 203–23.

8   Derived from Proverbs 31 and appearing on the cover of the Massachusetts SPCA publication *Our Dumb Animals* starting in 1868, the motto "We speak for those who cannot speak for themselves" soon became a stock phrase within the movement.

9   Duncan McEachran, "Why Every Student of Veterinary Medicine Should Study Psychology," *Can Animals Reason? Opening Address, Society of Comparative Psychology* (Montreal: Gazette Printing Company by Request of the Society for Prevention of Cruelty to Animals, Montreal, 1888).

10 Canadian SPCA. *Fourth Annual Report* (Montreal: Protestant Institution for Deaf-Mutes, 1873), 1–2.

11 For discussion of women in the context of the movement's more radical aspects see Elston, "Women and Anti-vivisection in Victorian

England, 1870-1900"; Lederer, "The Controversy over Animal Experimentation in America, 1880–1914"; Kean, "'The Smooth, Cool Men of Science'"; Craig Buettinger, "Women and Antivivisection in Late Nineteenth-Century America," *Journal of Social History* 30, no. 4 (1997): 857–72; Chien-hui Li, "An Unnatural Alliance? Political Radicalism and the Animal Defence Movement in Late Victorian and Edwardian Britain," *EurAmerica* 42, no. 1 (2012): 1–43.

12   Edna Healey, "Coutts, Angela Georgina Burdett-," *Oxford Dictionary of National Biography*, online edition, http://www.oxforddnb.com.proxy.bib.uottawa.ca/view/article/32175.

13   Canadian SPCA. *Seventh Annual Report* (Montreal: Protestant Institution for Deaf-Mutes, 1876), 4.

14   Studies of women within this segment of Montreal society include Bettina Bradbury, *Wife to Widow: Lives, Laws, and Politics in Nineteenth Century Montreal* (Vancouver: University of British Columbia Press, 2011; Joanna Dean, *Religious Experience and the New Woman: The Life of Lily Dougall* (Bloomington: Indiana University Press, 2007); Elizabeth Kirkland, "Mothering Citizens: Elite Women in Montreal 1890–1914" (PhD diss., McGill University, 2012); Janice Harvey, "The Protestant Orphan Asylum and the Montreal Ladies' Benevolent Society: A Case Study in Protestant Child Charity in Montreal, 1822–1900" (PhD diss., McGill University, 2001).

15   Montreal Ladies' Educational Association, *Report of the Montreal Ladies' Educational Association:*

Second Session, 1872–73 (Montreal: Gazette Printing House, 1873).

16   Ontario SPCA, *First Annual Report* (Toronto: n.p., 1874), 10.

17   Ingram, "Beastly Measures," 232–33.

18   On the more conservative character of first wave feminism in Canada see Alison Prentice, Paula Bourne, Gail Cuthbert Brandt, Beth Light, Wendy Mitchinson, and Naomi Black, *Canadian Women: A History* (Toronto: Harcourt Brace Jovanovich, 1988), 170.

19   On these three organizations see Sharon A. Cook, *Through Sunshine and Shadow: the Women's Christian Temperance Union, Evangelicalism, and Reform in Ontario, 1874–1930* (Montreal: McGill-Queen's University Press, 1995); Nina Mjagkij and Margaret Spratt, *Men and Women Adrift: The YMCA and the YWCA in the City* (New York: New York University Press, 1997); Veronica Strong-Boag, *The Parliament of Women: The National Council of Women of Canada, 1893–1929* (Ottawa: National Museum, 1976). See also Mariana Valverde, *The Age of Light, Soap, and Water: Moral Reform in English Canada, 1885–1925* (Toronto: University of Toronto Press, 2008).

20   Nova Scotia Society for the Prevention of Cruelty, *Ninth Annual Report* (Halifax: *Morning Herald*, 1885), 16; Nova Scotia Society for the Prevention of Cruelty, *11th Annual Report* (Halifax, n.p., 1888); "The SPCA: Organization of a Ladies' Auxiliary," Halifax *Morning Herald*, 22 August 1879.

21   Nova Scotia Archives, Nova Scotia Society for the Prevention of

Cruelty fonds, MG20 517 1, *Minute Book March 1888–February 1907*, 8 March 1898, 42.

22   Ibid., MG 20 16, Letter Books, No. 1, September 1877–April 1886, letter to New Brunswick SPCA, 15 November 1881, 337.

23   National Council of Women of Canada, *Women of Canada: Their Life and Work* (Ottawa: Queen's Printer, 1900), 390.

24   Toronto Humane Society, *Officers of the Toronto Humane Society* (Toronto: n.p., 1888).

25   *Toronto City Directory for 1888* (Toronto: R. L. Polk & Co., 1888); J. J. Kelso, *Early History of the Humane and Children's Aid Movement in Ontario, 1886–1893* (Toronto: L. K. Cameron, 1911), 15–16.

26   City of Toronto Archives, 1409, Toronto Humane Society Fonds, 147918, *Minutes of the Toronto Humane Society, 1887–1906*, 30 November 1893, 127; 14 May 1894, 140; 30 May 1895, 179. On the National Council of Women see Strong-Boag, *The Parliament of Women*. On the workings of Humane Societies during this period see Pearson, *The Rights of the Defenseless*.

27   Hamilton SPCA, *First Annual Report* (n.p., 1888).

28   National Council of Women of Canada, *Women of Canada*, 391. While the Victoria SPCA began in 1888, the society's fonds at the British Columbia archives indicate that the attempted province-wide association of BCSPCA chapters struggled well into the twentieth century just to stay afloat.

29   Sarah Ritchie was married to Supreme Court Justice Sir William Ritchie; Julia Gwynne was the wife of Supreme Court Justice John Wellington Gwynne.

30   Ottawa Humane Society, Sixth Annual Report, 1893–94 (Ottawa: C.W. Mitchell, 1894); Ottawa Humane Society, Eighth Annual Report, 1895–96 (Ottawa: C.W. Mitchell, 1896); Vivian Astroff, *The Humane Society of Ottawa-Carleton: The First 100 Years of Caring for the Abused and Abandoned, 1888–1988* (Ottawa: Humane Society of Ottawa-Carleton, 1888), 91.

31   City of Toronto Archives, 1409, Toronto Humane Society Fonds, 147918, *Minutes of the Toronto Humane Society, 1887–1906*, 21 March 1895, 175.

32   Though not prominent in THS records after the society's founding, Smith remained an important voice within the animal welfare movement in Toronto, in particular on vivisection. On his views regarding women's suffrage see Goldwin Smith, *Female Suffrage* (London: MacMillan and Co., 1875). On Smith's antivivisection views see Ingram, "Beastly Measures," 239; Connor, "Cruel Knives," 55.

33   Specifically, the Humane Societies based in Toronto, Ottawa, and Winnipeg, and the SPCAs operating out of Montreal, Victoria, and Saint John. See National Council of Women of Canada, *Women of Canada*, 382–92.

34   James Haverson, "Cat Worshippers," *The World*, undated newsclipping, 1891, in Library and Archives Canada (hereafter LAC), MG30, C97, J.J. Kelso fonds, vol. 2, file folder: Diary 1885–1891.

35 A sport that involves shooting pigeons released from cages, trap shooting was the subject of considerable debate in the Anglo-American world during the late nineteenth and early twentieth centuries.

36 Political biographies of Brown, Tisdale, and others can be found at the Parliament of Canada website: www.parl.gc.ca.

37 House of Commons, *Debates*, 6th Parliament, 3rd Session, vol. 27, 20 February 1889 (Ottawa: Brown Chamberlin, 1889).

38 Catherine L. Cleverdon, *The Woman Suffrage Movement in Canada* (Toronto: University of Toronto Press, 1974), 105–9.

39 House of Commons. *Debates*, 6th Parliament, 4th Session, vol. 29, 27 February 1890 (Ottawa: Brown Chamberlin, 1890).

40 Ibid..

41 Ibid.

42 Ibid., 12 March 1890.

43 Cleverdon, *Woman Suffrage Movement*, 110.

44 House of Commons, *Debates*, 6th Parliament, 4th Session, vol. 29, 12 March 1890.

45 For an overview of this controversy see Anthony N. Penna, *Nature's Bounty: Historical and Modern Environmental Perspectives* (New York: Routledge, 2015), 97–99.

46 House of Commons, *Debates*, 7th Parliament, 4th Session, vol. 38, 18 June 1894 (Ottawa: S.E. Dawson, 1894).

47 House of Commons, *Debates*, 6th Parliament, 3rd Session, vol. 27, 20 February 1889.

48 Ibid.

49 House of Commons. *Debates*, 6th Parliament, 4th Session, vol. 29, 27 February 1890.

50 Ibid.

51 "The Motley Fool." *Life*, 26 May 1888, newsclipping in LAC, MG30, C97, J.J. Kelso fonds, vol. 2, file folder: Diary 1885–1891.

52 LAC, MG30, C97, J.J. Kelso fonds, vol. 2, file folder: Diary 1885–1891: June 1891; City of Toronto Archives, 1409, Toronto Humane Society fonds, 147918, *Minutes of the Toronto Humane Society, 1887–1906*, 21 June 1892, 75

53 For an overview of first wave feminism in Canada see Jacquetta Newman and Linda A. White, *Women, Politics, and Public Policy: The Political Struggles of Canadian Women* (Don Mills, ON: Oxford University Press, 2006), 68–73. See also Cleverdon, *Woman Suffrage Movement*; Strong-Boag, *The Parliament of Women*; and Valverde, *The Age of Light, Soap, and Water*.

Fish out of Water: Fish Exhibition in Late Nineteenth-Century Canada

WILLIAM KNIGHT

In the nineteenth century, animal display proliferated. People peered at a myriad of animals – living and dead – in museums, international exhibitions, circuses, and zoos. Benefiting from collecting networks that extended across empires and nations, these spectacular sites exhibited animals to satisfy appetites for entertainment and science. While the growing literature on animal display documents this rich history, one class of creatures is routinely ignored: fish.[1] Remote, if not invisible to most people, fish were nonetheless the subject of intense interest in Europe and North America in the last half of the nineteenth century. Public aquariums, international fisheries exhibitions, and fish-culture displays reflected and sustained a pervasive exhibitionary interest in fish.

Curiosity about fish overlapped with their increasing commercial and recreational exploitation: it also coincided in North America with emerging regimes of state fisheries administration that harnessed fish reproduction through the technology of fish culture. Joseph Taylor called fisheries exhibitions (which presented fish-culture apparatus alongside mounted fish and fishing equipment) "didactic dioramas" that rationalized government fish culture and projected the state's mastery over fisheries and, by extension, nature.[2] In Canada, this rhetorical work is exemplified in the work of Samuel Wilmot. Wilmot was a private fish culturist appointed a federal Canadian fisheries officer in 1868 who integrated fish culture into the state's routine business, building a national fish-hatchery system designed to sustain Canada's fisheries. In support of this project, Wilmot became an impresario of fisheries exhibits. He transformed his private hatchery into a public attraction and, as a government official, mounted successively more spectacular displays at local and international exhibitions. Wilmot's most notable successes were Canada's massive showing at the 1883 London International Fisheries Exhibition and its conversion afterward into a permanent exhibit, the Canadian Fisheries Museum in Ottawa, in 1884.

This chapter presents Wilmot's exhibitionary work as a case study in nineteenth-century animal exhibition, one that explores the material culture and challenges of fisheries exhibits. Wilmot and his successors, Edward Prince and Andrew Halkett, confronted, as one museum official termed it, the "question of fish exhibition," the critical problem of transforming live and dead fish into authoritative representations of state power.[3] Keeping fish alive in aquariums was difficult and expensive, as was creating lifelike models from dead fish. These Canadian fisheries officials also contended with inadequate museum buildings and exhibition spaces – which cast into doubt the Fisheries Museum's scientific legitimacy – and struggled to satisfy a growing demand for fish exhibits even as questions emerged about fish culture's efficacy. From Wilmot's first exhibits to Prince and Halkett's futile attempts to rescue the Canadian Fisheries Museum from demolition in 1918, fish exhibition in Canada proved to be a decidedly problematic enterprise.

Fish Exhibition

Animal exhibition expanded in the mid-nineteenth century. Zoos, circuses, and natural-history museums flourished along with networks of animal collectors. Fish exhibition was an element of this trend and drew currency from two developments: fish culture and aquariums, which revealed aquatic life for public inspection, education, and entertainment. Modern fish culture – the practice of raising fish from eggs under controlled conditions – originated in France in the 1840s when experimenters developed techniques for reproducing fish, particularly salmon and trout. While raising fish in ponds was an old practice, nineteenth-century fish culture was a new approach that extended control over reproduction. Fish culturists captured fish during spawning season and stripped them of eggs and sperm, which they mixed to initiate fertilization. Hatchery workers then carefully nurtured the fertilized eggs. Once fish hatched, they were raised in hatchery buildings until ready for release. Proponents hailed fish culture as an improvement on nature because it increased the rate of fish survival by eliminating several risks for mortality, including predation.[4]

North Americans adopted the practice – widely disseminated through books, periodicals, and personal contacts – during the 1840s and 1850s, viewing fish culture as a solution to overfishing. Private fish-culture enthusiasts were in the vanguard. They proved, and promoted, the technology's efficacy, which attracted government officials who sought help establishing fish-hatchery programs. Samuel Wilmot was one such individual. Wilmot was a member of Upper Canada's middle-class elite who experimented with fish-culture methods to propagate Lake Ontario's Atlantic salmon in the 1860s. A staple of Native and settler fisheries, salmon had declined from the accumulated impacts of agriculture, dam building, deforestation, and invasive species. In the 1860s, Wilmot began building a hatchery on his rural property near Newcastle, east of Toronto. Enclosing a salmon stream, this property allowed Wilmot to capture salmon and attempt their restoration. On the strength of his efforts, Wilmot was appointed a federal fisheries officer in 1868.[5]

Wilmot was an adept entrepreneur. After his apparent (albeit short-lived) success in restoring Lake Ontario salmon, Wilmot was named Dominion Fish Culturist in 1876 and went on to construct a national fish-culture system that annually produced millions of fish. His entrepreneurial skills also extended to exhibitions. Wilmot, who gained substantial power within Canada's fisheries establishment, sought to promote and defend fish culture through public displays, borrowing techniques from other fish culturists. In England, for example, fish-culture advocate Frank Buckland drew throngs of curious observers with fish-culture displays. At a London dog show, Buckland's exhibit of hatching salmon – "pretty silver-coated little creatures" – attracted "many thousands of people who have certainly never seen a salmon alive before."[6] In 1865, Buckland established the "Museum of Economic Fish Culture," a large display of mounted fish alongside a working fish hatchery in London's South Kensington Museum.

Wilmot found similar opportunities to exhibit fish culture. In 1870, he exhibited his "breeding apparatus filled with salmon ova" at the Toronto Industrial Exhibition. The display, according to the Toronto *Globe*, demonstrated Wilmot's technological capacity to reverse the clock of settlement and repopulate Canadian waters with a never-ending supply of fish. "In a few years all our rivers and streams may be stocked with fish," the newspaper reported, repeating Wilmot's own confident predictions, "and salmon become as cheap and abundant as they were in the days of the first settlers." The fish-culture demonstration was accompanied by aquarium displays that showed the development of fish "in their different stages" – a lesson that reinforced Wilmot's claim that fish culture was a scientific enterprise that deserved public support.[7]

Wilmot's use of aquarium displays shows how fish culture and aquariums converged in fish exhibits. Used initially by English zoologists to study shore-bound marine life, aquariums were popularized as a domestic pastime in Victorian England. Naturalists such as Philip Henry Gosse helped launch this pastime with books that offered practical advice about aquarium keeping and philosophized about it as a form of domestic nature study.[8] If "parlour oceans" relocated natural-history observation from the field into the domestic sphere, then public aquariums extended this experience to an even wider audience on a more spectacular scale. Within twenty years of the opening of the first public aquarium in London's Regent Park in 1853, aquariums had grown to "colossal proportions," as an author of a manual on aquarium management noted. The launch of oceanographic expeditions and biological stations in Europe and the United States in the 1870s also contributed to the transformation of aquariums into spectacular public sites. In cities such as Naples, Berlin, Paris, New York, and Boston, the mysteries of the deep were revealed for pleasure, education, and profit.[9]

Some aquariums offered circus-like entertainments. The Boston Aquarial Gardens, opened in 1859, enticed visitors with a beluga whale that had been trained to tow a young woman, perched Venus-like in an oversized shell, around a large tank.[10] In Canada, where permanent aquariums were not established until the early twentieth century, people might have been more familiar with aquariums in travelling circuses. Fish tanks appeared alongside wild-animal displays and other curiosities, promising views of exotic and unseen creatures from the watery depths. An itinerant circus stopping in Toronto promised a "Deep Sea Aquarium"; another boasted of an "Aquarium of Oceanic Marvels." Aquarium displays also help promoted business. A water-works manufacturer used aquariums at

4.1 Canada, *Report of Fish-Breeding in the Dominion of Canada 1877* (Ottawa: Queen's Printer, 1878). Digital image courtesy of Stephen Crawford.

the Toronto Industrial Exhibition to demonstrate that its equipment could produce water pure enough to sustain speckled trout, a fish with exacting requirements for water quality. A fish merchant during the Manitoba exhibition in Winnipeg used an aquarium, an object of "considerable interest," to attract visitors. A live sea lion and pelican, however, may have distracted people's attention: they were displayed beside the fish tank and caused a commotion when the sea lion attempted to eat the pelican.[11]

Wilmot likewise used aquariums to lure visitors to his fish hatchery near Newcastle, Ontario. The hatchery was the centerpiece of the federal hatchery system that Wilmot created during the last half of the nineteenth century. Easily accessible by rail from Toronto, the hatchery promoted fish culture, and Wilmot's mastery of the craft, through a variety of exhibit forms. Contemporary illustrations, commissioned by Wilmot in the late 1870s, depict the Newcastle hatchery as a hybrid of zoological garden, aquarium, and industrial exhibition – a thoroughly genteel and pastoral setting for "rational recreation." The hatchery was nestled amid landscaped grounds where visitors could observe adult salmon in the holding ponds, "dotted here and there with miniature islands." Visitors could also inspect the "Reception House" where Wilmot's patented egg-hatching apparatus nurtured new fish into life. Aquariums helped educate visitors. Some tanks displayed commonly misidentified fish species to clear up confusion over species; another aquarium was kept cold to demonstrate how some fish became torpid during winter.[12]

Wilmot crowned his hatchery with a small natural-history museum. Upstairs from the hatching room, Wilmot offered an eclectic collection of spectacular taxidermied specimens. These included a 600-pound tuna, a 10-foot-long Greenland shark, and the "Pickering Ox," a locally famous prize bull. The museum added to the hatchery's exhibitionary appeal and reinforced Wilmot's identity as a natural-history expert. The complex also blurred the line separating Wilmot the private entrepreneur from Wilmot the state fisheries official. The hatchery's "handsome and commanding appearance" helped demonstrate that fish culture was, according to Wilmot, a "national enterprise." At the same time, the exhibition was a testament to Wilmot's own abilities, "proof throughout," he argued, "of the exercise of practical ingenuity and personal industry."[13]

Wilmot also continued to mount displays at the annual Toronto Industrial Exhibition. In 1879, Wilmot presented an ambitious display of "stuffed and live fish, along with the process of artificial breeding" that occupied almost an entire wing of the exhibition's main building. The *Globe* called the exhibit "by all odds the greatest attraction in the Main Building."[14] It included fourteen aquariums that displayed a variety of species, including Lake Ontario salmon and "California salmon," or chinook salmon from the Pacific, that Wilmot was then attempting to naturalize in Lake Ontario. These two salmon species, however, implicitly suggested the limits to fish culture, despite Wilmot's own optimistic promises.

By 1879, for example, salmon runs in Wilmot Creek were in decline. In 1881, only half a dozen adult fish returned despite Wilmot's efforts. "I fear that the time is now gone by," he admitted, "for the production and growth [of salmon] in the frontier streams of Ontario."[15] Some years earlier, Wilmot had obtained chinook salmon from the US Fish Commission, hoping that they could replace the disappearing Atlantic salmon. The tank of chinook in Toronto at once acknowledged both the reality of the decline in Atlantic salmon and Wilmot's evergreen belief that he could renew decimated fisheries through fish culture and exotic species.

However these displays were read, they built Wilmot's experience and reputation as an exhibition impresario. In 1882, the federal government appointed Wilmot as the organizer-in-chief of Canada's exhibit for the London International Fisheries Exhibition. Fisheries exhibitions had been previously held in Netherlands, France, Norway, and Germany. Like "universal" fairs, these exhibitions celebrated progress and the nation-state, but through a fisheries lens. They indexed profound changes in fisheries, including industrialization and the expansion of fishing effort, state administration, and scientific investigation.[16] Steam technology extended the range and catching capacity of fishing fleets. Fishing gear changed: larger trawl nets, adapted for steam vessels, could capture more fish. State administration expanded through fish culture, inspection, and statistical investigation, while state commissions investigated specific problems, such as gear impacts. Fisheries research increased with scientific expeditions and biological stations investigating the dynamics of ocean life. In 1883, the London Fisheries Exhibition provided a nexus, a "centre of calculation," where new questions and technologies could be posed and tested.[17]

The London exhibition began in May 1883 and ran for six months. It marked Canada's debut on the international stage of fisheries exhibitions, and Wilmot produced a display equal to the moment. He shipped 500 tons of objects to London and arranged them into an arresting display that covered 10,000 square feet of space. Mounted fish appeared alongside boats and fishing gear, as well as fish commodities and an assortment of models, dioramas, and other objects. At the heart of the Canadian Court (as the space was called) stood a spectacular focal point: a towering trophy, a pyramid of tinned fish, fishing gear, and nets, surmounted with the flags of Canada and topped by a stuffed 50-pound beaver. A trope of Victorian exhibition and retail display, the trophy marked Canada's pride as a consumer and exporter nation, while symbolizing the state's power to organize and administer the fisheries.

Fish culture also featured prominently in Wilmot's display. Visitors entering the court's main entrance first encountered a working model of Wilmot's fish hatchery containing 50,000 salmon eggs that hatched before visitors' eyes. Beside it stood Wilmot's patented "Self-Picking and Self-Cleaning Canadian Fish Egg Incubator," a device that automated the tedious labour of sorting and cleaning fish eggs. The display also contained scale models of the hatchery buildings at Newcastle. The display drew such crowds that one official claimed it made the Canadian Court "impassable," and won the exhibition's gold medal for fish culture. The display represented not only Wilmot's ability to produce fish at an industrial scale but also his ability to stage fish exhibitions at ever more spectacular levels.[18]

4.2 "Canada Court, showing Stuffed Fishes, Refrigerators etc." The Great International Fisheries Exhibition, London, 1883. Mikan No. 4111986. Courtesy of Library and Archives Canada.

While the display presented a progressive picture of the Canadian fisheries administration – and Wilmot's centrality – it was a representation that was not universally accepted. W.F. Whitcher, the Canadian fisheries official who had originally supported Wilmot's appointment as a fisheries officer, raised uncomfortable questions about fish culture during the London exhibition. Writing in the American journal *Forest and Stream*, Whitcher compared hatchery production to commercial catches and concluded that fish culture made no contribution to catches. While acknowledging that fish culturists produced fish far exceeding "the produce of natural operations," Whitcher doubted that hatchery-reared fish "re-appeared in commercial and industrial channels as a commodity of trade and an article of supply." His critique was also a veiled attack on Wilmot's reliance on government support. Noting that fish culturists were then gathered in London, Whitcher hoped they would "give assurance to the public tax-payer that we are reaping or shall sooner or later reap the fruits of so much zealous and expensive labor."[19]

This attack embarrassed Wilmot: it may have also sharpened his exhibitionary ambitions. After the London exhibition Wilmot lobbied to establish the Canadian exhibit as a permanent museum in Ottawa. In 1884, the museum opened in a former meeting hall, renamed the Fisheries Building for the occasion. Part of the late nineteenth-century boom in natural-history museums, the Canadian Fisheries Museum fixed a temporary exhibit into a permanent display that helped formalize Ottawa as the nation's repository of natural-history knowledge. More immediately, the museum marked the ascendancy of fish culture and Samuel Wilmot's position in Canadian fisheries administration. Although the museum could display only a fraction of the London exhibit, it drew thousands of annual visitors. The museum also served as a repository for international exhibitions, supplying material for the Colonial and Indian Exhibition in London in 1886 and the Columbian Exposition in Chicago in 1893.

For several years, the Fisheries Museum lacked a vital component – a live fish-culture demonstration. Wilmot rectified this in 1890 when he installed a fish hatchery in the museum's cellar. Wilmot had first proposed a hatchery in 1885 soon after the museum opened. Not content with a collection of inanimate objects, Wilmot wanted to unite "dead and living specimens of the products of the waters of Canada" in one place to create "a great National Fisheries Museum for the Dominion of Canada."[20] With the hatchery in place, Wilmot had reproduced all the elements of his Newcastle hatchery – an exhibitionary nexus of fish culture and natural history – in the heart of the national capital.

The hatchery, when it opened, was the fourteenth in Wilmot's national fish-culture system but differed from others in its explicit exhibitionary purpose. Wilmot used the hatchery to expose federal politicians to "both ocular and practical demonstrations of the *modus operandi* of propagating and rearing fish by the artificial methods."[21] Unlike other hatcheries, which secured eggs from wild fish, the Ottawa hatchery was supplied with eggs from other fish hatcheries. Spared the difficulties of egg collection, the Ottawa hatchery was thus free to focus on exhibition as well as the distribution of fish, including exotic game-fish species such as rainbow trout, to local fishing clubs.

The hatchery and its live fish may have overshadowed the museum's collection of taxidermied fish. An Ottawa tourist guide pointed out the museum but directed visitors to the hatchery. "What will most interest the many," the guide suggested, "is The Ottawa Fish Hatchery, especially if the 'many' come while the millions of little fish are busy getting ready for the rivers, brooks, and lakes of the Dominion."[22] The guide inadvertently touched a sore point – and ongoing challenge – for curators working on fish exhibitions: while live fish animated fish-culture displays and aquariums, mounted fish lacked "life-likeness," a problem framed as the "question of fish exhibition."

The "question of fish exhibition"

For curators and taxidermists, "life-likeness" was the gold standard of animal display. Taxidermists in the late nineteenth century used the same methods to mount fish as they did to mount birds and mammals: they removed the skins from dead animals and fitted them over moulds or models of their bodies. These techniques had been developed earlier in the nineteenth century, and by the 1880s museum and commercial taxidermists were constructing more vividly modelled mounted animals.[23] Although achieving "life-likeness" was a challenge common to all animal taxidermy, it was especially pertinent to fish. The aquatic origin of fish frustrated attempts by taxidermists to preserve them in the same way as terrestrial animals. Fish not only lost their vivid colours after death but their fins and scales were prone to shrivelling and fraying after mounting. "The great objection to mounted fish," wrote John Rowley, chief taxidermist at the American Museum of Natural History, "are the shrinkage and mummification of the fins and head in drying."[24]

Well-known taxidermist, museum administrator, and conservationist William T. Hornaday warned that fish were the most difficult animal of all to mount, and the most certain to disappoint. "In nearly every large zoological museum," advised Hornaday, "the stuffed fishes are the least attractive, and the least life like of all the vertebrates."[25] And certain fish were more difficult than others. Hornaday dreaded mounting cartilaginous fish such as sharks and rays. Rays, with their wing-like bodies and long tails, frustrated taxidermists in particular. "The rays are the meanest of all subjects that vex the soul of the taxidermist. Shun them as you would the small-pox or the devil," Hornaday warned, advising budding taxidermists to avoid them altogether. "The best way to mount a ray is to make a nice plaster cast of it," suggested Hornaday, "paint it, and then bury the accursed ray in a compost heap."[26]

For Ray Miner, curator at the American Museum of Natural History (AMNH), the question of fish exhibition came down to this: fish were simply too "refractory and difficult to prepare effectively for exhibition."[27] Fish taxidermists nevertheless rose to the challenge. Many tried, as Hornaday had suggested for rays, to make casts. John Rowley specified a complex process of moulding and casting fish in plaster. A mould produced a "perfectly formed manikin" over which the taxidermist glued the fish's skin. Once dry, the fish could be painted and varnished. But as Michael Rossi notes, "casting could produce an incredibly *precise* mold . . . while nevertheless yielding a terribly *inaccurate* impression of the animal in life."[28] Plaster casts required considerable finishing, and taxidermists struggled to perfect methods that created the illusion of life. New York taxidermist Dwight Franklin claimed success in 1908 with plaster moulds to produce translucent wax models. Franklin then painted them in "vibrant and life-like colours." Another museum taxidermist experimented with electroplating plaster-cast fish with copper and silver. This technique, he claimed, gave his models "the natural sheen" and reproduced what Ray Miner said was missing in most models: "the surface bloom of the living fish."[29]

This "bloom" was also lacking in alcohol-preserved wet specimens or "alcoholics." These were fish captured during collecting expeditions and preserved in jars containing alcohol or a formaldehyde solution. Wet preservation saved fish for close anatomical study and was the standard for museum-quality fish specimens. Some curators, however, blanched at exhibiting alcohol specimens. An American curator described them as "discolored, dead, ghastly, [and] of no general resemblance to nature." The cylindrical jars used to store alcohol specimens also caused visual distortion, "another serious disadvantage" to their exhibition. Alcohol specimens "must be replaced by something worthwhile," the curator declared, "something that is representative of life."[30]

This material problem was also a conceptual one. The failure to model "life-likeness" undermined the validity of both model and museum. A discoloured wet specimen or cracked mounted fish that failed to show the animal as it once lived undermined the museum's authority. A mount that failed to look "real" satisfied neither the curatorial requirement for accuracy nor visitors' expectations of attractive exhibits. Specimens had to "be an exact copy, as if it were a cast of the animal as fashioned by nature's cunning hand," declared R.W. Shufeldt, who surveyed American museum taxidermy in 1892. A museum specimen not only had to withstand visual scrutiny but do so over time. Specimens that failed these tests, because they had the wrong eyes or were visibly decaying, diminished a museum's credibility.[31]

Such was the case with the Canadian Fisheries Museum by the end of the nineteenth century. The museum's collection of objects, particularly its collection of mounted fish, showed the accumulated wear-and-tear of seventeen years of exhibition in Ottawa and at various venues in Europe and the United States. After the collection returned from the 1893 Columbian Exhibition in Chicago, Samuel Wilmot described it as "lying about the room in the most confused state."[32] In 1901, Ottawa taxidermist W.J. Henry gave an unvarnished account of the museum's mounted fish. In a long litany, Henry observed how the specimens, amateurishly made, lacked verisimilitude and gave an overall impression of tiredness and decay. Specimens were "twisted and warped out of shape" because they had not first been properly cleaned. Others had been "stretched several inches longer than when they were in the flesh." Henry went on:

> The fins and tails were badly set and broken. The material used in mounting them is running out into the case. Many of them have bird's eyes instead of fish eyes. Some have plain transparent eyes, not colored at all, and what coloring is done is very bad. The grease and oil is running out of the specimens. The alcohol specimens were very badly done, and unless they are remedied soon, they will be lost.[33]

By 1901, however, the museum was no longer Samuel Wilmot's problem. He retired in 1895 and his successor, Edward Prince, assumed responsibility for it. Prince was an English fisheries scientist who had been recruited in 1892 to place the Canadian fisheries department on a "scientific footing." Prince was part of an emerging class of male middle-class zoologists in the late nineteenth century. He represented the professionalization of scientific expertise within government and the shift toward the "rule of experts," a hallmark of the Progressive movement and state formation at that time.[34] Prince championed and established biological stations, which undertook fisheries-related research in the field and in labs. Prince sought to remake the Canadian Fisheries Museums into a scientific institution and plotted, even before Wilmot's retirement, its renewal. "The opportunity now occurs," Prince wrote in 1894, "for making such arrangements as will vastly increase the value and interest of the Fisheries Exhibit." The museum, Prince noted, had to be both "attractive and interesting," while having "real educational and scientific value."[35]

Prince later enumerated in more detail his frustrations with Wilmot's collection. "None of the stuffed fish in the Museum have ever been properly and scientifically labelled," wrote Prince. "The names are in many cases scientifically erroneous, and the localities which were placed on the cases some years ago are manifestly wrong."[36] A stuffed paddlefish, for example, was reported to have been captured near Sarnia on Lake Ontario, a geographical error that cast doubt on an unusual record of a fish found beyond its normal range. A specimen of a purported Atlantic salmon was labelled "Female, species doubtful; locality not stated." Such a collection could not, in Prince's eyes, "adequately represent the Fisheries of Canada." It lacked authority and "such educational and scientific utility as it ought to possess."[37]

Prince turned to another man, Andrew Halkett, to renew the collection and establish its scientific credibility. Born in Scotland in 1854, Halkett emigrated to Canada in 1872 and joined the fisheries department in 1878 as a clerk. In the late 1890s, Prince began assigning Halkett to curatorial and naturalist duties, an elevation that may have arisen out of their mutual acquaintance in Ottawa's natural-history society, the Ottawa Field Naturalists' Club. In 1903, Halkett was formally appointed curator of the Fisheries Museum and served in this capacity until the museum closed in 1918. Halkett collected and catalogued fish specimens, corresponded with collectors and other curators, and designed and supervised exhibits. And he had to contend with a collection of mounted fish that, as W.J. Henry had made clear, was visibly decaying before the public's eyes.[38]

From his confirmation as curator in 1903 to the museum's closure in 1918, Halkett confronted the material difficulties of managing an impermanent collection in an ostensibly permanent museum. During his tenure, Halkett struggled to renovate both the collection and the museum space. His first efforts stalled when he was named naturalist to Canada's 1904 "Neptune" expedition to the Arctic. The journey afforded an important collecting opportunity, but the year-long expedition also delayed the museum's renewal. On his return, Halkett also had to deal with an unexpected problem: a growing demand from regional exhibitions for fisheries exhibits, particularly aquarium displays.

Since its opening, the Fisheries Museum had functioned as an exhibit repository, supplying materials for Canadian fisheries displays at international exhibitions. After the 1893 Columbian Exposition in Chicago – where the US Fish Commission had sponsored a massive aquarium – the volume of requests from regional exhibitions across Canada for fisheries exhibits and aquariums increased. The fisheries department initially tried to satisfy such demands. Although wary about loaning mounted fish from the museum, the department often provided a model hatchery or aquarium tanks. Aquarium displays satisfied exhibition officials, who sought to attract visitors, and the fisheries department, which continued to promote "the great benefits to be derived from the artificial propagation of fish."[39]

Once word circulated that the fisheries department was supplying such exhibits, however, exhibition organizers began importuning for them. The Saint John Exhibition Association, for example, lobbied the fisheries department for a live-fish display after it learned that the Toronto exhibition had been granted one. And when the Halifax exhibition learned that the New Brunswick fair had been successful, it asked for one too. Exhibition officials hoped that such exhibits would boost attendance; in British Columbia, officials from the New Westminster exhibition believed that an aquarium display would help their fair recover from a disastrous fire the previous year. The fisheries department could not meet the demand because tanks and equipment were expensive. Instead the department began to offer live fish, supplied from the closest federal fish hatchery, and left exhibition organizers to supply aquarium tanks.[40]

An exception made for the New Westminster exhibition caused conflict. In 1907, curator Halkett went to the New Westminster exhibition and mounted a display of the Fisheries Museum's mounted fish and an aquarium display, which he stocked with fish that he had collected in local waters. The exhibit proved so popular that New Westminster officials constructed a permanent fisheries hall, which opened in 1909. When the City of Vancouver launched its own fair in 1910, it sought a similar exhibit.

Vancouver exhibition officials promised, in contrast to the seasonal New Westminster fair, to provide a year-round attraction that would comprehensively display British Columbia's resources. The fisheries department refused. Since Vancouver was only 12 miles from New Westminster, it could not justify fisheries exhibits in both places.[41]

Despite the lack of support, the Vancouver Exhibition proceeded with its plans and opened what may have been the first purpose-built aquarium in Canada in 1913. The aquarium was modest, with two small rooms, but it remained unfinished and understocked. The fisheries department supplied taxidermied fish for display but refused further pleas for financial assistance to complete the project.[42] The fisheries department had also refused earlier requests. The Halifax exhibition, which had been lobbying for an aquarium for more than a decade, was turned down in 1910 and again in 1911. So was the Manitoba government, which sought one for its provincial exhibition. Even a private park operator in Montreal asked the government for an aquarium installation. The fisheries department recognized the educational value of such exhibits but claimed that it had no funds to support them. Granting one exhibition an aquarium "would form a precedent," department officials warned, "that would surely lead to difficulties."[43]

Impermanence at the Fisheries Museum

The growing demand for aquarium displays indicated a shift in exhibitionary expectations, one that the Fisheries Museum itself struggled to meet. In 1911, the museum hatchery suddenly closed. A typhoid epidemic in Ottawa forced municipal officials to chemically treat the city's water supply, which was drawn from the Ottawa River. This change proved fatal to hatching eggs and fry, and ultimately to the hatchery's viability.[44] Without live fish, the question of fish exhibition became pronounced: as Halkett noted, the museum lacked animation and suffered from an "immobile effect engendered by mounted and prepared objects." The closure also highlighted other issues with the museum's physical arrangements: the question of fish exhibition extended from the modelling of fish to the museum's space, all of which affected the museum's legitimacy.

Around the time of the hatchery's demise, Halkett publically aired his frustrations with the Fisheries Building. As Halkett noted, the building

4.3 "Fisheries Building at the corner of Queen and O'Connor Streets." Photograph. Public Works Department, PA-046882. Courtesy of Library and Archives Canada.

was originally a meeting hall and was "entirely unadapted for the purposes of a natural history museum." The museum lacked the "appurtenances" of science: "a proper laboratory" equipped with scientific instruments and a zoological library without which "no museum of natural history is complete." Halkett exclaimed "violently against the present condition of things," and proposed a solution: a purpose-built museum building to house "a national fisheries collection which would be in every way creditable to the department."[45]

Behind Halkett's proposal was another disappointment: the Fisheries Museum's exclusion from the newly constructed Victoria Memorial Museum in Ottawa. Proposed in 1901 and completed ten years later, the structure was only the second purpose-built museum constructed in Canada. The building's Scotch Baronial design wrapped its principal tenant, the

Geological Survey of Canada and its natural history collection, in a stately exterior that marked their national importance. Early in the museum's planning, officials had proposed to also accommodate, along with the Supreme Court and National Art Gallery, the Fisheries Museum.[46] This plan was never realized; one government minister doubted there were enough fish specimens to fill a display case, let alone a museum wing. In the new museum's modelling of Canada's dominion over nature, fish and fisheries had no place.[47]

The Victoria Memorial Museum nevertheless provided an opportunity to address the Fisheries Museum's challenges. The National Gallery of Canada, which had occupied the Fisheries Building since 1888, vacated the building's top floor when it moved to the new museum. The Fisheries Museum was permitted to expand into this space, a voluminous high-ceilinged room with abundant natural light. The fisheries department also increased the Fisheries Museum's budget, allowing for renovation of the building's interior and the museum collection.[48] While workers replaced wiring and display cases, Halkett burned the museum's old "worthless" specimens and commissioned an American taxidermist, Sherman Denton, to make new examples of mounted fish.

Denton came recommended by Frederic Lucas, the director of the American Museum of Natural History. Denton, like other taxidermists, had confronted the question of fish exhibition. "A 'stuffed' fish is perhaps the ugliest thing in the way of decoration one can find in a day's search," Denton exclaimed in an essay. "When gazing on the dried and wrinkled skin without beauty of form or color, how difficult it is to realize that this wretched object was once a graceful, glittering fish." He claimed to have answered the vexing question of fish exhibition by placing fish skins over *papier maché* forms or moulds. This method, the taxidermist claimed, preserved the specimens as "real fishes."[49]

Once engaged, Denton began shipping freshly mounted specimens to Halkett. In 1912, Denton went on a collecting expedition to British Columbia, gathering rare and unusual species of fish. Denton helped Halkett to renew the collection and to complete his longstanding project of publishing a complete list of Canadian fish. In 1913, after a decade of work, Halkett's *Check List of the Fishes of the Dominion of Canada and Newfoundland* appeared. In addition to new specimens, Halkett commissioned expensive scale models of fishing boats and fishing gear, which provided authoritative representations of Canadian fisheries. Halkett also obtained a 50-foot whale skeleton that was hung in the museum's upper gallery. The skeleton placed the Fisheries Museum in a select company of grand metropolitan natural-history museums, including New York's American Museum of Natural History and London's Natural History Museum. Massive skeletal reconstructions of whales and dinosaurs attracted visitors fascinated by gigantic creatures – they also served museums as powerful emblems of scientific prestige.[50]

In 1914, the renovated Fisheries Museum reopened with new models, specimens, and exhibits. Halkett's work had renewed the museum and bolstered its status as a major scientific institution. Yet the museum still struggled to authoritatively answer the question of fish exhibition. Even though Denton's mounted fish represented the latest in model making, his mounted specimens suffered the same fate as the old collection: they decayed. In the spring of 1914, Halkett complained to Denton that a "Man-eating Shark" that the taxidermist had mounted "is becoming so cracked that it will soon be unfit for display." A specimen of an Ocean sunfish was also showing signs of collapse. Halkett was able "with the use of putty and paint" to conceal these defects, but a year later Halkett reported further damage:[51]

> I regret to advise you that some of the specimens supplied by you are seriously cracking. The two large Skates are cracking across the back. The green sturgeon is cracking practically all over. A large halibut is cracking close to the head, and the sword-fish is falling away from the board to which it is attached. The cast of the whale is cracking in several places and the maskinonge and blue shark are cracking about the head. Scales are falling off the two specimens of California herring, as well as off the shad.[52]

Denton repaired these specimens and continued to mount fish for the museum. Although Halkett had secured funding for the museum's renovation, and for a new collection of mounted fish, the Canadian Fisheries Museum did not long survive. Compounding the hatchery closure and ongoing problems with mounted fish was a shift in the fisheries department's exhibitionary strategy. Beginning in 1913, it started to mount consumer-themed exhibits at Toronto's Canadian National Exhibition. These displays focused on promoting fresh fish as a consumer item, schooling retailers and consumers in its handling and cookery. While the Fisheries Museum provided mounted-fish exhibits, they were soon overshadowed by a model fish-retail shop and fish restaurant that the fisheries department first presented in 1914. Against these interactive exhibits, displays of mounted fish appeared stale and out of date. "The restaurant has proved an eminent success," advised a fisheries department memorandum, "and is possibly far more efficacious in advertising fish than the exhibit."[53] *The Canadian Fisherman* shared this view and extended it to the museum itself. "It is true many of us have never heard of [the Canadian Fisheries Museum]," the publication claimed, "and those few who have discovered its location have failed to find anything of educational value to fisheries in it."[54]

Such criticisms forecast the museum's demise. In February 1918, the federal public works department advised fisheries officials that "it will be necessary to remove the Fisheries Exhibit" as the Fisheries Building was to be demolished.[55] In its place, a modern office building and a new headquarters for the fisheries department would be constructed. Halkett and other fisheries officials initially believed the museum's closure was temporary. Halkett arranged to loan the museum's fish collection to the Victoria Memorial Museum, while he waited upon the time "when we shall have a proper Fisheries Museum." After it became apparent that the museum would not reopen, Halkett began to freely distribute the museum's mounted fish. They were "worthless for scientific purposes," Halkett admitted, but "might be serviceable as natural history object lessons for educational institutions." The museum's demolition appeared to have surprised Halkett, who packed up the collection amidst the ensuing confusion. "The work of pulling down the museum building was underway," Halkett reported, "even when the material was being removed."[56]

Between 1919 and 1922, the collection was moved several times from one storage location to another in Ottawa. In 1922 the fisheries department instructed Public Works to complete the "final disposal of the residue ... of the Canadian Fisheries Museum."[57] The remaining objects were itemized for auction or destruction. Some objects – such as valuable ship models – were returned to the fisheries department for display in various government offices. A few rare specimens were saved for long-term storage, including a "left-eyed Halibut." Others, including the prized whale skeleton, were thrown out.[58]

The demolition of the Canadian Fisheries Museum ended a chapter in Canadian fish exhibitions that began with Samuel Wilmot in the 1860s. Wilmot launched fish displays in Canada and became a successful impresario of them. Working to promote fish culture, he also promoted himself. But Wilmot's legacy did not last long. Curator Andrew Halkett inherited a decaying collection and problematic museum space, while also having to negotiate a changing exhibitionary landscape. Questions of permanency – and legitimacy – dogged the museum's modelling of fish and its existence. Its demise in 1918 dramatizes the multiple material challenges that fish exhibitions posed. Only in the 1950s were Canadians ready to reconsider and reinvest in this type of display. The Canadian fisheries department sponsored a sleek fisheries gallery in the Royal Ontario Museum in Toronto, while in Quebec City and Vancouver, civic officials established Canada's first large civic aquariums. The question of fish exhibition, however, continued to challenge curators and aquarium keepers as they sought, for a new generation of audiences, to reveal life below the waves.

Notes

1   The literature on animal display is growing: recent contributions include Samuel J. M. M. Alberti, ed., *The Afterlives of Animals* (Charlottesville and London: University of Virginia Press, 2011); Joan B. Landes, Paula Young Lee, and Paul Youngquist, eds., *Gorgeous Beasts: Animal Bodies in Historical Perspective*, (University Park: Pennsylvania State Press, 2012); and Rachel Poliquin, *The Breathless Zoo: Taxidermy and the Cultures of Longing* (University Park: Pennsylvania State Press, 2012).

2   Joseph E. Taylor III, *Making Salmon: An Environmental History of the Northwest Fisheries Crisis* (Seattle: University of Washington Press, 1999), 95.

3   R W. Miner, "A Plan for an Educational Exhibit of Fishes," in *Bulletin of the Bureau of Fisheries* (Washington: Government Printing Office, 1908), 1317.

4   Darin Kinsey, "'Seeding the Water as the Earth:' The Epicenter and Peripheries of a Western Aquacultural Revolution." *Environmental History* 11 (2006): 535–36.

5   William Knight, "Samuel Wilmot, Fish Culture, and Recreational Fisheries in Late 19th Century Ontario." *Scientia Canadensis* 30, no. 1 (2007): 75–90; A.B. McCullough, "Samuel Wilmot," in *Dictionary of Canadian Biography* (Toronto: University of Toronto Press, 1990),

1106–7, also online at http://www.
biographi.ca/en/bio/wilmot_sam-
uel_12E.html.

6   George C. Bompas, *Life of Frank
Buckland* (London: Smith, Elder, &
Co., 1885), 127; 103–4; see Bernard
Lightman on "Frank Buckland and
the Culture of Display," in Bernard
Lightman, "Lecturing in the Spatial
Economy of Science," in *Science in
the Marketplace: Nineteenth-Cen-
tury Sites and Experiences*, ed.
Aileen Fyfe and Bernard Lightman
(Chicago: University of Chicago
Press, 2009), 110.

7   "Provincial Exhibition," *The Globe*,
8 October 1870, 3.

8   See Philip Henry Gosse, *The
Aquarium: An Unveiling of the
Wonders of the Deep Sea*, 2nd ed.
(London: John van Voorst, 1856);
Bernd Brunner, *The Ocean at
Home: An Illustrated History of the
Aquarium* (Baltimore and London:
Princeton Architectural Press,
2005); Rebecca Stott, "Through a
Glass Darkly: Aquarium Col-
onies and Nineteenth-Century
Narratives of Marine Monstrosity."
Gothic Studies 2, no. 3 (2000):
305–27; Vernon N. Kisling, Jr.,
"Zoological Gardens of the United
States," in *Zoo and Aquarium His-
tory: Ancient Animals Collections
to Zoological Gardens*, ed. Vernon
N. Kisling Jr. (Boca Raton, FL: CRC
Press 2001), 155.

9   J.E. Taylor, *The Aquarium; Its
Inhabitants, Structure, and
Management*, 2nd ed. (London:
David Bogue, 1881), 18. The Bright-
on Aquarium, for example, opened
in 1872 and featured massive tanks,
including one that held 110,000
gallons of sea water, "big enough
for the evolutions of porpoises,

full-grown sturgeons, sharks,
sea-lions, turtles, and other large
marine animals."

10 Jerry Ryan, *The Forgotten Aquariums of Boston* (Boston: Finley
Aquatic Books, 2002), 41–43.

11 See circus advertisements in *The
Globe*'s classified section for 2 June
1873; 21 August 1878; 21 May 1885;
and 20 June 1885. "Exhibition
Notices," *The Globe*, 24 September 1887, 13; "Annual Exhibition
of Manitoba Agricultural and
Industrial Society," *The Globe*, 13
October 1881, 7.

12 Canada, *Report of Fish-Breeding in
the Dominion of Canada 1877* (Ottawa: Queen's Printer, 1878), 24–26;
The Globe, Thursday, 15 December
1881, 5.

13 Canada, *Report of Fish Breeding*,
25.

14 "Dominion Exhibition," *The Globe*,
26 September 1879, 4.

15 Samuel Wilmot, "Introduction of
California Salmon into Ontario,"
*Bulletin of the United States Fish
Commission 1881* (Washington:
Government Printing Office, 1882),
3.

16 E.A. Heamen, *The Inglorious Arts
of Peace: Exhibitions in Canadian
Society during the Nineteenth
Century* (Toronto: University of
Toronto Press, 1999), 180; Paul
Greenhalgh, *Ephemeral Vistas:
The Expositions Universelles, Great
Exhibitions and World's Fairs,
1851–1939* (Manchester: Manches-
ter University Press, 1988), 77.

17 See Eric Mills, *Biological Oceanog-
raphy: A Early History, 1870–1960*
(Toronto: University of Toronto
Press, 1989); Tim D. Smith, *Scaling
Fisheries: The Science of Measuring*

the Effects of Fishing, 1855–1955 (Cambridge, UK: Cambridge University Press, 1994); W. Jeffrey Bolster, *The Mortal Sea: Fishing the Atlantic in the Age of Sail* (Cambridge, MA: Harvard University Press, 2012), 165–67; Bruno Latour, *Science in Action: How to Follow Scientists and Engineers Through Society* (Milton Keynes, UK: Open University Press, 1987), 237.

18   Canada, "Canada at the Great International Fisheries Exhibition, London," xxix. Canada, "Appendix B: Canada at the Great International Fisheries Exhibition, London," *Preliminary Report on the Fisheries of Canada for the year 1884* (Ottawa: Queen's Printer, 1885), xxix.

19   W.F. Whitcher, "Practical Results of Fish Culture in the Dominion of Canada," *Forest and Stream* 20 (1883): 408.

20   Canada, *Report on Fish-Breeding in the Dominion of Canada 1885* (Ottawa: Queen's Printer, 1886), 16.

21   Canada, *Report on Fish-Breeding in the Dominion of Canada 1889* (Ottawa: Queen's Printer, 1890), 6.

22   Anson A. Gard, *The Hub and the Spokes or, The Capital and its Environs* (Ottawa and New York: Emerson Press, 1914), 34.

23   Karen Wonders, *Habitat Dioramas: Illusions of Wilderness in Museums of Natural History* (Uppsala, Sweden: Acta Universitatis Upsaliensis, 1993), 23.

24   John Rowley, *The Art of Taxidermy* (New York: D. Appleton and Company, 1898), 173.

25   William T. Hornaday, *Taxidermy and Zoological Collecting*, 4th ed.

(New York: Charles Scribner's Sons, 1894), 208.

26   Ibid., 215–16.

27   Miner, "A Plan for an Educational Exhibit of Fishes," 1317.

28   Michael Rossi, "Fabricating Authenticity: Modeling a Whale at the American Museum of Natural History, 1906–1974," *Isis* 101, no. 2 (2010): 352.

29   Dwight Franklin, "A Method of Preparing Fishes for Museum and Exhibition Purposes," in *Bulletin of the Bureau of Fisheries* (Washington: Government Printing Office, 1908), 1355; Boyd P. Rothrock, "A New Method of Preparing Exhibits of Fishes," *Proceedings of the American Association of Museums* 9 (1914): 88; Miner, "A Plan for an Educational Exhibit of Fishes," 1317–18.

30   Charles F. Millspaugh, "Botanical Installation," *Proceedings of the American Association of Museums* 4 (1910): 56.

31   R.W. Shufeldt, *Scientific Taxidermy for Museums* (Washington: Government Printing Office, 1894), 381; Victoria Cain, "The Art of Authority: Exhibits, Exhibit-Makers, and the Contest for Scientific Status in the American Museum of Natural History, 1920–1940," *Science in Context* 24, no. 2 (2011): 219; Rossi, "Fabricating Authenticity," 354.

32   Samuel Wilmot, memorandum, 10 January 1895, RG 23, vol. 158, file 497, Library and Archives Canada (LAC).

33   W.J. Henry to Louis Davies, 8 May 1901, RG 23, vol. 226, file 271, LAC.

34   Jennifer Hubbard, *A Science on the Scales: The Rise of Canadian*

Atlantic Fisheries Biology, 1898–1939 (Toronto: University of Toronto Press, 2006), 18; Patrick Carroll, *Science, Culture, and Modern State Formation* (Berkeley: University of California Press, 2006), 13.

35   Memorandum, 25 August 1894, RG 23, vol. 260, file 1708, LAC; E.E. Prince to L.H Davies, 23 August 1894, RG 23, vol. 260, file 1708, LAC.

36   E.E. Prince, memorandum, 11 December 1895, RG 23, vol. 260, file 1708, LAC.

37   Memorandum, 25 August 1894, RG 23, vol. 260, file 1708, LAC; E.E. Prince to L.H Davies, 23 August 1894, RG 23, vol. 260, file 1708, LAC.

38   William Knight, "Modeling Authority at the Canadian Fisheries Museum" (PhD diss., Carleton University, 2014), 131–37; Hoyes Lloyd, "Andrew Halkett, Naturalist, 1854–1937," *The Canadian Field-Naturalist* 53, no. 3 (March 1939): 31–32.

39   E.E. Prince, memorandum, 4 July 1894, RG 23, vol. 232, file 1353, LAC; Canada, *Thirty-Seventh Annual Report of the Department of Marine and Fisheries 1904* (Ottawa: King's Printer, 1905), 233.

40   Charles Everett to J.D. Ellis, MP, 19 April 1898, RG 23, vol. 157, file 470, LAC; *The Globe*, Tuesday, 6 September 1904, 9; Memorandum, 7 April 1906, RG 23, vol. 157, file 470, LAC.

41   Andrew Halkett, memorandum, 10 December 1907, RG 23, vol. 311, file 2359, LAC; W.H. Neary to R.N. Venning, 4 November 1908, RG 23, vol. 311, file 2359, LAC; W.H. Neary to F.H. Cunningham, 3 July 1909, RG 23, vol. 311, file 2359, LAC; H.A. Ralston to Alderman Campbell, 24 May 1910, RG 23, vol. 311, file 2359, LAC; H.A. Ralston Vancouver Exhibition Association to Minister of Marine and Fisheries, 12 June 1911, RG 23, vol. 311, file 2359, LAC; F.H. Cunningham to J.A. Rodd, 9 March 1910, RG 23, vol. 311, file 2359, LAC.

42   J.D. Hazen to H.H. Stevens, 30 March 1914, RG 23, vol. 1148, file 722-5-8, LAC; H.S. Ralston to H.H. Stevens, 24 February 1914, RG 23, vol. 1148, file 722-5-8, LAC; H.S. Ralston to J.D. Hazen, 17 July 1914, RG 23, vol. 1148, file 722-5-8, LAC. Rolston suspected that the fisheries department favoured the New Westminster exhibition because the chief federal fisheries inspector in British Columbia, F.H. Cunningham, sat on the New Westminster exhibition committee.

43   Memorandum, 14 May 1910, RG 23, vol. 157, file 470, LAC; J.D. Hazen to G.W. Lawrence, 22 June 1912, RG 23, vol. 400, file 4068, LAC; A. Johnston to E.A. Saunders, 20 May 1911, RG 23, vol. 157, file 470, LAC; Memorandum, 25 February 1911, RG 23, vol. 389, file 3577, LAC.

44   Chris Warfe, "The Search for Pure Water in Ottawa: 1910–1915," *Urban History Review* 1 (1979): 93; Assistant Deputy Minister of Marine and Fisheries to J.A. Ewart, Chief Architect, Department of Public Works, 7 September 1911, RG 23, vol. 158, file 497, LAC.

45   "Natural History Report," *Forty-Fourth Annual Report of the Department of Marine and Fisheries 1910–11* (Ottawa: King's Printer, 1911), 418–20.

46 Morris Zaslow, *Reading the Rocks: The Story of the Geological Survey of Canada, 1842–1972* (Toronto: Macmillan Canada, 1975), 266; Susan Sheets-Pyenson, *Cathedrals of Science: The Development of Colonial National History Museums During the Late Nineteenth Century* (Kingston and Montreal: McGill-Queen's University Press, 1988); Canada, *Official Report of the Debates of the House of Commons*, vol. 53 (Ottawa: Queen's Printer, 1900), 7934.

47 William Templeman to Louis Brodeur, 22 July 1910, RG 23, vol. 158, file 497, LAC. On museum architecture, see Sophie Forgan, "The Architecture of Display: Museums, Universities and Objects in Nineteenth-Century Britain," *History of Science* 32 (1994): 143.

48 J.B. Hunter to C. Stanton, 11 March 1911, RG 23, vol. 158, file 497, LAC.; "Natural History Report," *Forty-Fifth Annual Report of the Department of Marine and Fisheries 1911–12* (Ottawa: King's Printer, 1912), 348.

49 Sherman Denton to W.A. Found, 7 August 1911, RG 23, vol. 226, file 1271, LAC; Sherman Denton, *Fish Mounting as an Art* (Wellesley Farms, MA: n.d.), 2.

50 William T. Stearn, *The Natural History Museum at South Kensington* (London: Natural History Museum, 1981), 118; S.J.M.M. Alberti, *Nature and Culture: Objects, Disciplines and the Manchester Museum* (Manchester, UK: Manchester University Press, 2009), 125.

51 W.A. Found to Sherman Denton, 18 March 1914 and 25 March 1914, RG 23, vol. 1146, file 722-3-2 [2], LAC.

52 W.A. Found to Sherman Denton, 12 May 1915, RG 23, vol. 1146, file 722-3-2 [3], LAC.

53 Memorandum, 27 March 1918, RG 23, vol. 1146, file 722-2-4, LAC.

54 "The Need for Technical Education in Our Fishing Industry," *The Canadian Fisherman* 5 (January 1918): 578

55 E.L. Horwood to G.J. Debarats, 15 February 1918, RG 23, vol. 1147, file 722-3-7, LAC.

56 Andrew Halkett, memorandum, 18 March 1918, RG 23, vol. 1147, file 722-3-7, LAC.

57 Memorandum, 29 May 1922, RG 23, vol. 1146, file 722-3-4, LAC.

58 Memorandum, 7 June 1922, RG 23, vol. 1147, file 722-3-7, LAC.

The Beavers of Stanley Park

Rachel Poliquin

Beavers have moved into Beaver Lake in Vancouver's Stanley Park. A single beaver arrived in 2008. No one knows where it came from. Stanley Park is at the end of a peninsula that protrudes into the Pacific Ocean like a stubby thumb. Hemmed by water on three sides and by Vancouver's downtown core on the fourth, the park is not particularly accessible to a migrating beaver. Perhaps it swam Burrard Inlet, a 2-kilometre stretch of water separating Vancouver from the wilderness of the North Shore Mountains. Beavers usually avoid salt water, but the distance is not impossible to swim. Perhaps it crossed the Lions Gate Bridge at night. A second beaver arrived shortly thereafter. The sex of the beavers was unknown (male and female beavers are indistinguishable by sight) until, unexpectedly, five beavers were spotted on a summer evening in 2013.

For most of the twentieth century, Beaver Lake had been devoid of beavers. In fact, around the time the lake acquired its name more than a century ago, its last beaver occupants were forcibly removed. But such irony is to be expected from any beaver tale. The long history of human–beaver relations has been plagued with inconsistencies and contradictions. The truth of the matter is that it is hard to see a beaver. Over the past century, the beavers of Stanley Park present the odd incongruity of being everywhere visible as traces, but nowhere to be seen in the flesh.

5.1 A tree that has been wrapped with wire mesh to prevent further beaver damage. Photograph by Rachel Poliquin.

Beaver Improvements

Vancouver is not an old city. The British naval captain George Vancouver was among the first Europeans to explore the area in 1792, having sailed all the way around Tierra del Fuego and Cape Horn. The first European to arrive overland came in 1808, and the first non-Native farm within what is now Vancouver was established in the early 1860s. A decade later in 1871, John A. Macdonald, Canada's first prime minister, wooed British Columbia to join Canada with the promise of bringing the railway all the way west to the Pacific Ocean. Vancouver was chosen as its terminus, and the first train arrived from Montreal in 1887. The population of Vancouver was at the time was only 5,000 people. Wilderness was everywhere. But yet, improbably, on 26 September 1888, city council designed a 1,000-acre park on the edge of Vancouver, making Stanley Park one of the oldest and most ostentatious urban parks in North America.

In his fascinating history, *Inventing Stanley Park: An Environmental History,* Sean Kheraj details the creation and ongoing management of the park's natural aesthetic. As Kheraj explains, a park is a human idea imposed upon a demarcated section of nature, and as such is always shaped by human intention. Even a supposedly pristine "wilderness" like Stanley Park has been profoundly shaped, reshaped, and reimagined by cultural forces, which are forever in tension with the ever-changing ecosystem.

As Kheraj outlines, from the park's earliest inception, the Park Board strove to create artfully shaped ecologies while simultaneously, and paradoxically, "masking evidence of human and non-human disturbances in order to produce a more naturalistic appearance."[1] Early improvements included building hardscapes such as paths and a seawall (to encourage strolling and forestall sea-wave erosion) as well as ecological interventions such as replacing western hemlock with Douglas fir (an outbreak of hemlock loopers had left many unsightly infected and dead trees) and forcibly modifying the park's animal populations.

In 1888, the peninsula was home to a wide variety of animal occupants, including squirrels, raccoons, skunks, beavers, and numerous species of ducks and geese, as well as humans and their domestic livestock such as pigs, horses, and cattle. After the area was designated a park, the Park Board had very specific ideas as to the proper sort of animals that should inhabit the new urban wilderness. As Kheraj explains, the board

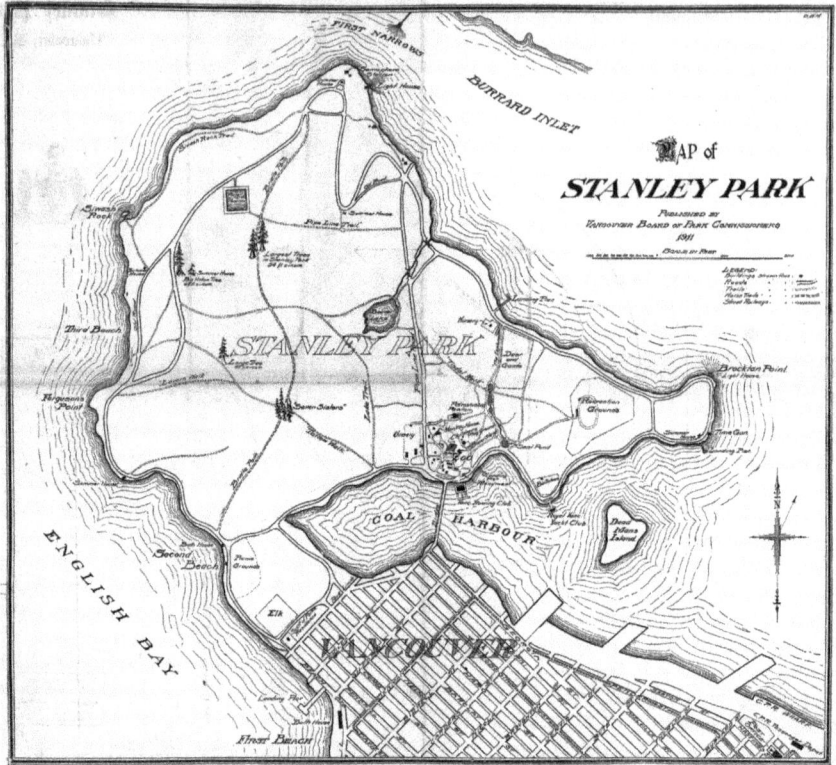

5.2 Map of Stanley Park, 1911. Map Cabinet C, Drawer 5. Courtesy of the City of Vancouver Archives.

encouraged "attractive species of gentle demeanour" to live within the park with the aim of entertaining visitors with "a sanitized and tamed wilderness."[2] Most birds and small animals were welcome to remain. Other animals were ousted or exterminated, while various exotic creatures were introduced either to roam freely about the park or within the confines of a zoo. At various times over the park's history, beavers have belonged to all categories of the Park Board's animal management.

At first glance, beavers might seem to conform perfectly to the Park Board's vision of a tamed wilderness. Beavers are gentle and retiring, unless provoked. They are among the most domesticated of creatures – they maintain a year-round abode, mate for life, and raise their kits well into adolescence. They are also large animals (beavers can easily weigh over 20 kilograms), which might suggest they offered abundant viewing opportunities, particularly as visitors always knew where to look – beavers never stray too far from the water's safety.

But Stanley Park's beavers did not cooperate with the Park Board's mandate in the early twentieth century. Firstly, they did not offer themselves for easy viewing. Beavers are secretive, nocturnal, and aquatic; it takes a patient observer with a sharp eye at dusk to catch even a glimpse of a beaver silently gliding by. But worse still, the beavers had their own version of "improved" nature. The animal embodiment of industry, beavers work tirelessly (some might say unrelentingly) to transform their environment to suit their lifestyle. While all animals are constantly modifying their surroundings, few animals have the vision and perseverance to build a new ecosystem. In that, beavers and humans are in a class of their own. But their ecological visions are often at odds. While the Park Board strove to mask its ecological interventions within the park, Stanley Park's beavers had no interest in such sleight of hand. Ironically, for an animal that is exceeding hard to see, beavers make their presence abundantly known.

Beavers are not simply builders. By felling trees, flooding an area and retaining stagnant water, they create wetland oases. And by changing the landscape's ecology, beaver craftsmanship directly controls the availability of resources for other organisms. In fact, biologists call beavers a keystone species or ecological engineers for their critical role in creating and sustaining ecosystems.[3]

As long as beavers have trees and water, they can remodel any landscape to suit their tastes. If the water is too shallow for safety, they construct a dam and build themselves a lodge in the middle of the ever-rising lake. Flooding often kills surrounding trees, and the slow-moving water entices a host of marsh-loving species and creatures that live in rotten wood. Beaver wetlands are associated with a more diverse and abundant bird communities, and the silt accumulation at the bottom provides ideal spawning grounds for golden trout. Although beavers deter certain species, by creating niche habitats and attracting different species than previously inhabited the area, beavers and their wetlands increase the overall species diversity of the area. Each year, the average adult beaver cuts approximately one metric tonne of wood – about 215 trees – for food and building materials, which means beavers can quickly transform a

5.3 A beaver gnawing on a tree, ca. 1920. Photograph by H. R. Stenton. AM54-S4: Misc P56, City of Vancouver Archives.

fast-flowing river into a stagnant and stump-studded haven for waterfowl, water-loving amphibians, insects, and the animals that eat them.[4]

In the early twentieth century, Stanley Park's beavers inhabited a small lake in a relatively isolated portion of the park. An early contour map of the park from 1890 identified the lake simply as "Marshy Pond." As the name suggests, the area had been thoroughly modified by beavers into the ideal castorine habitat. The water was stagnant, and the surrounding forest was filled with dead and fallen trees that had either died from insect infestation or been chewed by beavers.

The lake hardly conformed to the Park Board's vision of crystal blue waters. Perhaps the stumps, broken branches, and marshy water echoed too closely that other uncontained and unrestrained wilderness pushing against the edges of young Vancouver. As it was the only body of water within the park's perimeter, the board hoped to beautify the lake and make the area more accessible to visitors. In 1911 the water was encircled with an embankment and a path. The area came to be known as Beaver Lake. But the beavers would have to go.

5.4 A postcard from Beaver Lake. Classic Postcards, Rootsweb.

The Right Sort of Beaver

The Park Board minutes from 1911 do not directly express frustration with the beavers, but letters to and from Stanley Park's Zoo hint at a fraught and mercurial relationship.

On 25 February 1911, the Superintendent of the Public Parks Board of Winnipeg wrote a letter to Stanley Park following up on an earlier verbal beaver offer made to the chairman of their board. "He tells me, that you gave him to understand you could give him a pair of beavers." The wording of the letter suggests Stanley Park was very keen to rid itself of beavers. A few months later, the Park Board also offered a pair of beavers to the Royal Zoological Society of Ireland. And in September, Horne's Zoological Arena, a wild animal importing outfit from Denver, Colorado, wrote asking for as many beavers as possible. "We have been advised," the letter begins, "that you have a number of surplus beavers you wish to dispose of."[5]

At the beginning of the twentieth century, both species of beaver were sadly diminished throughout their indigenous range. Eight isolated populations totalling a mere 1,200 animals were all that remained of the Eurasian beaver (*Castor fiber*).[6] North American beavers (*Castor canadensis*) fared only slightly better; beavers were threatened from coast to coast. For example, when the 45,000 square kilometres of Wood Buffalo National Park was established in northern Alberta in 1922, largely to protect the world's largest herd of free-roaming wood bison, the area was barren of beavers.[7] By the 1930s, beavers were all but extinct in Canada's vast northern territories, which prompted the Hudson's Bay Company, the largest fur trading monopoly the world has ever seen, to initiate conservation programs in hopes of rehabilitating the species and saving their trade.[8] Grey Owl's powerful advocacy for beavers also came in the 1930s. In other words, in 1911 a thriving population of beavers was a precious rarity.

And a lucrative one. A price list from Horne's zoological catalogue included in City of Vancouver Archives among letters to and from the Stanley Park Zoo (which suggests the beavers for sale may have been trapped in Beaver Lake) offered beavers for $150 a pair. If cost reflected audience appeal, a $75 beaver was less in demand than an African lion ($450) or a male hyena ($180), but not far from the allure of a German wild boar, "male, very large," offered for $90. Armadillos were listed at $6 each.

Although beavers were not officially appointed as Canada's national animal until 1975, they have always been synonymous with the nation. Canada, after all, was built on the back of beaver, and the Hudson's Bay Company was practically its first government. Beavers were the motivating cause for North America's first white settler colonies, and the quest for a steady supply of beaver skins to make beaver felt hats was one of the main drivers of expansion toward the Pacific coast. But beaver obliteration and beaver appreciation have never been mutually exclusive activities. At precisely the moment beavers were being slaughtered by the hundreds of thousands, those same beavers ascended as the supreme animal model of hard work, integrity, and perseverance. The industrious beaver began to gnaw during the eighteenth century and has never stopped. Endowed with an ever-willing, ever-ready work ethic, beavers became synonymous with busy-ness. As the English novelist William Kingston put it in 1884, "the beaver has fitly been selected as the representative animal of Canada, on account of its industry, perseverance, and hardihood, and the resolute way in which it overcomes difficulty."[9]

5.5 The Beaver Enclosure in the Stanley Park Zoo, ca. 1911. Photograph by Major James Skitt Matthews. AM54-S4, City of Vancouver Archives.

It was perhaps that nationalized symbol, the beaver of Canadian backwoods, industrious living, and tireless perseverance, that the foreign zoos wanted to display. And perhaps it was such international appreciation that changed the Park Board's opinion of their beavers. Whereas in February, it had been trying to rid the park of beavers, by July a beaver display was suggested for the Stanley Park Zoo. In November, the board voted to build a beaver enclosure for the extravagant sum of $1,450.[10] The beavers of Beaver Lake were live-trapped to be displayed in the zoo.

The plan solved two challenges with one enclosure: it corralled the beavers' "messy" ecological behaviour and put the hard-to-see animals on conspicuous display, at least in theory. In practice, the idea was a failure.

The beaver display consisted of an artificial pond encircled with a wooden and wire fence. A photograph of the enclosure shows it to be wholly insufficient to the task of containing the animals. A beaver could easily chew through or burrow under the fence, and they did. The pond also had a spouting fountain in the middle "to irrigate the surface and prevent stagnation or vegetable growth," which only further accentuates the ignorance – whether wilful or not – of beaver behaviour.[11] Stagnant water and vegetable growth are precisely what makes a beaver happy, while the sound of water constantly running through the fountain would have driven the beavers wild with damming desire.[12]

The idea of relocating problematic beavers in order to curb their ability to transform their surroundings and better facilitate visitor encounters is a striking example of Stanley Park's mandate to offer visitors pleasing encounters with a tidied and tamed wilderness. As Kheraj puts it, the Park Board believed that "human modifications of the animal composition of the park was a necessary improvement for the pleasure of tourists." Inhibiting the beavers' ability to make their own ecological modifications was believed to be crucial for visitors' experience. Blue waters and living trees were vastly more charming than swamps and stumps.

However, the wild beavers of Beaver Lake were not quite eradicated. Perhaps some escaped the zoo enclosure back to the lake, or perhaps not all the beavers were captured in the first place. Unfortunately there is no record of their numbers, except what can be determined obliquely from letters to and from the zoo negotiating sales and animal exchanges. In 1912, for example, a local pheasant dealer wrote offering a male pheasant to breed with the park's population in exchange for a pair of beavers. In December 1912, the Seattle Park Board exchanged an elk for a pair of kangaroos and a pair of beavers. And in 1913, the Vancouver Exhibition Association wrote an exasperated letter to Mr. Balmer, the Superintendent of Stanley Park Zoo, saying, "I have been trying to get you for some time, in reference to the beavers that you promised me." "The Superintendent has requested me to state," came the reply, "that he is endeavouring to obtain a pair of beavers from the lake. They are very difficult to catch, but as soon as they can be trapped Mr Balmer will communicate with you."[13]

In 1916 Beaver Lake was dredged to remove the mud and debris and transform the marsh into a blue-watered lake. It would seem the beavers were finally eradicated. The Park Board had a long-term plan of establishing a fishery in Beaver Lake. After multiple attempts over several decades, the fishery was finally abandoned. But the beavers did not return.

Living with Beavers

The return of wild beavers to Stanley Park plays into a new paradigm of urban park management. In contrast to earlier interventionist strategies, contemporary policies encourage indigenous animals and foster their habitats as sanctuaries for wildlife observation.[14] Encountering "wild" nature within urban parks – as long as the animals are not too wild – encourages proximity, and proximity – as long as it is not too close – has the potential to nurture awareness, appreciation, and respect.

Such encounters, although spontaneous and unpredictable, are nevertheless highly choreographed and ideologically laden, which is to say, the nature we see is the nature we are conditioned to see. As the editors of *Gorgeous Beasts: Animal Bodies in Historical Perspective* aptly put it, "animals are never just there to be seen, felt, or known. History situates them. Culture appropriates them. Science defines them in one way, affection in another." Then again, animals are forever more than the objects we choose to contemplate. Animals will always exceed human reckoning because they "realize a life that exceeds the small circle of our so-called humanity, a full and feral life irreducible to reason and its pale twin, propriety."[15]

Propriety is a key word for urban animals. Scavengers, marauders, hunters, rummagers and opportunists, urban animals do not always play by the rules. Coyotes kill pets. Racoons break into garbage cans. Swallows, mice, and rats invade attics and tear into roves. But beavers go one step better by radically transforming the ecology of their surroundings. And in that fashion, beavers are challenging neighbours.

It is true enough to say that humans and beavers never really cohabitated until the mid-twentieth century, when beaver populations began to recover. Eurasian beaver populations were driven into extinction as medieval towns grew into cities, and in North America, white settlement followed the fur trade – trappers and traders had usually already depleted the beaver populations before homesteaders arrived. Since beavers were last abundant, modern cities have sprawled across the landscape. Roads, rail lines, highways, sewer systems, and housing developments criss-cross what was once prime beaver territory, which means humans and beavers are forced to cohabitate in ways that are not altogether agreeable for either species.

Stanley Park would seem to be an ideal landscape for humans and beavers to share. But the same difficulties beavers presented to the park's

5.6 The beavers' lodge is the mound on the left, covered with shrubberies. Photograph by Tobias Slezak.

management in 1911 still plague twenty-first-century wardens. Beavers have not changed their ways, and while gnawed branches and stumps are no longer deemed unattractive or the wrong kind of nature, the beavers of Beaver Lake require daily management if humans and beavers are going to share the park peaceably.

The vast majority of visitors (myself included) arrive during the day, when the beavers are safely out of view in their lodge, and most of us will only know ever know beavers from the traces they leave from their nightly constructions. Ironically, the only readily visible beaver in the park is a stuffed beaver in the Stanley Park Nature House, an educational centre run by the park's ecological society. But even that beaver is only visible on Saturday and Sunday between 10 a.m. and p.m., and is otherwise covered in a cloth to protect it from sun damage – although damage has already been done. The beaver's fur has been sun-bleached from chestnut brown to a tawny gold.

So what precisely do visitors see at Beaver Lake? The evidence is easy to miss, unless one knows where to look. The beavers have built themselves a lodge in the lake quite close to the pathway. But the lodge is completely

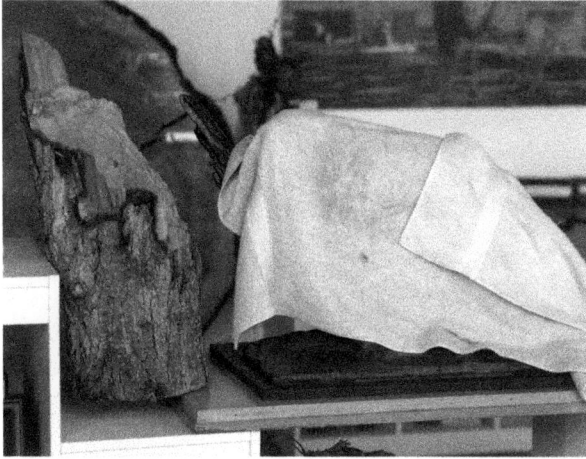

5.7 The veiled beaver of Stanley Park's Nature House. Photograph by Tobias Slezak.

overgrown with shrubs and grasses and easily mistaken for a clump of reeds. A hundred yards or so away, around the curve of the pond, the beavers have severely gnawed several large trees. The trees have been wrapped with steel mesh by park wardens to prevent the beavers from felling them and causing soil erosion. As tree roots undergird the path, losing the trees could mean losing a section of the path.

The beavers have also cleared a large section of water lilies. For Stanley Park's half-centennial celebration in 1936, water lilies were introduced to the lake. Over the years, the invasive plants have all but eliminated open water. The returning beavers have removed (and likely eaten) the plants to expedite the swim between their lodge and the culvert. And that lily-free swimming lane leads us to the most extraordinary and most oblique evidence of the Stanley Park's beavers.

Every night the beavers dam up the culvert with branches and mud. As the culvert drains the lake's overflow and prevents the surrounding path and forest from flooding, every morning park wardens unclog the culvert again. And so it has gone, night by morning, morning by night, since the beavers' arrival in 2008. A fortress of branches and mud now stretches about 8 feet high and 40 feet along the trail to Beaver Lake. Yet there is no interpretative sign explaining the wall of branches. It is stands as a mute testament – overtly visible yet bizarrely easy to miss or mistake – to the efforts both beavers and humans will exert to realize their vision of a perfected nature.

5.8 Beaver Lake's culvert, unplugged. Photograph by Tobias Slezak.

5.9 A wall build from branches and mud made from debris removed from the culvert. Photograph by Tobias Slezak.

The history of the beavers in Stanley Park is a story of shifting policies on the proper management of the park's creaturely inhabitants. It is a story of how nature is always being "improved" upon, whether by humans or other animals. And most crucially it speaks to ever-changing interplay between nature and animal desire. The treatment of the park's beavers over the past century highlights that the park's primary purpose was and remains a place for human recreation. The beavers will be allowed to stay as long as wardens are willing to unclog the culvert, which means that Beaver Lake remains a profoundly humanized landscape. And whether the beavers have been trapped, sold, penned in, or accommodated, they have always offered a reflection of the nature humans most yearn to see, all the while barely being seen themselves.

Notes

1 Sean Kheraj, *Inventing Stanley Park: An Environmental History* (Vancouver: University of British Columbia Press, 2013), 4, 6.

2 Kheraj, *Inventing Stanley Park*, 129.

3 See Justin P. Wright, Clive G. Jones, and Alexander S. Flecker, "An Ecosystem Engineer, the Beaver, Increases Species Richness at the Landscape," *Oecologia* 132, no. 1 (2002): 96–101.

4 Robert J. Naiman, Jerry M. Melillo, and John E. Hobbie, "Ecosystem Alteration of Boreal Forest Streams by Beaver (Castor Canadensis), *Ecology* 67, no. 5 (1986): 1254–69.

5 City of Vancouver Archives (hereafter CVA), Park Board Correspondence, Stanley Park Zoo, 1911–1913, box 48-E-2, folder 4, p. 2.

6 D. J. Halley and Frank Rosell, "The Beaver's Reconquest of Eurasia: Status, Population Development and Management of a Conservation Success," *Mammal Review* 32, no. 3 (2002): 153–78.

7 Glynnis Hood, *The Beaver Manifesto* (Victoria, BC: Rocky Mountain Books, 2011), 58.

8 See Tina Loo, *States of Nature: Conserving Canada's Wildlife in the Twentieth Century* (Vancouver: University of British Columbia Press, 2006), 102–11.

9 William Kingston, *The Western World: Picturesque Sketches of Nature* (London: T. Nelson and Sons, 1884), 123.

10 CVA, Park Board Minutes, box 48-A-2, folder 1.

11 CVA, Park Board Correspondence, Stanley Park Beaver Pond, box 48-C-5, folder 18.

12 In 1972, Stanley Park mounted another beaver display within the zoo. An artificial pond, named Beaver Pond in distinction from Beaver Lake, was dug in the park's upper zoo. The bottom was lined with a heavy-gauge steel mesh in an effort to contain the ever-industrious occupants. It was only after the road

alongside the pond collapsed under the weight of a park service truck that zoo staff discovered the beavers had chewed through the wire and burrowed beneath the road to cut down maple saplings across the road. Presumably the beavers then dragged the saplings back through the tunnel to their pond. The wire mesh was patched and the road repaired, but shortly thereafter the miniature train tracks running alongside the pond began to sag. Thwarted in one direction, beavers had dug a new tunnel. Finally the pond was temporarily drained and lined with concrete. See Richard M. Steele, *The Stanley Park Explorers* (Vancouver: Whitecap Books, 1985), 125–26.

13   CVA, Park Board Correspondence, Stanley Park Zoo, 1911–1913, box 48-E-2, folder 4.

14   Sean Kheraj, "Demonstration Wildlife: Negotiating the Animal Landscape of Vancouver's Stanley Park, 1888–1996," *Environment and History* 18, no. 4 (2012): 501.

15   Joan B. Landes, Paula Young Lee, and Paul Youngquist, *Gorgeous Beasts: Animals in Historical Perspective* (University Park: Pennsylvania State University Press, 2012), 3, 1.

Species at Risk: *C. Tetani*, the Horse, and the Human

JOANNA DEAN

The agonizing death of an Ottawa man was noted on 11 September 1885:

> Mr Jno Crabtree, of the firm Robertson and Crabtree, builders,
> Ottawa, died at his residence on Tuesday morning last week
> under particularly distressing circumstances. Some ten days
> ago while laying a brick floor in a new building a nail accident-
> ally penetrated his great toe. Nothing serious was anticipated
> at the time, but on Tuesday last lockjaw set in, which termin-
> ated in his death after suffering intense agony from tetanic
> convulsions.[1]

Crabtree was one of innumerable individuals whose death from lockjaw,
or tetanus as we now know it, was recounted in the pages of late nineteenth-century newspapers. The accounts followed a similar narrative
arc, beginning with a minor wound, typically a rusty nail or splinter, or
a kick from horse. Then there was a momentous lull – "nothing serious
was anticipated at the time." The lull could last three days, or twenty-one,
but usually about eight days after the injury the first symptoms of lockjaw appeared, and then culminated in the horrific denouement of tetanic
convulsions.

Crabtree's death can be traced back to the number of horses employed in Canadian cities in the 1880s. Many horses carried the spores of

Clostridium tetani in their intestines and distributed them liberally into the urban environment in their manure. We might trace Crabtree's death to the horses hauling people and goods on the streets of Ottawa; his death might be traced to the horses that turned the pugmills mixing the clay for the brick floor he was laying, or it might be traced to one of the horses working on his construction site. It might have been any of one these horses, or a horse that was long gone. *C. tetani* spores lurked in urban soil for many decades.[2] A deep injury left to fester, like that caused by the nail piercing Crabtree's toe, created the anaerobic conditions for the dormant tetanus spores to become active, and release their deadly toxin.

This chapter looks at the three species that produced lockjaw in the city: the bacilli, the horse, and the human. In an attempt to foreground the bacilli, and bring the horse into the picture as a sentient, if not agential, being, it considers them as part of an assemblage or, to use Gilles Deleuze and Felix Guattari's original French term, *agencement*. In agencement, the human is not at the centre but is one part of an interactive whole. As Vinciane Despret explains, "Each living being renders other creatures capable (of affecting and of being affected) and they are entangled in a myriad of rapports of forces, all of which are 'agencements.'"[3] The story of the tetanus bacilli's trajectory through the equine and human bodies provides a window into the entangled animal world of Canadian cities.[4] Agencement is an idea that emphasizes movement and becoming, and this chapter follows *C. tetani* from the streets and into the Connaught Laboratories on the outskirts of Toronto, where a new concatenation of bacilli, horse, and human was put in place with the production of antibodies for human use from the blood of tetanus horses.[5] Photographs distributed by the Connaught Laboratories accustomed the public to the new agencement of laboratory animal, scientist, and bacilli. Photographs made the invisible bacilli visible, and the unnatural natural, familiarizing the readers to the new uses to which animals were put, especially the intimate role of the horse as the "heroic" donor of biomedical products.

The agony of lockjaw

Before the discovery of the bacilli as the causative agent, lockjaw was understood as an inexorable sequence of symptoms: a narrative. The story line was set with Hippocrates' account of a ship captain's death: "The master of a large ship mashed the index finger of his right hand with the anchor. Seven days later a somewhat foul discharge appeared; then trouble with his tongue – he complained he could not speak properly." At this point lockjaw was diagnosed: "His jaws became pressed together, his teeth were locked, then symptoms appeared in his neck; on the third day opisthotonos [spasms] appeared with sweating. Six days after the diagnosis was made he died."[6] The horrors of the lockjaw narrative, in various permutations, run through the long history of intimate connections between human and horse. It was most commonly associated with the battlefield, where the assemblage of horse, human, mud, and weapon led to deep, unwashed wounds that were fertile ground for the bacilli.

The most famous Canadian death by lockjaw was that of Lord Sydenham, governor general of British North America, who died in 1841 after falling from his horse in Kingston in front of the Parliament buildings. His demise was made the stuff of political drama by historians like Adam Shortt and Archibald MacMechan. It is said that Sydenham composed a speech while in the agonies of the disease: his last thoughts were on the state he had served so well.[7] Working-class men and youth were more typical victims, and their deaths were described in newspapers in spare but harrowing narratives that stressed the suspense of the lull, and the pain of the death.

> John Marek, a young man who resided in Streator, died at his home there this week in great agony from lockjaw. Several days ago he received a slight scratch on the cheek from a wire, but the little mark did not appear serious and no attention was paid to it. The latter part of the week it began to pain and physicians were called but they could afford no relief. Sunday morning lockjaw resulted and within a few hours death relieved the young man of his sufferings.

Death by lockjaw was not common, but the stories were widely disseminated as sensational filler for the columns of newspapers across North America. Children often suffered; death came from the most innocent of childhood activities, and the stories recount the familiar trajectory with chilling specifics.[8]

DIED OF BLOOD POISONING
Orlo B. Dicken of the South Side Dies Sunday Morning

Orlo B. Dicken, the five year old son of Mr. and Mrs. Charles Dicken, died at their home on the south side Sunday morning of lockjaw, after an illness of twenty-four hours. The boy went barefoot on Thursday and accidentally stepped on a rusty nail, inflicting a severe wound. As it did not pain him greatly, he said nothing about it to his parents and they were not informed of his condition until Saturday when lockjaw set in. The best of medical attendance was secured but proved of no avail. It was even found impossible to pry the boy's jaws apart to insert food.

MAY DIE OF LOCKJAW
Water Street Boy Suffering Intense Pain in Water Street Hospital

A fourteen-year-old boy named Talon, living on Water Street, was taken to the General Hospital suffering from a severe attack of tetanus or lockjaw. But slight hopes are held out for his recovery by the hospital staff and he is suffering from severe spasms. The lad was playing about ten days ago when he got a piece of glass in his right foot. The injury was attended to but symptoms of tetanus showed themselves yesterday and the lad was immediately moved to hospital for treatment. He is a delicate lad and apparently unable to stand severe pain.[9]

Horses were also known to suffer from lockjaw. Most North American horse-care books devoted a page or two to the disease. As Everett Miller notes, "They related how the disease would occur in the horse which was newly shod (nail prick), lamed (picked up nail) operated on (docked, nicked, gelded) or severely wounded, and seven to ten days later the horse would exhibit signs such as closed jaws, flared nostrils, cocked ears, and opisthotonos (stretched out muzzle, rigid neck, and back muscles and set tail) and a sawhorse like stance." *The Canadian Horse and His Diseases* (1867) noted that lockjaw was not uncommon in Canada, especially in the summer, and described the equine agony: "A horse laboring under this awful disease is one of the most pitiable objects we can look at. He stands with his legs wide apart, like four posts, to support his body; which, from the head to the tail, is rigid and quivering."[10] Newspapers carried occasional accounts of equine lockjaw, usually recounting the deaths among the equine elite of well-loved carriage horses and expensive racing horses.

FAITHFUL HORSE DIES OF LOCKJAW

The sorrel horse which has done such faithful service for Mr. M.G. Willis for so many years, and has been such a familiar object on the streets, was taken with lockjaw Wednesday and died Thursday. When Mr. Willis was mayor this good, old, reliable horse knew just when nine o'clock came every morning and stood ready to convey his owner to the office to transact his official business. Mr. Willis had used him as a driving horse for a number of years.[11]

The medical care provided for horses and humans was similar, and similarly ineffective. The abundance of folk remedies, such as smoke or copper pennies on the wound, testify to the inability of regular physicians to furnish any real assistance.[12] Fluids and nourishment had to be forced through the clenched jaws. The horse might be fed a liquid mash through closed teeth; the humans soup or oatmeal. Any nervous stimulation set off the convulsions, so horses were to be kept in a dark, quiet stable, people in a muffled room. If the patient could be nursed through the bout, then recovery was possible. Death came from exhaustion, respiratory failure due to convulsions, or the direct action of the toxin. The fatality rate for horses was 80 per cent; survivors would take weeks or months to recover. Among humans, the spasms could continue for weeks, and full recovery could take months. Even today the case fatality rate in the United States is 13 per cent.[13]

Nineteenth-century lockjaw narratives were the product of a particular assemblage of inert and sentient entities: the unprecedented numbers of horses on city streets, the heavy application of their manure to suburban gardens and fields, the wide use of metal tools capable of slicing into human flesh, and the number of human and equine bodies susceptible to the potent toxin. Until the 1880s the critical agent, the bacilli, coursing through the various animal bodies, was unknown and invisible.

"That Awful Microbe"

In the 1880s *Clostridium tetani* emerged in European laboratories, made apparent by its impact on the bodies of small animals. In 1884 Antonio Carle and Giorgio Rattone injected pus from a fatal human case of lockjaw into the sciatic nerve of a rabbit to produce the typical symptoms of lockjaw in the animal. The disease was then transmitted from this rabbit to other rabbits. That same year Arthur Nicolaier injected soil into animals and produced lockjaw. In 1886 *C. tetani* came into view when a spore-forming bacillus was observed in human exudate: rod-shaped with a terminal spore at one end, the bacterium is often compared to a drumstick or tennis racket. In 1889 the spores were shown to be resistant to heat, and to germinate into the vegetative (and toxin-producing) state if placed in anaerobic conditions. The toxin, tetanospasmin, was produced in 1890.[14]

Laboratory research turned lockjaw, a disease that had been identified clinically with a set of symptoms, into tetanus, a disease associated with a bacillus.[15] The discoveries were disseminated rapidly, if with variable accuracy, in the North American daily press.[16] A Canadian nursing text published in 1893 said of tetanus: "formerly thought to be nervous in origin we now know is peculiar kind of bacillus species found most often in garden earth, manure or putrefying fluids, the poison being conveyed by the earth or dirt that is carried into the wound."[17] As scientists discovered the presence of spores in soil, and the anaerobic conditions necessary for *C. tetani*'s proliferation, it became clear why deep wounds caused by rusty nails and dirty tools were particularly dangerous, and why careful cleaning of the wound would reduce the likelihood that tetanus would develop.

A French scientist, Aristide Verneuil, drew the connection between horses and *C. tetani*. In an article entitled "That Awful Microbe," the *Toronto Daily Mail* reported in 1888: "The microbe theory seems destined to be held responsible for all the ills that flesh is heir to. M. Verneuil a French scientist . . . asserts that the hitherto respected horse is responsible for the lockjaw microbe and that it is from the docile and useful animal that man 'catches' the disease." Verneuil's evidence was epidemiological: "the greatest proportion of cases of tetanus being those of stablemen, coaches and grooms."[18] The medical journal *Canada Lancet* provided the details in June 1889. Verneuil had examined 380 cases of lockjaw, of which 222, or 58 per cent, were among those working with horses. Other victims, like the three doctors in his list, were discovered on investigation to care for their own horses. In the face of evidence of earth or dirt causing the disease, Verneuil argued that the earth acted as an intermediate agent.[19] News of Verneuil's association of the horse with lockjaw travelled quickly, possibly because his epidemiological studies confirmed existing anxieties about human–animal intimacy. The *Canada Health Journal* cited his work in an article on the "Diseases of Domestic Animals: Their Relation to the Human Family and Hygiene." The *Ottawa Journal* linked the faithful horse with the dread disease in 1900: "When the silent and swift automobile glides through Ottawa's streets and the horse is used only for pleasure lockjaw will be an almost unknown disease, says a well known physician."[20]

We now understand that all mammals can carry tetanus, although the horse is the most susceptible. The number of horses in the city, the prodigious amount of manure produced per horse, and the wide distribution of this manure suggest that horse manure was the likely source of much, if not all, urban lockjaw at the turn of the century. Horses were essential to the functioning of the modern city, and their numbers had been increasing as the railway brought more goods needing distribution into the city. The Canadian census indicates that almost two thousand horses lived in Toronto in 1871, one for every 28 human residents; by 1891 there was one for every 25 humans. The number of horses continued to rise, but the proportion of horse to human dropped dramatically in the 1890s when the electric streetcar replaced the horse-drawn streetcar. There was only one horse for every 62 people in 1901, though this rose again to one to every 51 in 1911.[21] At the same time as their numbers were growing, draft horses nearly doubled in size to meet the growing demand for muscle.[22] Horses are recalled with fond nostalgia today, but they occupied a more complicated and more prosaic place in the nineteenth-century imaginary. Many owners cared deeply about individual horses, admiration for the fire horses was almost universal, and the very public suffering of carthorses met with sympathy. But the forced intimacy and the smells, occasional unruliness, and sheer massive sweaty animality of the labouring beast also produced distaste bred of too close a familiarity. Manure was the biggest problem. Each horse produced roughly five tons of manure a year, much of it distributed along city streets, where it was ground into a fine choking dust in the summer and churned into the muddy streets in the spring and fall. As Joel Tarr has shown, the smell and filth was only tolerated because of the necessity of the horse to urban transportation.[23] Other domestic animals, such as pigs and cows, had been removed from most Canadian cities by the end of the nineteenth century.[24] Pet dogs were regulated through muzzles, leases, and licensing, and stray dogs were eradicated from cities because of the threat of rabies.[25] Horses, however, were absolutely critical to the functioning of the modern city, and although the management of the manure was debated and regulated, the horse remained on the streets. Until the advent of the electric streetcar in the 1890s, and then the widespread adoption of the internal combustion engine after the First World War, there was quite simply no other way to move goods from train station to store, or carry people from place to place.

Producing Antitoxin

The first steps in combatting *C. tetani* involved a more intimate rather than a more distant relation with the horse. In 1890, Shibasaburo Kitasato and Emil Adoph von Behring injected sub-lethal doses of tetanus toxin into rabbits and demonstrated the prophylactic action of the resulting antitoxin. (Terminology has changed: what was initially called an antitoxin, and subsequently an antibody, is now called tetanus immune globulin, or TIG. The terminology used here – antitoxin, bacilli, germ – is that of the period.) Two years later von Behring immunized sheep and horses to produce commercial quantities of antitoxin. Horses were injected with gradually increasing doses of tetanus toxin over a number of weeks or months and built up high levels of antitoxin in their blood. This antitoxin was extracted from the blood, purified, and injected into a human, where it provided temporary immunity. A similar process produced diphtheria antitoxin.

A young Canadian doctor brought the new immunological science to Toronto. John Gerald FitzGerald, a graduate of the medical school at the University of Toronto, studied bacteriology at Harvard, and then at the Pasteur Institute in Paris and the University of Freiburg. He developed a close relationship with Dr. William H. Park, the director of the New York City Health Department's Laboratories, during postgraduate studies. He returned to the University of Toronto in 1913 as an assistant professor of hygiene, and immediately began producing Pasteur Preventative Treatment for rabies, derived from the spines of infected rabbits, at the provincial laboratory. His main interest, however, was in combatting diphtheria, the leading cause of death for children under the age of fourteen, and he built a stable in his assistant's yard on Barton St. to house five horses, named Crestfallen, Surprise, Fireman, and J.H.C. and Goliath, for the production of diphtheria antitoxin.[26] FitzGerald subsequently received university funding for a serum institute modelled on the Pasteur Institute: the Antitoxin Laboratory's three goals were, like those of the Pasteur Institute, to prepare and distribute public health serums and vaccines, to conduct research into new biological products, and teach.[27]

The First World War turned FitzGerald's focus from diphtheria to tetanus. Horses and humans fought side by side in the war, and the deep injuries caused by modern explosives led to high rates of tetanus in both species. In the fall of 1914, on the urging of Colonel A.E. Gooderham, chairman of the Canadian Red Cross Society, FitzGerald turned to the production of tetanus antitoxin. With $5,000 in funding from the Department of National Defence, he hired Robert Defries to oversee the immunization of eighteen tetanus horses, housed in the former stables of the Ontario Veterinary College on Temperance Street. The following summer, Gooderham purchased 58 acres of land 12 miles north of the university campus and donated the farm to the university to be used for the production of antitoxins. The province provided an endowment of $75,000, and, perhaps more important, ensured a steady market for the serums.[28] The horses were moved there in 1916, and Connaught Laboratories, with a new central building constructed in an English cottage style, were officially opened with great ceremony in October 1917.

The term "laboratory" is slightly misleading: the Connaught was originally referred to as a farm as well as a laboratory, and might best be understood as a hybrid space, where the animality of the horse met the modern technology of science. Stables dominated. Most of the space on the main floor of the new Connaught building was taken up with twelve wide standing stalls and three box stalls, and a large paddock extended behind the building.[29] Horses were not the only experimental animals housed at the laboratory. A research colony of 500 guinea pigs, for the testing of the antitoxin, were initially to have been accommodated upstairs in the hayloft, calves were kept in one corner for the production of smallpox vaccine, and over time as research expanded many thousands of small mammals – mice, rabbits, dogs, and cats – were also housed on the property.[30] The human technicians were also to have been housed in the same building: at the far end of the loft from the guinea pigs was an apartment provided for the family of the "technical bacteriologist," and an additional bedroom. But horses dominated. The fifteen stalls were inadequate even before the building opened. In addition to tetanus antitoxin, the laboratories used horses to produce anti-meningitis serum, diphtheria antitoxin, anti-pneumococcus serum, and serum for the prevention of gas gangrene, and by 1918 there were, in all, fifty horses for the production of the various serums, housed in an old barn on the property and two temporary stables as well as the laboratory building.[31] The 58 rolling acres provided extensive pastures.

The science took place in the corners of the new building. Tucked into the southeast corner, in one of the smaller rooms, was the laboratory proper with sinks, work tables, sterilizers, and other apparatus. Other laboratories were eventually built on the second floor where the guinea pigs and the bacteriologist were to have been housed. Science and stable met in the northwest corner, where an "operating room" provided for the injecting and bleeding of the horses.

Laboratory reports in the Connaught Archives provide some sense of the experiences of horses involved in antitoxin production. Some early tetanus horses were identified by name (as were all of the diphtheria horses) – Tom and Bert appear in the record book on 21 December 1915 – but very quickly a system of numbers was put in place. A chart, *Report of Tetanus Horses*, for the month ending March 1918, identifies 20 horses, numbered T#1, T#6, T#8, T#17, T#21, and then consecutively T#25 through T#27 and T#29 through T#32 and T#34 through T#42. The horses were injected with gradually increasing amounts of tetanus toxin, and over a few months gradually gained immunity through the production of antibodies. They were then "bled." Large amounts of blood were withdrawn and the antitoxin extracted. A few of the Connaught horses were very productive: horse T#21 had been bled 35 times over three years. Horse T#17 had been bled 30 times. T#1 had been bled 15 times.[32] A second laboratory record, a manual kept by FitzGerald, shows steady bleeding, on a par with that of T#17 and T#21, of horses numbered, more simply, 10, 11, 12, 13, 14, 15, 16,

19, and 20.[33] It appears from this book that about ten tetanus horses were bled every month.

These records show that horses at the Connaught Laboratories routinely had about 6,000 cc of blood removed at a single time, although amounts as low as 2,000 cc and as high as 11,000 cc were recorded. This amount meant that the horses could recover and produce more serum in a month's time. Horses that had reached the end of their productivity as serum horses were bled out. Connaught records show three horses, numbered 11, 16, and 19, being bled out in 1917. The records note of the procedure for number 16: "Large amount of salt solution with sod. citrate run into jugular vein after 4 bottles of blood had been withdrawn total plasma 22,400 [sic]." Tom and Bert appear to have been bled out on 21 December 1915, as they produced 38,000 cc and 14,000 cc respectively. As this record book ends on 22 February 1917, and horses 10, 12, 13, 14, 15, and 20 do not appear in the "Report of Tetanus Horses" for 1918, we can speculate that the other horses had also been bled out as they reached the end of their serviceability.[34] A pamphlet produced a number of years later by the Connaught describes the process: "In a separate room with an autopsy room adjoining, an operating-table is installed. When a producing horse is disposed of, it is anaesthetized and 'bled out' on this table. In other words, as much as possible of its blood is removed and preserved."[35] The procedure was more fraught than this clinical account suggests: one employee, whose memory dates back to the early 1950s, remembers the struggle to strap the horse to the operating table, and hold the horse in place as the table and horse were tilted from an upright position to the horizontal. He recalled holding anesthesia in a rag to the horse's nose. The process may also have been emotionally difficult for technicians who had become familiar with the individual horses. Number 16 is identified by only number until 16 December 1917, the day she was bled out, when she is given a name, Molly, in the laboratory records.

Antitoxin serum was revolutionary in its impact during the First World War, when thousands of men who would have died from minor wounds inflicted on the manure-filled fields of battle were given a series of antitoxin injections. The British military epidemiologist, Sir David Bruce, concluded that the injections reduced the death rate from tetanus from 50 per cent to 19 per cent.[36] More recently epidemiologists have concluded that "anti-tetanus serum undoubtedly prevented life threatening tetanus among several hundred thousands of wounded men, making it one of the most successful preventive interventions in wartime medicine."[37] Much of the credit for protection of the British forces from tetanus infection goes to the Connaught Laboratories. By 25 October 1917, when the laboratories were formally opened, they were producing all of the antitoxins for the second British Army Corps, which included all the men in the Canadian Expeditionary Force.[38] FitzGerald subsequently claimed that over the course of the war they produced one fifth of the tetanus antitoxin required by the British forces, and did it at a fraction of the cost of the commercial laboratories south of the border.[39] (The Department of National Defence had been paying $1.35 for antitoxin from American commercial laboratories, but Connaught Laboratories provided a dose of antitoxin, of high quality, for 34 cents.[40])

Vaccine Farms

There were no national standards for the production of biological products in Canada until 1928, and in the early years the Connaught Laboratories struggled to overcome the controversial legacy of "vaccine farms," where cowpox vaccine had been produced from infected calves under questionable circumstances. A 1917 article on the Connaught Laboratories in the *Contract Record* emphasized that their new stables were hygienic spaces: "One feature of the building is the arrangement to secure sanitary conditions. The walls in the stables and laboratory rooms are lined with glazed brick dado, which can easily be kept clean. All internal angles are coved, so as to avoid dust-catching conditions, and all corners are bull-nosed."[41] A manure trolley removed waste to the outside, and floor level ventilators removed foul air. A similar article, in *Construction*, also emphasized cleanliness and modernity.[42]

Vaccine farms had not been particularly scientific or hygienic locations. The cowpox vaccine was produced from an infected calf: the calf was shaved and scarified with vaccine; five days later large vesicles formed, and when they were considered ripe they were broken and the lymph used to coat ivory "points," sealed with a protective coating of egg white. As Jennifer Keelan has observed, the science of vaccine production was unreliable: bad lymph could cause painful side effects, even (rarely) death, and the protection offered was variable.[43] Canadian vaccine was sourced from the Montreal Cowpox Institute (from 1878) and the Ontario Vaccine Farm (from 1885) as well as from American vaccine farms, such as the New England Vaccine Company.[44] The Ontario Farm was, like the American farms, a private initiative. It was subsidized, and inspected, by the Government of Ontario, but there were ongoing concerns about hygiene, and demands for higher-quality glycerinated vaccine. In 1916, probably in response to these concerns, the Connaught Laboratories purchased the calves and equipment from the Ontario Farm and took over production of the vaccine. The calves were housed separately in one corner of the laboratory building, with their own operating room, a large enamel bath for bathing the calves, laboratories "for vaccine work only," and a separate entrance.[45]

Opposition to smallpox vaccination had been heated. In 1887 Montreal had erupted in riots, and protests took place in Toronto before and after the opening of the Connaught: in 1906, five thousand Toronto residents signed a petition to repeal the mandatory vaccination of schoolchildren, and a second successful campaign was waged in 1919.[46] The antivaccination groups were dismissed by public health officials – in his 1899 annual report Toronto's chief medical officer, Dr. Charles Sheard, called them "ignorant and superstitious" – and historians have, until recently, largely followed suit.[47] Michael Bliss dismissed antivaccinators as, simply, "wrong."[48] Recently historians have been more sympathetic. Katherine Arnup points out that fears of contamination by unhygienic vaccines, opposition to compulsion, and the accusations of class bias in the administration of vaccines in Toronto had some legitimacy. Jennifer Keelan argues from a careful study of the medical literature that the fears of the antivaccinators were often legitimate; she points out that in the early twentieth century science was not the prerogative of pro-vaccinators.[49] Whether historians will remain as sympathetic in the coming years, with new concerns about vaccination levels emerging, remains to be seen.

Much of the public anger was directed at the arrogance of the medical profession and the compulsion involved in mandatory health measures, but there was a distaste, even repugnance, at the use of animal products in human medicine. In *Bodily Matters: The Anti Vaccination Movement in England, 1853–1907*, Nadja Durbach notes: "Anti vaccinators repeatedly characterized vaccine matter as a 'loathsome virus derived from the blood of a brute' which could harbor animal diseases as yet unknown to humans."[50] The original vaccine matter was supposed by some to have come from a horse: "the stinking heels of an emaciated horse in the later stages of phthisis."[51] She describes widespread fears in the 1890s that the calf lymph would cause cow-like tendencies in children. Similarly, in the United States, Dr. J.F. Banton wrote that vaccination introduces a "bioplasm, death laden – carrying all the vices, passions and diseases of the cow."[52] In 1906 a Toronto school board trustee echoed these concerns, demanding that "the arbitrary pollution of children's bodies in Toronto with animal matter be abandoned."[53]

A public health disaster in St. Louis in 1901 heightened anxieties about the animal source of biomedical products. Antitoxin derived from a diphtheria horse called Jim killed several children, and it emerged that he was carrying tetanus. A report published in the *Canadian Journal of Medicine and Surgery* absolved Jim, but blamed the unhygienic conditions of the laboratory for the deaths, citing a *New York Times* editorial: "The business of producing virus and serum . . . cannot be carried on without immeasurable risk to life and health with worn-out horses and sickly calves, nor in dirty stables or improvised annexes to vermin infested barns. Healthy animals, perfect plants constructed and managed under expert supervision, and the assurance of pure cultures with entire freedom from pus organisms are the essential conditions."[54] In response, serum producers began to account for the origins, the history, and the health of their horses, and new standards for serum production were set in the United States.[55]

Distaste for the animality of the vaccine co-existed with concern for the welfare of the calf donor. In 1882 Henry Bergh, the president of the American Society for the Prevention of Cruelty to Animals, had raised the "barbarous and unnatural treatment to which animals are subjected" in his discussion of "the loathsome pestilence" that was vaccine in the *North American Review*.[56] The British *Vaccination Inquirer* wrote in 1895: "The luckless calves must be no longer strapped and fixed and shaved and scarified and poisoned and fastened in their stalls with fourscore aging sores on their bellies, and their tails tied over their backs, lest in seeking alleviation of their miseries for themselves they rupture their vesicles and ruin the stock-in-trade of the virus-mongers."[57] More research is needed to establish the connections, but it appears that antivaccination sentiments contributed to the rise of antivivisection movements in Canada. In 1920, when the Anti Vaccination League of Canada was restructured to become the Medical Liberty League, the antivivisectors created a separate entity, the Canadian Anti Vivisection League. Both movements appear to have collapsed in the 1920s with the success of diphtheria and tetanus antitoxin and the ascendancy of medical science.[58]

In 1906, the *Toronto Star* called for the medical profession to address the antivaccinators' concerns and make the case for vaccination: "If, therefor, medical scientists wish people to retain their faith in vaccination they must keep them constantly supplied with facts and arguments, and be ready to meet the opposition, not angrily, but patiently."[59] A few years later, as the Connaught opened, they did exactly that, providing the public with facts, as well as photographs, to reassure them of the hygiene, health, and happiness of the animals used to produce smallpox vaccine and tetanus and diphtheria antitoxins.

Reassuring the Public

Tetanus antitoxin was not itself controversial but the patriotic production of tetanus antitoxin served to build support for the laboratories' other activities, and accustom readers to the use of animals in the production of biomedical products. On Saturday, 25 November 1916, almost a year before the official opening of the Connaught, an article appeared on the front page of the *Toronto Star* with a headline in red ink, "Anti toxin for Canadian Soldiers All Made at Toronto University," and a subtitle, "STAGES IN ANTI-TOXIN MANUFACTURE ILLUSTRATED FOR OUR READERS," with four photographs of handsome horses and clean laboratories. The article takes the reader through the process of antitoxin production, emphasizing the healthiness, and also the happiness, of the horses, and the scientific and hygienic methods. It first describes the production of tetanus toxin from the bacilli, describing it as a kind of alchemy taking place at the medical school in a "mysterious-looking room with long tables, glass cupboards filled with strange looking flasks and tubes." An accompanying photograph shows a white-coated man sitting at a lab table at the University of Toronto.[60] The scientific origins of the germ are established (the tetanus originated from Washington Laboratories), and the various germs are made familiar through domestic metaphors : tetanus and diphtheria germs are fed veal broth, and the meningitis germ "must, as the doctor said, change its boarding house every other day." Diphtheria,

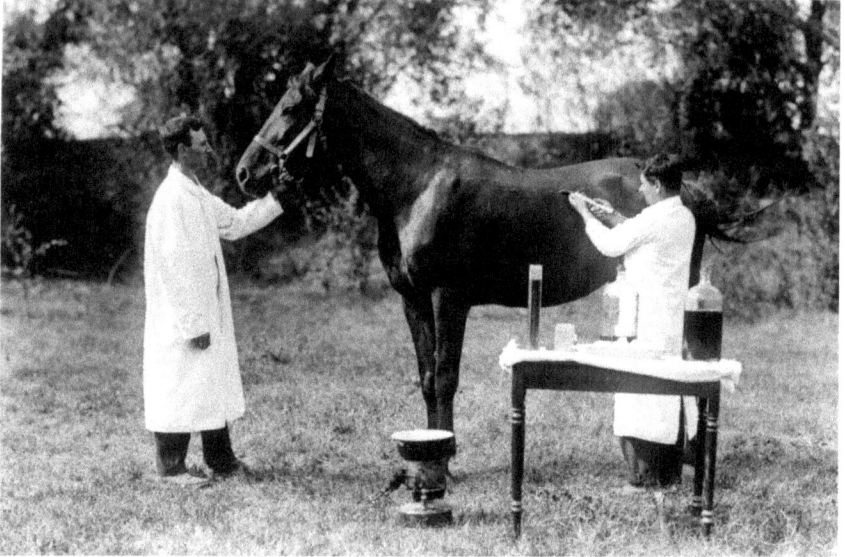

6.1 "Injecting Toxin." Photographs familiarised the readers to the new uses to which animals were put, especially the intimate role of the horse as the heroic donor of biomedical products. This photograph, "Injecting Toxin," was published on the front page of the *Toronto Star*, 25 November 1916 to promote the war work of the laboratory. It is not likely that the photograph reflects the normal procedures. Acc1076. Courtesy of Sanofi Pasteur Canada (Connaught Campus) Toronto Archives.

tetanus, and meningitis germs are described as fussy children: "germs are very particular and must have things to their taste if they are to grow up to be fine hardy germs." At the end of three weeks, the article explains, each flask holds billions of germs.

The toxins are extracted from the flask and injected into the horse. After a few months, when the horse has accumulated enough "poison counteracting fluid," one to two gallons of blood is taken from the animal. The author is reassuring: "Now most people think that the bleeding causes the horse to suffer. As a matter of fact the horse hardly seems to notice the procedure but stands quietly and patiently while the blood is being taken. Of course, he may feel a little weak, but a good rest and several good feeds soon remedy that." An article published the same month in the Australian *Sydney Herald* makes the same point even more emphatically of tetanus horses at the Danish Serum Institute: "They feel well, and they are so well looked after that even old weak horses, which otherwise would

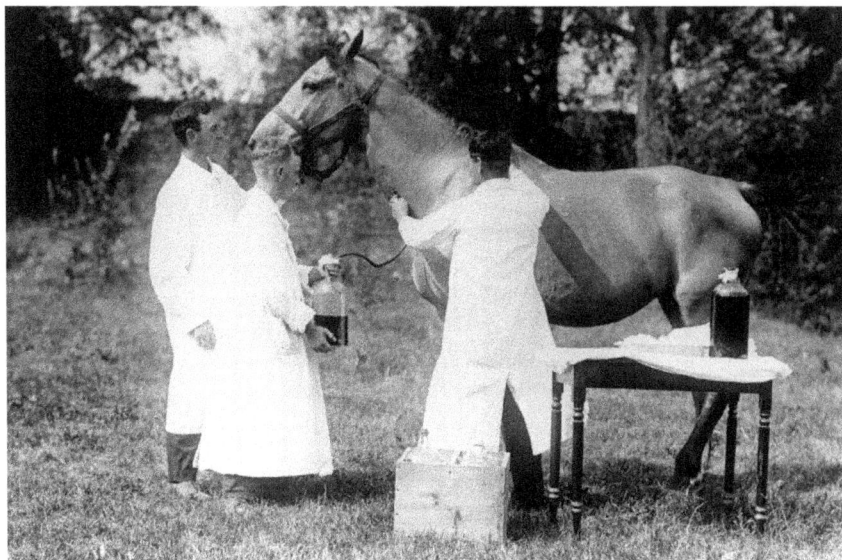

6.2 "Bleeding a Horse." This photograph was published on the front page of the *Toronto Star* on 25 November 1916 to promote the war work of the laboratory. It was probably staged for this purpose; horses were normally restrained for this procedure. Acc1080A. Courtesy of Sanofi Pasteur Canada (Connaught Campus), Toronto Archives.

have been used for the manufacture of 'guliasch' now live, thrive and increase in weigh and even regain some of the friskiness of their youth."[61] Accompanying photographs in the *Star* show white-coated scientists "inoculating a horse with tetanus germs" (this was an error: the toxin was injected) and then "drawing off some blood from the animal."[62] The horses are large handsome creatures. A third photograph in the series, available in the Connaught Archives but not used in the *Star*, depicts a handsome horse with the caption "A Typical Antitoxin Horse."[63]

The *Toronto Star* then followed the "great bottles of blood" to the laboratories at the University of Toronto, where it reported that the plasma was drawn off, and the antitoxin precipitated, filtered, scraped off, and tied into paper bags to be dissolved into water. Here the reporter strains to make the laboratory procedures familiar, describing paper bags of antitoxin as being "like Christmas puddings ready for boiling." The final photograph shows a clean white laboratory room with a long line of flasks with paper filters in funnels with the caption "Filtering Anti-Toxin to Ensure its Purity."[64] The flasks make the invisible antitoxin visible, and the white filter papers remind the reader once again of its purity. The description of the process created distance between the blood and the antitoxin: the red corpuscles were removed, leaving a bloodless yellow serum. As the antitoxin was precipitated, dried, and dissolved, the bloodiness and the horsiness disappeared, leaving only the active agent, the antitoxin. (Enough horse remained, however, to trigger allergic reactions in a percentage of the population.[65])

One year later, J.G. FitzGerald, director of the laboratories, wrote a similar article for the University of Toronto *Varsity Magazine* Supplement describing the opening of the laboratories. He emphasized the contribution made to the war effort, and the honour of their lab being selected as a reliable source for antitoxin. Photographs depict the horses in the new Connaught stables, a scientist in the lab, a horse being bled, antitoxin preparation, and the shipping room.[66] Another collage of photographs positioned prominently above FitzGerald's desk in the laboratories presents these laboratory images in the context of bucolic photographs of country estate–type cottages and herds of tetanus horses, anti-meningitis horses, and diphtheria horses grazing on rolling meadows.[67]

The following year, his assistant director, Robert Defries, contributed another article to the *Varsity*. His message is much same as in the *Star*: he emphasizes the healthiness of the horses and purity of the toxin.

> In preparing this serum, healthy horses are selected and injected with increasing doses of the lockjaw poison. To obtain this poison, which is one the most powerful known, the germs are grown in a special broth for two weeks. The germs are removed by careful filtering, and the clear broth contains the poison. The poison is so powerful, that less than one thousandth of a drop will kill a small guinea pig. The horse, as the treatment is continued, produces an antitoxin to neutralise the poison, and finally after six or eight months is not in the least affected by very large amounts of the poison. The serum is then obtained from the blood of these horses, at regular intervals, and during the whole treatment the horses maintain good health.[68]

6.3 Photographs distributed by the Connaught Laboratories accustomed the public to the new assemblage of bacilli, laboratory animal, and scientist. They emphasised the hygiene of the laboratory procedures and the health of the horses. Robert Defries, "The War Work of the Connaught and Antitoxin Laboratories, University of Toronto," The Varsity Magazine Supplement (1918), 94-96. Courtesy of Sanofi Pasteur Canada (Connaught Campus) Toronto Archives.

The invisible agents, *C. tetani*, toxin, and antitoxin, are made visible by their containment in gleaming glass flasks in a series of photographs. A photograph titled "Horses During Treatment" shows horses grazing under trees by a stream. "Withdrawing the Serum" shows a horse being bled in a spotless room. "A Ton of Tetanus Antitoxin" shows stacked boxes of anti-toxin ready for shipment to the front. The photographs are professionally shot. They make the bacilli visible, the horses' role natural, and the scientists authoritative.[69] The glass flasks in the toxin laboratory contain, and define, the microbe. The antitoxin is made apparent by the rubber tubing running from the horse, the line of bottles labelled Tetanus Serum, and the boxes of antitoxin destined for soldiers in France. They serve to make the new *agencement* of bacilli, horse, and human familiar to readers.

Photographs

The photographs of horses disseminated by the Connaught Laboratories were elements in an emerging iconography of serum production. As Bert Hansen has observed, images of a healthy horse surrounded by white-coated scientists were a common trope of American serum therapy, intended to reassure the reader of the health of the animal, the hygiene of the procedure, and the purity of the final product. He traces their origin to November 1894, when *Scientific American* used three images of serum production that, as Hansen observes, "established the leading visual elements for all the successive depictions": a child being treated, laboratory technicians with glass flasks and tanks, and "docile and dignified horses patiently receiving injections or allowing their blood to be drawn."[70] These images were recirculated by the *New York Herald* in a campaign for the funding of a laboratory and stables for the New York Health Department. As the iconography developed, certain norms emerged. The horses are usually handsome animals, and stand calmly during the treatment, secured by metal railing. The technicians and handlers are white-coated, serious professionals. The glass bottles and instruments shine. The images culminate in a 1950s painting, *The Era of Biologicals,* by Robert A. Thom for the Parke-Davis series Great Moments in Pharmacy, depicting three anonymous technicians in white jackets, pants, and hats drawing blood from two horses.

J.G. FitzGerald had worked with the New York Health Department, and the Connaught campaign echoes that in the *Herald*. The initial photographs in the *Star* were, however, obviously and awkwardly staged. The horse stands on a rough lawn, secured only by a lead rope, and the scientific instruments are perched precariously on a side table on a white cloth. The first photograph, depicting the inoculation of the horse, is the most curious. Robert Defries described toxin injection as a hazardous procedure: "a slip of the injecting needle might result in the death of an operator, for the fatal dose of tetanus toxin for man is an infinitesimal amount," and he explains the precautions taken at the Connaught Laboratories: "Mr. Double developed the technique of injecting the horses and trained his assistants to exercise great care."[71] It seems unlikely that Defries would have authorized an injection of such a toxic agent in these circumstances: without any restraints, outside, where the horse could easily be startled. An article in the *New York Herald* in 1894 showed a "refractory" diphtheria horse strapped down on its side for inoculation, and the classic photograph shows a horse restrained by a stall of iron piping, and several attendants.[72] The second photograph, of the horse being bled, also depicts an unlikely scenario. It shows a full bottle of dark fluids, presumably blood, perched on the narrow table only inches from the horse, well within reach of a good kick, which the horse seems poised to deliver. Were the garden images an attempt to naturalize the procedure? Was the location necessitated by the lack of appropriate indoor spaces in 1916? Were the existing buildings on the Connaught property too barn-like, too unhygienic to be featured in a newspaper story whose intent was to reassure? The photograph used in FitzGerald's subsequent 1917 article is a classic serum horse photograph. The photograph is cropped to show only the horse's head and flank, restrained by iron pipes, and two men in white coats holding tubing of blood. Defries's 1918 collage also shows a much more likely image of a handsome horse restrained by iron piping in bright, clean, large windowed operating room, a safe and hygienic location for the inoculating and bleeding of horses.[73]

At the conclusion of Defries's article, however, is a separate, and somewhat incongruous photograph of an ungainly little horse, with the caption: " 'BRICK TOP.' A REAL WAR HORSE. Has supplied sufficient serum for 15,000 soldiers in his four years of service." Brick Top is awkwardly posed beside the brick wall of the stable on a dirty tile floor. His hipbones are

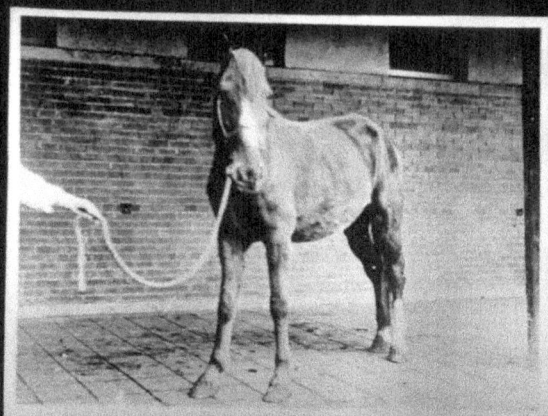

"Brick Top" A Real "War Horse" Produced sufficient Tetanus Serum for more than 15,000 wound soldiers

6.4 "Brick Top: A Real War Horse." Photograph from Connaught Laboratory photo album. Acc0708A. Courtesy of Sanofi Pasteur Canada (Connaught Campus) Toronto Archives.

visible and his coat dull. His handler stands off camera, loosely holding the lead rope.[74] Brick Top also appears in two Connaught photo albums. Brick Top is such an unlikely candidate that the only explanation for his selection as a poster boy for the laboratory is that Brick Top was actually the horse that produced serum for 15,000 soldiers. There is no record of a Brick Top in the laboratory records, where most of the tetanus horses were identified by number, but it is possible he was T#17, who had at this point been bled 35 times over the course of three years.[75] The decision to give Brick Top a name, and a personality as a war hero, was typical of the equine serum narrative. In the United States, Dan, "the retired fire horse," was given credit for saving 100,000 soldiers.[76] In his ordinary heroism Brick Top may have served as a stand-in for the maimed and worn veterans of the First World War.[77]

The serum horse imagery was intended to reassure the public of the health of the horse, the hygiene of the facilities, and the naturalness of the procedure. The awkwardness of the early Connaught photographs, and the transition to the image of the iconic serum horse, reveals the work

Seeing her true friend ~ An Antitoxin producing horse at the Connaught Laboratory Farm

6.5 "Seeing her true friend. An Antitoxin producing horse at the Connaught Laboratory Farm." Color Lantern Slide. Ags020. Courtesy of Sanofi Pasteur Canada (Connaught Campus), Toronto Archives.

underlying this image. The tetanus horse images were later used in a colourized lantern slide on diphtheria horses, with photographs of beautiful horses and pretty children, and such headings as "Jack and Tom have produced Antitoxin for 3 years, saving many children's lives," and "Seeing her true friend. An Antitoxin producing horse at the Connaught Laboratory Farm."[78] The photographs build on much older, heroic, narratives of war horses and fire horses. They work with animal welfare narratives, like *Black Beauty*, to show animals in willing service to mankind. These ideas become woven into new narratives of science and modernity.

Canadians no longer live in terror of lockjaw. The assemblages described in this chapter no longer exist. We do not have horses, humans, and *C. tetani* jostling one another on city streets; nor do we have horses, scientists, and germs circulating through laboratory spaces. In 1927, scientists developed the tetanus vaccine. The weakened toxins in the vaccine induced the recipient to develop their own antibodies, conferring long-term immunity, and making antitoxin necessary only for the rare unvaccinated victim. The vaccine was widely available by 1938, just in time for the next world war, and it is now a routine part of childhood and adult immunization.[79] Curiously, the narratives and visual images continued to circulate long after the bacilli was defeated. The serum horse, like the fire horse, continues to serve as a potent image of animals in heroic service to humankind.

Notes

1   *Huron Expositor*, 11 September 1885.

2   Other species also shed tetanus spores, but the horse was the animal that did so most prolifically in the late nineteenth-century city.

3   Vinciane Despret, "From Secret Agents to Interagency," *History and Theory* 52, no. 4 (2013): 37. Although most of the literature in animal studies literature uses the English translation, "assemblage," this chapter follows Vinciane Despret and John Phillips in using Deleuze and Guattari's original French term *agencement*. Assemblage evokes a static collection of things, and does not fully capture the interactive and evolving nature of Deleuze and Guatarri's model. See John Phillips, "Agencement/assemblage," *Theory, Culture & Society* 23, nos. 2–3 (2006): 108–9, and Gilles Deleuze and Felix Guattari, *A Thousand Plateaus*, trans. B. Massumi (Minneapolis: University of Minnesota Press, 1987).

4   The story of tetanus has largely gone untold, as historians of immunological medicine have focused upon the parallel history of diphtheria, which Terra Ziporyn calls the darling of the bacteriological revolution. See Ziporyn, *Disease in the Popular American Press: The Case of Diphtheria, Typhoid Fever, and Syphilis, 1870–1920* (New York, Westport, CT, and London: Greenwood Press, 1988). See also Evelynn Maxine Hammonds, *Childhood's Deadly Scourge: The Campaign to Control Diphtheria in New York City, 1880–1930* (Baltimore and London: Johns Hopkins University Press, 1999).

5   I would like to thank Sanofi Pasteur Limited (Connaught Campus) for access to the records in their archives, and the invaluable assistance of archivist Christopher Rutty.

6   J.M.S. Pearce, "Notes on Tetanus (Lockjaw)," *Journal of Neurology, Neurosurgery, and Psychiatry* 60 (1996): 332.

7   Archibald MacMechan, *The Winning of Popular Government: A Chronicle of the Union of 1841* (Toronto, 1920), reprinted in *The Chronicles of Canada, Volume VII: The Struggle for Political Freedom*, ed. George Wrong and H.H. Langon, 235. See also Adam Shortt, *Lord Sydenham* (Toronto: Morang,

1908), 340: "Yet in the intervals of his suffering he continued, with characteristic fortitude, to devote himself to his duties, public and private." Even the dispassionate account of Sydenham's life in the *Dictionary of Canadian Biography* notes the agony of his death. Phillip Buckner, "Thomson, Charles Edward Poulett, 1st Baron Sydenham," *Dictionary of Canadian Biography*, http://www.biographi.ca/en/bio/thomson_charles_edward_poulett_7E.html (accessed 17 December 2015).

8   Statistics for the incidence of tetanus prior to the twentieth century are not available. The focus in this chapter is on generalized tetanus, which produced the classic symptoms of lockjaw. Neonatal tetanus was not understood at the time to be the same disease. See Sally G. McMillen, "No Uncommon Disease: Neonatal Tetanus, Slave Infants, and the Southern Medical Profession," *Journal of the History of Medicine and Allied Sciences* 46, no. 3 (July 1991): 291–314. See also Stephen J. Kenny, "'I can do the child no good': Dr. Sims and the Enslaved Infants of Montgomery, Alabama," *Social History of Medicine* 20, no. 2 (August 2007): 223–41. There are two other rare types of tetanus: localized tetanus and cephalic tetanus.

9   "DIED OF BLOOD POISONING: Orlo B. Dicken of the South Side Dies Sunday Morning," "MAY DIE OF LOCKJAW: Water Street Boy Suffering Intense Pain in Water Street Hospital," *Ottawa Citizen*, 3 August 1899.

10   Everett B. Miller, "Comparative Medicine: American Experience from Equine Tetanus – From

Benjamin Rush to Toxoid," *Bulletin of the History of Medicine* 57, no. 1 (1983): 141; D. McEachran and Andrew Smith, *The Canadian Horse and His Diseases* (Toronto: J. Campbell 1867), 152. "Tetanus or Lockjaw in Horses," *The Canada Farmer* 3, no. 2 (15 January 1866): 23, describes how to treat a horse.

11   See accounts of horses' deaths in *The Canada Farmer*, 1, no. 11 (15 June 1864): 165, and "Disease of Horses and Cattle," *The Canadian Gentleman's Journal and Sporting Times* 7, no. 385 (10 January 1879): 1, and *The Illustrated Journal of Agriculture* 4, no. 7 (November 1882): 106. The last article describes the loss of a valuable team of draft horses and calls for the removal of nails from city streets. One article lists the causes of equine death, in cases with insurance in New York over five years, with tetanus coming 7th with 37 causes. *The Monetary Times, Trade Review and Insurance Chronicle* 24, no. 38 (20 March 1891): 1155.

12   See, for example, recommendations for smoke in the wound in "A Cure for the Most Dangerous of Wounds," *Northern Messenger* 24, no. 19 (20 September 1889): 3; "Cure for Lockjaw," *The Canadian Mute* 7, no. 18 (14 June 1889); and in *Newcastle Farmer* 3, no. 3 (November 1948). A warning against the use of cobwebs in wounds was published in "Death in the Cobweb," *The Northwest Review* 15, no. 51 (26 September 1900): 3. A tarnished copper penny was advised in "Remedy for Lockjaw," *The British American Cultivator* 2, no. 3 (March 1846). The *Journal of Agriculture and Horticulture* 2, no. 19 (1899): 4511, published in

Montreal, recommended salt pork on the wound.

13 *Epidemiology and the Prevention of Vaccine-Preventable Deaths*, 13th ed. (May 2015), available through the Centers for Disease Control, http://www.cdc.gov/vaccines/pubs/pinkbook/tetanus.html (accessed 17 December 2015).

14 *C. tetani* is now known to produce two exotoxins: tetanospasmin, which is one of the most potent toxins known and causes the symptoms of lockjaw, and tetanolysin, the function of which is still unknown.

15 Andrew Cunningham and Perry Williams, eds., *The Laboratory Revolution in Medicine* (Cambridge, UK: Cambridge University Press, 2002). For another perspective, see Morten Hammerborg, "The Laboratory and the Clinic Revisited: The Introduction of Laboratory Medicine into the Bergen General Hospital, Norway," *Social History of Medicine* 24, no. 3 (2011): 758–75.

16 Terra Ziporyn tracks the inconsistencies in media accounts of diphtheria in *Disease in the Popular American Press*.

17 Isabel Robb, *Nursing: Its Principles and Practice for Hospital and Private Use* (Montreal: W. Briggs, 1893), 435–36.

18 "That Awful Microbe," *Toronto Daily Mail*, 27 February 1888, 4. The story was attributed to the *New York Times*.

19 "The Nature of Tetanus," *Canada Lancet* (June 1889): 310.

20 "Diseases of Domestic Animals, Their Relation to the Human Family and Hygiene," *The Canada Health Journal: A Monthly Magazine of Preventative Medicine* 10, no. 2 (February 1888): 66; *Ottawa Journal*, 25 January 1900. The *Ottawa Journal* story continues: "Tetanus – the lockjaw germ – will, he says, disappear almost completely. It is in fodder that the germ is introduced into cities, and with the elimination of the horse that dread disease, lockjaw, will probably almost disappear." The story goes on build the case against the horse, arguing that in Paris, France, where the new automobile was being adopted, the horse caused more traffic fatalities than the automobile. An American newspaper, *Spokesman Review,* made the point more forcefully in 1913, in "Why Horses Are Among Man's Worst Enemies," *Spokesman Review*, 14 September 1913. For an interesting discussion of the incidence of tetanus in the decades following the disappearance of the horse, see "Tetanus in the United States, 1900–1969, Analysis by Cohorts," *American Journal of Epidemiology* 96, no. 4 (1972): 306.

21 The statistics can be found in the Canadian census. The ratio of horse to human was also high in other Canadian cities in 1891, ranging between 1 to 18 in Ottawa and 1 to 41 in Saint John. Margaret Derry estimates that the world population of horses peaked between 1910 and 1920 at 110 million horses, double the horse population of a century earlier, and four times that of 1720, before the industrial age: Margaret Derry, *Horses in Society: A Story of Animal Breeding and Marketing Culture, 1800–1920* (Toronto: University of Toronto Press, 2006), 47. Derry cites Harold B. Barclay, *The Role of the Horse in Human Culture*

(London: J.A. Allan, 1980), 339. For US statistics see Clay McShane and Joel A. Tarr, *The Horse in the City: Living Machines in the Nineteenth Century* (Baltimore: Johns Hopkins University Press, 2007), 16, and Ann Norton Greene, *Horses at Work: Harnessing Power in Industrial America* (Harvard University Press, 2008), 166. For British numbers see F.M.L. Thompson, "Horses and Hay," in *Horses in European Economic History: A Preliminary Canter*, ed. F.M.L. Thompson (Reading, UK: British Agricultural History Society, 1983). Thompson has calculated that the ratio of urban horse to urban human in England rose from 1 to 30 in 1830 to 1 to 20 in 1900. For a discussion of the many ways that horses powered the modern city, and their impact on urban life, see Joanna Dean and Lucas Wilson, "Horse Power in the Modern City," in *Powering Up: A Social History of Power, Fuel and Energy from 1600*, ed. Ruth Sandwell (Montreal and Kingston: McGill-Queens University Press, 2016).

22   Ann Greene estimates that in the United States the average draft horse increased in size from 900–11,000 pounds in 1860 to 1,800–2,000 pounds in 1880. Greene, *Horses at Work*, 174. Leah Grandy has observed that photographs show noticeably larger horses in the streets of Saint John, New Brunswick, after 1901. Leah Grandy, "The Era of the Urban Horse: Saint John, New Brunswick, 1871–1901" (MA thesis, University of New Brunswick, 2004).

23   Joel Tarr, "Urban Pollution: Many Long Years Ago," *American Heritage Magazine* (October 1971),

available at http://www.banhdc.org/archives/ch-hist-19711000.html (accessed 26 January 2015). Toronto's attempts to manage manure are described in P.M. Hall, "Disposal of Manure," Paper read before the Section of Public Officials, American Public Health Association, September 1913. For discussion of stable flies, see Nigel Morgan, "Infant Mortality, Flies and Horses in Later-Nineteenth-Century Towns: A Case Study of Preston," *Continuity and Change* 17, no. 1 (May 2002): 97–132, and Patricia Thornton and Sherry Olsen, "Mortality in Late Nineteenth Century Montreal: Geographic Pathways of Contagion," *Population Studies* 65, no. 2 (2011): 157–81.

24   In Toronto, for example, there were 1,102 dairy cows in 1861, 500 in 1891, and 29 in 1911. Sean Kheraj, "Living and Working with Animals in Nineteenth-Century Toronto," in *Urban Explorations: Environmental Histories of the Toronto Region*, ed. L. Anders Sandberg, Stephen Bocking, Colin Coates, and Ken Cruikshank (Hamilton, ON: L.R. Wilson Institute for Canadian History, 2013), 120–40, esp. 126.

25   For a description of the regulation of dogs in Toronto during this period, see Amanda Sauermann, "Breeding and Exhibition of the Canine Body in Canada" (MA thesis, Carleton University, 2011).

26   In 1914, 443 deaths from diphtheria were reported in Ontario (16.7 per 100,000 population) and 654 in Quebec (31 per 100,000). The story of FitzGgerald funding his laboratory from his wife's dowry is widely told.

27 This account of the early history of the Connaught Laboratories is drawn largely from Robert D. Defries, *The First Forty Years, 1914-1955: Connaught Medical Research Laboratories, University of Toronto* (Toronto: University of Toronto Press, 1968). See also Paul A. Bator and A.J. Rhodes, *Within Reach of Everyone: A History of the University of Toronto School of Hygiene and the Connaught Laboratories, Vol. 1, 1927-1955* (Ottawa: Canadian Public Health Association, 1990), and Paul A. Bator, *Within Reach of Everyone: A History of the University of Toronto School of Hygiene and the Connaught Laboratories, Vol. 2, 1955-1975, With an Update to 1994* (Ottawa: Canadian Public Health Association, 1995); Christopher J. Rutty, "Robert Davies Defries (1889-1975)," in *Doctors, Nurses and Medical Practitioners: A Bio-Bibliographical Sourcebook*, ed. L.N. Magner (Westport, CT: Greenwood Press, 1997), 62-69; Pierrick Malissard, "Quand les universitaires se font entrepreneurs: les laboratoires Connaught et l'Institut de Microbiologie et d'hygiène de l'Université de Montréal, 1914-1972" (PhD diss., Université du Québec à Montréal, 1999).

28 Pierrick Malissard describes multipurpose laboratories as ingenious devices for ensuring research funding. Pierrick Malissard, "Les 'start up' de jadis: la production de vaccins au Canada," *Sociologie et societes*, 32, no. 1 (2000): 93-106.

29 Defries repeatedly states in *The First Forty Years* that the Connaught Laboratory building housed 20 horses, but the floor plan shows only 15 stalls.

30 A full accounting of the assemblage in the Connaught Laboratories should include the humble guinea pig. These small animals would be infected with tetanus, and then given varying doses of antitoxin. The amount required to save the guinea pig would determine the strength of the antitoxin. By the time the building was opened the guinea pig room had been redesignated for future laboratory space, and two neighbouring buildings were cobbled together to house the colony. Defries notes that the colony had thrived in the original Barton Street stable, where it had grown to 500 guinea pigs, but struggled in the new location, and eventually succumbed to a streptococcic infection. It was replaced by a new strain from the Lister Institute in London in 1930. Defries, *The First Forty Years*, 315. Guinea pigs appear once in FitzGerald's laboratory book, when it is recorded that the guinea pig given 450 units of antitoxin lived 8 hours longer than the untreated guinea pig, and the pig given 500 units lived for 88 hours. Record book labelled, "Dept Hygiene, Record Diphtheria and Tetanus Antitoxin Refining. Book 2. Commencing October 12, 1917 Ending Feb 22, 1917," Sanofi Pasteur Limited (Connaught Campus) Archives. A newspaper article on "the humble guinea pig" made no reference to the guinea pig's heroism: "The horse actually supplies the serum but the little pig acts as a meter, in order the mixture may be of the right strength. A group of guinea pigs would be given a fatal dose of toxin, and varying amounts of antitoxin," *The Globe*, 21 November 1925, 14. For background on the standardization of serum, see

Christoph Gradmann and Jonathan Simon, eds., *Evaluating and Standardizing Therapeutic Agents, 1890–1950* (London: Palgrave Macmillan, 2010).

31   Robert D. Defries, "The War Work of the Connaught and Antitoxin Laboratories, University of Toronto," *The University of Toronto Varsity Magazine Supplement* (1918), 94–96.

32   "Report of Tetanus Cases, for the month ending March 1918," Sanofi Pasteur Limited (Connaught Campus) Archives. The chart notes: Toxin Dose; Date Started; No. of Bleedings; Date of Last Bleeding. The earliest horse, T#21, started on April 7, 1915, and had been bled 35 times by March 1918. T#17 started May 31, 1915 and had been bled 30 times; T#1 started January 1916, and had been bled 15 times; T#6 was also started January 1916 and had been bled 17 times; T#25 had been bled 9 times; T#26 had been bled 4 times. Of T#29 through T#34, who had been started 5 or 6 September 1917: T#30 and T#31 had been bled 3 times, T#32 had been bled once, T#29 had not yet been bled. Nor had T#8, who had been started 3 August 1917, or horses T#34 through T#42, started in early 1918, presumably because their antibody levels were not yet high enough. The chart also has a column for General Condition, which is not filled out.

33   Record book labelled "Dept Hygiene, Record Diphtheria and Tetanus Antitoxin Refining. Book 2. Commencing October 12, 1917 Ending Feb 22, 1917," Sanofi Pasteur Limited (Connaught Campus) Archives.

34   There is some confusion in the record book, as horse 11 is bled out on 13 November (10,600 cc) but appears once again in the record book on 28 November, when 9,700 cc is recorded as having been taken. However, horse 11 does not appear again. Horse 19 is bled out on 20 June 20 1917, when 24,800 cc was taken.

35   "Connaught Laboratories, University of Toronto," pamphlet at Sanofi Pasteur Limited (Connaught Campus) Archives. Undated, but the reference to three brick stables (p. 49) dates it after the period under discussion here.

36   David Bruce, "Tetanus: Analysis of One Thousand Cases," Presidential Address, *Transactions of the Royal Society of Tropical Medicine and Hygiene* 11, no. 1 (November 1917): 1–53.

37   P.C. Wever and L. van Bergen, "Prevention of Tetanus during the First World War," *Med. Humani* 38, no. 2 (December 2012): 78–82.

38   "Splendid Gift to the University," *Mail and Empire*, 26 October 1917.

39   *The Globe*, 25 October 1927, 13.

40   Defries, *The First Forty Years*, 24. The lab also supplied the needs of the Armed Services for smallpox vaccine.

41   *Contract Record*, 24 October 1917, 882.

42   *Construction* 11, no. 5 (May 1918). The photographs are attributed to Stevens and Lee, Architects, and a blueprint is included.

43   This description is drawn from Jennifer Keelan's excellent thesis. Jennifer Keelan, "The Canadian Anti-Vaccination Leagues, 1872–1892"

(PhD thesis, University of Toronto, 2004). The process of smallpox vaccine production had changed in the late nineteenth century. In "arm to arm" vaccination with human lymph, lymph was taken from the pustules of cows infected with cowpox and used to initiate a chain of infection that was passed directly from vaccinated child to unvaccinated child. Concerns about sharing human disease through the lymph led to its replacement by the use of vaccine points impregnated with animal lymph. Keelan notes that the history of the shift in methods is still poorly understood. See also Keelan, "Risk, Efficacy, and Viral Attenuation in Debates over Smallpox Vaccination in Montreal, 1870-1877," in *Crafting Immunity: Working Histories of Clinical Immunology*, ed. Kenton Kroker, Jennifer Keelan, and Pauline M.H. Mazumdar (Aldershot, UK: Ashgate, 2008), 29-54.

44   W.B. Spaulding, "The Ontario Vaccine Farm, 1885-1916," *Canadian Bulletin of Medical History* 6 (1989): 45-56. See also Pierrick Malissard, "'Pharming' à l'ancienne: les fermes vaccinales canadiennes," *Canadian Historical Review* 85, no. 1 (2004): 35-62.

45   One photograph in the Connaught collection shows the calf splayed on the operating table, with the white-coated scientist harvesting serum. Photograph Acc1125. Photographs from an album, labelled CAL 1918 album – B3 Smallpox 2 and Smallpox1, show the operating table and enamel bath for the calves. Another, a collage, shows the white-coated technicians "Bathing Calf before Vaccination, "Acc0094. This photograph appears

in Robert Defries's 1918 article in the *Varsity Magazine Supplement*, along with photographs with the captions, "Vaccine Unit," and "Feeding the calf after vaccination." Photographs in Sanofi Pasteur Limited (Connaught Campus) Archives. For a discussion of these photographs, see Joanna Dean, "Animal Matter: The Making of Pure Bovine Vaccine at the Connaught Farm and Laboratory at the Turn of the Century," blog post, *Active History*, 2 April 2015, http: http://activehistory.ca/2015/04/ animal-matter-the-making-of-pure-bovine-vaccine-at-the-connaught-laboratories-and-farm-at-the-turn-of-the-century/ (accessed 17 December 2015).

46   See Paul Adolphus Bator, "The Health Reformers versus the Common Canadian: The Controversy Over Compulsory Vaccination against Smallpox in Toronto and Ontario, 1900-1920," *Ontario History* 75 (1983): 348-73; Barbara Tunis, "Public Vaccination in Lower Canada, 1815-1823: Controversy and a Dilemma," *Historical Reflections* 9, nos. 1/2 (Winter 1982): 264-278; Katherine Arnup, "Victims of Vaccination?: Opposition to Compulsory Immunization in Ontario, 1900-1990," *Bulletin canadien d'histoire de la médecine* 9, no. 2 (1997): 159-76; Jennifer Keelan, "Risk Efficacy and Viral Attenuation in Debates over Smallpox Vaccination in Montreal, 1870-1877," 29-54, and Christopher J. Rutty, "Canadian Vaccine Research, Production and International Regulation: Connaught Laboratories and Smallpox Vaccines, 1962-1980," 273-300, in *Crafting Immunity*; Heather MacDougall, *Activists and Advocates:*

Toronto's Health Department 1883–1983 (Toronto: Dundurn, 1990), and Keelan, "The Canadian AntiVaccination Leagues, 1872–1892." For earlier, scattered opposition see Barbara Lazenby Craig, "State Medicine in Transition: Battling Smallpox in Ontario, 1882–1885," *Ontario History* 75, no. 4 (December 1983): 319–47; and Barbara Craig, "Smallpox in Ontario: Public and Professional Perceptions of Disease, 1884–1885," in *Health, Disease and Medicine: Essays in Canadian History*, ed. Charles G. Roland (Toronto: Hannah Institute for the History of Medicine, 1984), 230. There are some slight discrepancies between Arnup's account and that of Heather MacDougall in *Activists and Advocates*. MacDougall describes the formation of the Toronto Anti-Compulsory Vaccination League by Dr. Alexander Ross in 1888, and says it re-emerged in 1900 as the Toronto Anti Vaccination League. Arnup describes the league as a national body. She says the league was renamed The Anti-Vaccination and Medical Liberty League in 1920; McDougall refers to this later organization as the Medical Liberty League, which may reflect common usage. For the United States, see Martin Kaufman, "The American Anti-Vaccinationists and Their Arguments," *Bulletin of the History of Medicine* 41 (1967): 463–78, esp. 470–71; James Colgrove, "'Science in a Democracy?' The Contested Status of Vaccination in the Progressive Era and the 1920's," *Isis* 96, no. 2 (2005): 167–91. For Britain see Nadja Durbach, *Bodily Matters: The Anti-Vaccination Movement in England, 1853–1907* (Durham, NC: Duke University Press, 2005), 113.

47   Sheard is cited in MacDougall, *Activists and Advocates*, 123.

48   Michael Bliss, *Plague: A Story of Smallpox in Montreal* (Toronto: Harper Collins, 1991), 212.

49   Durbach is not unsympathetic to the charges by the *Vaccination Inquirer* that "the vaccinators not only come into [the Englishman's home], but they get inside his skin, and invade his veins, so his blood is not his own," *Vaccination Inquirer*, June 1881, 50. Cited in Durbach, *Bodily Matters*, 113.

50   Gibbs, *Our Medical Liberties*, 8, cited in Durbach, *Bodily Matters*, 125.

51   Eadon, *Vaccination*, I, cited in Durbach, *Bodily Matters*, 125. Human-derived lymph was understood to have exposed children to a range of human diseases, notably syphilis.

52   Cited in Kaufman, "The American Anti-Vaccinationists," 471.

53   "Vaccination Optional Now, " *Toronto Daily Star*, 2 March 1906, 7. Cited in Arnup, "Victims of Vaccination," 161.

54   W.R. Inge Dalton, MD, "Responsibility for the Recent Deaths from the Use of Impure Antitoxins and Vaccine Virus," *Canadian Journal of Medicine and Surgery* 11, no. 1 (1902): 36.

55   See, for example, the *Pittsburgh Press*, 3 November 1901. The article says that all the horses from which serums are taken for making diphtheria and other antitoxins are obtained from the fire and police departments. "The majority had been used by the city for some time so it is well known where they come from and what their

associations have been previous to being turned over to the health bureau."

56   H. Bergh, "The Lancet and the Law," *North American Review* 134, no. 303 (February 1882): 161–70. He writes: "In the period of less than one hundred years, millions upon millions of sound and healthy human beings have been inoculated with the most loathsome pestilence, doomed to carry to the grave bodies wasted by consumption, or marred and deformed by scrofula, cancer and innumerable ills." For Canadian antivivisection sentiment, see J.T.H. Connor, "Vivisection and Biomedical Research in Victorian English Canada," *Canadian Bulletin of Medical History* 14 (1997): 37–64.

57   *Vaccination Inquirer*, 1 July 1895. Cited in Durbach, *Bodily Matters*, 144.

58   The discovery of antitoxin has been described by James Turner, Harriet Ritvo, and Susan Lederer as a critical moment in the history of animal welfare movements. As Ritvo says: "Continuing advances in immunology and other areas protected biomedical research from antivivisectionist protest for much of the first part of this century, as did the prestige enveloping the entire scientific enterprise." Harriet Ritvo, "Plus ca Change: Antivivisection Then and Now," *Bioscience* 34 (1984): 626–33, esp. 630; Susan E. Lederer, "Political Animals: The Shaping of Biomedical Research Literature in Twentieth-Century America," *Isis*, 83, no. 1 (1992): 61–79; James Turner, *Reckoning with the Beast* (Baltimore: Johns Hopkins University Press, 1980). See also Nicolaas A. Rupke, ed.,

Vivisection in Historical Perspective (London: Routledge, 1987). Terra Ziporyn notes of diphtheria antitoxin that "few articles about immunization technique failed to reassure the readers that the horses were well treated." Many, she notes, concluded with a dig at antivivisectionists: "the wondrous antitoxin alone, they proclaimed, should end any concerns about the horrors of animal sacrifice." Ziporyn, *Disease in the Popular American Press*, 35.

59   "Vaccination," *Toronto Daily Star*, 7 March 1906, 6. Cited in Arnup, "Victims of Vaccination," 163.

60   This appears to be the room used for toxin production. The large cupboard to the left appears in two photographs of the toxin production laboratory at the Connaught. Photograph CAL 1918, album-B3LAB, Sanofi Pasteur Limited (Connaught Campus) Archives. The article does not distinguish between the "germ" and the spore, saying only that the tetanus germ has been known to live fifty years, and survive boiling.

61   *Sydney Herald*, 22 November 1916. The article continues: "Before the war nobody was sure as to the importance of this serum. Now it is quite certain that the effect of it is wonderful. After having introduced the rule that all wounded are to receive an injection of serum – and it has been introduced, both with the Central Powers as well as the British and French, and it is also being introduced with the Russian army – tetanus has, to all practical purposes, disappeared. Thousands and thousands of human lives have been saved in this manner." A similar feature article in the *New York Times* extolled a

diphtheria horse with this series of headlines in 1895: " 'No. 7' A Valuable Horse. Has Furnished the Health Board with 15 Quarts of Antitoxine. Bought for $10; Worth $5,000. Gaining Flesh While Losing Blood and Does Not Appear to Be at All Dissatisfied in His New Role." *New York Times*, 26 March 1895, p. 3, col. 4. Cited in Bert Hansen, *Picturing Medical Progress from Pasteur to Polio: A History of Mass Media Images and Popular Attitudes in America* (New Brunswick, NJ: Rutgers University Press, 2009), 291.

62   The original photographs are Acc1077A (toxin injection), and Acc1080S (bleeding), Sanofi Pasteur Limited (Connaught Campus) Archives. The text notes correctly that it was the tetanus toxin that was injected, rather than tetanus germs.

63   The third photograph is CAL 1918 Album, Sanofi Pasteur Limited (Connaught Campus) Archives. The photograph does not appear in the *Star* but it has the same background, and is positioned in a photograph album with the photographs used in the Star.

64   A similar photograph is Acc0995, Sanofi Pasteur Limited (Connaught Campus) Archives.

65   British military policy was to give injured soldiers four doses, once every seven days, to keep the level of antitoxin high. Because the first dose could activate an allergy to the horse, the reactions to the second and third doses could be fatal, and the army found that the effectiveness of the antitoxin had to be factored against the allergies it created. Sir David Bruce, "Tetanus:

Analysis of 1458 cases, which occurred in Home Military Hospitals during the years 1914–1918," *Journal of Hygiene* 19, no. 1 (July 1920): 1–32.

66   J.G. FitzGerald, Director, "The War-Work of the Connaught and Antitoxin Laboratories," *The Varsity Magazine Supplement*, 3rd ed. (1917), 54–56. The photograph of antitoxin preparation depicts a demonstration table, probably at the opening ceremonies for the laboratory, with a young woman demonstrating the various stages of antitoxin purification.

67   The collage is photograph Acc0094. The collage can be seen above FitzGerald's desk in an early photograph of the laboratory, Acc0690. Sanofi Pasteur Limited (Connaught Campus) Archives.

68   Robt. D. Defries, MD, DPH, Associate Director, "The War Work of the Connaught and Antitoxin Laboratories, University of Toronto," *The Varsity Magazine Supplement*, 4th ed. (1918), 94–96.

69   Kenton Kroker describes the process of making the invisible visible: "Extraction, filtration, cultivation and inoculation produced cultures of microbes of considerable purity, which could be then be viewed with light microscopes and their associated technologies of stains and filters." Kenton Kroker, "Immunology in the Clinics: Reductionism, Holism or Both?," in *Crafting Immunity*, 107–44.

70   "The New Cure for Diphtheria: Drawing the Serum from the Horse," *Scientific American* 71, no. 20 (17 November 1895): 309. Cited in Hansen, *Picturing Medical Progress*, 93. The image recirculated,

appearing in the *New York Herald*, 12 December 1894, and *Leslies Illustrated Weekly*, 17 January 1895.

71 Defries, *The First Forty Years*, 23.

72 "Inoculating a Refractory Horse," *New York Herald*, 17 December 1894, 4. Cited in Bert Hansen, "New Images of a New Medicine: Visual Evidence for the Widespread Popularity of Therapeutic Discoveries in America after 1885," *Bulletin of the History of Medicine* 73. no. 4 (1999): 629–78.

73 Photograph Acc1076, Sanofi Pasteur Limited (Connaught Campus) Archives. See also Plate 38 in Defries, *The First Forty Years*, which shows a new animal operating room, built in 1928, with a large tilt table prominently positioned.

74 Photograph Acc0708C, and Acc0708A, Sanofi Pasteur Limited (Connaught Campus) Archives.

75 One American story was titled "Exfire Horse Saves Many Lives." Dan the retired fire horse had, according to the story, saved 100,000 European soldiers through his serum, and a Dr. Parks was quoted as saying that the example of the horses at Otisville was a consummate example of service which no human ever excelled. *Gettysburg Times*, 3 January 1917, 3.

76 After the war J.G. FitzGerald made an even greater claim for what was presumably another horse: "To have saved the lives of between 20,000 and 30,000 men is a record of which any man might be justly proud, and this is the record of a horse at the farm of the University of Toronto, which is run by the Connaught Research Laboratories."

77 Credit for this observation should go to Ann Greene, at the 2015 annual meeting of the American Society for Environment History.

78 The lantern slide image of a tetanus horse is identified as Ags288, Sanofi Pasteur Limited (Connaught Campus) Archives. It is likely that these were the images were used in promotional lectures given by FitzGerald in 1927. The photographs with the captions quoted are Ags019, Ags020, Sanofi Pasteur Limited (Connaught Campus) Archives.

79 David W. Fraser, "Tetanus in the United States, 1900–1969," *American Journal of Epidemiology* 96, no. 4 (1972): 306–12. Fraser documents a steady decline in the incidence of deaths from tetanus from 1900, and argues: "Decreasing exposure to tetanus spores or improvement in non specific wound care may have had more effect than immunization in lowering tetanus mortality rates over the last 70 years." This is hard to reconcile with what we know of horse populations. Urban horse populations declined with the invention of the electric streetcar in the 1890s, but their numbers continued strong until after the First World War, and the bacilli remained active for a number of years in the soil.

Got Milk? Dirty Cows, Unfit Mothers, and Infant Mortality, 1880–1940

CARLA HUSTAK

In its current cultural context, milk is a site of entangled feminist, coloni-al, and capitalist politics. Milk travels in our time in multiple networks, congealing and drawing together human breasts, cows' udders, infant health, racialized and colonized digestive tracts, technological apparat-uses, capitalist profits, nutritional science laboratories, bioengineering, and communal milk banks. Social media such as Twitter and Facebook sites have been incorporated into the circulation and formation of milk communities as milk spills into virtual space. The politics of breastfeeding have currently highlighted the place of breast milk within environment-al politics. Recently, feminist concerns surrounding breast milk toxicity from the absorption of DDT have generated a possible trajectory for the advocacy of breastfeeding rights.[1] This has complicated traditional fem-inist agendas which have been preoccupied with concerns over moth-er-blaming in injunctions to maternal sacrifice or the social reprobation over the exposure of breasts in public. Significantly, feminist attention to breast milk toxicity has highlighted the intimacies of human breasts with nonhuman environmental actors. At the same time, the issue of breast-feeding has intricately entangled human and animal bodies at the level of the production of cow's milk. Both the cleanliness of cow's milk and the failure of breastfeeding have been linked to notions of unfit motherhood.

On a global capitalist scale, the demands for cow's milk and artifi-cial formulas have been intertwined in Western capitalist markets and in national and colonial politics. The Nestlé scandal, for example, involved the Western marketing of infant formulas in Africa and India, which resulted in infant suffering from diarrhea, malnutrition, and even death. This essentially occurred through the uneven distribution of resources given that mothers in these areas lacked sterilizing equipment, clean water, and the literacy skills to read the package directions.[2] Cows, too, have been implicated in the colonial politics of infant health insofar as the marketing of milk privileges European breeds and uses of cattle in contrast to indigenous cows and buffalo that are poor milk producers. Capitalist marketing of milk in "Got Milk" ads propagandizes its nutritional value, intertwining the provision of milk with maternal responsibility for infant health.

Milk's flow can also be tracked in the circuits of genetics as demands for milk have prompted the use of bovine growth hormones in cows and the Western hegemony of exporting milk's status as nature's perfect food in spite of the indigestibility of milk in some populations. One anthropologist has gone so far as to divide the world into lactophiles and lactophobes.[3] Mammalian maternity interlocks the bodies of human and cow mothers through the flow of milk, entangling their connectedness yet with asymmetrical costs. Cow mothers have been shown to produce more milk in the presence of calves in comparison to machine-milked cows.[4] The body of the cow mother has also been significantly altered through technological apparatuses employed to meet demands for capitalist profits on milk. Industrially milked cows, for example, live only four to five years despite a typical lifespan of twenty to twenty-five years. The fluidity of milk in social, economic, and political channels highlights the fluidity of animal and human bodies in their mutual material entanglements.

The intricate connections between cows, mothers, and infants in the circuits of milk's flow have a long history. From the late nineteenth century to the 1930s, public health reformers were at the forefront of campaigns that addressed the conditions of cows, the contamination of milk, responsible mothers, and infant mortality. These concerns specifically dovetailed with urbanization, prompting reformers to address issues of milk supply for larger urban populations and the dirt of the city in contaminating the milk supply.[5] Canadian public health reformers were part of a transnational network of reformers in Britain, the United States, and Europe who collectively addressed infant mortality and pure milk questions.

Notably, Toronto and Hamilton were among the first Canadian cities to implement milk depots to ensure a safe supply of milk. While reformers addressed concerns over milk quality, they also voiced concerns over reforming maternity, namely the insistence on the application of scientific principles to motherhood.

Historians have amply demonstrated that this period witnessed the rise of "scientific motherhood," but this story often leaves out the significance of the cow as a crucial factor in implications for breastfeeding.[6] Similarly, histories of farming and cows have left out the intimacies of cows' histories with those of infants and motherhood.[7] Moreover, the cow has been an overlooked actor in histories of sanitary reform, given that public health reformers devoted attention to the construction of barns and specifically addressed conditions of sewage disposal, ventilation, and overcrowding.[8] In a compelling history of milk, Peter Atkins has argued that milk's very ontology was called into question as scientists, public health reformers, politicians, physicians, and farmers assessed and intervened in the composition of milk. He has contended that "we may need to revise our human-centered narrative and see the cows themselves as experts."[9] While Atkins suggests that milk should be considered as a historically mutating epistemic object, I seize on milk as a productive site for challenging ontological divides between human and cow maternities. Similarly, Marilyn Yalom historicizes the breast in its shifting cultural meanings, only gesturing to cow's milk as one brief strand in this history.[10] I suggest that breasts and udders entered into important new relationships in the context of late nineteenth and early twentieth-century urbanization and milk politics. In doing so, I excavate the traces of the cow in archives of public health, scientific motherhood, and the reproductive body.[11] The space of the city presented unique and pressing challenges. Sanitary reformers approached the city as a space of contagion that intertwined the life conditions and maternity of lactating cows and lactating mothers. This chapter addresses the theme of the cow in the city as an intervention in historiographies of motherhood, infant health, agriculture, and sanitary reform.

By tracking the flow of milk, I situate udders and breasts in the wider environmental context of historically specific anxieties over urbanization and the contamination of the milk supply. Reformers' concerns over milk impurities cut across the contamination of cow bodies and the allegedly unclean breasts and feeding practices of lower-class and racialized mothers. Yet this story draws attention to a specific genealogical moment in a longer environmental history that has intimately interlocked and situated breasts and udders in wider ecologies. I focus on early twentieth-century milk sanitation and urbanization as a significant chapter that should be considered in relation to other twentieth-century moments in a changing narrative of entanglements of breasts and udders at the site of technological risk and improvement of milk, whether these technologies are mechanical, industrial, chemical, or genetic. Beyond this early twentieth-century moment, milk impurities transformed into concerns over corporate chemical pollutants in the form of DDT and DES. In the 1940s and 1950s, the reproductive lives of cows and women became entangled at the site of concerns over DES toxicity in breast milk and cow's milk. Women took DES to prevent miscarriages and treat menopause, whereas cows were given DES to stimulate growth.[12] In 1962, Rachel Carson's *Silent Spring* condemned the use of DDT, noting breast milk's toxicity due to women's exposure to DDT and the contamination of cattle from feeding on plants sprayed with pesticides.[13] In the present, feminist concerns over breast milk toxicity have reached a level where one woman has described her body as a "toxic waste site," wondering whether she should breastfeed.[14] This historic changing relationship between breasts and udders highlights the significance of milk's flow for grasping the ecological context of cow/human intimacies in their mutual susceptibility to toxicity. Indeed, this historical context also highlights the changing meaning of what counts as toxicity, impurity, and environmental pollutants.

I approach the story of Canadian cows and the city through three lenses. The first lens involves the conditions of cows in the city and the spectre of the cow's health and living conditions as milk was pursued, delivered, dispersed, and consumed. The second lens turns to the centrality of the cow in breastfeeding and, more broadly, maternity advice and practices. The third lens explores how concerns over the conditions of cows were interwoven with public health concerns over infant health. This drew together human and cow maternity in the prospects and stakes of child health in the future of the nation. In the early twentieth century, as cows began to be moved out of the city, rising new technologies, food science, and pasteurization and "certified" milk debates over policing cows, milk, and farmers continued to raise the spectre of dirty cows and vulnerable, porous human bodies.

The Cow in the City: Reforming Dirty Milk and Dirty Cows

Amid late nineteenth-century processes of urbanization, cows were prominently featured among the concerns of municipal officials. As cities formed, reformers duly noted dramatic contrasts between an idyllic rural landscape of green pastures, pure air, and open space and the urban conditions of poor sewage removal, impure water, crowded space, industrial filth, noise, and pollution.[15] Reformers associated this changing landscape of the urban built environment not only with the health of humans but also the health of cows. In fact, cows increasingly came under scrutiny as not only contaminated in this urban environment but also contributing to the unsanitary conditions of the city in terms of manure and drifting odours between the homes of cow owners and their neighbours. Sanitary reformers devoted attention to the condition of barns and the proximities of cows and people. For the most part, the interest in the living conditions of cows not only mirrored the reform efforts of tenements for the lower classes but closely connected the cow's environment, pure milk, and human digestive tracts.[16] As historians have shown, the nineteenth century witnessed particular anxieties over "swill" milk, which came from cows that were fed distillery slop.[17] At the local level, there were individual private citizens who kept cows and sought their own milk licences. City officials inspected their barns and judged such conditions according to many of the same criteria as those applied to tenements.

From the late nineteenth century into the 1930s, cow's milk made the agenda of public health reformers as one of the most dangerous, contaminated foods and turned intense attention to the conditions of cows. By the mid-1920s, the federal government established food inspection regulations, bringing the body of the cow under growing surveillance. During the 1880s, Toronto passed laws to regulate dairy barns. In 1908, Ottawa had strict laws for inspecting cattle that supplied milk. In 1911, Ontario's Milk Act stipulated the inspection of herds and proper facilities for dairy production. In 1922, The *Hamilton Spectator* ran an ad to reassure Hamiltonians that the Wentworth Co. Dairy's quarters were sanitary and used milk from government-approved cows (see Figure 7.1). The passage of these laws dovetailed with growing curtailment of the presence of cows in the city. The process of urbanization introduced new issues of transportation

Sanitary headquarters of the Wentworth Dairy Co., John street south. The building, now nearing completion, is modern in every respect. Equipment is of the latest design. Milk from government tested herds will be sold exclusively. The Wentworth Dairy is the only concern in the city offering for exclusive sale milk from government tested herds.

7.1 Wentworth Dairy advertising its sanitary construction and selection of cows during the milk reform campaigns in 1922. Originally published 7 September 1922 in the *Hamilton Spectator*.

and heightened anxieties over the fact that conditions out of sight could not be scrutinized. The spectre of the cow moved along with milk to infant mouths in the city. This spectre haunted the practice of breastfeeding, which had declined by the 1920s.[18] Public health reformers emphasized the conditions of the cow in a shared discourse on how these conditions contributed to contaminating the milk supply and endangering infant life.

A work on *Keeping One Cow* in 1880 suggests the common practice of keeping a cow in the city.[19] According to one writer, Mrs. Bourniot of Ottawa, the average citizen could keep a cow shed in addition to raising vegetables. She specified that a cow stable would be approximately 15 by 15 feet in the backyard. Mrs. Bourniot further stipulated the proper conditions for the cow. Bourniot maintained that "she must be fed and milked at regular times, be kept thoroughly clean, have plenty of fresh air and water, and her food composed of those substances that will keep her always in good condition."[20] In the late nineteenth century, many of these conditions echoed sanitary reform campaigns for better tenements. Mrs. Bourniot also drew attention to the growing concern over contaminated milk, traced back to feeding brewers' slop or grains to cows.[21] As late as 1923, this practice of keeping one's own cow did not entirely disappear in spite of municipal

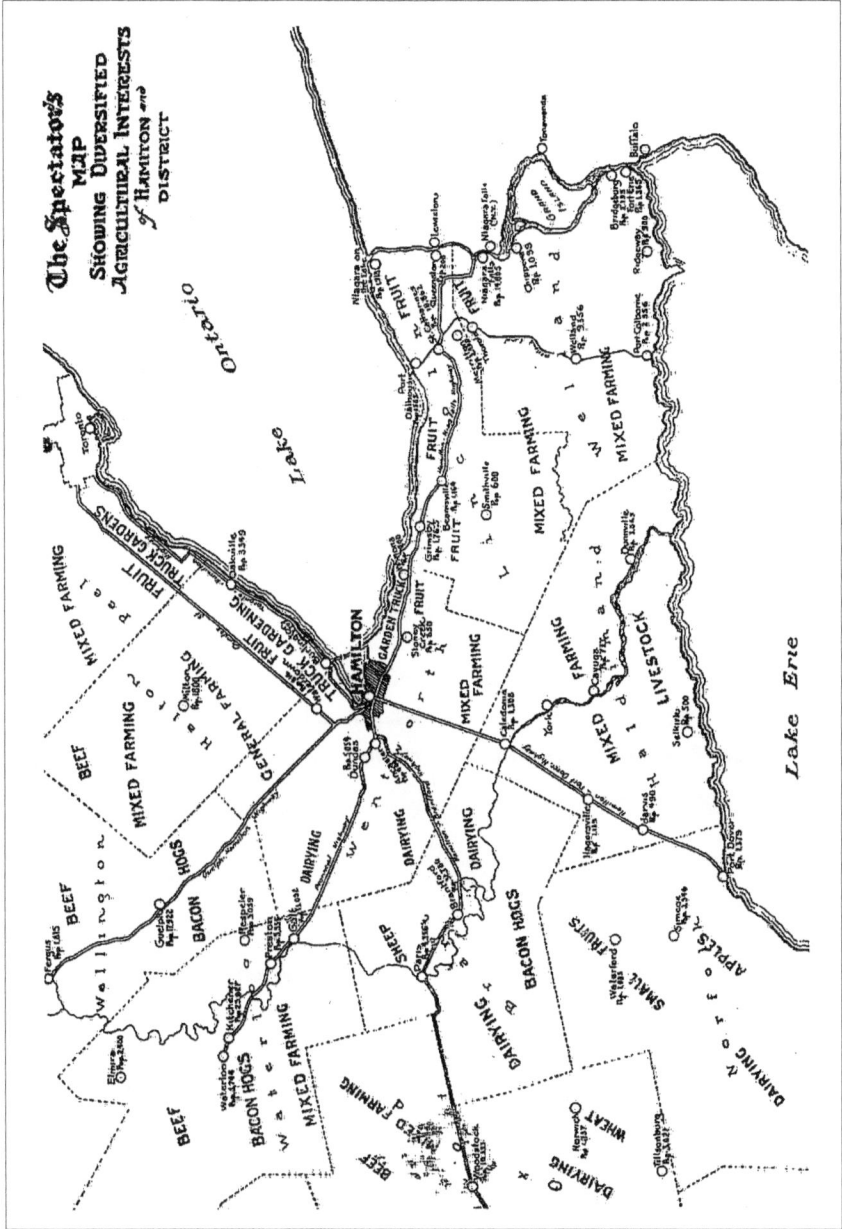

7.2 Distribution of Dairying in Hamilton and its surrounding areas in 1922.
Originally published 7 September 1922 in the *Hamilton Spectator*.

officials' anxieties over cows in the city. Helen MacMurchy, recognized for her expert advice to mothers and her avid involvement in child welfare, also mentioned cows in her popular Little Blue Books. She highlighted the problem of contaminated milk but drew attention to the possibility of keeping one's own cow.[22] MacMurchy's advice drew on themes that had been circulating since the late nineteenth century over clean stables, clean udders, and healthy cows.

In late nineteenth and early twentieth-century Hamilton, municipal officials scrutinized the environmental health of cows, firmly linking the improvement of life for cows to the purity of milk and human health. Dairying was concentrated in the immediate and surrounding areas of Hamilton (see Figure 7.2). The issue of "swill" milk preoccupied public health officials. In February 1888, the *Hamilton Spectator* reported that dairymen and vendors of milk would be required to register with a medical health officer at least once a year and make "a statement . . . as to the kind of food supplied to their cows, whether of brewers' grain, distillery slops, starch factory refuse, ensilage or oil-cake."[23] Within a climate of urban reform, the case of Mrs. Corbett came before Hamilton's city council in 1889. At the time, city councillors debated the possibility of a milk bylaw. During this year, Inspector Nixon investigated Mrs. Corbett's property on Barton Street to assess whether she would be eligible for a milk licence. Mrs. Corbett was eventually granted her milk licence approximately eight months after the council met. Nixon noted the good condition of the barn, the poor drainage, the good condition of the milk house, and the implementation of city water.[24] Municipal politics took cows into account insofar as the human consumption of milk rendered the human intensely vulnerable and vitally intertwined with the conditions of the cow.

Cows entered into the social relations of neighbours in the city, prompting municipal regulations of space while highlighting the intimate proximities of people and cows. Within the next few years, municipal officials continued to inspect cow byres in Hamilton. However, others were not as fortunate as Mrs. Corbett. In April 1896, the city council discussed whether a cow should be removed from the premises of Mr. D. Evans, who also kept a sow.[25] Although Mr. Evans maintained that the premises were clean, a Medical Health Officer recommended the removal of the cow. The Council ultimately concluded that Inspector Peacock should measure the distance between the cow byre and the nearest dwelling. A month later, Dr. Ryall came before the council to insist that cow byres be abolished or that a distance of 50 to 70 feet be enforced between the byre and the closest residence.[26] Cow byres were evidently not abolished, given that cases of cows in Hamilton persisted well beyond May 1896.[27] In November 1896, Mr. Ballentine reported on cow byres. The Committee on Cow Byres concluded that clean cows posed no danger to public health in terms of milk. However, the committee insisted that manure and disagreeable odors drifting into neighbouring doors and windows required the enforcement of a 50 to 70–foot distance between residences and cow byres. While the report also considered "humane action" to ensure that cows slept on decent bedding instead of on planks, the inspections largely reduced concerns for cow health to anticipated milk consumption.[28] In April 1897, this same Mr. Ballentine moved a motion for adopting public inspections of cow byres in conjunction with meat and milk inspections. At this same session, it was decided that the board should be permitted to publish the findings of any milk tests in the event of the milk being of an "inferior quality."[29] Although cows in the city presented contentious public health issues, as late as January 1931 city hall approved the motion to allow Acme Farmers Dairy Co. to maintain stables on Barton Street.[30]

The case of Hamilton was far from exceptional. Government reports highlighted the problem of dirty stables, dirty cows, and dirty milk on a national and often international scale. The issue of dirty milk went far beyond Ontario's borders. W.A. Wilson with the Department of Agriculture in Saskatchewan considered the dangers of milk that "turned" to traces of the cow's habitation. Wilson referred to "damp, filthy, dark, unventilated stables" and "wet and dusty milking corrals" as possible sources of contaminated milk.[31] In Saint John, New Brunswick's municipal politics, physician William Roberts who was trained at New York City's Bellevue Hospital, addressed milk pasteurization upon his re-election. Roberts attributed high infant mortality rates to impure water and milk. Across Canada, the passage of pasteurization regulations was uneven, with Saint John passing such laws in 1923, Toronto in 1915, and Hamilton in 1928.[32]

Imperial Cows: City Milk in Global Circuits of Transnational Whiteness

During this period, Canadian cows also gained attention from distant regions like Britain and South Africa. Situated within imperial circuits of sanitation and environmental health, Canadian cows were historical actors in colonizing projects and populations. The milk question was also a question of Empire. Helen MacMurchy, a Toronto physician, eugenicist, and public health reformer, positioned infant health within imperial discourses. MacMurchy claimed that "we are only now discovering that Empires and States are built up of babies."[33] Milk reformers participated in a Western hegemonic nexus of practices differentiated by the absence of milking domestic animals in areas such as indigenous America, Southeast Asia, and Africa.[34] These practices framed the milk question in terms of close ties across Canada, the United States, Britain, and Europe. As transnational public health reformers collaborated on the milk question, the whiteness of milk also materially and politically whitened Canadian cows. Duncan Ferguson, a Medical Officer in South Africa's Port Elizabeth, published a report in 1936 on behalf of the Carnegie Corporation Visitors' Committee. Corporate giant Andrew Carnegie's involvement in public health marked one form of American imperialism by claiming superior scientific knowledge to justify reform efforts. During the early twentieth century, business tycoon John D. Rockefeller was also well known for engaging in the uses of science and capital to export American influence and control.[35] In Ferguson's report, he emphasized efficiency, pasteurization, and sufficient capital for the dairy business in Canada and the United States. In the case of South Africa, however, Ferguson emphasized inadequate knowledge of pasteurization and the incompetency of milkers.[36] When Ferguson turned to the subject of the meat industry, he maintained that "as in the milk industry, the labour appeared to be of a superior type, intelligent and courteous and mostly of the white race."[37] Ferguson's report traced clean milk as a material flow that brought clean cows and white bodies into intimate imperial relations.

Canadian public health officials collaborated with American officials across borders on the question of clean milk. Public health reformers in both the United States and Canada devoted their attention to the issue of impure milk. In 1908, when Toronto reformers began launching organized efforts for milk depots, American President Theodore Roosevelt consented to an investigation of milk under Milton Rosenau's direction. In 1910, Canadian and American milk reformers attended a Conference on Milk Problems initiated by the New York Milk Committee. Evan Perry's report to the Canadian Department of Health, *Pasteurization of Milk For Small Communities,* cited the work of S.D. Belcher, who was involved with the Medical Division of the Rochester Institute. Belcher noted poorly venti-lated stables, dirty barns, urine saturated sidings, the presence of odours, dirty clothing of workers, dirty cans, dust, flies, and contaminated water.

As government officials paid close attention to cows' bodies and their homes, they vitally interlocked cow health with human health at a time when milk was seen as a dangerous liquid. Just as sanitary reformers as-sociated clean homes with clean people, public health officials applied such logic to cows while highlighting the responsibility of farmers and milk vendors. As historians have shown in the case of sanitary reformers, cleanliness and purity amounted to a racial and class politics of the white middle class as exemplars of cleanliness.[38] Similarly, government officials who stressed the importance of clean cows also noted the incompetence of milkmen. In 1936, Duncan Ferguson's *Public Health Control* associated the bacterial contamination of milk with the failure of farmers to obtain white men to do the milking because of the early morning hours required for such work. In an earlier investigation of cows in Canada, the Milk Commission of 1909 blamed the problem of dirty milk on "a slovenly carelessness characterized by the premises and naturally also the people responsible therefor."[39] The commission visited over one hundred dairy farms, observing that in 10 per cent of the farms, the barns were dark and ventilation poor. J.H. Grisdale, the Director of Experimental Farms, also insisted that pure water was a necessary condition for cleanliness in the production of milk.[40] Public health officials cared whether cows were in the dark, had spacious accommodations, and proper ventilation.

Canadian public health officials devoted attention to the environ-mental health of cows largely for the purposes of regulating a clean milk supply and maximizing the economic potential of the cow. In the 1909 Milk Commission Report, Frank Herns, the Chief Dairy Instructor for Western Ontario, is cited for encouraging clean and ventilated stables and proper feed in contrast to distillery slop in the interests of maximizing milk production. A few years later, Charles F. Whitley of the Department of Agriculture attended the Dairymen's Convention of Ontario. In his report, Whitley highlighted an intimate connection between cows, owners, and profit "as the cow impresses her needs on the mind of her owner, he reaches out for more information on the best dairy practice regarding suitable and better field crops, improved conditions in the stables, and better products."[41] Yet, for some government officials, business competition could jeopardize the necessary caution required in selling milk. In 1902, J.A. Ruddick, as Minister of Agriculture, asserted that "unbusinesslike competition" among creameries could involve accepting any milk without considering its quality.[42] Ruddick attributed milk impurities to cows drinking out of muddy ponds, germs and dirt on the flanks and udders, and vile odours absorbed by the milk. For Ruddick, capitalist competition in milk production could prompt carelessness.

Where and how cows lived became pressing questions for municipal politicians, public health reformers, physicians, mothers, and infants in late nineteenth and early twentieth-century Canada. Cows emerged as prominent and significant actors within city council debates, neighbourly disputes, public health inspections, and transnational collaborations. Public health reformers' efforts to purify milk, then seen as a deadly substance, involved shifting attention to the environmental health of cows living in dingy, cramped, poorly ventilated sheds. The fate of cows involved a historically specific late nineteenth and early twentieth-century climate of sanitary reform combined with the faith in the science of bacteriology. By this time, Robert Koch's tuberculin test pervaded debates on cow's milk as part of milk's role in the era's panic over germs.[43] In this period, the goals of improving milk quality inspired a narrative of sanitary reform for dirty cows that overlapped with tenement reforms tying dirty mothers to dirty living quarters.[44] The cleanliness of cows, mothers, living quarters, and milk were intertwined in this urban narrative of the milk question.[45]

Fluid Embodiments: Milk's Spillage Across Human and Cow Maternities

As the public health campaign for better milk coincided with the rise of "scientific motherhood," the bodies of cows and mothers converged at the site of improving the quality and supply of milk. From its emergence as part of an American diet in the mid-nineteenth century, milk

Milk of Guaranteed Quality and Absolute Safety

Hamilton Dairy offers you in highest degree the two essentials in milk. It is rich in butterfat --- absolutely pure and safe.

No farm can supply Hamilton Dairy unless the herds are carefully selected and regularly inspected. Unless rigid sanitary standards are strictly adhered to.

Our splendid dairy is equipped with the most scientific devices for assuring absolute purity and safety in Hamilton Dairy milk. No expense has been spared in securing costly clarifying, pasteurizing, bottling and other equipment to secure this end.

As a result, through years of constant testing by the Department of Public Health, not the slightest trace of T. B. germs has ever been found in Hamilton Dairy Milk.

Isn't the assurance of such a guarantee of milk---the most important food you use --- worth while? Tele-phone Regent 170 or stop our salesman as he passes your door. Our delivery service covers every section of Hamilton, West Hamilton, the Beach and the Highway beyond Burlington "before breakfast daily."

12 Cents a Quart

7 Cents a Pint

7.3 Advertisement highlighting the dangers of impure milk to children. Originally published 23 October 1922 in the *Hamilton Spectator.*

was interrelated with practices of breastfeeding as a plausible substitute.[46] At a time of public health reformers' warnings of the dangers of milk, mothers who substituted cow's milk for breastfeeding could be construed as harming their children. As tactics for improving milk developed in terms of pasteurization or "certification" of herds, the notion of scientific motherhood came to encompass the education of mothers for these tasks. Some dairy companies such as Hamilton Dairy pitched ads directly associating their provision of pure milk with the welfare of children (see Figure 7.3). During this period, what came to be considered "responsible motherhood" included the scientific techniques of the care of children in addition to the responsible breeding of fit children. Historically, the fitness and quality of milk was tied to the racial and class status of mothers, with concerns surrounding the passage of undesirable qualities to children through the flow of milk.[47] Similarly, cows were incorporated and affected by the eugenics movement, with particular breeds seen as fitter, producing better quality milk, capable of a higher yield of milk to meet growing urban demands, and, as it travelled to human mouths, integrally tied to responsible motherhood and infant health.

Eugenics shaped attention to both better mothers and better cows in the early twentieth century.[48] At a time of baby contests to display eugenic maternity and popular discussions of mate selection, breeders' associations devoting attention to pedigreed animals provided the foundational organization for American eugenics. In Canada, the problem of infant mortality raised eugenic fears of race suicide among both Anglo and French Canadians.[49] As such, cows and the quality of their milk were part of eugenic narratives of better breeding.[50] Cows were not homogeneous but carefully demarcated by their breed. Breeders separated breeds of cattle for beef from breeds of cattle for dairy with Holstein-Friesians, Jerseys, and Ayrshires deemed quality dairy breeds. The Ayrshire, a Scottish breed known for good milk yields, became available in Ontario in 1882.[51] Holstein-Friesians emerged in Ontario in the 1880s, originating in Holland. In Hamilton, dairy farmers also turned to "high-class Scotch" Shorthorns as an ideal breed for milk production (see Figure 7.4). Breeds of cattle, therefore, embodied Canada's immersion in transnational networks of the dairy industry.

To some extent, the racial politics of eugenics in Canada influenced the opinions of public health reformers in associating the purity of cow bodies and the purity of milk. J.H. Grisdale commended "the hardy and useful race of Ayrshire cattle."[52] The Ayrshire, according to Grisdale, was "one of the principal breeds of dairy cattle."[53] He described the Ayrshire as medium-sized with red, white, or brown spots. In terms of character, the Ayrshire "possess great vitality, are of a nervous disposition."[54] For Grisdale, the breeding of cattle mattered insofar as the breed could maximize milk production which, in the case of the Ayrshire, would yield good quality milk of approximately 8,000 pounds in nine or ten months. The Ayrshire, however, bore defects of small teats and the likelihood of

7.4 Hamilton's use of Scottish-bred Shorthorn "matrons" for pure milk. Originally published 7 September 1922 in the *Hamilton Spectator.*

beefiness. When mating cattle, Grisdale suggested selecting a bull of good milking stock but "no animal strikingly weak, or of very faulty conformation should be used even when coming from heavy milking stock."[55] Grisdale recognized the significance of breeding cattle as one factor in milk production which continued to occur in cities among the herds of milkmen. In breeding dairy cattle, cows were further tied to women's bodies through breeders' association of these breeds with femininity because of lactation.[56] As Margaret Derry has noted, breeders took into account the size of the cow's udder.[57]

While Harriet Ritvo has shown that breeding cows has a long history, the late nineteenth and early twentieth centuries introduced new intimacies between the bodies of cows and nursing mothers which converged at the site of pure milk.[58] Both the surveillance of cow's udders and women's breasts occurred in the context of anxieties over contaminated milk from contaminated surfaces. Cows and mothers were subjected to similar scrutiny over the insistence on cleanliness for the purpose of ensuring pure milk. Helen MacMurchy's advice to mothers urged massaging breasts and sponging them with water. MacMurchy also suggested the importance of using an absorbent cotton swab and applying Castile soap to the nipples of the mother.[59] While MacMurchy also praised breastfeeding as the only way to save the baby, she also clearly insisted on keeping breasts clean. In the *Canadian Mother's Book*, MacMurchy drew from the warnings surrounding dirty milk. She told mothers that "no formula with bottles and rubber nipples, and measuring spoons and milk-sugar and sterilizing, and no one knows what else, for the Canadian Mother. These things will get dirty, and dirt in milk is death to the baby." MacMurchy's urging for clean nipples also circulated within a public health discourse shared with American reformers, and visiting nurses worried over the transmission of germs from mothers' breasts to infant mouths.[60] Breast milk, while exalted by reformers as healthy for children, could also bear the taint of contamination, which persuaded mothers to put their faith in pediatricians, nurses, and other experts.

During this period, MacMurchy's warnings occurred in the context of concerns over the effects of modernity on "civilized" breasts in the form of lactation failure, which was perceived as another urban public health issue alongside the impurity of cow's milk.[61] Public health reformers and pediatricians engaged in prominent discourses on neurasthenia, emphasizing the proneness of white middle-class women's bodies to nervousness, which registered at the level of breastfeeding. Reformers warned that overly emotional female bodies could affect the quality of breast milk. MacMurchy, for example, noted that "passion or temper or any other bad feeling should never enter the mother's room. Great emotion spoils the nursing milk and the milk secreted under such circumstances makes the child ill."[62] While pediatricians exalted the importance of breastfeeding during this period, they also suggested that breast milk could be of poor quality depending on the emotional conditions and diet of the mother.[63] These concerns over the bodies of mothers occurred within the context of exalting white upper- and middle-class mothers as paragons of cleanliness and healthy responsible motherhood.

In a report to the Department of Health titled "Canadians Need Milk," MacMurchy also specifically noted many of the same concerns voiced in agricultural and dairy reports on dirty udders, the dirty hands of milkmen and dirty pails, bottles, and utensils. While devoting attention to the proper feeding of babies, MacMurchy also noted the proper feeding of cows. She insisted that milk would be "almost a perfect food, if the cows are healthy, well fed and have some green fodder."[64] In her work on *How to Take Care of the Baby*, MacMurchy situated the cow within the broader scope of a human/nonhuman maternity in light of lactating functions.[65] She ascribed a maternal status to the cow, indicating that "the cow has been well called 'the foster mother of the human race.'"[66] Although MacMurchy emphasized the dangers of cows' milk by insisting that "the poor babies that die are nearly all bottle-fed," she nonetheless highlighted a particularly vital relationship between mothers and the consumption of milk.[67] According to MacMurchy, for mothers, milk was not only the best food but would also stimulate further milk production for the baby.[68] This accessibility to milk, however, also suggested a class politics of nutrition insofar as MacMurchy felt compelled to urge mothers that milk was affordable.[69] Cow's milk and mother's milk were integrally tied, as these bodies flowed together as cow's milk stimulated mother's milk.

As urbanization called into question the issue of pure milk, it prompted historically specific conditions that registered intimate associations of nursing breasts and cows' udders. Mastitis provided a site of physiological interconnections of nursing mothers and cows. Public health reformers' attention to clean cows to ensure clean milk inspired studies of the cow's udder. M.E. Whalley, who published a report on *Mastitis in Cows* indicated that "efforts to produce milk of good quality have led to investigations of various contributing factors, including a study of the udder. Mastitis was found to be prevalent, an insidious disease, frequently escaping detection."[70] The growth of cities, with an associated heightened demand for milk, generated profound physiological effects on cows resulting from greater capitalist efforts to maximize the udder – and thus maximize profits. This higher production of milk increased the susceptibility of cows to mastitis. Whalley, however, also noted many of the conditions discussed by sanitary reformers that infected the udder, such as improper milking and poor stable conditions.[71] A nursing cow mother, much like a nursing human mother, should have a clean udder/breast to feed the young.

According to Whalley, calves feeding from infected cows were found to contract the germs.[72] In this report, recommendations similar to those made for extracting pure milk were made because of the concern over potential mastitis in cows.[73]

"The Maternity Problem": Public Health Configurations of Unfit Mothers and Unfit Cows

The question whether milk for infants came from the mother's breast or the cow's udder ultimately intertwined women's bodies and the body of the cow in webs of social responsibility. Milk flowed across material and discursive aspects of these bodies as the spectre of dirty or clean cows, responsible or irresponsible mothers, thickened milk's social textures. At a Hamilton City Hall meeting in January 1931, councillors took note of a Board of Health report from 1909–1910. This report declared that "the milk question is but an outgrowth of a larger and more difficult problem – the maternity problem."[74] This same report referred to the necessary training of men and women to carry out the duties of parenthood. One Hamilton newspaper visually conveyed this formulation of pure milk as a maternity problem, joining cow mothers and human mothers in the sanitary or unsanitary space of the kitchen (see Figure 7.5). Such visual images circulated and reinforced popular connections between cows, mothers, lactating capacities, and pure milk.

In this period, the use of cow's milk carried implications for the suitability of the mother to the extent that choices for feeding infants became vital ones. According to the Milk Commission of 1909, most infant deaths could be attributed to mothers' decisions to artificially feed their children. Dr. James Roberts, Hamilton's Medical Health Officer, hinted at the responsibilities of mothers in attributing infant intestinal diseases to "unclean milk and improper feeding."[75] At Hamilton's City Hall, a report on the milk question for 1909–1910 was discussed in connection with grave maternal responsibility in providing pure milk.[76] This report lamented the tendency of many politicians to treat the milk question as less important than water, land, or mineral issues. It satirically claimed that such an attitude suggested that "the child murdering potencies of dirty milk must not be interfered with."[77] Leading authority on pediatric advice to mothers, L.E. Holt, also addressed the milk question. The Canadian Milk

7.5 Borden's St. Charles Milk connecting the cow to the housewife's kitchen with the provision of pure milk connecting cows and women's bodies in the space of the kitchen. Originally published 7 September 1922 in the *Hamilton Spectator*.

Commission cited the involvement of Holt in a study on the effects of pure and impure milk on infants born to mothers in tenement house dwellings in New York City.[78] Targeting mothers of tenement house dwellings, these reformers drew on assumptions that associated unfit mothers with feeding children dirty milk from dirty cows. In this period, the knowledge of milk's proper sterilization was one of the qualities of scientific motherhood, largely associated with white middle-class mothers.

Public health reformers made concerted efforts to ensure a pure milk supply in both Hamilton and Toronto. In 1908, public health reformers began to launch organized campaigns for milk reform. James Acton organized the Pure Milk League, "certified" milk was ensured at Price Farm at Erindale, and two milk stations were established in 1909. In Toronto,

J. Ross Robertson was at the forefront of implementing a pasteurization plant for the Hospital for Sick Children. Many of these milk depots also drew on the transnational connections of the milk question in looking to French "gouttes de laits" (milk stations), first developed in 1893, and the American movement for pure milk led by wealthy philanthropist, businessman, and R.H. Macy's department store owner, Nathan Straus.[79] Across England, the United States, and Canada, the education and training of maternity built on assumptions of motherhood performed in the right way by educated middle-class women. The Milk Commission in 1909 cited the cohort of "lady visitors" going to homes in England and the United States to convey knowledge of milk to mothers. In Hamilton, the Victorian Order of Nurses exemplified this tradition of "lady visitors" in milk reform.[80]

Although public health reformers drew particular attention to the milk problem as one of dirty milk and unfit mothers in the city, breast-feeding and cows also took on patriotic tones. In the early twentieth century, public health reformers like Helen MacMurchy aligned infant health with the future of the nation. Helen MacMurchy's advice to mothers cast the proper knowledge of feeding in nationalistic terms. MacMurchy dedicated her book for the mother as "the first servant of the state."[81] On the milk question, MacMurchy insisted on maternal responsibility as national responsibility, telling mothers that "you can nurse the baby, and you will do it for you know it is better for the baby, better for you and better for Canada."[82] In her book addressed to the Canadian mother, MacMurchy situated breastfeeding within concerns over beauty, insisting that "nursing will not harm the delicate mother, and, indeed, her health will be better, and the maternal organs will return to their former shape and size more quickly, when she nurses the baby."[83]

Udders and breasts entered into new relationships through early twentieth-century campaigns for pure milk. Tracing the purity of milk to its origins, public health reformers contributed to new discourses and practices which tightened connections between cow and human maternities. Public health reformers contributed to intensifying concerns surrounding impure milk. These concerns heightened the surveillance of both the body of the cow and the body of the human mother. Mothers were increasingly subjected to advice on home techniques of pasteurization or urged to pay vigilant consumer attention to "certified" milk. Moreover, the impurities of cow's milk raised the stakes for breastfeeding for mothers who were confronted with the guilty prospects of feeding their babies contaminated milk. Cow mothers and human mothers became inextricably linked within the class, racial, and sexual politics of late nineteenth and early twentieth-century Canada. Pedigreed cows were ranked along eugenic lines partly for the quality of their milk. Similarly, early twentieth-century eugenics in Canada posited fitter mothers as those among the white middle class.[84] Pedigree and quality of milk has a long history that has entangled the body of the cow and the body of the human mother. The milk question intertwined cow and human bodies in addition to urban and rural spaces as milk spilled across these terrains.

Conclusion

Amid late nineteenth and early twentieth-century movements for pure milk in urban conditions, milk overflowed beyond human/animal maternities, rural/urban space, and barn/tenement dwellings. Framed as a dangerous and potentially lethal substance, milk signified much more than a liquid but also a site for social reform, scientific knowledge, and the entangled surveillance of human and cow mothers. Milk's history is one of the problematization and fracturing of its status as nature's perfect food. Cows and human mothers have shared this history as cow barns and tenement dwellings both came onto the agenda of sanitary reform and pure milk movements. In the case of tenements, this involved the education of mothers in addition to the facilities for providing clean milk. In the case of the intertwined physiologies of cows and mothers, clean udders and nursing nipples, in addition to potential mastitis, joined these bodies through anxieties over pure milk. These historical strands of the story of milk, cows, and human mothers linger, albeit in different forms, in the present.

Currently, milk continues to be a site entrenching the reproductive bodies of women and cows in concerns over environmental conditions, global capitalist production, and sexual politics. Intimate ties across cow and human maternities are being formed in the present. The choices between breast milk and cow's milk continue to shape issues of food security. In 2010, for example, the presence of breast milk in cheese for consumers prompted the New York Health Department to shut down the Klee

Brasserie.[85] The London *Daily Mail* reported on ice cream being sold with breast milk in it. Within the last ten years, breast milk has also undergone commodification. In 2005, Prolacta Bioscience in California sold a brand of breast milk, Prolact-22, at ten times the cost of milk banks.[86] In both Canada and the United States, what has been termed the "breast milk black market" has formed through the growing commodification and biotechnological interventions in breast milk.[87] Like cow's udders, breasts have also been commodified in corporate marketing strategies in transnational networks that capitalize on associations of the breast with white middle-class motherhood, the nuclear family, and nurturing. As Samantha King has shown, corporations like Avon have seized on breast cancer advocacy as a marketing tool.[88] King shows new circuits for the flow of milk into racial and class politics, with breast cancer campaigns privileging white middle-class women survivors, obscuring the uneven distribution of access to resources for early breast cancer detection which render some breasts more important than others. Women and cow bodies also currently share the costs of intensified capitalist production, mired in new technologies that re-articulate and re-channel the flow of milk.

In addition to concerns over consumer protection, pure milk politics have drawn cow and human maternities into the politics of biotechnologies. Cows have been implicated in the prospects and dangers of biotechnologies in terms of food security in addition to the costs to the health of the cow. Dairy farmers' use of bovine growth hormones to meet growing demands for milk production has generated concerns over pure milk. Canada, in fact, followed the European Union in banning the use of an FDA-approved Monsanto drug on cows.[89] Biotechnologies have also surfaced in efforts to manipulate sex and select for female gender to ensure the birth of a milk producer and reproducer. Recently, scientists have genetically modified cow's milk to replicate human breast milk, with the first transgenic dairy bull, Herman, created to eventually produce female cows that will possess milk with human proteins.[90] The strands of eugenics for cows continue today in the valuation of the Holstein-Friesian breed for better and higher quantity milk production.

In addition, the capitalist exploitation of the body of the cow has prompted further linkages to new concerns over pure milk, infection, and the living conditions of cows. For example, mastitis in cows has been linked to the conditions of cows hooked to electronic milking machines in concrete stalls for most of their lives. Capitalist agendas of higher production have intertwined options between cow's milk and breastfeeding insofar as maternity leave policies impact on mothers' choices. Breast milk has also been mired in contemporary concerns over impure milk in the case of the greater exposure of lower-class and non-white women to the pollutants of corporations. The Mothers' Milk Project began with the protest of General Motors' dumping of pollutants, which resulted in traces of DDT in both Mohawk mothers' breast milk and the fat of Beluga whales.[91] On a global scale, the Western capitalist marketing of formula had confronted protests in the 1970s and 1980s. This marketing exalted Western superiority in feeding children over the resources and knowledge of poorer women in countries such as India.

Much as with organic food concerns over contaminants, advocates for pure milk have also interlocked human and cow bodies at the site of emotions and milk. One Wisconsin motto has urged the need to "speak to a cow as you would a lady," intimately tying the emotional sensitivity of cows to better milk production and their shared lactating kinship with nursing mothers. In 2009, an Ig Nobel Prize, a parody of the Nobel Prize, was awarded to Newcastle University researchers Catherine Douglas and Peter Rowlinson for their findings on improved milk production by cows that are given names and affection. Other research has extended maternal love to cows, indicating that cows kept among their calves also produce more milk.[92] As Deborah Valenze has claimed, "cow love is intimately tied to milk history and always has been."[93] Of course, such attention to the emotional lives of cows has drawn particular connections to mothers through priorities placed on exploiting cow maternity for milk yields. In a recent condemnation of inhumane Canadian dairy practices, Olivier Berreville has discussed the emotional trauma experienced by cows and calves at early separation to ensure that milk is not wasted on the calf.[94] This diversion of cow maternal resources further resonates with the colonial politics of the drain of maternal resources of nannies from poorer countries for the benefit of white Western middle-class families. Through a shared common fluid of milk, cow and human maternities continue to flow together.

Notes

1   Maia Boswell-Penc, *Tainted Milk: Breastmilk, Feminisms, and the Politics of Environmental Degradation* (Albany: State University of New York Press, 2006). Also, see Florence Williams, *Breasts: A Natural and Unnatural History* (New York & London: W.W. Norton, 2012).

2   Greta Gaard, "Toward a Feminist Postcolonial Milk Studies," *American Quarterly* 65, no. 3 (September 2013): 604.

3   Andrea Wiley notes that Marvin Harris divided societies into lactophiles and lactophobes. See Andrea Wiley, "Milk for 'Growth': Global and Local Meanings of Milk Consumption in China, India, and the United States," *Food and Foodways: History & Culture of Human Nourishment* 19, nos. 1/2 (January–June 2011): 11–33. Wiley shows recent shifts from earlier patterns of milk consumption when milk was symbolic of US modernity and lactase impersistence in China and India shaped the lack of milk in dietary regimens. Wiley notes that milk consumption has increased in India and China, highlighting the global spread and marketing of milk drinking.

4   Gaard, "Toward a Feminist Postcolonial Milk Studies," 609.

5   Pure milk continues to be a contentious issue in contemporary concerns over organic food, specifically calls for access to raw milk. Ron Schmid has written *The Untold Story of Milk* to highlight the changing composition of milk to make a larger point to advocate for the rights to raw milk. See Ron Schmid, *The Untold Story of Milk*, rev. ed. (Washington, DC: NewTrends, 2009).

6   Rima Apple, *Perfect Motherhood: Science and Childrearing in America* (New Brunswick, NJ: Rutgers University Press, 2006); Alice Boardman Smuts, *Science in the Service of Children, 1893-1935* (New Haven, CT: Yale University Press, 2006); Jacqueline Wolf, *Don't Kill Your Baby: Public Health and the Decline of Breastfeeding in the Nineteenth and Twentieth Centuries* (Columbus: Ohio State University Press, 2001); Katherine Arnup, *Education for Motherhood: Advice for Mothers in Twentieth-Century Canada* (Toronto: University of Toronto Press, 1994).

7   See, for example, Margaret Derry, *Ontario's Cattle Kingdom: Purebred Breeders and Their World, 1870-1920* (Toronto: University of Toronto Press, 2001); Harriet Ritvo, *Noble Cows & Hybrid Zebras* (Charlottesville and London: University of Virginia Press, 2010).

8   See, for example, Megan Davies, "Night Soil, Cesspools and Smelly Hogs on the Streets: Sanitation, Race, and Governance in Early British Columbia," *Social History/Histoire sociale* 38, no. 75 (2005): 1–35; James Opp, "Re-Imaging the Moral Order of Urban Space: Religion and Photography in Winnipeg, 1900–1914," *Journal of the Canadian Historical Association* 13, no. 1 (2002): 73–93; Ruth Engs, *Clean Living Movements: American Cycles of Health Reform* (Westport, CT: Greenwood, 2000); John Duffy, *The Sanitarians: A History of American Public Health* (Urbana: University of Illinois Press, 1990).

9   Peter Atkins, *Liquid Materialities: A History of Milk, Science, and the Law* (Burlington, VT: Ashgate, 2010), 113.

10 Marilyn Yalom, *A History of the Breast* (New York: Alfred A. Knopf, 1997).

11 On the methodology of pursuing animal history in the archives and the concept of "trace," see Etienne Benson, "Animal Writes: Historiography, Disciplinarity, and the Animal Trace," in *Making Animal Meaning*, ed. Linda Kalof and Georgina M. Montgomery (East Lansing: Michigan State University Press, 2011), 3–16. Also, see Susan J. Bearson and Mary Weismantel, "Does 'The Animal' Exist? Toward a Theory of Social Life with Animals," in *Beastly Natures: Animals, Humans and the Study of History*, ed. Dorothee Brantz (Charlottesville: University of Virginia Press, 2010), 17–37.

12 Nancy Langston, *Toxic Bodies: Hormone Disruptors and the Legacy of DES* (New Haven, CT: Yale University Press, 2010).

13 Rachel Carson, *Silent Spring* (Boston: Houghton Mifflin 1962), 23, 159, 168–69.

14 Langston, *Toxic Bodies*, viii.

15 Olivier Berreville has indicated that this mythic rural idyll of healthy happy cows in red barns and feeding in green pastures continues today in popular misconceptions of the dairy industry. Berreville notes how the dairy industry has capitalized on such scenes to promote milk consumption. See Olivier Berreville, "Animal Welfare Issues in the Canadian Dairy Industry," in *Critical Animal Studies:*

Thinking the Unthinkable, ed. John Sorenson (Toronto: Canadian Scholars' Press, 2014), 186.

16 Aleck Ostry indicates that the Canadian urban poor bore a disproportionate cost of impure milk's health effects in large cities. See Ostry, *Nutrition Policy in Canada, 1870–1939* (Vancouver: University of British Columbia Press, 2007).

17 E. Melanie Dupuis, *Nature's Perfect Food: How Milk Became America's Drink* (New York: New York University Press, 2002), 5; Michael Egan, "Organizing Protest in the Changing City: Swill Milk and Social Activism in New York City," *New York History* 86, no. 3 (Summer 2005): 205–25.

18 Ostry, *Nutrition Policy in Canada, 1870–1939*, 36.

19 E. Melanie Dupuis has indicated that keeping a "family cow" was fairly common in America's Northeast, where cows were part of the scene of towns. Dupuis, *Nature's Perfect Food*, 5.

20 Mrs. Bourniot, "Keeping One Cow, The Family Cow at the North," in *Keeping One Cow: Being the Experience of a Number of Practical Writers In a Clear and Condensed Form Upon the Management of a Single Milch Cow* (New York: Orange Judd, 1880), 9.

21 Ibid., 9–10.

22 Helen MacMurchy, "Canadians Need Milk," Department of Health, Publication No. 12 (Ottawa: F.A. Acland, 1923), 6.

23 "Milk Inspection: The Board of Health Takes a Step in This Direction." *Hamilton Spectator*, February 1888. *Milk Scrapbook*, Hamilton

Archives, Hamilton Public Library, Hamilton, Ontario.

24　Hamilton City Council Minutes, 1884–1896, 72, 84, 85. Hamilton Archives, Hamilton Public Library, Hamilton, Ontario.

25　Hamilton City Council Minutes, 1896–1907, 7. Hamilton Archives, Hamilton Public Library, Hamilton, Ontario.

26　Ibid., 9.

27　These transitions in concerns over milk and the presence of cows in the city were also taking place in Los Angeles and other cities in the United States. In 1908, the Los Angeles City Council passed an ordinance to restrict the presence of cows. There were also petitions to the council to remove cows. See, for example, Jennifer Lisa Koslow, *Cultivating Health: Los Angeles Women and Public Health Reform* (New Brunswick, NJ: Rutgers University Press, 2009), 77–79, 86–95. Also, on the association of women as mothers and the public activism of the milk question, see Jennifer Koslow, "Putting It to a Vote: The Provision of Pure Milk in Progressive Era Los Angeles," *Journal of the Gilded Age and Progressive Era* 3, no. 2 (April 2004): 111–44; Julie Guard, "The Politics of Milk: Canadian Housewives Organize in the 1930s," in *Edible Histories, Cultural Politics: Towards a Canadian Food History*, ed. Franca Iacovetta, Valorie J. Korinek, and Marlene Epp (Toronto: University of Toronto Press, 2012), 271–85.

28　Hamilton City Council Minutes, 1896–1907, 22–24.

29　Ibid., 38.

30　Hamilton City Council Minutes, 1922–1947, 118. Hamilton Archives, Hamilton Public Library, Hamilton, Ontario.

31　W.A. Wilson, *Causes of Contamination and the Care and Preservation of Milk and Cream on the Farm*, Saskatchewan Department of Agriculture Bulletin No. 15 (Regina: J.W. Reid, Government Printer, 1914), 5.

32　On milk reform politics in Saint John, New Brunswick, see Jane Jenkins, "Politics, Pasteurization, and the Naturalizing Myth of Pure Milk in 1920s Saint John, New Brunswick," *Acadiensis* 37, no. 2 (2008): 86–105.

33　Helen MacMurchy, *Special Report on Infant Mortality* (Toronto: L.K. Cameron,, 1910), 3.

34　Dupuis, *Nature's Perfect Food*, 27.

35　Elizabeth Fee points out the role of the Rockefeller foundation in the Johns Hopkins School of Hygiene. See Elizabeth Fee, *Disease and Discovery: A History of the Johns Hopkins School of Hygiene and Public Health, 1916–1939* (Baltimore and London: Johns Hopkins University Press, 1987).

36　Duncan Ferguson, *Public Health Control: Of Milk & Other Food Supplies, Combined with The Problem of Housing & Slums Elimination* (Pretoria, South Africa: Carnegie Corporation Visitors' Committee, 1936).

37　Ibid., 20.

38　Anne McClintock, *Imperial Leather* (New York: Routledge, 1995); Seth Koven, chapter 4: "The Politics and Erotics of Dirt: Cross-Class Sisterhood in the Slums," in *Slumming: Sexual and Social Politics in*

Victorian London (Princeton, NJ: Princeton University Press, 2004); Duffy, *The Sanitarians.*

39 Report of the Milk Commission 1909 (Toronto: L.K. Cameron, 1910), 40.

40 J.H. Grisdale, *Milk Production in Canada: Crop Rotations, Dairy Barns, Breeding Dairy Cattle, Feeding Care and Management of Milch Cows*, Bulletin No. 72 (Ottawa: Government Printing Bureau, 1913), 7.

41 Charles F. Whitley, *Some Notes Gleaned from the Work of the Dairy Record Centres in 1912* (Ottawa: Dairy Cold Storage Commission, 1913), 7.

42 J.A. Ruddick, *Milk for Creameries*, 2nd ed. (Ottawa: Department of Agriculture, 1902), 3.

43 Madeleine Ferrières has claimed that fears of the tubercular cow and its effects on human health did not begin to emerge until the mid to late nineteenth century, when the possibility of contamination began to be conceived. Madeleine Ferrières, *Sacred Cow, Mad Cow: A History of Food Fears*, trans. Jody Gladding (New York: Columbia University Press, 2006), 286. On this cultural role of germs, see, for example, Nancy Tomes, *The Gospel of Germs: Men, Women, and the Microbe in American Life* (Cambridge, MA: Harvard University Press, 1998).

44 Ostry notes how the urban poor were targeted as particularly prone to unsanitary living and the use of impure milk. See Ostry, *Nutrition Policy in Canada, 1870–1939*, 26, 42.

45 In the case of milk reform in Chicago, Daniel Block has made a similar claim that the milk question was feminized in the common connections between the lactating functions of cows and mothers in the particular context of urbanization. Block has addressed this issue within the larger argument that predominantly male public health reformers appropriated the authority over reproduction in consolidating their expertise over milk, simultaneously asserting patriarchal claims over cows and women. See Daniel Block, "Saving Milk Through Masculinity: Public Health Officers and Pure Milk, 1880–1930," *Food & Foodways: History & Culture of Human Nourishment* 13. nos. 1/2 (January–June 2005): 115–34. Similarly, Kara Swanson has argued that male medical practitioners engaged in the question of 'pure milk' ultimately disciplined lactating bodies, specifically in the case of technologically perfecting milk. See Kara Swanson, "Human Milk As Technology and Technologies of Human Milk: Medical Imaginings in the Early Twentieth Century United States," *Women's Studies Quarterly* 37, nos. 1/2 (Spring/Summer 2009): 21–37.

46 Dupuis, *Nature's Perfect Food*, 5. Aleck Ostry's work on nutrition policy in Canada situates prominent advocacy for breastfeeding in the context of the anxieties surrounding cow's milk. Ostry also suggests that milk depots in Toronto, Hamilton, Ottawa, and London emerged as centres for educating mothers and made the transition to child welfare clinics. See Ostry, *Nutrition Policy in Canada, 1870–1939*, 3, 35, 42–43.

47   On the concerns over wet nursing, see, for example, Jacqueline Wolf, "'Mercenary Hirelings' or 'A Great Blessing'? Doctors and Mothers and Conflicted Perceptions of Wet Nursing and the Ramifications for Infant Feeding in Chicago 1871–1961," *Journal of Social History* 33, no. 1 (Fall 1999): 97–120. On the longer history of wet nursing in the context of the eighteenth century and the racial and class politics of impure breast milk, see Ruth Perry, "Colonizing the Breast: Sexuality and Maternity in Eighteenth-Century England," *Journal of the History of Sexuality* 2, no. 2 (1991): 204–34; and Elisabeth Badinter, *The Myth of Motherhood: An Historical View of the Maternal Instinct*, trans. Roger DeGaris (London: Souvenir Press, 1981). In this eighteenth-century context, debates surrounding impure milk centred on the conditions of the wet nurse rather than conditions of the cow, focusing particularly on the importance for white middle- and upper-class mothers to breastfeed.

48   Angus McLaren, *Our Own Master Race: Eugenics in Canada, 1885–1945* (Toronto: McClelland & Stewart, 1990).

49   Tasnim Nathoo and Aleck Ostry, *The One Best Way? Breastfeeding History, Politics, and Policy in Canada* (Waterloo, ON: Wilfrid Laurier University Press, 2009),35.

50   Margaret Derry has indicated how breeding was treated as an art for generating better-quality cattle for beef or dairy purposes. Derry notes the eugenic ties to improving herds, with Mendelian genetics slowly taking effect after 1900 and the American Breeders'

Association being overtaken by eugenicists. See Derry, *Ontario's Cattle Kingdom*, 24–25.

51   On breeding Scottish cattle and Canadian connections, see M.R. Montgomery, *A Cow's Life: The Surprising History of Cattle and How the Black Angus Came to Be Home on the Range* (New York: Walker & Company, 2004), 23, 109, 113–14, 79.

52   Grisdale, *Milk Production in Canada*, 13.

53   Ibid.

54   Ibid.

55   Ibid., 19.

56   Derry, *Ontario's Cattle Kingdom*, 28.

57   Ibid.

58   Harriet Ritvo, "Possessing Mother Nature: Genetic Capital in Eighteenth-Century Britain," in *Noble Cows & Hybrid Zebras* (Charlottesville and London: University of Virginia Press, 2010), 157–76.

59   Helen MacMurchy, *The Canadian Mother's Book* (Ottawa: F.A. Acland, 1923), 69.

60   Wolf, *Don't Kill Your Baby*, 108.

61   Wolf, *Don't Kill Your Baby*, 30, 97, 92. Also, see Nathoo and Ostry, *The One Best Way?*, 30–31.

62   MacMurchy, *The Canadian Mother's Book*, 32.

63   Nathoo and Ostry, *The One Best Way?*, 29.

64   Helen MacMurchy, *Canadians Need Milk* (Ottawa: F.A. Acland, 1923), 10.

65   As Londa Schiebinger has shown, since the eighteenth century with the Linnaean classification

of mammals, lactating function became an important criterion for considering human/nonhuman kinship. In particular, Schiebinger highlights milk and the wet nursing debates as the political conditions shaping Linnaeus's choice of the term mammal, meaning "of the breast," to bind humans to animals. See Londa Schiebinger, "Chapter 2: Why Mammals Are Called Mammals," in *Nature's Body: Gender in the Making of Modern Science* (Boston: Beacon Press, 1993), 40–74.

66 Helen MacMurchy, *How To Take Care of the Baby* (Ottawa: F.A. Acland, 1923), 21.

67 MacMurchy, *The Canadian Mother's Book*, 30.

68 Ibid., 76.

69 Andrew Ebejer has noted that by the 1930s, milk was generally affordable to most low-income families. Yet rising prices after the market stabilized prompted protests that showed how milk by this time came to be regarded as essential to health. See Andrew Ebejer, "'Milking' the Consumer?: Consumer Dissatisfaction and Regulatory Intervention in the Ontario Milk Industry during the Great Depression," *Ontario History* 102, no. 1 (Spring 2010): 20–39.

70 M.E. Whalley, *Mastitis in Cows* (Ottawa: National Research Council, 1932), 1.

71 Ibid., 21.

72 Ibid., 18.

73 Kendra Smith Howard has shown that the 'pure milk' debates shifted in the mid-twentieth century to a focus on the contaminating effects of antibiotics used to treat mastitis in cows, which was associated with the dangers of human poisoning from the bacteria of the infected udder. See Kendra Smith Howard, "Antibiotics and Agricultural Change: Purifying Milk and Protecting Health in the Postwar Era," *Agricultural History* 84, no. 3 (Summer 2010): 327–51.

74 Hamilton City Council Minutes, 1922–1947, 8. Hamilton Archives, Hamilton Public Library, Hamilton, Ontario.

75 "Pure Milk for Babies – Child Life-Saving on Scientific Lines – Godsend to Mothers." *Hamilton Times*, 17 July 1909.

76 In the case of early twentieth-century Quebec, Denyse Baillargeon discusses how women's failure to breastfeed came to be construed as failed maternal and national responsibility. She notes that women had given reasons for not breastfeeding ranging from personal choice to fears of milk harming the infant to lack of milk due to overwork. See Denyse Baillargeon, *Babies for the Nation: The Medicalization of Motherhood in Quebec, 1910–1970*, trans. W. Donald Wilson (Waterloo, ON: Wilfrid Laurier Press, 2009), 34–35, 76.

77 Hamilton City Council Minutes, 1922–1947, 8. Hamilton Archives, Hamilton Public Library, Hamilton, Ontario.

78 Report of the Milk Commission 1909, 54.

79 Lawrence Weaver shows these transnational connections across Europe and the United States in terms of the different methods devised for purifying milk. See Lawrence Weaver, "Growing Babies: Defining the Milk Requirements of

Infants, 1890–1910." *Social History of Medicine* 23, no. 2 (August 2010): 320–37. Also, on the transnational dimensions of "humanizing milk," see T.B. Mepham, "'Humanizing' Milk: The Formulation of Artificial Feeds for Infants (1850–1910)," *Medical History* 37, no. 1 (July 1993): 225–49. On Nathan Straus's initiation of pure milk activism in New York City, see Julie Miller, "To Stop the Slaughter of the Babies: Nathan Straus and the Drive for Pasteurized Milk, 1893–1920," *New York History* 74, no. 2 (April 1993): 158–84.

80 "To Continue Clean Milk – Victorian Order Will Again Cooperate in the Movement," *Hamilton Times*, February 1910.

81 MacMurchy, *The Canadian Mother's Book*.

82 Ibid., 31.

83 Ibid., 30–31.

84 McLaren, *Our Own Master Race*, 32, 81.

85 Gaard, "Toward a Feminist Postcolonial Milk Studies," 602.

86 Nathoo and Ostry, *The One Best Way?*, 195. On the history of milk banks in early twentieth-century America, see Janet Golden, "From Commodity to Gift: Gender, Class,

and the Meaning of Breast Milk in the Twentieth Century," *The Historian* 37, no. 1 (Fall 1996): 75–87.

87 Nathoo and Ostry, *The One Best Way?*, 195.

88 Samantha King, *Pink Ribbons Inc.: Breast Cancer and the Politics of Philanthropy* (Minneapolis: University of Minnesota Press, 2006).

89 Deborah Valenze, *Milk: A Local and Global History* (New Haven, CT: Yale University Press, 2011), 284.

90 Nathoo and Ostry, *The One Best Way?*, 197.

91 Gaard, "Toward a Feminist Postcolonial Milk Studies," 595.

92 Ibid., 609.

93 Valenze, *Milk*, 3.

94 Berreville, "Animal Welfare Issues in the Canadian Dairy Industry," *Critical Animal Studies*, 186–207. Also, see the recent video of animal cruelty on dairy farms. "Canada's Largest Dairy Farm Employees Accused of Animal Cruelty," *Huffington Post*, 9 June 2014, http://www. huffingtonpost.ca/2014/06/09/ chilliwack- dairy–farm–animal– cruelty_n_5475953.html (accessed 22 June 2014).

Howl: The 1952–56 Rabies Crisis and the Creation of the Urban Wild at Banff

George Colpitts

In 1948, a young husky dog appeared sick and useless in its team in Cambridge Bay, Northwest Territories. Inuit hunter "Eskimo Jack" Ehakataitok pointed out the dog to Sam Carter, the local interpreter at the Hudson's Bay Company store. When Carter saw the animal running in circles and foaming at the mouth, he picked up his .30-30 rifle and shot it between the eyes.[1] A number of months later, Ottawa agricultural scientists confirmed it had been rabid. Between 1947 and 1952, a large number of sled dogs had been acting strangely after being bitten by Arctic foxes. As part of a global resurgence of rabies just after the Second World War,[2] rabies had apparently begun vectoring for some time between wild furbearers, especially as "crazy fox disease," and northern working sled dogs.[3] By 1952, it was confirmed in northern Alberta. An Arctic fox bit four sled dogs in Fort Fitzgerald that year, all later testing rabid. When foxes, wolves, and coyotes then bit large numbers of domestic cattle, hogs, and farm dogs in the Fort Vermilion region soon afterward by 1953,[4] the disease seemed to have spread well into parts of northern British Columbia, Saskatchewan, and Manitoba.

Although rabies was effectively contained in the north until 1955, when a fox strain broke out in Ontario's Little North and reached even southern Ontario districts, Alberta's northern fox rabies outbreak nevertheless constituted the largest and most complex occurrence in Canada to date.[5] Unlike earlier manifestations of the disease fought within dog populations, the 1952 outbreak was notable not only for its epidemic extent but also its more complex arcing from large and dispersed northern wildlife population pools on the peripheries of metropolitan and settled areas of Canada. For the first time, as the federal agricultural veterinarian, K.F. Wells, pointed out in 1957, rabies was pooling "in our Canadian wild animals."[6] For that very reason, the 1952–53 crisis posed great quandaries in Banff, Jasper, and Field, British Columbia. National Park towns went into a veritable red alert status with the first reports of rabies at Fort Fitzgerald, despite the considerable geographic distance to that northern Albertan town. The reasons were evident. In Rocky Mountain park towns, wildlife had gained considerable tourist and scientific value. The occasional glimpse of wildlife in towns certified an anti-modern ideal. Park superintendents and the National Parks' chief veterinarian, B.I. Love, took very seriously the possibility that rabies might infect wildlife populations so iconic in tourist experience and inestimably valuable for science. But the rabies outbreak also provided an occasion for authorities and townies to take up its chief vector, domestic dogs, and, to a lesser extent, cats, and debate exactly what place domesticated animals played in towns situated within natural national parks. The rabies crisis prompted far greater public scrutiny over these animals' roaming. If Rex the Dog, or Snowball the Cat, had always been given freedom in Banff's "pristine" nature, public attitudes began to change after 1953, and a new human ecology and relationship between animals and humans within park townsites, and other settled spaces, likely emerged thereafter.

This held especially true in that most wild metropolis, Banff. Located in the Rocky Mountains and central to Canada's emerging National Parks system after the town's establishment as a whistle stop on the Canadian Pacific Railway in 1886, Banff and its townsite had complicated the park's wilderness metanarrative from its beginnings. Many townies owned dogs, and domestic animals undoubtedly struck an ecological balance with wild animal populations nearby. In the case of Banff, the free agency and prevalence of roaming domestic dogs spatially limited, and indeed helped create, the largely ornamental wilderness experience cherished in Banff life. Dogs harried mule deer, and certainly white-tailed deer that would otherwise thrive in the edge environment of town; they drove elk from the town almost entirely; and dogs marginalized problematic wolves, coyotes, and foxes from human communities. In that respect, beyond changing popular understandings of urban animals, rabies control measures reined in dogs and cats in Banff, but in doing so, further problematized the wild–human encounter by encouraging unprecedented wildlife incursions into town life. As happened with so many parks issues in the postwar period, then, these metropolitan natures by necessity had to become more "managed" because of the medicalized threat of rabies. Indeed, what occurred in Banff and other park towns framed the larger debate around urban wildlife for most of Canada in the later twentieth century.[7]

The 1952–53 Rabies Crisis in Northern Alberta

Given the horrific suffering and death following human "hydrophobia" infection, Ottawa bureaucrats and northerners took very seriously reports of sled dog disease in 1947–49. Rabies is a viral type of the *Lyssavirus* genus. In humans, a bite from an infected host, usually through its saliva, enters the bloodstream. Although a victim initially suffers only mild symptoms of itching and prickling on the skin where biting has occurred, a fever and headache soon follows. The disease worsens as it is carried in the bloodstream to the brain, where it begins to cause inflammation and affect cognitive functions, mood, and behaviour.[8] The acute period of the disease is characterized by agonizing and largely untreatable pain and delirium. The virus colonizes the salivary glands to allow for its chief animal transmission through biting. It also, for that reason, causes muscle spasms in the throat and larynx of the infected animal or human, causing pain when swallowing. Drinking water becomes excruciating painful, eliciting an aversion in both infected animals and humans to drinking water, hence the term "hydrophobia," the historical name for the disease. Once infection has occurred, and if it is not addressed immediately with vaccines that build up a victim's immunity, the disease's incubation in the human brain is largely untreatable and death is almost always certain.[9]

Complicating the history of rabies was the wide range of behaviours exhibited by its victims. Historically, rabies panics in England from the 1830s onward coincided with moral reform movements that saw the behaviours of "wild" and "unruly" elements of society, both human and urban canine, as a larger problem of unseemly and uncontrolled behaviour in urban environments. Anti-rabies measures, whether quarantine or muzzling, enacted in legislation to eliminate rabies threats were often applied wholesale to dog populations even in areas unaffected by rabies.[10] Rabies itself could take on a number of symptomatic faces because of the wide range of its behavioural manifestation. Dogs or other animals infected with "rage" rabies turned classically "mad," acting strangely, uncharacteristically aggressively and violent. Their difficulty in swallowing made an animal foam at the mouth and bite for no reason other animals or humans; by contrast, "dumb" rabies could cause an animal to exhibit gregariousness, strong affection toward strangers, or associate itself closely with other animals with seemingly friendly intentions. This long period of amicability then changed suddenly when the animal succumbed to the mental deterioration of the disease and turned, in the end, violent and wildly aggressive.[11]

It was Louis Pasteur who, in 1885, successfully developed a vaccine to treat infected victims of rabies, using the brain tissue of infected rabbits to obtain an attenuated (or modified and therefore less virulent) strain that, once introduced through vaccine into the human body, allowed an individual to develop immunity before the infection from a bite fully incubated within the brain. At the turn of the century, vaccines improved. When the brain tissue from a human victim of rabies was finally used and repeatedly reproduced in chicken embryos, the wild virus's incubation time was reduced significantly (or "fixed") and its severity attenuated. With multiple injections of the resulting vaccine, a victim could build up resistance to a wild form of the virus that, though infecting the body, was still following a slower incubation period. This breakthrough also allowed the first dog vaccines to be developed as a key means of combatting rabies outbreaks, since dogs were traditionally the most common carrier of the virus.[12]

The outbreak of rabies among northern sled dogs in the late 1940s was taken more seriously after agriculture scientists confirmed the above-mentioned case of a rabid Arctic fox biting and infecting four sled dogs in Fort Fitzgerald in Alberta in 1952. At that point, authorities recognized that a quite unprecedented rabies pool existed in wildlife.[13] By early 1953, the disease had apparently spread via wolves, coyotes, or foxes to Fort Vermilion, located farther south and west of Fort Fitzgerald (see Figure 8.1). Vermilion had a population of approximately 30,000 people. In a community economically wedded to mixed agriculture and fur trapping, and an edge environment harbouring sizable local wildlife populations ("the whole country is lousy" with foxes, as one Fort Vermilion resident lamented in

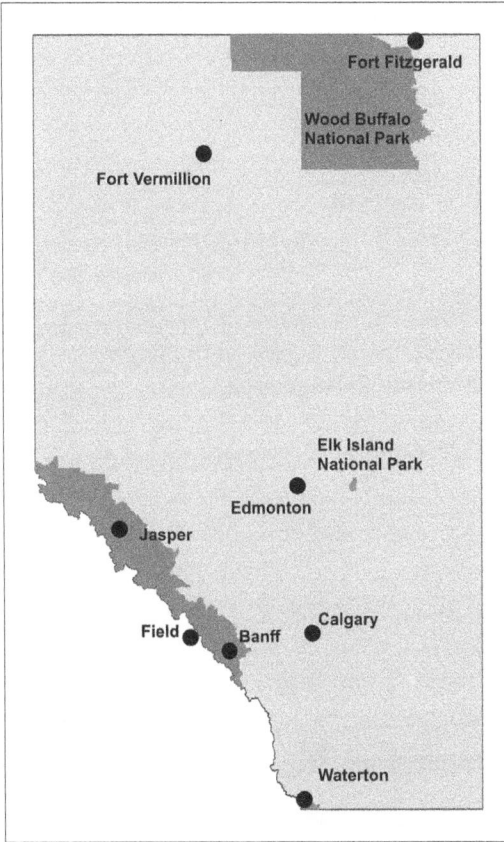

8.1 Alberta's National Park Towns, Cities, and Settlements.

the midst of the crisis in 1953),[14] the federal government struck an interdepartmental rabies task force;[15] the Alberta government, given the lead in management, mustered the Alberta Central Rabies Control Committee. Both federal and provincial committees began work just as quite alarming reports emerged from northern Alberta. By September 1952, some forty dogs, hogs, and cattle had been bitten apparently by rabid foxes, coyotes, or wolves.[16] The stories challenged the idealized and peaceable animal kingdom in Disney films of the era:[17] one wolf acting erratically and aggressively attacked the bumper of a truck driving the road to Peace River. A completely deranged 150 lb. wolf tried to chew its way through a cabin door behind which cowered a Fort Vermilion farming family.[18] In December 1952, a single rabid dog in Peace River country bit no fewer than fifteen people, all requiring the painful and multi-dose "Pasteur" treatment afterward, administered in a course of twelve doses deep into the stomach.[19] Eventually some 180 people in Alberta required the same anti-rabies vaccination after being possibly infected by suspect animals.

Veterinary and medical authorities largely contained the 1952–53 crises (ending officially in 1956 with the last confirmed laboratory case). Public education campaigns proved key in averting complete panic throughout the period.[20] It is interesting that the rabies outbreak coincided with Alberta's recently launched Norway rat control efforts, which entailed not only extensive poster campaigns but also displays of killed Norway rats at schools, fairs, rodeos, and exhibitions. Headed by the same Department of Agriculture, Alberta's anti-rat campaign focused attention on the animal itself and its relationship with humans and, above all, sought to educate Albertans to recognize and therefore kill rats they encountered. Within the visual rendering of the rat as a subject, images of the rodent elicited a broad array of emotions and responses from their audiences, from fear to vulnerability or to imagining human power to control what was presented as an economic and unhygienic pest in Alberta farm environs.[21] Unlike the rat campaign, the Alberta government's rabies information was text-based, its visualizations in brochures more often showing maps of the virus's spread from a wild north through Alberta's more settled, civilized south, and specifying remedial actions on the main potential vector in settled areas: dogs.

However, though the Alberta government's public education diverted attention away from the virus itself, textual information, bulletins, and news reports redirected most attention to wildlife. In that respect, it likely changed human–animal relationships, especially attitudes in urban settings toward wildlife. Unlike in the United States, where authorities fought a similar 1950s rabies strain primarily through a massive dog vaccination program, in Canada, and in Alberta in particular, as Christopher Rutty has pointed out, state authorities hesitated to follow suit with vaccine as a sole strategy.[22] Canadians instead used vaccine – for the first time in a widespread program – coupled with dog control programs, and, in Alberta and later Ontario, and with some controversy, wildlife "depopulation."[23]

In Canada, both federal and provincial authorities had long used leash and licensing laws as means of controlling the movement of domesticated pets in the midst of rabies outbreaks. Dogs were always part of settled communities in Canada, but their numbers usually exceeded any local capacity to control them. Beginning in the early nineteenth century, urban reform and sanitary movements often prioritized for the state the surveillance, regulation, and control of urban dogs and cats, along with horses, as part of a larger attempt to bring better order and improvement to cities.[24] In urban Toronto, efforts to assess taxes on dogs in the city started in 1832 and mandatory licensing followed in 1855. Such measures raised city revenues, identified the dogs in the urban space, and controlled their numbers.[25] Regulations sought to limit dogs from running at large and without muzzle in public places, and licensed dogs, in summer months, were required to be muzzled, with the understanding that the rabies outbreaks occurred in the hottest and driest months of the year.[26] At the same time, into much of the twentieth century, dog owners, especially those without money to pay for licences or simply lax in keeping dogs on their property or leashed, continued to make room for what can be termed as the "roaming domestic," an always-criticized free agent in urban settings. Dog agency was suddenly curtailed in periods of rabies outbreaks when authorities eliminated "strays" within settled areas.[27] Increased use of pounds in Toronto meant that more strays and unaccompanied licensed dogs could be rounded up, kept over a period of time, and destroyed if not claimed by owners.[28] However, even in 1884, the sporadic use of dog catchers, even in the summer months when the "dog nuisance" was considered most threatening, were often found wanting. Toronto could still be "overrun" with strays during these periods.[29] Certainly, the ongoing fear of rabies being carried by "curs" and strays within city limits led, at times, to hysteria and mass culls.[30]

Although dog vaccines employing attenuated and shorter incubating, "fixed" rabies strains were developed by the 1910s and used famously in Hungary and later in Japan in the interwar period, the uncertain effectiveness of early vaccines and the need for multiple injections made most Canadian medical authorities believe that the best means of controlling rabies outbreaks among dogs in settled areas was through quarantine.[31] They understood that rabies was usually imported from the United States via dogs crossing the border, often in automobile tourism. In Gatineau-Ottawa in 1925–26 and Kingston in 1927–28, public health authorities had successfully used quarantine programs to contain quite serious outbreaks, coupling them with selective animal vaccinations in farming districts. The protocol was simple. Authorities killed thousands of strays while forcing owners to tie up their domestic animals during the course of the outbreak. The common expression was to muzzle and leash "respectable" dogs during an outbreak while destroying "vagrants."[32]

A different response was needed in the 1952 outbreak. Reports indicated that rabies was pooling within wildlife, particularly fox. Although authorities were concerned that wolves, coyotes, and other predators might serve also as carriers, the particular epidemiological characteristics of northern rabies, the seemingly peculiar behaviour exhibited by foxes, and their aggressive and non-specific biting of many other domestic or wild animals made the northern fox outbreak particularly alarming.

In what is now regarded as a controversial decision, the federal government passed by 1953 an ambitious mandatory leash law across northern Canada and, for the first time, mobilized a mass, mandatory sled dog vaccination requirement (eventually administering some 100,000 doses in the north supplied by the Connaught Laboratories at the University of Toronto).[33] The campaign, implemented without Inuit and northern Aboriginal consultation, coincided with another outbreak of what was likely distemper that killed many sled teams. Inuit oral history still views the rabies campaign as a case of misguided colonization to modernize the north by moving hunting and trapping cultures dependent on dog teams into towns. Inuit memory links these early rabies vaccination programs with the ill health of their sled dogs at the time.[34]

The federal government continued to recognize the outbreak as a "dog problem" requiring traditional quarantine measures. However, since rabies was apparently pooling in wildlife, other measures were necessary. The Alberta government, headed by the agriculture department's chief veterinarian, Dr. A.A. Ballantyne, therefore also used wildlife "depopulation" (used in small programs in US states like Maine) as a means of reducing the overall disease pool. Although not intending to eliminate wildlife, depopulation as a program attempted to reduce the virus's carrying capacity into settled districts. Ballantyne employed the program on a scale never undertaken before or since. Using only recently appreciated understandings of wildlife population cycles, and recognizing the disease's vectors in fox, and potentially wolf, coyote, bear, and lynx populations, Ballantyne worked with the province's forestry branch to employ about 170 trappers to work a twinned trapline to stop the disease's southward spread.[35] By 1953, their traplines extended some 5,000 miles in length that, if stretched out end to end, as the province's media-releases emphasized, could connect Edmonton to St. John's, Newfoundland.[36] Within a year and a half, trappers killed whatever they could within their allotted lines. Although it is difficult to enumerate with certainty, the province reported that its hired trappers had trapped, shot, or poisoned some 54,000 foxes, 45,000 coyotes, 5,000 wolves, 9,850 lynx, 3,440 bears, 670 skunks, and 64 cougars.[37] By 1954, a concurrent cull in southern districts of the province hunted another 60,000 to 80,000 coyotes.[38] Using relatively new pellet strychnine guns and cyanide capsules, and now versed in medical knowledge on the safe handling of wildlife, even the roughest employed trapper was fully drawn into a High Modern, state-directed wildlife control effort.[39]

The government expert provided leadership and coordinated the state's intergovernmental response to the crisis. Government press releases, radio and newspaper stories, and the widely circulated 1953 information brochure, "Rabies," all written by Ballantyne himself, communicated the tenets of High Modernism. The brochure's text and illustrations emphasized the role of the scientific expert in diagnosing suspected cases. The text provided surprising detail on the disease's epidemiology (specifying the difference between "rage" and "dumb" strains of rabies in animals), and protocols for wardens, farmers, and even the province's hired trappers to follow when handling suspect animals. Authorities were to segregate for two weeks a dog showing odd behaviour, handle carcasses of destroyed suspected animals with rubber gloves, pack heads in leakproof containers, and dispatch them with brains intact to the Lethbridge, Alberta, provincial veterinarian laboratory. The brochure insisted that as a matter of course, all dogs should be kept on leash; they were also to be vaccinated. And in cases where suspected dogs were destroyed, their carcasses were to be buried deeply so that other animals could not consume them as carrion.[40]

The agriculture department concurrently controlled and quarantined dogs in large urban communities far from the source of infection. In Edmonton and Calgary, veterinarians, physicians, and nurses led publicity campaigns to promote annual dog and cat licensing programs, as well as to encourage owners to voluntarily have their animals vaccinated. The rabies scare certainly helped authorities tighten urban licensing programs. They also more effectively rounded up, pounded, and destroyed strays within communities. Perhaps most importantly, the 1952–56 period shifted popular understandings, if not misgivings, about wildlife in urban areas. Wild animals were explicitly understood as potential carriers of rabies. Medical authorities, reaching for the first time many rural, First Nations, and Metis communities in the early 1950s, similarly sharpened sensibilities toward wildlife as a potential medical threat. By May 1953, veterinarian experts had briefed thousands of Albertans at information sessions; many had heard of "an increase in rabies among lynx," a "rabid fox" cornering a Fort Vermilion farmer, a "queer bear" roaming near Keg River ("queer" connoting at the time abnormal behaviour in the animal), moose at Upper Hay River acting strangely, and even suspect mice biting trappers' toes in their beds.[41] Experts in Calgary, Edmonton, and Banff also stressed how the fox rabies could be carried by wild birds and animals, meaning that, effectively, all wildlife could be understood as wild viral carriers. Lethbridge laboratory testing further demonstrated that virtually all forms of wildlife had been affected by the northern rabies, including beaver, fox, coyote, wolves, bear, lynx, moose, rabbit, cats, dogs, cows, and pigs (see Figure 8.2).[42] The potential disease pool, then, was massive, as suggested in a news report, ghostwritten by Ballantyne himself, that "Cow, Bear, Fox are Stricken; Proven Rabid Animals Total 57."[43]

In community halls and church basements, nurses, doctors, and veterinary authorities used persuasive visual evidence in slide presentations and films to drive home the point. By the end of information meetings, authorities urged those attending to pick up rifles and shoot any coyote or wolf on sight. Such experts also had on hand for distribution, free of charge, modern "coyote getter" traps and strychnine bait equipment. By Ballantyne's own admission, the information sessions were to visually and even emotionally move audiences. Whatever its traumatic consequences, Ballantyne included an 8-minute 1929 Britannia film (long out of circulation but reprinted for the purpose) in his travelling information settings. For viewing only when "a medical doctor, public health nurse or veterinarian is in attendance," the footage showed a rabies-infected child in the United States six hours before his death from the disease. It "isn't pleasant to look at but on the other hand it isn't too gruesome," Ballantyne told the Deputy Minister of Agriculture approving the film's purchase. If used "judiciously" the film could help "where people are not tying up their dogs or taking no action in poisoning coyotes."[44] Besides the showings in northern

Species	June 1952 to December 31, 1953		1954		1955	
	Lab.	Clinical (Approx.)	Lab.	Clinical (Approx.)	Lab.	Clinical (Approx.)
Cattle	10	70	11	8	7	1
Hogs	5	150	8	6	6	6
Horses	0	20	1			
Sheep	2	20	4	3		
Dogs	30		9		7	
Cats	8		2		3	
Bear	1					
Beaver	2					
Coyote	18		13		20	
Fox	23		2		3	
Lynx	3				1	
Moose	1					
Rabbit	1					
Weasel	1					
Wolf	1					
TOTAL	106	260	50	17	47	7
GRAND TOTAL—	1952-53—approx. **366;**		1954—approx. **67;**		1955—approx. **54.**	

8.2 Laboratory and clinical testing for rabies in Alberta wildlife, 1953–55, *Annual Report of the Department of Agriculture of the Province of Alberta for the year 1955* (Edmonton; 1955).

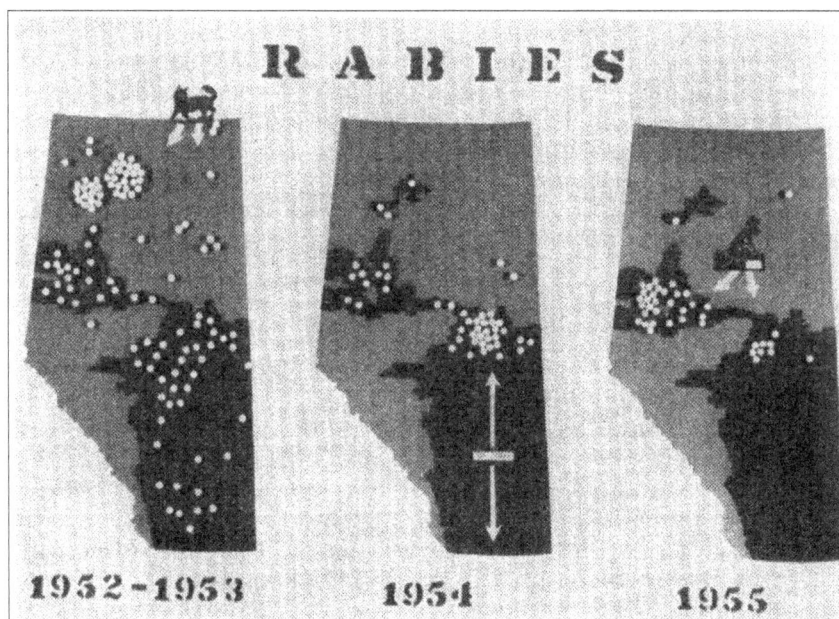

8.3 The Alberta Agriculture Department's visual depiction of the rabies "front" and the apparent success of its "wildlife depopulation" efforts to contain the outbreak. The white dots represent clinical and laboratory confirmations of rabid animals. Report of the Veterinary Services Branch, *Annual Report of the Department of Agriculture of the Province of Alberta for the year 1955* (Edmonton; 1955).

Alberta, the film was part of the information sessions in Lethbridge, Calgary, Red Deer, Edmonton, and Grand Prairie.[45]

The publicity around the epidemic, then, had a significant imaginative dimension (see Figure 8.3). It helped sustain a poison-baiting predator program in settled areas and northern affected places for years afterward. First Nations' own understanding of wildlife, particularly of Arctic fox, was likely affected by such work.[46] Education campaigns likely explain the popular suspicion that a bear, mauling one Banff family in 1958, could be thought of as rabid until proven otherwise.[47] At the very least, the public education programs, and later medical and veterinarian studies confirming the cyclical nature of rabies in urban park species such as raccoon and other wild animal and bird populations, helped sharpen public sensibilities.[48] It is no exaggeration to say that from 1953 onward, Canadians began to think of wildlife and wildlife in urban spaces, whatever their intrinsic and ecological value, as potentially rabid.

National Parks and metropolitan animals in Banff, Jasper, and Field

Central to rabies control campaigns was a mandatory leash law in both farm rural and town settings in northern Alberta. It was also promoted in urban areas such as Calgary and Edmonton. It was understood as absolutely essential in the National Parks. Mandatory leashing could prove to be "a blessing to get rid of a large number of stray dogs," Ballantyne wrote at one point, pleased that some sixty strays had been killed in the Peace River townsite as a precaution by September 1953. He believed that such rabies control would help rid problematic strays from all areas of the province, as "this could apply to most cities, towns and villages in Alberta."[49]

In Fort Vermilion, where the leash law was particularly enforced by RCMP and forest rangers, and especially among sled dogs within the community, however, mandatory leashing challenged longstanding relationships between domestic dogs, farmer/trapper populations, and the comparatively large numbers of wild animals that thrived in the forest edge within settled environments. In a region where only up to half of land was being taxed and only half of that was actually in cultivation, these northern spaces had much room for large populations of wild animals, including coyotes, wolves, and bears.[50] Dogs in Fort Vermilion and in the outlying farm community went largely off leash in such circumstances. They kept wild animals out of farm and town properties; off-leash dogs accompanied and protected children walking to school in the morning. The roaming domesticate was, as a government appointee in the Fort Vermilion area pointed out – complaining of the leash law now applied in his environs – central to life in these settlements. "Farmers want their dogs free, because dogs keep coyotes and bears and other dogs away from their farmsteads, because dogs keep livestock where farmers intend them to stay, because trained dogs watch for hawks and other birds ready to pounce on chickens."[51]

But nowhere was the debate about the "free roaming" domestic more acute than in Canada's western National Parks. News of the positive rabies diagnosis in Fort Fitzgerald, though actually distant from any of the southern National Parks in Alberta, was sent immediately in a circular letter to all western parks superintendents in 1952, along with an American information pamphlet on the characteristics and epidemiology of rabies.[52]

The circular's arrival at Jasper deeply alarmed townsite officials. When the Alberta government extended its "quarantine" zone north to the 55th parallel by early 1953, ordering all dogs leashed or chained, and vaccinated, the superintendent understood that his park, closest to the affected area, was most vulnerable to infection if the virus escaped such measures. He immediately asked Dr. B.I. Love, the superintendent and veterinarian expert at Elk Island National Park, to head up a control program for Jasper. Love had already taken measures to protect domestic and wild animals at his own park, including a coordinated trapline system. He circulated a lengthy report on the disease's manifestations in dogs, cats, horses, and wild animals, as well as brief summaries of the behaviour of rabid foxes in northern Alberta. Love also stressed the importance of preserving and sending heads of suspected animals to the province's veterinarian service for testing.[53]

Jasper wardens and the RCMP began rounding up and destroying strays within the park, a policy encouraged in the other parks nearby, including Yoho and Banff.[54] The superintendent also ordered that wolves, coyotes, and foxes be destroyed. Wardens were to shoot on sight such animals, especially around settled spaces, and "special efforts must be taken to destroy any of these animals which have become tame and are accustomed to feed on refuse near wardens' cabins."[55] With a mandatory vaccination program now planned, park gate staff demanded from visitors to see a recently issued certificate indicating that a dog or cat entering the park had been vaccinated in the previous six months. In the case of dogs, owners were required to purchase a park licence (reduced to a $1) for their animal; and owners of cats and dogs were made aware of the rule that they could not be off leash at any time.[56]

By February 1953, Ottawa's rabies control committee had advised the National Parks branch to reanimate a long-dormant leash law for all resident dogs and order their mandatory vaccination. Such vaccines, supplied either by the American Lederle Laboratory in the United States or Toronto's Connaught Laboratories, benefited from recent breakthroughs in attenuating live rabies strains, and delivering it in three rather than multiple doses.[57] Dr. Love accordingly headed up the parks' vaccination program, initially sending some 400 doses of vaccine to Yoho by rail from Vancouver. He coordinated dates to administer the vaccine thereafter at Jasper, Field, Radium Hot Springs, and Banff. In the town of Banff, the mandatory vaccine program in fact went a long way to better implementing the licensing program, long on the books but often overlooked by pet owners. There was immediately a 72 per cent increase in dog licensing when owners followed the mandatory vaccination under Love's supervision.[58]

All dog owners presented their pooches at the appointed time for the first of three vaccines. For Yoho, the park superintendent prepared his own park's publicity for the mandatory vaccination, and included cats, "due to the fact that many persons in western Canada have been bitten by rabid cats."[59] In February 1953, Love vaccinated some 40 dogs in that town alone;[60] 36 received their third vaccination in August.[61]

In Banff, there were many more dogs. The mandatory vaccination program caught the attention of the *Calgary Herald*, which carried front-page coverage, including a photograph of dogs lining up for treatment (see Figure 8.4). "Big dogs, little dogs, dogs with pedigrees and dogs without," the *Calgary Herald* reported, "in fact all dogs" made their way to Banff's warden equipment depot on the Saturday of the first of three vaccines. About 200 dogs were vaccinated on the first day.[62] This "veritable parade of local canines – all on leashes, chains or bits of string," waited about 45 minutes for Love's vaccination, the *Crag and Canyon*, Banff's own local newspaper, reported.[63]

WITH RABIES MOVING SOUTH AMONG INFECTED WILDLIFE in the north of the province at the rate of about 40 miles a month, dogs are being vaccinated against the dread disease. Here, dog-owners bring their pets to the mass vaccination program Saturday at Banff. Dogs are regarded as the most likely contact between humans and infected wildlife, though the disease, which affects all warm-blooded animals, may be transmitted by any animal which bites — including horses.

8.4 The *Calgary Herald*'s coverage of Banff's mandatory dog vaccination program, February 23, 1953. Courtesy of Glenbow Archives.

Vaccination was one thing. Keeping dogs leashed and cats indoors, however, was another. The related order that "no dogs are to be allowed to run free and must remain on a leash or otherwise confined. No movement of dogs into the park will be allowed" was more difficult to see through.[64] Often accompanying tourists with the advent of the automobiles in the park system, dogs and cats had fit problematically into the wild animal patina developed in the National Parks, especially in town settings. Licensing regulations were harsh against domesticated animals from the start, since from an official perspective they threatened the sanctuary offered to wildlife in parks. Quite simply, the domesticated animal ran amok in paradise. A 1946 park regulation was clear: dogs found chasing game were to be shot on sight by wardens. Specific breeds could not be licensed in the National Park system: "any breed termed as a hunter, such as police, husky, Airedale, hound or crosses of any such breed," could not be licensed for Canada's park system at all, since these breeds were suspected of making the greatest impact on resident wildlife.[65]

There is little evidence that wardens applied earlier legislation against certain breeds or even interfered a great deal with dog owners, especially those arriving in summer as tourist pet owners. But with the rabies threat in 1953, parks branch officials resolved not to discriminate between hunting and other dog breeds, since "under conditions of freedom, almost any dog follows a natural instinct to hunt" and to apply the controls against them without exception, by implication meaning that all dogs would require greater control and leashing within the park at all times.[66]

The crisis certainly raised to a head the need to better control cats, largely ignored altogether by parks officials and tolerated only because townspeople insisted on bringing them with them to their park lifestyle. Traditionally viewed as inappropriate in the parks, cats were licensed only at a rate set intentionally high – a whopping $5 a year – to deter town citizen cat ownership altogether. By 1953, all admitted that the high licence fee had no deterrent effect; Banff officials had stopped enforcing cat licensing altogether,[67] and town residents simply saw the fee as unjust and usually did not buy one. All the same, since it was still seen that cats "are generally hunters and in the vast majority of cases are a menace to bird life and small mammals," parks officials still saw licensing as a means of limiting cat numbers. Initially, it was thought prudent to allow only one cat licence per household, a view later changed to two, and the cat licence fee was dropped to a still relatively high fee of $3.[68]

The *Calgary Herald*, reporting on the vaccination, however, caught the spirit of the urgency of the measures. It noted that a 24-hour watch was in effect at Banff's townsite for rabid animals; coyotes were being culled, and Elk Island National Park was maintaining a five-man trapline of some 75 miles through its woodlands to depopulate it of potential wild carriers.[69] In Yoho, the chief warden reported six coyotes shot on sight along the *cordon sanitaire* it had established near Field townsite, "under instructions as precautionary measure against possible means of spreading rabies."[70] Wolf and coyote culling, mostly through trapping but also through poisoning, was carried largely near settlements, as they "might be a possible danger should rabies develop in the wildlife in the park."[71]

The Problem of Off-Leash Dogs and Cats

The fundamental problem was, however, that despite leash laws on the books, wardens had long not enforced them and town residents had grown accustomed to flouting them in Canada's parks. Wardens back to 1943 acknowledged their concern that resident dogs, especially, were running free and doing considerable damage to wildlife. Unlike the tourist's dog, one warden stated, it was resident dogs, "those whose permanent homes are in or near one of the parks [that] do much more harm throughout the year if permitted to run at large." He stated that it was not necessary to demonstrate that they ran deer, bear, and other large animals, since everyone knew that they did. In writing yet more instructions to wardens to clamp down on the situation, he pointed out that unleashed dogs were able to "chase small mammals or birds, to find and destroy birds' nests, to alarm visitors or to cause other mischief."[72] However, by the eve of the outbreak, there is every indication that whatever official sanctions existed against animals roaming free, there was little control over Banff's dog populations. Culturally wired into Banff life was a tradition of owning dogs and allowing them to roam.

Whatever officials wanted, dog owners rarely curbed their animals' freedom. In 1951, before the rabies outbreak, a concerned citizen was peeved by the "large number of dogs running loose in Banff and out of control . . . upsetting garbage, running and chasing the deer and even attacking people." The same citizen reported many individuals breeding dogs and raising puppies for sale to other Banff citizenry in a largely underground trade.[73] In 1953, now with rabies a new threat to wildlife, a member of the Banff Advisory Council was frank in admitting that "a large number of people" in Banff "were not co-operating in the control measure." He said that "previous to now all dogs in the townsite have been running at large" and wardens who might have applied the leash law tended to return dogs "to the owners with an apology, rather than having the owners prosecuted."[74]

In 1954, the Banff superintendent continued the policy of returning loose dogs and charging owners rather than impounding their pooches.[75] The town's position was to simply fine dog owners after impounding and returning off-leash dogs, without formally charging owners.[76] Even by February 1955, the Banff Advisory council, composed of citizen leaders and the parks superintendent, received "a number of complaints" from dog owners when they received phoned rather than hand-delivered summonses to appear in court after wardens saw their dogs running at large.[77] Many cited dog owners were clearly ready to test the law in the courts if need be since they had not had an opportunity of reviewing the evidence or contesting the citations handed them.

Even in 1957, one citizen complained about "the large number of dogs which are running loose in his particular area of the townsite," to which the park superintendent assured him that "wardens now have a drive on to eliminate this nuisance."[78] The superintendent at Yoho found Field residents initially non-compliant in the rabies control measure, to the point where "there have been several dogs roaming unrestrained throughout the town." In 1954, wardens attempting to enforce the leash law were contending with one woman who, despite their "verbal warnings" on 16, 18, and 19 February in 1954, still let her dog run at large. The wardens finally destroyed the dog on 23 February 1954.[79] No less uncooperative was another woman whose dog was reported by wardens at large on 16 and 18 February, then sighted it at 9:10 a.m. on the 22nd. Wardens then made early morning and late evening sightings of the same dog running around town on the following 23, 24, 25, 27 February and 1 March.[80] The superintendent records indicate just how many dogs were off leash in mountain park towns as wardens attempted to enforce the leash law. In Field, wardens sighted five dogs running free in town on 16 February alone.[81] It is no surprise that the same dog owners letting dogs off leash were also reported on lists of dog owners not licensing their animals in Yoho as well.[82]

Having already taken the step of barring all domestic dogs and cats from restaurants and eateries in September 1952,[83] the Banff Advisory Council supported the more robust application of leash laws. The superintendent initially briefed the council in October about the rabies outbreak and the threat it posed to parks wildlife. One councilman stated that "it was about time some dog control measures were adopted in the park."[84]

The council even wondered whether the large numbers of crows and magpies in the town presented a possible rabies threat as carriers, suggesting that an organized cull should be mounted.[85]

But it was the cat populations in parks that were the first to really be affected by the turn toward greater regulation. The Banff council was alarmed that immediately after the rabies outbreak was announced, apparently with no warning to Banff citizens, wardens began enforcing the leash law against cats. The council was alarmed by reports that wardens were applying "the control measures to cats and proceeded with a program of capture and destroying cats running at large."[86] The Banff *Crag and Canyon* then fully blew the lid off the cat killing occurring.[87] As an outraged citizen wrote in the *Crag and Canyon*, admittedly, "there were too many stray cats in Banff," but she was aghast at the "high handed action of pursuing an order to shoot all cats" not on their owner's property, "regardless of whether they were well-bred and valuable pets, or not."[88] The letter writer urged all Banff citizenry "who love justice," whether they loved cats or not, to attend the next Banff Advisory Council meeting, where citizens were given a forum to air grievances with parks officials.

The very question of the "rights of cats and cat owners in a national park" thereafter began to animate council meetings.[89] Similarly controversial was the council's attempt to redress the high cat licensing fee, when the superintendent defending the rate said that it discouraged cat ownership in Banff "because cats were not welcome in the National Park." The *Crag and Canyon* also reported parks officials' comments that wardens had a right to enter any home in Banff and remove unlicensed pets from "door steps or even inside homes." One "authority" had apparently even stated that since home owners were renters within the townsite "residents have no rights in this matter" to say otherwise.[90]

A townsperson attending one meeting claimed that wardens were using steel traps to take the free-roaming cats, "the speaker claiming to have found a cat in one . . . in an alley between Banff Avenue and Bear Street."[91] Although the parks superintendent disclaimed "all knowledge" that wardens were resorting to steel traps, he did admit that wardens were using "box traps" humanely before destroying the animals.[92] That meeting coming to a close ("one of the liveliest and most heated public discussions of the year," as the *Crag and Canyon* reporter attending it said[93]), the commissioner finally relented. He stated that "in view of the opposition which had developed," he would delay cat measures until 1 April, in the meanwhile "giving the matter thorough publicity."[94] The time would permit cat owners to have their animals properly licensed, and after that wardens would "trap and destroy any unlicensed cats." The *Crag and Canyon* ran a front-page article headlined "Cat Trapping Stops 'Til April 1st"[95]

However offensive the park's measures against cats were, the *Crag and Canyon* largely defended the warden service's clamp-down. Its editorial chided letter writers who sneered at the "brave wardens going after people's pets with guns," when pet owners should consider the horrid nature of rabies as a threat to human life if loosed within Banff's wildlife population. The newspaper repeated what parks officials were stressing, that once introduced, rabies could be carried in all of the parks' wildlife and bird populations, and wreak havoc on one of the parks' most important tourist assets.[96]

But the newspaper could not stifle Elsie McCowan, a Banff citizen. She dismissed the park's stance against strays simply as "a poor excuse to get rid of cats" in the park. She intended to license her own cat, but "I have no intention of keeping my pet chained up. So What?"[97] And there is much evidence that, at least initially, many Banff citizens followed suit. In November 1953, a letter writer by the name of "Fed Up" noted that despite the recent announcement by the chief superintendent to see dogs leashed in the community, "the Town of Banff is still infested with free running cats both stray and otherwise . . . These cruel, slinking creatures are allowed to run free and stalk and kill hundreds of song birds and semi-tame squirrels every year."[98] The writer queried whether anyone else in the town had noticed that there were hardly any song birds to be heard. As far as the leash law, it "had long been a law in the park" but rarely enforced, and "there are probably very few Banff people, pet owner or not, who have not breathed a sigh of relief at the conspicuous absence of stray and loose dogs about the streets the past few weeks"[99] as wardens now began enforcing it.

Rabies Controls and the New Urban Wild

The *Crag and Canyon* welcomed the enforcement of the leash law now being applied against cats. Its editor, Norman Luxton, was also relieved that there was an indication that wardens were taking more seriously the dog regulations. With dog owners "threatened with destruction of their pets if they were found unleashed," the newspaper pointed out that the "streets devoid of dogs this week were testimony that residents paid careful heed to the warning."[100] By March 1953, the RCMP were at least making test cases out of six local residents running their dogs free by prosecuting them.[101] Indeed, by 1958, wardens were no longer issuing just warnings. They were convicting with greater consistency and reporting at each Advisory Council meeting the numbers of warnings and prosecutions given to animal owners, and how many cats and dogs they destroyed. That year, one meeting learned that seven warnings were issued to animal owners, one resident was fined, and four unlicensed cats were destroyed. The administration had identified "habitual offenders" who would to be instructed to remove their animals from the park if they continued to allow them off leash.[102] In the first months of 1958, wardens had "considerably tightened" the leash law, with three prosecutions and ten warnings given to dog owners allowing them freedom off the leash, and destroying "four loose cats."[103] In February, they issued eight warnings and three prosecutions for "loose animals in the townsite,"[104] and in April, they destroyed one dog and two cats, and laid two charges against dog owners and four warnings.[105] When the council took up the case of a woman walking her dog on leash being knocked down by two off-leash dogs, the superintendent reassured members that "the problem of dogs roaming the streets has been considerably reduced," and that wardens would be instructed to enforce the regulations "more severely."[106] The superintendent was likely anxious to see his wardens doing the job before some citizens did it for them. At least one Banff citizen seems to have poisoned two dogs, likely running off leash, in the townsite in 1957.[107] Between the last months of 1958 to 1960, wardens consistently enforced the leash law. Convictions were highest in winter months, when dog owners likely ran their dogs free instead of walking them. But the overall decline in convictions in summer months suggests that dog owners, in particular, were responding to the new requirement[108] (see Figure 8.5). By 1960, when there were 3,000 year-round residents at Banff, its summer population grew to 18,000. There were now 223 licensed dogs and 220 licensed cats; and perhaps 3,266 "transient" dogs and cats brought by tourists into the park, practically all of them procuring park licences.[109]

The citation written to a dog owner in the period suggests the new expectations. In one of its only letters written as a warning in 1958 to

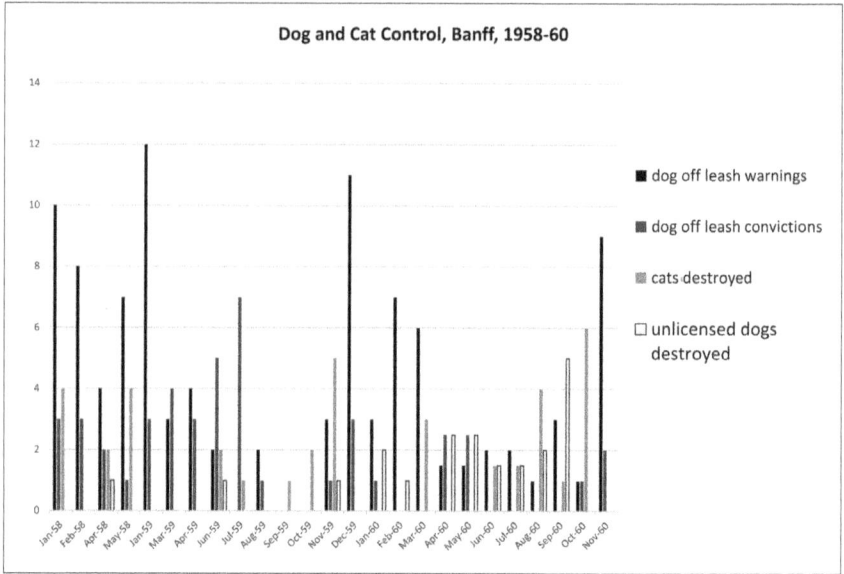

Dog and Cat Control, Banff, 1958-60

Legend:
- dog off leash warnings
- dog off leash convictions
- cats destroyed
- unlicensed dogs destroyed

8.5 Dog and Cat control in Banff, 1958–60. Compiled from Banff Advisory Council Minutes, RG 84, A-2-a, vol. 966, File B155, parts 5-8. Library and Archives Canada.

a Field resident, the superintendent pointed out that "your dog running at large has been the source of many complaints. Yesterday afternoon at about 5:15, I witnessed your dog chasing a deer. The deer crashed through a fence causing injury and suffering to the deer, and extensive property damage to a neighbour's fence. This cannot be tolerated in a park."[110] By the 1960s, the warden service had clearly raised the issue of dogs "worrying" the deer within the townsite.[111] It became something of a celebrated case in Field when a young fawn "was savaged by dogs in the Township" and the superintendent appealed to the public to identify the dogs in question in order to prosecute their owners.[112]

But leashing dogs likely brought in train numerous human ecological changes to townsites. Dogs enjoying their liberty had run out deer. They had eliminated most elk in towns like Banff for decades, even when their numbers rose elsewhere in the park. Because they were pack animals and could hold some of their own against large dog populations, there seems to have been a "heavy" coyote population of likely around twenty-five animals in Banff by 1951. They were "harassing and probably destroying mule deer" seen in the townsite and the golf course. "These deer are an attraction for visitors and it is very desirable that the small population, not in excess of twenty scattered animals" were protected from coyote that year.[113] Soon after, eleven coyotes were shot by rangers. However, coyotes likely maintained at best a small "resident" presence throughout its history and it was likely the large number of dogs roaming Banff townsite that kept coyote numbers so low and mule deer numbers miniscule. Indeed, there were only eleven reported sightings of such deer – and none of white-tailed – by rangers in 1953 while dogs still ran off leash in large numbers;[114] elk was nonexistent in the townsite, whereas the animals could be sighted in numbers of 250 and more in the Ya Ha Tinda area in March of that year, 39 in Cascade in November, and 65 at Bankhead in April.[115] Moose were seen only as close as the Bow Valley, but not in town at all. There were about 16 black bear sighted at the Banff dump.[116]

As the leash law was more regularly enforced, wildlife not harassed by free-roaming domestic dogs appeared in larger numbers in town. In 1957, at least one property owner in Banff felt the Banff townsite should pay for "repairs to property damaged by big game."[117] The Advisory Council soon asked for the Department's policy "regarding property damaged by wild animals," and that the question was not dismissed outright likely reflects some of the changing human and wildlife ecology of town life.[118]

A growing problem with greater dog control was that coyotes now enjoyed greater liberty in Banff.[119] By 1958, the Banff Advisory Council had received "several" complaints regarding the "annoyance caused by coyotes." The council took from the reports that the animals were "infesting the town in considerable numbers." They usually came into the town at night and went into backyards looking for food, "and when one of them starts to howl he seems to set off all the others, they thus cause a good deal of annoyance to the residents of the town throughout the night." They had apparently grown in such numbers that they were, ironically, attacking dogs tied up out of doors during the night.[120] In 1959, the park service had shifted from selective culling (requesting to kill a certain number of animals) into believing that "there is only one course of action to be taken to reduce the number of coyotes in and around the townsite and that is to destroy them." The methods to be adopted: strychnine and shooting.[121] Coyotes now "roaming the streets of Banff" near the Bow River were so prevalent during the night and early morning that Banff's citizens were in an uproar; a persistent rumour, disavowed by parks officials but given credence from the *Crag and Canyon*, was that a wolf was also ranging within the townsite as well.[122] The newspaper even reported that mothers along Cave Avenue were keeping preschool children indoors "for fear they will be attacked by coyotes which are roaming the area." One resident on Cave Avenue even saw a pack of six coyotes "feeding on the carcass of a deer which they had dragged onto the street in front of her house."[123]

The other, obvious issue, was more threatening: a growing "nuisance" bear population. Now a "much discussed problem," bears were upsetting garbage containers along town alleys, having expanded their frequentation of the nearby dump.[124] It was indeed in 1959 when the parks branch began more assiduously prosecuting "residents or park visitors molesting or feeding the bears."[125] They likely needed to do so. That year, youths in town used firecrackers to startle a black bear likely nosing around garbage for food, causing it to crash through a fence on Lynx Street.[126]

Bears and coyotes were only a part of a larger, complex, wildlife invasion. Banff citizenry were contending with a sizable and growing elk population in town limits. In 1955, the Banff Advisory Council was concerned that "a large bull elk with a deformed antler has been roaming the streets,"[127] and in the next year it took up the unsubstantiated report that "someone had been attacked by an elk" near a local establishment.[128] When the national park began to slaughter elk to reduce the park's overall herd numbers in 1958 and 1959, it was slaughtering animals right within town limits. Citizens were "offended" on more than one occasion having to step over the slaughter offal wardens left on Banff streets.[129] Wardens began formally culling problem elk populations in 1959. It is indicative that they killed no fewer than 36 animals in the Banff townsite that year: 12 adult males, 12 adult females, 3 male calves and 4 female calves. There were another 5 males and 2 females killed on the Banff Springs Hotel golf course.[130]

Conclusion

Scholars have only begun to examine the 1952–56 rabies crisis in northern Canada.[131] In the present historiography, Alberta was "allegedly threatened" by wolf rabies in this outbreak, and the undue fear prompted National Parks administrators to carry out intensive wolf and coyote culling and "blanket" Jasper and Banff with poison.[132] Predator control in parks like Banff, moreover, is perceived to have "owed more to lupophobia than hydrophobia. Humans appeared far more frenzied than wolves" in the response of officials to rid the parks of the rabies threat in its wild canid carriers.[133] However, scholars risk obscuring the reality of the outbreak and even its magnitude by such an approach.[134] The 1952–56 outbreak was the first of many rabies outbreaks vectoring from wildlife populations, and, in the subsequent years, vectoring from wildlife within urban and settled spaces. Campaigns to control its various manifestations arguably developed a new relationship between humans with wildlife, especially in urban environments. Although even at the time Ballantyne's program of wildlife depopulation, on such a large scale, was questioned in terms of its efficacy, it was likely his agriculture department's widespread publicity about the threat of wildlife rabies that impacted popular imaginations and, in turn, understandings of wildlife. In urban and rural areas, information campaigns had reinforced a very different conceptualization of wildlife as a potential disease threat.

For better or worse, this medicalized understanding of wildlife suggests some of the ways humans have accommodated, if at arm's length, wild creatures in their settled spaces. National Park towns present an early example of the new urban wild that became idealized in postwar planning to provide more ecologically diverse town and urban spaces. Banff and other National Park towns located within wildlife refuges and sanctuaries were, ironically, very different places in periods when dogs still ran off leash. Since leash laws and restrictions were rarely applied to residents and high-paying tourists during summer months, dogs likely shaped ecologies of these mountain town wonderlands. Rabies changed all that. The 1952–56 crisis made dog and cat control a priority for the Banff Advisory Council and the chief superintendent. Wardens finally enforcing leash laws, however, inadvertently prompted an ecological transformation in the same towns. Undoubtedly the larger numbers of deer, elk, bear, and coyote that made their way into townsites changed tourist and resident expectations. The myriad of postwar postcards and tourist pictures of deer, elk, and even bears within Banff, Jasper, Field, or Waterton suggests what visitors came to take for granted in a National Park experience. Now even in populated centres, tourists encountered wild animals right at the very doors of their town hotels and within town green spaces.

But that poses further questions about similar wildlife invasions in other urban areas. New and growing wildlife populations within urban spaces in the postwar period have enlarged potential disease pools. As a recent study indicates, urban planning that encourages ecological diversity has prompted the setting aside and management of more greenbelts, parks, and walking trails. That has increased the potential pooling of rabies, West Nile virus, and bovine tuberculosis within newly re-established and very urbanized wild animal populations. Humans now in "greener" cities are, in fact, at greater risk of diseases pooling in coyotes, raccoons, skunks, and red foxes, either through their direct contacts with these animals or their own pets'.[135] Ironically, while rabies vaccination and control legislation in the twentieth century has led to a remarkable decline in dog rabies cases, wildlife rabies cases have increased significantly.[136] The very large population densities of such species as raccoons in urban contexts, likely far greater than in their rural and "wild" environments, allow for significant rabies pooling within urban populations that pose threats to humans and non-urban wildlife populations.[137]

Authorities, then, undoubtedly contained rabies by the mid-1950s in Alberta. But in so doing, they did much to change attitudes and understandings of wildlife in urban and rural settings. Alan MacEachern argues that National Parks always balance use with preservation, and the greater use of natural spaces required greater management;[138] rabies control as part of that management entailed a new imagination of wildlife within towns. In addition to greater predator control, the state promoted new public sensibilities to discourage feeding problematic "highway bum" bears now more prevalent in townsites; it tried to keep tourists from getting too close to highly dangerous elk and moose now showing up regularly in dog-controlled towns. And residents were now constantly reminded to mind their own business as they shared space with a greater variety of wildlife from skunks to red foxes ornamenting town life.[139] Most metropolitan spaces now control domestic animals far more effectively than they have in the past. In many settings, that has only invited a new wildlife presence, and with it, a new complex relationship with wildlife-carried rabies at the very doorsteps, and within the mindsets, of Canadians in settled, town, and urban settings.

Notes

1 Library and Archives Canada (hereafter LAC), RCMP G Division to Mitchell, 16 February 1948, RG 17, vol. 4362, file 71, "Rabies 1946–1953," f. 106380.

2 Horrific rabies outbreaks had occurred in eastern Europe during the war. Afterward, Hungary undertook a massive dog vaccination program. See Christopher J. Rutty, "Rabies Vaccines in Canada" (copy of paper provided to author), in *Taking the Bite Out of Rabies: The Evolution of Rabies Management in Canada*, ed. David Gregory and Rory Tinline (forthcoming), 14.

3 LAC, Ralph Williams to M. Barker, 9 January 1946, RG 17, vol. 4362, file 71, "Rabies 1946–1953," f. 106333. Ibid., Charles Mitchell to R.D. Defries, 7 May 1947, f. 106352.

4 See E.E. Ballantyne's overview of rabies in Alberta, where foxes, wolves, and coyotes were all responsible for biting animals and proved positive to rabies infection. Provincial Archives of Alberta (hereafter PAA), "Rabies" Memorandum by E.E. Ballantyne, in Rabies 1954 file, Acc. 67.31/629.

5 Rutty, "Rabies Vaccines in Canada", 15–18. See Christopher J. Rutty, "Personality, Politics, and Canadian Public Health: The Origins of Connaught Medical Research Laboratories, University of Toronto, 1888–1917," in *Essays in Honour of Michael Bliss: Figuring the Social*, ed. Alison Li, Elsbeth Heaman, and Shelley McKellar (Toronto: University of Toronto Press, 2008), 273–303; a summative overview of the significance of the outbreak as "the most extensive enzootic of rabies ever known in Canada" happening in 1952–54 is provided by P.J.G. Plummer, "Rabies in Canada, with Special Reference to Wildlife Reservoirs," *Bulletin of the World Health Organization* 10 (1954): 767.

6 K.F. Wells, "The Rabies Menace in Canada," *Canadian Journal of Public Health* 48 (1957): 239.

7 On government and science in the postwar period, see Stephen Bocking, "Science and Spaces in the Northern Environment," *Environmental History* 12, no. 4 (2007): 867–94.

8 Karen Brown, *Mad Dogs and Meerkats: A History of Resurgent Rabies in Southern Africa* (Athens: Ohio University Press, 2011): 2–6; John Douglas Blaisdell, *A Frightful, But Not Necessarily Fatal, Madness: Rabies in Eighteenth-Century England and English North America* (PhD diss., Iowa State University, 1995). On treating rabies, see Susan D. Jones, *Valuing Animals: Veterinarians and Their Patients in Modern America* (Baltimore: Johns Hopkins University Press, 2003).

9 See the disease's description offered by the US Center for Disease Control and Prevention, Rabies Bulletin, http://www.cdc.gov/rabies/symptoms/.

10 See Philip Howell, "Between the Muzzle and the Leash: Dog-Walking, Discipline and the Modern City," in *Animal Cities: Beastly Urban Histories*, ed. Peter Atkins (Burlington, VT: Ashgate, 2012), 228–29.

11 "Rage" and "dumb" rabies are described by E.E. Ballantyne, "Rabies Control Programme in Alberta,"

Journal of the American Veterinary Medical Association, 20, no. 1 (February 1956): 21–30.

12 Rutty, "Rabies Vaccines in Canada," 1–10.

13 Ballantyne, "Rabies Control Programme in Alberta," 21–30.

14 PAA, Jackson to Ballantyne, 2 February 1953, in "Rabies – General 1952–53," Acc. 67/31/432. Plummer provides an ecological context to the regions above and below the 55th parallel, heavily populated with wildlife. Plummer, "Wildlife Reservoirs," 768.

15 LAC, "Interdepartmental Meeting" Memorandum, 29 December 1952, RG 17, Department of Health, Rabies – General, 311-R1-1, vol. 1, ff. 116–17. The federal rabies committee minutes are found in LAC, RG 29, Department of Health and Welfare, Rabies, 1953-1077, vol. 2970, file 851-4-094.

16 PAA, Dr. R. Rankin Report, 22 September 1952, Fort Vermilion Meeting, Rabies 1954 file, Acc. 67.31/629.

17 See Ralph H. Lutts, "The Trouble with Bambi: Disney's 'Bambi' and the American Vision of Nature," *Forest and Conservation history* 36, no. 4 (1992): 150–71; Gregg Mitman, *Reel Nature: America's Romance with Wildlife in Film* (Cambridge, MA: Harvard University Press, 1999).

18 PAA, E.E. Ballantyne to C.E. Longman, 26 September 1952, C.E. Longman, Deputy Minister of Agriculture Files, Acc. 67.31/437.

19 PAA, Ranger Powell telegram to A.A. Ballantyne, 19 December 1952, Rabies 1954 file, Acc. 67.31/629.

20 Neil Pemberton and Michael Worboys, *Mad Dogs & Englishmen: Rabies in Britain, 1830–2000*; *Historical Perspectives of Rabies in Europe & the Mediterranean Basin*, and *Rabies* (Basingstoke and New York: Palgrave Macmillan, 2007); Eric T. Jennings, "Confronting Rabies and its Treatments in Colonial Madagascar, 1899–1910," *Social History of Medicine* 22, no. 2 (August 2009): 263–82. On the ways that scientific and medical intervention offered hope in rabies outbreaks, see Bert Hansen, "America's First Medical Breakthrough: How Popular Excitement about a French Rabies Cure in 1885 Raised New Expectations for Medical Progress," *American Historical Review* 103, no. 2 (April 1998): 373–418.

21 Lianne McTavish and Jingjing Zheng, "Rats in Alberta: Looking at Pest-Control Posters from the 1950s," *Canadian Historical Review* 92, no. 3 (2011): 515–46.

22 Rutty, "Rabies Vaccines in Canada," 15–16. It was the position of Charles Mitchell, the Chief Veterinarian officer in the Department of Agriculture, that "it is quite true that the disease has found its way into the wild animal population but this has resulted from the improper control of dogs." LAC, Mitchell to A.F.W. Peart, 6 September 1950, RG 17, Department of Health, Rabies – General, 311-R1-1, vol. 1, ff. 172–73.

23 The approach taken in Canada was laid out in the provincial and federal plan of action, 13 January 1953, including dog control, vaccine, and "wildlife depopulation." LAC, "Report of Meeting of Federal and Provincial Officials Held,

Edmonton, Alberta, RE: Rabies Control, 13 January 1953," RG 17, Department of Health, Rabies – General, 311-R1-1, vol. 1.

24   Howell, "Between the Muzzle and the Leash," 226–33.

25   Amanda Anne Margaret Sauermann, "Regulating and Representing Vagrant Curs and Purebred Dogs in Toronto, 1867–1910" (MA thesis, Department of History, Carleton University, 2010), 27–28.

26   Ibid., 27–28, 42–43.

27   Wells suggests that control measures in Canada until June 1952 "were based solely upon dog control with elimination of strays." K.F. Wells, "Control of Rabies," *Canadian Journal of Comparative Medicine* 18 (1954): 305.

28   Sauermann, "Regulating and Representing Vagrant Curs," 49–50.

29   Ibid., 51

30   Ibid., 72–73.

31   Rutty, "Rabies Vaccines in Canada," 4–6. On breakthroughs in chloroform-killed vaccines in the 1930s in the US, see Jones, *Valuing Animals,* 131–33. A contemporary account of the new fixed virus vaccines being developed for dogs in Hungary and Japan is offered in "The Etiology and Prevention of Rabies," *The British Medical Journal,* 14 June 1924, 1059–60. Canadian authorities following quarantine in such circumstances were emulating their British counterparts who effectively controlled the virus with a six-month quarantine of all dogs coming through its ports. See K.F. Wells, "Control of Rabies," 303.

32   Rutty, "Rabies Vaccines in Canada," 10.

33   LAC, James. G. Gardiner order, 16 January 1953, RG 17, Department of Health, Rabies – General, 311-R1-1, vol. 1, ff. 110–11. Wells cites this "first major change in Canada's rabies control policy": "Control of Rabies," 307; Wells, "Rabies Menace in Canada," 240.

34   See *Qikiqtani Truth Commission: Community Histories, 1950–1975* (Iqaluit: Inhabit Media Inc., 2013), 27, 76, 143.

35   The decision to create a "crash" in the wildlife populations over a two-year period was made on 17 January 1953: see PAA, Minutes of Meeting, Rabies 1954 file, Acc. 67.31/629. Wells suggests that "the part played by normal wild life cycles in rabies spread is fully appreciated" in reducing wildlife "below the threshold level" to carry the disease. Wells, "Control of Rabies," 308–9.

36   PAA, Ballantyne to Childs, Rabies Report Ending February 21, 1953; PAA, Rabies – Health of Animals 1952–53, 67.31/439; and PAA, "Rabies Control in Alberta" prepared by the Alberta Central Rabies Control Committee, Agriculture and Veterinarian Services Boxes, Acc. 69.67, file 4 of 4.

37   PAA, Department of Forestry Returns from Trappers, 1953–54; "Rabies Control in Alberta," prepared by the Alberta Central Rabies Control Committee, Agriculture, Veterinarian Services Boxes, Acc. 69.67, file 4 of 4.

38   PAA, J.J. Ballantyne, "Rabies Control in Alberta" Media Release Article, 1954, p. 3, Agriculture,

Veterinarian Services Boxes, Acc. 69.675, file 4.

39 High modernism is explored by Arn Keeling in "'A Dynamic, Not a Static Conception': The Conservation thought of Roderick Haig-Brown," *Pacific Historical Review* 71, no. 2 (2002): 239–68; Tina Loo, "Disturbing the Peace: Environmental Change and the Scales of Justice on a Northern River," *Environmental History* 12, no. 4 (October 2007): 895–919; and Tina Loo, "People in the Way: Modernity, Environment, and Society on the Arrow Lakes," *BC Studies* 142/143 (Summer/Autumn 2004): 161–96.

40 "Rabies," Central Rabies Control Committee, Edmonton, January 1953. See also L.P. Gauthier, "Notes on Rabies Control, 7 February 1953," distributed to forestry department trappers in northern Alberta, pp. 1–3, PAA, Acc. 1991.0270, box 61, file R3, vol. 1.

41 PAA, E.E. Ballantyne, Rabies Report Ending Week, May 23, 1953, PAA, Rabies – Health of Animals 1952–53, Acc. 67.31/439. On mice biting trappers' toes, PAA, Ballantyne to Childs, 27 March 1953, Rabies Report for Week ending March 28, Rabies – Health of Animals 1952–53, Acc. 67.31/439.

42 PAA, Ballantyne to Longman, 15 April 1953, C.E. Longman, Deputy Minister of Agriculture Files, Acc. 67.31/437. For press reports appearing in newspapers, see "95 Rabies Cases Said Confirmed," *Edmonton Journal,* 25 June 1953; "Anti-Rabies Vaccine Earmarked for the Arctic," *Calgary Herald,* 23 June 1953; "Rabies Outbreak in Alberta Spreads to Edmonton Area," *Sudbury Star,*

23 June 1953; "Albertans Treated Against rabies," *Edmonton Journal,* 22 April 1953.

43 PAA, "Cow, Bear, Fox are Stricken; Proven Rabid Animals Total 57," and "Rabid Fox, Bear Battle to Death on North Trail," clippings in Fish and Wildlife Files, 1991/0270, box 61, file R3, vol. 1.

44 Ballantyne said, "It'll be a very resolute individual who'll get up at a public meeting after showing the film and oppose whether or both of above [tying up a dog or coyote culling]. These would be used in our educational meetings." PAA, Ballantyne to Longman, 5 March 1953, C.E. Longman, Deputy Minister of Agriculture Files, Acc. 67.31/437. On the film's earlier release by Britannia and its status as out of circulation, see PAA, H.R. Lamberton to Ballantyne, 24 February 1953, Film File, Acc. 67.37/557.

45 PAA, E.E. Ballantyne, Rabies Report for week ending April 11, 1953, PAA, Rabies – Health of Animals 1952–53, Acc. 67.31/439.

46 Hence the decline in Arctic fox consumption noted by Kassam, where "one respondent stated that he was concerned about rabies and therefore chooses not to eat the fox anymore." Karim-Aly S. Kassam, *Biocultural Diversity and Indigenous Ways of Knowing: Human Ecology in the Arctic* (Calgary: University of Calgary Press, 2009), 138. Wells notes that in the Arctic "for 50 or 60 years rabies was known as 'Wild Fox Disease.'" Wells, "Control of Rabies," 306. Plummer, an epidemiologist with the federal government, believed that the northern rabies strains

affected fox differently, creating a dumb (or amicable) behaviour that sometimes prompted foxes to run alongside dog teams. Trappers and other northerners saw them as "crazy animals." Plummer, "Wildlife Reservoirs," 771. Inuit now use "rabies" to understand their own observations of "crazy" fox behaviour and the disease's epidemiology, particularly its cycling in fox and sled dog populations. See summation of testimony, *Qikiqtani Truth Commission: Thematic Reports and Special Studies 1950–1975* (Iqaluit: Inhabit Media, 2013), 333–34; on subsequent outbreaks and the issue of sled dog vaccination, see *Qikiqtani Truth Commission: Community Histories, 1950–1975* (Iqaluit: Inhabit Media, 2013), 27, 76, 143.

47   The head of the bear that killed a girl and mauled her mother in 1958 in Jasper was sent to Lethbridge "to determine whether it is rabid, a disease which swept through Alberta wildlife about four years ago." "Jasper's Killer Bear Bold Camp Scavenger," *Windsor Daily Star,* 11 August 1958.

48   Seth P.D. Riley, John Hadidian, and David A. Manski, "Population Density, Survival, and Rabies in Raccoons in an Urban National Park," *Canadian Journal of Zoology* 76 (1998): 1153–64.

49   PAA, Ballantyne to Longman, 25 September 1953, C.E. Longman, Deputy Minister of Agriculture Files, Acc. 67.31/437.

50   PAA, V. Breckenbridge, Chairman of the Agricultural Service Board of MD of Athabasca No. 103, 3 March 1953, Rabies – Health of Animals 1952–53, Acc. 67.31/439.

51   V. Breckenbridge, Chairman of the Agricultural Service Board of MD of Athabasca No. 103, 3 March 1953, PAA, Rabies – Health of Animals 1952–53, Acc. 67.31/439.

52   LAC, Winnipeg Depot (hereafter LAC-WD), Circular, 7 August 1952, Department of Resources and Development, Yoho Files, March 1952–December 1966, Health of Animals, Y210-1.

53   Ibid., 7 January 1953.

54   Ibid., J.H. Hutchinson to the Superintendent of Yoho, 18 March 1953, Y210-1

55   Ibid., J. Smart Circular Memorandum, 6 February 1953, P.2, Y201-1.

56   Ibid., J.R.B. Coleman to A.M.S. McGaw, Eastern Gateway, Banff, 17 February 1953, Y210-1. The policy endured as a problem in tourism, since many auto travellers did not anticipate the need to have dogs and cats vaccinated, and at least one Banff citizen could use the vaccination in the popular criticism of the federal government in the townsite: "If you bring any parliamentary pets to Banff, Mr. Government, don't forget the anti-rabies vaccination rules." Ernie Smith, "Mountain Lines," *Crag and Canyon,* 23 May 1956. The need for a rabies certificate for cat and dog visitors had been made law in PC 1963-449. Resident dogs and cats were required to have vaccination in 1953; however, the vaccine required three doses. By 1956 an improved dog vaccine made a single annual rabies shot necessary for resident and visiting animals. Regulations were changed in PC 1956-712. In 1960, with rabies no longer a threat, the annual vaccination requirement was not enforced

but applied only in the case of dogs and cats coming from rabies-infected areas. LAC, JRB Coleman letter, RG 84, A-2-a, vol. 2131, file U229, part 2, f. 1403.

57 PAA, "A New Approach to the Control of Canine Rabies," n.d., published by Lederer, in PAA Rabies 1954 file, Acc. 67.31/629. The switch from the "Pasteur method" to "fixed," or phenol-killed vaccines in the 1920s, and finally to the avianized, "Flury" strain in vaccines, is described Robert D. Defries, *The First Forty Years: 1914–1955, Connaught Medical Research Laboratories, University of Toronto* (Toronto: University of Toronto Press, 1968), 119, 160, 232.

58 There were only 142 dogs licensed before the program; 200 dogs were licensed with the vaccine campaign. LAC-WD, J.R.B. Coleman to B.I. Love, 13 February 1953, Y210-1.

59 Ibid., Memorandum, "To All Dog and Cat Owners," R.J.J. Steeves, 28 April 1953, Y210-1.

60 Ibid., "Dogs and Cats Inoculated on May 13th at Field," Y201-1.

61 Ibid., "Dogs Inoculated at Field on August 6, 1953." Y201-1.

62 "Precaution against Rabies: All Banff Dogs Treated in Free Vaccination," *Calgary Herald*, 23 February 1953, 1 and 8.

63 "Banff Dogs Parade for 1st Vaccination," *Crag and Canyon*, 27 February 1953, 1.

64 LAC-WD, R.J.J. Steeves, Superintendent, Yoho, 16 February 1953, Y210-1.

65 LAC-WD, National Park Dog License, Dogs and Cats, Acc.

1998-00796-0, box 137, file Y229, part 1.

66 LAC-WD, J.A. Hutchison letter to Acting Superintendent, 13 March 1953, Dogs and Cats, Acc. 1998-00796-0, box 137, file Y229, part 1. The change in policy didn't agree with F.A. Bryant, superintendent in Kootenay, who saw hunting dogs as "more aggressive" and "natural killers." He didn't believe that controlling all dogs would be possible, since there "are times during severe weather when owners cannot exercise their dogs and the dog, when turned loose for exercise, will return to the owner within a few minutes. The hunting dogs are usually tougher and withstand more cold and hunt as soon as given liberty. Dogs in parks have a high nuisance value. . . . The larger the dog, the greater is his nuuisance value." LAC, Bryant to Director, 20 March 1953, RG 84, A-2-a, vol. 1665, file K210-1, part 1.

67 BIM Strong pointed out that "insofar as this Park is concerned . . . we are not enforcing the present cat licensing regulations nor is any action being taken toward disposing of presumably stray cats." LAC, Strong to Chief Superintendent, 15 June 1953, RG 84, A-2-a, vol. 166, file U229, part 1.

68 LAC-WD, J.A. Hutchison, Circular, 13 March 1953, Dogs and Cats, Acc. 1998-00796-0, box 137, file Y229, part 1. The regulations by 1959 did not specify how many cats a person owned; the licence fee was $3.00. dogs were licensed at $3.00, and unspayed bitches at $5.00; the park allowed for first offences but animals pounded the second time could have their licences cancelled and the animal destroyed or

removed from the park. LAC, "Extracts from National Parks Game Regulations – Cats and Dogs" 1959, "Dogs and Cats – General" – RG 84, A-2-a, vol. 2131, file U229, part 2, f. 1430.

69 "Precaution against Rabies," *Calgary Herald,* 23 February 1953, 8.

70 LAC-WD. T.G. Nelles, Chief Warden, Yoho, 29 April 1953, Y210-1.

71 Ibid.

72 LAC-WD, J. Smart, memorandum, "Re: Dogs Running at Large," 12 December 1943, "Dogs & Cats," Acc. 1998-00796-0, box U7, file Y229, part 1.

73 LAC-WD, Stamped 28 March 1951, "Dogs and Cats," 1997-01159-X, box 111, file 229, part 1.

74 LAC-WD, 19 May 1953, Banff Advisory Council Minutes, Acc. 1997-01159-X, box 104, file 155, part 2.

75 LAC. Banff Advisory Council Meeting, 11 May 1954, RG 84, A-2-a, vol. 966, file B155, part 5, p. 2.

76 LAC. Banff Advisory Council Meeting, 20 April 1954, RG 84, A-2-a, vol. 966, file B155, part 5, p. 2.

77 LAC-WD, 6 February 1955, Banff Advisory Council Minutes, Acc. 1997-01159-X, box 104, file 155, part 2.

78 LAC. Banff Advisory Council Meeting, 12 November 1957, RG 84, A-2-a, vol. 966, file B155, part 6, p. 4.

79 LAC-WD, J.J. Stevens memorandum, dated February 1954, Yoho Files, March 1952–December 1966, Y210-1.

80 Ibid.

81 Ibid.

82 LAC-WD, "Dogs Which Have Not Been Licensed, 1954–55," Yoho Files, March 1952–December 1966, Y210-1.

83 LAC-WD, 9 September 1952, Banff Advisory Council minute books, Acc. 1997-01159-X, box 104, file 155, part 2.

84 LAC-WD, 21 October 1952, Banff Advisory Council minute books, Acc. 1997-01159-X, box 104, file 155, part 2.

85 Ibid.

86 LAC-WD, R.W. Webster to Love, Elk Island, 13 March 1953, Y210-1.

87 Ibid.; "Banff Dogs Parade for 1st Vaccination," *Crag and Canyon,* 27 February 1953, 1.

88 Letter, "In Defence of Cats," *Crag and Canyon,* 27 February 1953.

89 LAC-WD, 17 February 1953, Banff Advisory Council minute books, Acc. 1997-01159-X, box 104, file 155, part 2.

90 "Public Furor Arises over Pets," *Crag and Canyon,* 6 March 1953.

91 "Cat Trapping Stops 'Til April 1st," *Crag and Canyon,* 13 March 1953.

92 LAC-WD, 17 February 1953, Banff Advisory Council minute books, Acc. 1997-01159-X, box 104, file 155, part 2.

93 "Public Furor Arises over Pets," *Crag and Canyon,* 6 March 1953.

94 Ibid.

95 "Cat Trapping Stops 'Til April 1st."

96 Editorial, "Pets and Predators in the Park, "*Crag and Canyon,* 27 February 1953.

97 "On Confining Cats," *Craig & Canyon,* 20 March 1953.

98   "Fed Up," Letter to the Editor, *Crag and Canyon,* 27 November 1953.

99   "Outcry against Restrictions Unreasonable," *Crag and Canyon,* 6 March 1953.

100 "Pets and Predators in the Park," *Crag and Canyon,* 27 February 1953.

101 "Dog Owners Prosecuted for Not Leashing Pets," *Craig & Canyon,* 20 March 1953.

102 LAC. Banff Advisory Council Meeting, 10 June 1958, RG 84, A-2-a, vol. 966, file B155, part 7, p. 3.

103 LAC, Banff Advisory Council Meeting, 21 January 1958, RG 84, A-2-a, vol. 966, file B155, part 7, p. 4.

104 Ibid., 11 February 1958, p. 4.

105 Ibid., 8 April 1958, p. 3.

106 Ibid., 13 May 1958, p. 2.

107 Ibid., 12 February 1957, part 6, p. 2.

108 In the month of August, only two warnings were issued to dog owners and only one person was charged for running a dog unleashed. Ibid., Banff Advisory Council Meeting, 17 September 1959, p. 2.

109 LAC-WD, Superintendent to Kramer 1 February 1960, Health of Animals, Acc. 1997-01159-X, box 111, file 210-1, part 1.

110 LAC-WD, Warden letter to Mrs. M. McKinnon, 7 November 1958 Dogs and Cats, Acc. 1998-00796-0, box 137, file Y229, part 1.

111 LAC-WD, R. H. Kendall to Townsite Residents, Field, 22 May 1964, Dogs and Cats, Acc. 1998-00796-0, box 137, file Y229, part 1.

112 LAC-WD, R.H. Kendall, "Circular to Residents of Field," 13 January 1965, Dogs and Cats, Acc. 1998-00796-0, box 137, file Y229, part 1.

113 LAC-WD, Herbert Green to Chief Park Warden, 12 October 1951, "Wolves," Acc. 1997-01159-X, box 112, file 226, part 1.

114 LAC-WD, "Summary of Wildlife Observations, Banff National Park, 1952," 'Game Animals' Files, Acc. 1997-01159-X, box 111, file 210, part 1.

115 Ibid.

116 Ibid.

117 LAC, Banff Advisory Council Meeting, 9 July 1957, RG 84, A-2-a, vol. 966, file B155, part 6, p. 2.

118 Ibid., 11 July 1957, RG 84, A-2-a, vol. 966, file B155, p. 2.

119 LAC, "Mr. Dempster informed Council that he has requested permission to destroy twenty of these animals," Banff Advisory Council Meeting, 18 March 1958, RG 84, A-2-a, vol. 966, file B155, p. 3.

120 LAC-WD, R.E. Edwards, to Mr. Dempster, 13 February 1958, "Wolves," Acc. 1997-01159-X, box 112, file 266, part 1.

121 LAC-WD, B.I.M. Strong, to Superintendent, 8 December 1959, "Wolves," Acc. 1997-01159-X, box 112, file 266, part 1.

122 "Coyotes Seen in the Town," *Crag and Canyon,* 9 December 1959.

123 "Mothers Alarmed at Coyote Menace," *Crag and Canyon,* 16 December 1959.

124 LAC, Banff Advisory Council Meeting, 13 May 1958, RG 84, A-2-a, vol. 966, file B155, p. 5.

125 LAC, Alvin Hamilton's letter to Banff Advisory Council, 30

September 1959, RG 84, A-2-a, vol. 966, file B155.

126 "Bedevilled Bruin Batters Boards," *Crag and Canyon* 5 August 1959, 1. See my "Films, Tourists, and Bears in the National Parks: Managing Park Use and the Problematic 'Highway Bum' Bear in the 1970s," in *A Century of Parks Canada, 1911–2011*, ed. Claire Elizabeth Campbell (Calgary: University of Calgary Press, 2011), 153–78.

127 LAC, Banff Advisory Council Meeting, 7 June 1955, RG 84, A-2-a, vol. 966, file B155, p. 2.

128 Ibid., 7 February 1956, RG 84, A-2-a, vol. 966, file B155, part 6, p. 2.

129 Ibid., 10 December 1957, RG 84, A-2-a, vol. 966, file B155, part 6, p. 3; 21 January 1958, RG 84, A-2-a, vol. 966, file B155, part 6, p. 2.

130 LAC, Elk Slaughter, December 1958–January 1959, RG 84, A-2-a, vol. 513, file B299, part 4.

131 John Sandlos does not provide this context for the NWT poison baiting programs, in *Hunters at the Margin: Native People and Wildlife Conservation in the Northwest Territories* (Vancouver: University of British Columbia Press, 2007), 206.

132 Tina Loo suggests that the parks department managers "blanketed Jasper and Banff with poison" in *States of Nature: Conserving Canada's Wildlife in the Twentieth Century* (Vancouver: University of British Columbia Press, 2006), 159.

133 Karen Jones, *Wolf Mountains: A History of Wolves along the Great Divide* (Calgary: University of Calgary Press, 2002), 134.

134 Plummer suggests statistics should be read as indicating disease pools: "When an infected animal is demonstrated in a district, this is looked upon as an infected area and very few other specimens are taken." Plummer, "Wildlife Reservoirs," 771.

135 Mike Dunbar, Ray T. Sterner, and Shylo Johnson, "Impacts of Wildlife Diseases in Urban Environments," *Proceedings of the 12th Wildlife Damage Management Conference* (Lincoln: University of Nebraska, 2007), 256, https://www.aphis.usda.gov/wildlife_damage/nwrc/publications/07pubs/dunbar073.pdf; see also Catherine A. Bradley and Sonia Altizer, "Urbanization and the Ecology of Wildlife Diseases," *Trends in Ecology and Evolution* 22, no. 2 (2006): 95–102.

136 Dunbar et. al., "Impacts of Wildlife Diseases," 256.

137 Bradley and Altizer, "Urbanization and the Ecology of Wildlife Diseases," 100.

138 Alan MacEachern, *Natural Selections: National Parks in Atlantic Canada 1935–1970* (Montreal and Kingston: McGill-Queen's University Press, 2001), 14–19. Ian McTaggart Cowan suggested the need for management in the growing complexity of Banff wildlife populations in "The Role of Ecology in the National Parks," in *Canadian Parks in Perspective*, ed. J.G. Nelson (Montreal: Harvest House, 1970), 321–28.

139 See my "Films, Tourists, and Bears," 153–78.

Arctic Capital: Managing Polar Bears in Churchill, Manitoba

Kristoffer Archibald

"The Polar Bear Capital of the World" is the slogan of Churchill, Manitoba, a town located on the western shore of Hudson Bay, where the polar bear has become the central attraction in the community's wildlife tourism–dependent economy.[1] Every autumn, polar bears congregate near Churchill while they wait in a semi-fasting state for Hudson Bay to freeze over so that they can begin seal hunting. While most bears remain outside town limits and pose no threat to residents, some do enter the community, curious about the human inhabitants or attracted by the presence of food. The relationship between polar bears and the town evolved through a combination of natural processes, human intervention, and popular media representations. Churchill, an urban space, has accepted the polar bears, and takes pride in identifying itself as the town that hosts them.

This chapter examines prominent Canadian and American media depictions of polar bears in the Churchill area in the 1970s and early 1980s and discusses how the famed Arctic animal was incorporated into the town's cultural identity. Although non-Arctic residents had historically perceived the Arctic as remote and isolated, Churchill's unique relationship with its bears was successfully marketed to domestic and international tourists who, yearning to engage with nature beyond the confines of zoos, began to arrive in the town each fall. Media coverage presented Churchill's polar bears through a variety of narratives: in some stories, the bears were wild animals, marauding around town and foraging for meals at the local dump; in others, the bears were subject to a host of wildlife control programs aimed at constructing a safe environment for them, as well as for the residents and tourists with whom they coexisted. Churchill's human–bear coexistence ultimately proved to be both possible and profitable, and illustrated the Arctic's growing accessibility within the popular imagination.

Since the sixteenth century, scholarship, natural histories, and visual art pertaining to polar bears have placed the animal in Arctic environments uninhabited by people, enforcing the perception that encounters with the animal occur in locations isolated from human societies.[2] From the late 1950s to the late 1970s, the popular press in North America presented many images of wildlife biologists studying the bear in its Arctic habitat.[3] Even when polar bears made their presence known in Churchill, scholars did not pay attention to the bears' role in an urban locale. They focused instead on issues related to wildlife tourism: visitors' experiences of the polar bears and the prospects for ecotourism.[4] Visitors witness and experience conservation efforts aimed at ensuring positive and sustainable human–bear cohabitation in the area. Polar bear tourism is not, however, simply about being educated on wildlife conservation tactics. In Churchill, as with other wildlife tourism ventures, the tourist's gaze alters human relationships with the bear. The focus of the activity is looking at and photographing the animal, and wildlife tourism scholars express concerns that the animal has become nothing more than an experience to capture, via cameras, in a manner that discourages humans from understanding its complexities or its interactions with its natural habitat.[5] As noted by the tourism scholar R. Harvey Lemelin, the impulse to photograph the bear can stimulate a desire for more exotic photographic collectibles,[6] presumably fuelling other wildlife tourism markets and situating charismatic megafauna as consumable experiences ever available for human entertainment.

The science that guides wildlife conservation, moreover, is ever-changing. It is updated based upon field and laboratory research, which alters how we go about seeing and interacting with wildlife. Environmental historians focusing on human–wildlife interactions have stressed humans' evolving ecological outlooks on animals, including bears, throughout the twentieth century. Both Alice Wondrak Biel and George Colpitts have noted that while national parks previously allowed visitors to feed bears, by the 1970s policies outlawed it.[7]

Yet one need not be in a national park to experience wild bears. This chapter joins a growing body of scholarship and journalism depicting the town of Churchill as a rich case study around which to think about human–wildlife relations. The importance of polar bears to Churchill's wildlife tourism economy is stressed in R. Harvey Lemelin's examination of the cooperative relationship between the parties responsible for polar bear management and the town's tourism entrepreneurs; he also highlights the media's role in popularizing the availability of polar bears in the area.[8] In 2014 Edward Struzik published *Arctic Icons*, a book that narrates the efforts of scientists and wildlife officers to manage human–polar bears coexistence each autumn. Struzik presents a town dependent upon wildlife management for the well-being of the animals and townspeople.[9] Jon Mooallem engages with Churchill's polar bears as a species representative of the complicated relationship between North Americans and wildlife. Mooallem's exploration of the stories Americans tell about animals demonstrates that conceptions of wildlife and wilderness depend upon human representation and intervention, and that human outlooks on wildlife conservation have been fluid. Moreover, he argues that the narratives presented by the media were of great importance in situating Churchill as a tourist destination.[10]

This chapter demonstrates that polar bears were not merely a creation of tourism boosters but rather held a central place in Churchill's urban history and local identity since the late 1960s. The assertion that animals are central to Canadian urban spaces is a recent addition to historical scholarship on wildlife. Whereas much work has discussed the relationship between wildlife and Canadians, it has tended to focus on animals living beyond urban boundaries.[11] Sean Kheraj argues, however, that everyday interactions between people and animals in urban environments have influenced modern attitudes toward wildlife – the beasts' autonomous behavior, he suggests, shaped urbanites' opinions on wildlife management: Kheraj examines Vancouver's Stanley Park, where, in the early twentieth century, predators, such as crows and cougars, were killed through sanctioned hunts because they preyed on wildlife valued by park administrators.[12] This chapter builds on such claims and establishes how an urban population's interactions with wild animals was exported through popular media and ultimately attracted tourists intent on encountering the creature in what they had previously considered to be its natural but inaccessible habitat.

An Absence of Polar Bears

Before the late 1960s, the polar bear is relatively absent from Churchill's historical record. European settlement of the area was initiated by the fur trade industry: in the late seventeenth century, the Hudson's Bay Company established Fort York as a trading post.[13] Native peoples from the area, including Cree, Dene, and Inuit, were important participants in the fur economy, bringing furs from the interior to the bayside outpost, including some polar bear pelts. The province of Manitoba, founded in 1870, formally established Aboriginal hunting rights for polar bears in 1930.[14] Recognition of the bear's importance in Inuit culture and economies was also evident in 1973, when Canada, Norway, Denmark, the Soviet Union, and the United States signed the Agreement on the Conservation of Polar Bears. Of the signatory countries, only Canada recognized its Indigenous peoples by allowing the Canadian Inuit subsistence access to the polar bear through a predetermined annual quota. Under that agreement, the Inuit held the right to allocate portions of that quota for use in non-Inuit sport hunts, which largely occurred in the Northwest Territories and what is now Nunavut.[15] Economic opportunities associated with the polar bear in those territories were attached to the sport hunting industry, a decidedly different form of tourism than Churchill ultimately produced.

The arrival of industrial infrastructure in Churchill expanded the town's economic base beyond the fur trade. In the 1930s a commercial port was constructed at Churchill and a rail line was built to link it with Winnipeg for the purposes of shipping grain from western Canada to European markets. The military's arrival in 1942 further boosted the local economy. That year the US Army Air Corps established Fort Churchill, a base that would go on to be jointly operated by Canadian and American forces during the Cold War. While a tourism industry emerged in the postwar era, Churchill's initial foray into wildlife tourism did not include the polar bear. The Canadian Travel Bureau sought to attract visitors to Churchill with the 1950 promotional film *North to Hudson Bay*, advertising the presence of caribou, white whales, and scientists studying cosmic rays as local attractions. For tourists interested in history, Churchill was home to Prince of Wales Fort, once the abode of Samuel Hearne, an eighteenth-century English explorer.[16] In the 1960s, birding also attracted visitors to the area;[17] however, while Churchill marketed itself as an Arctic locale well suited to the adventurous tourist, the polar bear was not mentioned as a tourist attraction.

Churchill's polar bears rose to prominence only as a result of the closure of two institutions that had long restricted them. One reason for the scarcity of polar bears in the Churchill area was that until 1957, the Hudson's Bay York Factory purchased polar bear pelts from local native hunters who hunted bears in the region's principal denning area. The shuttering of the York Factory curtailed the hunts, which allowed the local bear population to increase in number.[18] The other reason was the 1964 closure of Fort Churchill. During their tenure in the area, the Canadian and American militaries practised land manoeuvres on the terrain surrounding Churchill, and encounters between soldiers and bears resulted in the fright or death of the latter. As a result, bears learned to avoid humans. The military's departure from Churchill, the outcome of shifting military priorities,[19] meant the bears' numbers grew and their conditioned fear of humans diminished. Additionally, the consequent loss of some 4,000 military personnel from the region[20] meant that the town required a new industry to help cushion the loss of military spending. The increase in the bear population and the growing public interest in the animal led Churchill to capitalize upon the animal's presence and embrace a wildlife tourism–based economy.

Polar Bears in Churchill

By the late 1960s, polar bears had colonized the Churchill area. In 1967, seventy-six bears were sighted in the area, a number that increased to two hundred a decade later.[21] The presence of this massive animal, the sovereign creature of the Arctic region, was firmly established in November 1968 when as many as forty polar bears were recorded by photojournalists at the town dump. That same month a polar bear killed a nineteen-year-old boy who had followed bear tracks near the school.[22] The boy's tragic death at the paws of a bear made the animal a local concern; any bear wandering through Churchill's school zone now represented an overlap between the urban and the natural worlds. Deaths from polar bears have proven to be relatively rare events in Churchill.[23] Most of the bears are lethargic and exist peacefully beyond urban limits; as of 2014 there were only two recorded human fatalities from polar bears in Churchill, one in 1968 and another in 1983.[24] Bear attacks on visitors and residents, however, continue to occur occasionally.[25]

In the early 1970s the International Fund for Animal Welfare (IFAW),[26] a Canadian animal protection organization, mobilized to protect polar bears that were causing problems around Churchill. Although established only in 1969, IFAW possessed some 8,000 members globally. Through a series of fundraising campaigns in Europe, the United States, and Canada, it was able to airlift nuisance bears away from Churchill.[27] At a cost of $500 per bear,[28] the airlift campaign[29] transported nearly one hundred bears between 1971 and 1978.[30] IFAW's campaign represented a dramatic effort to conserve the polar bear, which was indicative of the desire in the early 1970s to protect wildlife. The airlift attracted significant media coverage to Churchill and cast a spotlight upon the town's Arctic animal resident, increasing the bear's celebrity nationally and internationally.[31]

From the 1970s into the 1980s, reporters and photojournalists showcased the issue of polar bears in Churchill to nature-oriented, and also more general, audiences in southern Canada and throughout the United States. Journalists visiting the tiny, windswept northern town told tales of bears wandering the streets, eating people's food and garbage, sleeping in awkward locations, and generally intruding on residents' day-to-day lives. This presentation conveyed the message that polar bears had become particularly accessible to human society. In 1978, the *Smithsonian* magazine published an article titled "Polar Bears Aren't Pets, But This Town Is Learning How To Live With Them" that included a photograph taken outside the Churchill airport at dusk. The picture shows a bear wandering freely outside the terminal. Dominated by the outline of the airport's buildings and an approaching car, the polar bear looks small and out of place in its urban surroundings.[32] That article was condensed and reprinted in *Reader's Digest* under the title "The Town That 'Hosts' Polar Bears." *Reader's Digest* opened the article by describing how "at the town's Legion Hall, a polar bear walked in at midday and ambled toward a crowd of dart players before being evicted – by an indignant shout from the club steward. Not far away, another bear leapt through a house window at dinnertime and started helping himself at the family table. The homeowner beat him off with a two-by-four."[33] A *Time* magazine article described living among polar bears, with one Churchill resident recalling that a polar bear "got into our porch where we kept our meat, and Mother chased him out with a broom."[34] Humorous portrayals like these capitalized upon the sensational image of polar bears as close neighbours. The large number of bears in the area, when combined with their curious personalities and their hunger, meant that some bears did cause problems for humans. Hungry bears were known to pillage and eat local livestock, such as pigs, chickens, and rabbits. In 1982, one resident who raised rabbits lost fifteen of the fluffy creatures to bears' jaws. Dogs were also at risk. In *Arctic Icons* Struzik explains that in the 1970s working sled dogs were left outside town, tethered to barrels filled with whale and seal meat to sustain them. Polar bears, presumably attracted by the rotting meat, killed some of these dogs.[35] By the early 1980s residents had altered this practice to prevent bears coming into contact with such dogs.[36] Still, negative accounts of the bears persisted; the majority concerned the bears' general mischief-making and tendency to damage property, contributing a level of unpredictability and drama to daily life.

While some bears ambled through the streets of Churchill, enjoying the smells, and at times, tastes of local cuisine, some preferred to loiter at the garbage dump outside the town.[37] By the late 1970s, photojournalists had been aware of the bears' presence at the garbage pile for a decade; the congregation of bears at the dump had been photographed and presented to the public by naturalist and news magazines. *Time* published one photograph of six bears rummaging in the dump amongst burning piles of garbage that had been lit ablaze to discourage that very activity. The photograph defines the white bears against background heaps of unidentifiable garbage and dark smoke.[38] *National Geographic* published a similar picture in an article examining the Hudson Bay region: this time a bear, with a large number "13" dyed on its fur for identification purposes, stands alone against the heat-induced shimmering backdrop of burning garbage. Flames and smoke rise up behind the bear, whose face is covered in grey soot. A mound of garbage appears in the foreground.[39] These photographs and reports presented to the public a polar bear that was far from majestic; rather, these images positioned the bear as an abject nuisance. Instead of a dignified Arctic monarch, the polar bear appeared similar to black and grizzly bears to the south whom audiences might have encountered in person.

Indeed, scavenging bears were not an unusual spectacle for those vacationing in Canada's Banff National Park or the United States' Yellowstone National Park, where the bears had become habituated to human visitors through feeding. These other species of bears had long been known to dig through garbage in national parks and suburban neighborhoods. In the case of Yellowstone National Park, Alice Wondrak Biel has shown that in the early decades of the twentieth century, bears were fed by park staff in a specially built auditorium as a form of nightly entertainment.[40] In Banff National Park, vacationers motoring along the scenic roads offered tasty treats to bears in the hope of facilitating a photograph and for personal entertainment.[41] Yet in the 1970s, changes in ecological thinking meant park staff changed their practices and also began re-educating tourists and resident bears. George Colpitts' work on the "'highway bum' bear" explains how Canada's parks staff turned to film as an educational medium in their efforts to alter human–bear relations. Feeding bears was discouraged; instead, visitors were encouraged to respect the bear's space.[42]

Unlike its southern cousins the black and brown bears, the polar bear had previously escaped the reputation of being habituated to humans, entrenched as it was within popular perceptions of a vast and uninhabited Arctic wilderness. In the early 1980s, however, the polar bear's meanderings amongst trash humans discarded diminished the image of a strong and fearsome animal. Instead, coverage of bears at Churchill's dump situated them as unhealthily fat and dirty, a disconcerting picture that expressly linked wild polar bears with the local human population. Wildlife biologists and Churchill's conservation officers acknowledged that while the story of polar bears growing obese from eating garbage might be upsetting from an ecological perspective, the situation was also disconcerting to employees at the dump. Polar bears, these experts argued, remained dangerous animals. Some bears returned to the dump year after year, even introducing younger bears to the rubbish heap and endangering workers.[43]

Concerns about wandering bears impacted many aspects of local life. For one, the Manitoba Government Employees' Association reached an unusual union agreement on behalf of sixty Churchill hospital workers. Public bear alerts sometimes prevented hospital employees from walking to work, which reduced their paychecks and compromised the town's health services. The solution was that any worker stranded as a result of polar bears was entitled to employer-provided transportation.[44] Public festivities were also affected: community members feared that polar bears might be unwelcome trick-or-treaters at Halloween, a situation potentially dangerous to costumed children. In 1981, *Time* magazine described how each Halloween, armed men checked the town's streets and back alleys before the children went out for the evening. "It was not ghosts and hobgoblins that were on their minds," the author observed, "but polar bears."[45]

Residents' relationships with the bears were complex. Bears were bothersome animals that posed inconveniences to Churchill's community at multiple levels. For "Mother" with her broom, the bear was simply an unwanted pest, best dealt with decisively. Yet polar bears were also acknowledged to be potentially lethal to people and as such required both management and caution. For Churchill residents to enjoy Halloween or walk to work, certain accommodations had to be made. As these examples demonstrate, people willingly took short- and long-term actions to ensure the safety of both humans and bears.

Churchill's human population became determined to coexist as harmoniously as possible with the bears. When journalists of the late 1970s related residents' stories, the theme of tolerance for polar bears was common. Statements such as "Bears were here long before people" and "Dogs are more trouble here than bears" alluded to the acceptance the town had developed for the animal.[46] Polar bears became a part of the community's identity and most folks took pride in having the bear nearby. Residents bonded over the common presence of bears: "Despite the very real dangers of polar bears, most Churchill residents wouldn't have it otherwise. Dr. Sharon Cohen of the Churchill Health Centre says: 'Nothing unites the people of this town as much as polar bears.'"[47] Residents also felt a sense of stewardship toward the animal. In interviews for documentaries and magazines and in local letters to the editor, locals expressed their willingness to resolve problems with the marauding bears peacefully.

In 1982 *National Geographic* produced a documentary for public television titled *Polar Bear Alert* that displayed Churchill's uneasy situation: residents' fondness for the bear was complicated by the dangers associated with it. The film suggested that residents were considerate of their shared habitat with the bears and lived alongside them using constant vigilance. In the documentary's opening scene, a bear stands in the middle of a street with power lines, parked cars, and several buildings clearly visible in the background. The narrator explains that Churchill is the "one place in the world where the great white bears roam the streets, immune to the presence of their only enemy, man." Later in the film, a man who lived on the outskirts of Churchill expresses that one has to exercise some caution because "they [polar bears] live here too."[48] Another scene featured a young couple pushing a baby carriage, out for a walk with their toddler. Other than their heavy winter clothing, there is little to distinguish them from any other urban North American couple walking with their child except that the man carries a hunting rifle on his shoulder. The mother comments: "I like to go out for walks and things, but it's awkward to carry the gun as well as the baby."[49] This documentary dramatized the town's polar bear issue for audiences and helped generate the notion that Churchill was a dangerous but exciting town in which to live. It also cast inhabitants as courageous, as they practised their daily urban activities in the possible presence of marauding beasts. Churchill residents were not going to remain captives of the bears.

Polar Bear Alert set ratings records and has been credited with "putting Churchill and its bears on the map."[50] However, some local residents criticized the documentary for the manner in which it sensationalized the cohabitation of people and polar bears. By presenting the bears as monstrous and the people as armed for their safety, the film downplayed the town's emphasis on treating the bears with caution and respect.[51] While rifles may have been necessary on occasion, Churchill's bear management drew on other tools and strategies that were devised to better ensure the bear's survival.

Managing Bears, Educating Residents

Churchill's residents were not alone in their efforts to protect themselves from polar bears. In 1980, the town instituted a Polar Bear Alert Program in conjunction with provincial wildlife officers to help prevent bears from wandering too close to humans. A 1969 initiative labelled the Polar Bear Control Program had emphasized killing those bears that entered the town; in contrast, Polar Bear Alert aimed to protect the lives of both humans and polar bears, to minimize property damage, and to minimize any food conditioning or human habituation of the bear.[52] The program

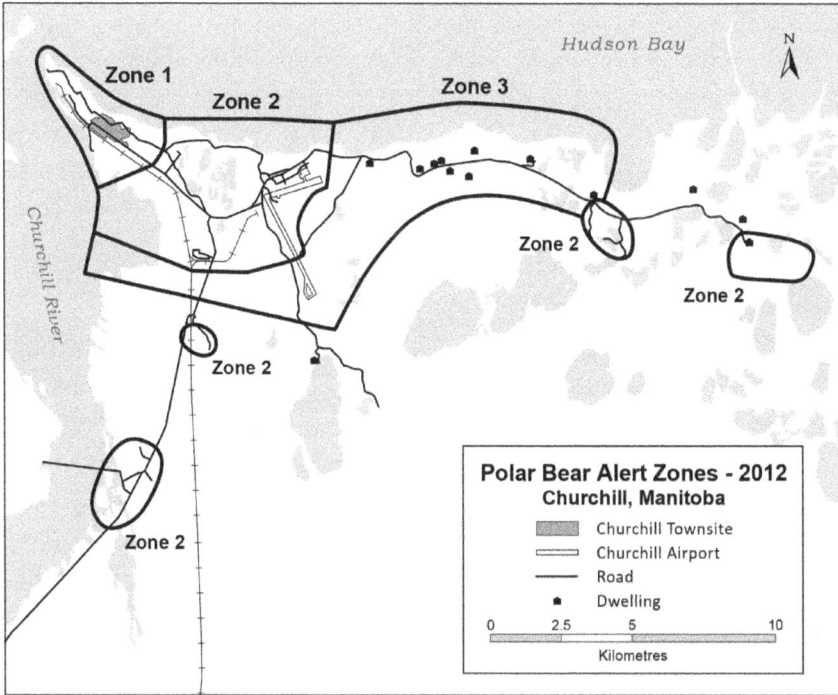

9.1 This map of the Churchill region depicts the Polar Bear Alert Program's zones. Churchill is located in Zone One, whereas the airport is located in Zone Two. Zone Three is largely uninhabited. Data courtesy of Bob Windsor, Manitoba's Department of Conservation and Water Stewardship.

resulted from residents and conservation officers realizing the economic value of live polar bears to the town as derived through wildlife tourism and recognizing that the animals could be managed using humane practices.[53] Central to the program was the establishment of three spatial zones that dictated different levels of tolerance for the presence of bears. In Zone One, the area encompassing Churchill's urban core, polar bears were promptly removed. Live traps were set on the outskirts of Zone One to prevent polar bears from wandering too close to many of the town's residences. Zone Two included the airport, and mobile traps were located as needed; however, this area's small number of dwellings diminished the opportunity for human–bear interactions. In Zone Three, polar bears were monitored but not removed from the area unless wildlife officers received a complaint.[54] A Bear Patrol comprised of wildlife officers enforced the zones to ensure that the bears remained a safe distance from the majority of Churchill's human population. Citizens aided the Bear Patrol by alerting the officers to bear sightings within the three zones.[55] Although various media represented the bear as frequently present within town limits, by the early 1980s the town was striving to ensure that humans and polar bears resided in separate spaces.

Under the Polar Bear Alert Program, Churchill took great efforts to avoid killing polar bears.[56] Officers used noise-making devices to scare them away, a tactic that attracted some condemnation and generated sympathy for the bears. Mrs. Carol MacKenzie's letter to the editor of Churchill's *Northport News* criticized the tactics officers used to scare a bear on the basis that excessive harrassment could produce a "mean" bear. She concluded by noting: "Despite my conservative outlook, I feel very strongly that a more liberal attitude could be adopted towards Churchill's Polar Bears."[57] To address the bears who repeatedly caused problems in the town, a polar bear holding compound – another component of the Polar Bear Alert Program – was trialed in 1979.[58] The compound, or, as the media dubbed it, the "bear jail," consisted of a metal building outside town that was renovated to accommodate sixteen individual bears and four family groups.[59] Chronic offenders were caught in live traps and placed in the facility until the ice formed on Hudson Bay and the animals were ready to leave town. The polar bear jail provided officers with a humane method of addressing the issue of nuisance bears and demonstrated that Churchill no longer viewed killing polar bears as an acceptable means of managing the species. The program has been considered a success because of the decreased number of both bear deaths and human maulings since its inception.[60]

Accompanying the physical work of scaring bears away and removing them from Churchill was a public education campaign aimed at improving the safety of human residents. Signs were erected along the borders of the zone system, informing people of where humans' space ended and that of the polar bears began, and deterring humans from entering the bears' zones. Signs on the outskirts of town stating "POLAR BEAR ALERT. STOP. DON'T WALK IN THIS AREA" warned people that that area was off-limits to humans. The signs featured an illustration of a large

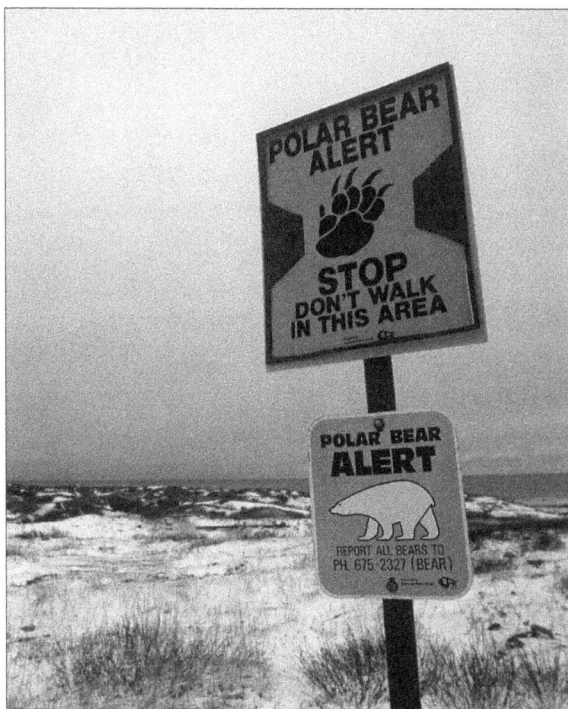

9.2 A sign warning Churchill's visitors and residents that they entering a polar bear zone. iStock.com/ IPGGutenbergUKLtd.

polar bear paw complete with sharp-looking claws to reinforce the idea that polar bears were dangerous.[61] Notices were also visible throughout town, instructing visitors and reminding locals of what to do when polar bears were spotted in town. Topping the list of actions one should take were "Get indoors and stay there" and "Call the RCMP or Conservation Office."[62] Another sign that read "Polar Bears and People Don't Mix" emphasized the importance of proper garbage disposal and provided advice for keeping bears away from garbage. "Odours attract bears – place all garbage in sealed plastic bags" and "Don't leave any loose garbage around" were tips deemed useful, though given the bear's famed sense of smell and sharp claws it seems unlikely that a plastic bag alone would have been an effective deterrent.[63] The local elementary school held an annual poster design contest aimed at educating Churchill's children about the dangers of their bear neighbours – the winning poster would best demonstrate that message. Children were also instructed on a safety position to assume in case they were attacked by a polar bear.[64] These public campaigns helped to prevent human–bear incidents. While people accepted the bear, they did so with caution evident in Churchill's commonsense slogan: "A safe polar bear is a distant polar bear."[65]

A range of print media publicized these successful campaigns to explain how a potentially dangerous situation might be defused. Audiences of naturalist magazines such as *Canadian Geographic, National Geographic*, and *International Wildlife* were shown a delicate relationship between a modern town and a magnificent and charismatic predator; thus, locals as well as readers who engaged with the relevant media were taught that polar bears were still dangerous, even if they looked benign. This print media offered a more balanced approach than the drama of *Polar Bear Alert*, but regardless of the manner in which the bears were presented, their presence in and around Churchill was common throughout the media coverage, and audiences soon began to consider visiting polar bears in the wild.

Churchill's Polar Bear Tourism

Churchill's polar bear tourism industry evolved during the 1970s and coincided with changing tourist demand and an increasingly consumerist attitude toward nature. The increased affluence of the postwar period enabled growing numbers of people to afford a holiday in remote Churchill, a destination that offered Canadians, Americans, and Europeans experiences of the natural world and an escape from their hectic day-to-day lives.[66] Initially, the polar bears and the town received visitors in the form of media personnel and wildlife biologists who photographed and studied the animals. Yet as Churchill's bears garnered more media attention for airlifts, their antics around town, and apparent cohabitation with local human residents, wildlife tourists began recognizing Churchill as a location offering access to an animal previously unavailable but to a select few sport hunters, scientists, and Arctic explorers. Photographers, cinematographers, and reporters transmitted an image of the bear as a guaranteed spectacle whose magnificence was available for viewing in a uniquely intimate atmosphere. Churchill's bear tourism offered a relatively undeveloped location and an ostensibly authentic experience of watching live bears in their natural habitat.[67]

The town and its entrepreneurs capitalized upon the attention the animal received in the media. Commenting on the best marketing approach for Churchill to take, a government-funded tourism and transportation study

9.3 A young bear sits before a Tundra Buggy. iStock.com/BLFink.

concluded: "Television programs and magazine articles provided many more visitors with information about Churchill, perhaps suggesting that forms of promotion other than the more traditional brochures and guidebooks may be more effective in disseminating tourism related information."[68] The diverse stakeholders involved in selling and promoting Churchill's polar bear tourism agreed on the media's importance in spreading the message of bear tourism and in fostering interest amongst potential visitors in viewing the bears in person. These stakeholders included management agencies such as the Canadian Wildlife Service and Manitoba Conservation; industry representatives composed of Churchill entrepreneurs involved directly in the industry as tour operators; representatives of Churchill's service sector and local government; non-profit environmental organizations; and various independent and commercial media.[69]

As the Churchill polar bears were being indirectly marketed to potential tourist audiences, a unique vehicle was constructed to facilitate large-scale bear tourism. Photographer Dan Guravich travelled to Churchill on assignment for the Smithsonian Institution in the 1970s to photograph the bears at the dump and was taken on an unplanned polar bear outing by local mechanic Len Smith. The two men became friends and together conceptualized what became known as "Tundra Buggies," giant wheeled contraptions that allow groups of tourists to venture onto the tundra comfortably, safely above the bears' reach, and with minimal impact on the land.[70] For a price, Tundra Buggies would transport small groups of tourists 21 kilometres away from town and onto the tundra to Gordon Point, within the Churchill Wildlife Management Area.[71] There, in a more natural setting than was achievable from sightings at the dump, tourists witnessed polar bears resting as they waited for Hudson Bay's waters to freeze.[72] Although the polar bear experience was marketed as limited to Churchill, visitors actually travelled beyond the town to witness the bear. Tundra Buggies became the vehicle of choice for Churchill's bear-seeking guests, and photographs of people photographing bears from the safety of these mammoth vehicles became common in tourist and wildlife magazines.[73]

By the late 1970s, Churchill's polar bears had been solidly commodified. Tourists able to afford the full Churchill experience, including the not-insignificant costs of travelling to Churchill, tour tickets, and northern accommodations, observed and photographed polar bears from the safety of Tundra Buggies.[74] Witnessing bears in their natural habitat, free from media manipulations or the cages of zoos, ostensibly provided visitors an authentic experience with one of nature's majestic creatures. By observing a polar bear firsthand, visitors hoped somehow to obtain a bit of the purity that the natural world has long been perceived to embody.[75] Just as wilderness enthusiasts had once argued in favour of the power of being immersed in a sublime and spectacular landscape, gazing on wild, free polar bears offered a means of purifying oneself from the ills associated with modern urban living. In addition to providing tours of wild polar bears, Churchill's tourism industry marketed an array of souvenirs. As of 1990, these included "Inuit carvings of polar bears in soapstone, bone, and ivory . . . polar bear place mats, polar bear pins, polar bear patches ('Churchill Household Pests'), polar bear postcards, polar bear posters, polar bear puppets, and beer mugs labeled 'Polar Bear Piss.'"[76] Tourists purchased memorabilia from this eclectic collection to adorn their homes, pass on as gifts, and entertain friends.

Accounts and images of people looking at and photographing polar bears presented the creature as an object for the consumption and pleasure of visitors seeking a genuine glimpse of the bear they had heard and seen so much about. In the early 1980s, magazines such as *Life* and *Canadian Geographic* included photographs showing polar bears grouped around Tundra Buggies while tourists competed for the best views. *Life* published a compelling photograph in which a young bear stands on its hind legs, with its enormous front paws on the tire of a Tundra Buggy and looking upward at the vehicle's windows. Hanging out a window a short distance away, a photographer's head and upper shoulder are turned to face the bear.[77] Later in the article was an image of a polar bear peering through the window at the tourists, looking more curious than dangerous. The photograph conveyed the sense of intimacy a tourist experienced with the bears when all that separated the species was a reinforced windowpane.[78] These and other images of bears and tourists demonstrated how physically close visitors could get to polar bears, in contrast to the image of potentially dangerous bears that had emerged from Churchill's public education campaigns. High up in machines that dominated the surrounding bears, humans appeared to have peacefully overcome the dangerous animal and ensured their own entertainment. Photos that captured tourists carrying their ever-present cameras reaffirmed the idea that this was a wildlife tourist venture. The close proximity of the bears assured those who made the trek to Churchill that bear watchers would be rewarded with a sort of trophy – a polar bear close up.

Bear watching as a tourist activity grew quickly. In 1984, figures from wholesale tour operators indicated that 41 per cent of the package tours sold for Churchill were concentrated in the weeks of polar bear season. Tour packages themselves accounted for a small percentage of the total visitors, and self-bookings constituted "some 70% of non-business travel to Churchill"; most of these travellers came for the polar bears or whales.[79] By 1985, those involved in the industry agreed that while room for growth existed, care had to be taken to ensure that the industry did not disrupt the bears' psychology. Beyond fears that large numbers of tourists could impact the bear's mental well-being, tour operators were cautious to keep tourist numbers in check to prevent any reduction in the quality of the

9.4 A lone polar bear on the snowy tundra. iStock.com/HuntedDuck.

experience – the perceived wildness and authenticity of the creature would be diminished when it was framed against another tundra vehicle filled with photo-snapping visitors. As such, it was in the tour operators' long-term interest to expand cautiously.[80] Writing in 1990, the geologist Charles Feazel observed that polar bear tourism contributed "at least $3 million a year into the local economy,"[81] supporting the town's hotels, restaurants, and shops in addition to the polar bear tours. Churchill's bear-watching industry understood the fine balance between the economics of Tundra Buggy tickets, the aesthetics of viewing bears in a landscape perceptibly devoid of humans, and ethical concerns for animal welfare when conceptualizing how to ensure a healthy population of bears and a satisfied wildlife tourist clientele. Striking this balance was not new to Churchill, as it had also been a concern in the early 1980s when the images of the polar bears at the garbage dump were published.

Concerns About Polar Bear Tourism

Although the town has benefited economically from bear tourism, some concerns remain, most notably the representation of First Nations groups within the tourism economy and the impact of climate change on Churchill's polar bear population. The Indigenous peoples of Churchill – Cree, Dene, and Inuit – have not played a large role in the town's polar bear tourism and did not appear prominently in publicity images either of polar bears or the local tourist industry; nonetheless, they are important actors in bear management in the wider Canadian Arctic. Indigenous knowledge of polar bear populations has gained recognition among scholars of northern Aboriginal communities and wildlife scientists, who as of 2001 began to acknowledge the Inuit and Manitoba's First Nations' significant contributions to scientific understandings of polar bears.[82]

Despite First Nations' historical engagement with polar bears in Arctic settings and their more recent involvement in bear management, the role of Churchill's Indigenous communities in polar bear tourism has been less prominent. Edward Struzik observes that initial efforts to attract tourists to Churchill were "multicultural in a unique way, with non-natives working with Cree, Chipewyan, Métis, and Inuit entrepreneurs. Recognizing an opportunity [the media's interest in Churchill's polar bears] . . . they all got together at the Chamber of Commerce level to see how they could turn this publicity into a successful economic venture."[83] To prospective visitors, however, the region's Indigenous peoples may be perceived as inherent to the north, just like the polar bear. Some tour companies do offer Indigenous elements to their polar bear tours; a highlight of Natural Habitat Adventures' "Ultimate Churchill Adventure" package is to "meet the Native peoples of Hudson Bay and learn about their age-old customs and traditions during special cultural presentations."[84] Since these cultural presentations are listed alongside Tundra Rover polar bear tours that feature the opportunity to crawl into an unoccupied polar bear den, one wonders to what extent Indigenous peoples and polar bears are portrayed similarly as wildlife tourist attractions.

While the Indigenous people of Churchill may not receive substantial profits from polar bear tourism, their cultural presence remains visible to visitors. A 2008 study on Canada's Inuit and polar bear hunting found "no evidence or suggestion that any of the polar bear viewing ecotourism companies were Inuit owned and because almost all tourists' needs are met by non-Inuit ecotourism companies, local people are likely to receive a reduced share of profits flowing from bear viewers."[85] The Eskimo Museum, an institution in Churchill since 1944, contains a collection of Indigenous artwork and cultural artifacts. A popular tourist attraction, the museum reminds visitors that Churchill's population consists of Indigenous peoples in addition to polar bears, whales, and birds.

Climate change, an issue that has increased public and political interest in the Arctic,[86] is perceived as a threat to polar bear tourism.[87] A changing Arctic climate could shorten the winter season, reduce the sea ice platform, and hamper the animal's ability to sustain itself through a prolonged summer season.[88] This link between the polar bear's future and a changing climate, combined with the beast's capacity to captivate the public, led the Center for Biological Diversity to propose in 2008 that the polar bear join the American listing of endangered species. The center reasoned that were the bear to achieve an endangered status, it would force the American government to acknowledge climate change as a legitimate threat. Ultimately, the American government classified the polar bear as "threatened." Wildlife conservationists portrayed it as a mighty animal that the world stood to lose if actions were not taken to alleviate climate change.[89]

The impact of climate change is difficult to predict; it may reduce the Hudson Bay polar bear population and result in thinner, less healthy animals.[90] In a 2010 study, over 60 per cent of polar bear tourists expressed their willingness to visit Churchill's polar bears in spite of the possibility of seeing unhealthy bears or fewer bears. Faced with the prospect of seeing no bears, however, only 50 per cent of respondents were willing to visit Churchill, a decline the community dreads.[91] Since at least 2004, Churchill's residents have treated the issue of climate change as a significant challenge for polar bear tourism and, by extension, the local economy.[92] In interviews with community members, the most common issue discussed in relation to climate change was the dangers it posed to the polar bear – a finding that reinforces the bear's importance to Churchill. Churchill's human population knows that a loss of the polar bear and the associated wildlife tourist industry would undermine the town's identity and disrupt the local economy. As one resident reasoned, "The main attraction is the polar bears; there is whaling and birding, but compared to the bears that is a side issue. The main tourist season is during bear season."[93]

Demand for polar bear tourism is forecast for the next twenty to thirty years.[94] Ironically, climate change may increase Churchill's wildlife tourism – at least in the short term – because visitors want to travel north to see and experience the animal before it disappears into extinction. As another Churchill resident articulated, "People come up here now with a lump in their throats because they think this bear is doomed . . . Not for the joy of being with a bear, and seeing a bear in the wild. That's secondary now."[95]

Conclusion

Churchill's wildlife tourism industry situated the polar bear as a wild and quintessential sight indigenous to the Arctic that is uniquely available to bear watchers. In spite of the emphasis Canadian and American media placed on the promise of unobstructed views of these urban polar bears, a range of human activity shaped this tourist experience. For example, Churchill initiated wildlife management and public education programs aimed at keeping the animal outside the town, allowing humans and bears to coexist safely. Furthermore, Churchill's bear watching, although depicted in early media accounts as an urban activity, ultimately emerged as a safari-style endeavour outside town limits, complete with specialized vehicles that protected tourists while allowing them to achieve closer physical proximity to the bear than was previously possible. The rise of polar bear tourism meant that the Arctic was available for consumption and entertainment, no longer beyond the reach of affluent tourists. Churchill's relationship with polar bears in the 1970s and 1980s demonstrated that in the face of a natural predator, a broad respect for wild animals could empower a town to manage creatively and ultimately profit from an unusual, potentially dangerous, natural phenomenon. Into the next few decades, the Churchill region will continue to be a setting through which wildlife tourists may experience the Arctic as a safe, accessible space, albeit one whose appeal faces an uncertain future.

Notes

1 "Everything Churchill," Travel Manitoba, www.everythingchurchill.com (accessed 23 July 2014). For an accessible discussion of the centrality of polar bear tourism to Churchill's economy, see Michael P. Chotka, *Climate Change and the Tourist Economy of Churchill: Perspectives of Local Residents* (Winnipeg: University of Winnipeg, May 2014), 1–33.

2 Richard Perry, *The World of the Polar Bear* (London: Cox and Wyman, 1966); Charles Feazel, *White Bear: Encounters with the Master of the Arctic* (New York: Ballantine, 1992); Ian Stirling, *Polar Bears: A Natural History of a Threatened Species* (Markham, ON: Fitzhenry & Whiteside, 2011); Kieran Mulvaney, *Ice Bear: A Natural and Unnatural History of the Polar Bear* (London: Hutchinson, 2011); Richard Ellis, *On Thin Ice: The Changing World of the Polar Bear* (New York: Vintage, 2010). While this scholarship gives some attention to the topic of Churchill and polar bears, there is little engagement from a historical perspective.

3 Kristoffer Archibald, "From Fierce to Adorable: Representations of Polar Bears in the Popular Imagination," *American Review of Canadian Studies* 45, no. 3 (2015): 266–82.

4 This literature includes studies on how tourists view the bear, how differing ecological outlooks generate tensions amongst bear watchers, and the influence of the visual sense in shaping perceptions of ecological degradation. R. Harvey Lemelin, "The Gawk, The Glance, and The Gaze: Ocular Consumption and Polar Bear Tourism in Churchill, Manitoba, Canada," *Current Issues in Tourism* 9, no. 6 (2006): 516–34; R. Harvey Lemelin and Elaine C. Wiersma, "Perceptions of Polar Bear Tourists: A Qualitative Analysis," *Human Dimensions of Wildlife* 12 (2007): 45–52; R. Harvey Lemelin, David, Fennell, and Bryan Smale, "Polar Bear Viewers as Deep Ecotourists: How Specialised Are They?," *Journal of Sustainable Tourism* 16, no. 1 (2008): 42–62.

5 Scholars critical of the polar bear tourists' gaze include Gerry Marvin, who writes that visitors "might see them close up but this is essentially a distant encounter from the safety of a vehicle. The polar bears are transformed, reduced to being a sight, another tourist attraction." Gerry Marvin, "Perpetuating Polar Bears: The Cultural Life of Dead Animals," in *Nanoq: Flat Out and Bluesome*, ed. Bryndís Snaebjörnsdóttir and Mark Wilson (London: Black Dog, 2006), 158. See also Lemelin, "The Gawk, The Glance, and The Gaze.".

6 Lemelin, "The Gawk, The Glance, and The Gaze," 517.

7 Alice Wondrak Biel, *Do (Not) Feed The Bears: The Fitful History of Wildlife and Tourists in Yellowstone* (Lawrence: University Press of Kansas, 2006); George Colpitts, "Films, Tourists, and Bears in the National Parks: Managing Park Use and the Problematic 'Highway Bum,'" in *A Century of Parks Canada, 1911–2011*, ed. Claire Elizabeth Campbell (Calgary: University of Calgary Press, 2011), 153–78.

8   R. Harvey Lemelin, "Wildlife Tour-
     ism at the Edge of Chaos: Complex
     Interactions Between Humans and
     Polar Bears in Churchill, Mani-
     toba," in *Breaking Ice: Renewable
     Resource and Ocean Management
     in the Canadian North*, ed. Fikret
     Berkes et al. (Calgary: University of
     Calgary Press, 2005): 192–93.

9   Edward Struzik, *Arctic Icons: How
     the Town of Churchill Learned to
     Love its Polar Bears* (Markham,
     ON: Fitzhenry & Whiteside, 2014).

10   Jon Mooallem, *Wild Ones: A Some-
     times Dismaying, Weirdly Reassur-
     ing Story About Looking at People
     Looking at Animals in America*
     (New York: Penguin, 2013).

11   Historical studies of wildlife in
     Canada, including Janet Foster,
     *Working for Wildlife: The Begin-
     nings of Preservation in Canada*
     (Toronto: University of Toronto
     Press, 1998); George Colpitts,
     *Game in the Garden: A Human His-
     tory of Wildlife in Western Canada
     to 1940* (Vancouver: University of
     British Columbia Press, 2002); Tina
     Loo, *States of Nature: Conserving
     Canada's Wildlife in the Twentieth
     Century* (Vancouver: University
     of British Columbia Press, 2006);
     John Sandlos, *Hunters at the
     Margin: Native Peoples and Wildlife
     Conservation in the Northwest
     Territories* (Vancouver, University
     of British Columbia Press, 2007),
     have tended to focus on human
     relationships to wildlife outside
     urban spaces.

12   Sean Kheraj, "Demonstration
     Wildlife: Negotiating the Animal
     Landscape of Vancouver's Stanley
     Park, 1888–1996," *Environment
     and History* 18 (2012): 497–527.

13   Shelagh Grant, *Polar Imperative:
     A History of Arctic Sovereignty in
     North America* (Vancouver: Doug-
     las & McIntyre, 2010), 78.

14   R. Harvey Lemelin, "Human–Polar
     Bear Interactions in Churchill,
     Manitoba: The Socio-ecological
     Perspective," in *Marine Wildlife
     and Tourism Management*, ed.
     James Higham and Michael Lück
     (Cambridge, MA: Cabi, 2007), 98.

15   This situation enabled some Inuit
     communities in Nunavut to profit
     from the sale of their guiding ex-
     pertise and quota. The sport hunt-
     ing industry was pursued cautious-
     ly, establishing itself prominently
     in Nunavut in the mid-1980s after
     the sealskin market had collapsed
     and residents sought alternative
     economic ventures. Like Chur-
     chill's polar bear tourism, it offered
     a means of attracting new capital
     to remote Arctic communities. Lee
     Foote and George Wenzel, "Con-
     servation Hunting Concepts, Cana-
     da's Inuit and Polar Bear Hunting,"
     in *Tourism and the Consumption
     of Wildlife: Hunting Shooting and
     Sport Fishing*, ed. Brent Lovelock
     (New York: Routledge, 2008), 366.

16   *North to Hudson Bay* (Canadian
     Government Travel Bureau, 1950).

17   Lemelin, "Wildlife Tourism at the
     Edge of Chaos," 188.

18   Stirling, *Polar Bears*, 157–58.

19   Shelagh Grant suggests, for exam-
     ple, that the American military's
     reduced Arctic presence after
     1965 is attributable to America's
     need for troops in Vietnam and a
     redeployment of military spending
     to space exploration. Grant, *Polar
     Imperative*, 337.

20   Lemelin, "Human–Polar Bear Interactions in Churchill, Manitoba," in *Marine Wildlife and Tourism Management*, 99.

21   Ibid., 100.

22   Stirling, *Polar Bears*, 158.

23   According to Polar Bears International, the leading conservation organization whose mission it is to protect the polar bear through protecting its sea ice habitat, there have only been two human fatalities in Churchill, the incident described above and the case of a local man in 1983 who stuffed his pockets with meat from a freezer in the ruins of the recently burnt Churchill Hotel and was killed by a bear. "Attacks and Encounters," Polar Bears International, http://www.polarbearsinternational.org/about-polar-bears/essentials/attacks-and-encounters (accessed 28 July 2014).

24   "Polar Bear Alert Program Frequently Asked Questions," 27 January 2014. Bob Windsor, email message to author, 23 December 2014.

25   In the fall of 2013, for example, a 30-year-old woman visiting Churchill was attacked by a polar bear in town. She was saved by a local 69-year-old man who in turn was also attacked by the bear. On Halloween night, after the trick-or-treating was finished, another man was attacked. "Woman Recounts Harrowing Attack by Churchill Polar Bear," *CBC News*, 19 December 2013; "Man, Woman Attacked by Polar Bear in Churchill," *CBC News*, 1 November 2013. Struzik overviews these maulings and Churchill's wildlife officers' response. Struzik, *Arctic Icons*, 283–87.

26   Alan Herscovici, *Second Nature: The Animal-Rights Controversy* (Toronto: CBC Enterprises, 1985), 71.

27   "Manitoba Receives Bid to Airlift Polar Bears from Churchill area," *Globe and Mail*, 8 October 1971; Martin O'Malley, "Into the White Horizon: Operation Bear Lift Finally Begins – With Barely Room for One Polar Bear on the Plane," *Globe and Mail*, 18 October 1971. The animal welfare organization campaigned worldwide for financial assistance, a process that included an advertisement in a prominent Canadian paper and the director, Brian Davies, travelling to Europe. "It's Time to Kill the Polar Bears Unless You Help Them [Advertisement]," *Globe and Mail*, 3 October 1971; "Funds for Airlifting Polar Bears Assured, Director Says After Trip," *Globe and Mail*, 4 November 1971.

28   Richard Davids, "The Town That 'Hosts' Polar Bears," *Reader's Digest*, June 1978, 122–25. The cost per bear was reported at $400 by the *New York Times*.

29   This interesting event in the life of Churchill's polar bears was not unique to the era. In Glacier National Park, grizzly bears were airlifted away from humans. Jeanne N. Clark, "Grizzlies and Tourists," *Society* 27 (1990): 30.

30   *Stranded Marine Animals*, pamphlet (International Fund For Animal Welfare, 1978). *Stranded Marine Animals* pamphlet obtained by author through e-mail message via IFAW's international office. For a greater discussion on IFAW and its philosophy, see Herscovici, *Second Nature*, 69–115.

31　IFAW's campaign was so well publicized that its arrival in Churchill "was attended by reporters from all over Canada, from London, Bonn and Paris, and by a television team from Chicago." "Polar Bears Airlifted Out, Return Because They Love the Dump," *New York Times*, 21 November 1971, 34. For a Churchill perspective on IFAW in the community, see "Davies Returns for Bearlift II," *Northport News* [Churchill], 28 October 1972.

32　Richard Davids, "Polar Bears Aren't Pets, but This Town Is Learning How to Live with Them," *Smithsonian*, February 1978, 70–79.

33　Richard Davids, "The Town That 'Hosts' Polar Bears," *Reader's Digest*, June 1978, 122.

34　Frederic Golden, "A Plethora of Polar Bears," *Time*, 21 December 1981, 70–71.

35　Struzik, *Arctic Icons*, 62.

36　Ibid., 106.

37　Sub-adult and female bears with young are the animals most likely to scavenge at the dump – adult males tend not to frequent the dump. This behaviour is explained by polar bear biologists Stirling and Lunn as resulting from the animals' nutritional needs and learned traits. Observations of bears at the dump reveal cases of juvenile bears returning to the dump until maturity, at which point it is thought that their hunting skills have advanced enough to provide them sufficient caloric levels until they can resume seal hunting on Hudson Bay. N.J. Lunn and Ian Stirling, "The Significance of Supplemental Food to Polar Bears During the Ice-Free Period of Hudson Bay,"

Canadian Journal of Zoology 63, no. 10 (October 1985): 2291–97.

38　Identifiable garbage included a package bearing the brand McCain, a multinational frozen foods corporation. The presence of such manufactured packaging reinforced the fact that these bears were scavenging among modern human garbage and that Churchill in northern Manitoba enjoyed the current conveniences of larger southern cities. Golden, "A Plethora of Polar Bears," 70–71.

39　Readers learnt that wildlife biologists dyed numbers on the fur of bears identified as "chronically aggressive." Bill Richards, "Henry Hudson's Changing Bay," *National Geographic*, March 1982, 395; *Canadian Geographic* expressed disgust at this situation, noting of one photograph how a "family of filthy bears has grown into obesity at the Churchill garbage dump." Fred Bruemmer, "Churchill: Polar Bear Capital of the World," *Canadian Geographic*, December 1983–January 1984, 24.

40　On the image of grizzly and black bears in Yellowstone National Park see Alice Wondrak Biel, *Do (Not) Feed The Bears: The Fitful History of Wildlife and Tourists in Yellowstone* (Lawrence: University Press of Kansas, 2006).

41　Colpitts, "Films, Tourists, and Bears in the National Parks," 158–60.

42　Ibid., 153–78.

43　Bear biologists were concerned that bears at the dump could become increasingly aggressive as they became ever more familiar with humans working in the area.

Stirling, *Polar Bears*, 169. Richard Davids reported on dump employees being harassed by polar bears in the course of their daily work. Davids, "The Town That Hosts Polar Bears," 123.

44   Peter Carlyle-Gordge, "The Dark Side of Winnie-the-Pooh," *MacLeans*, 22 September 1980, 33; "Polar Bear Clause in Union Contract," *Globe and Mail*, 4 September 1960.

45   Golden, "A Plethora of Polar Bears," 70–71.

46   Davids, "Town That 'Hosts' Polar Bears," 122–25.

47   Ibid.

48   *Polar Bear Alert*, narrated by Jason Robards (National Geographic Society, 1982).

49   Ibid.

50   Mooallem, *Wild Ones*, 29.

51   Ibid., 29–31.

52   The Control Program changed names to the Alert Program to better reflect its broader mandate of protecting both bears and humans. Feazel, *White Bear*, 158.

53   See the video interview with Manitoba Wildlife Manager Daryll Hedman on the Polar Bears International website. "Churchill, Canada's Polar Bear Alert Program," Polar Bears International, http:// www.polarbearsinternational. org/media/video/churchill-canadas-polar-bear-alert-program (accessed 7 August 2014).

54   The Polar Bear Alert Program continues to exist and has been recognized globally for its success in protecting humans and bears – a 2014 article championing the program's success reports that on average less than one bear is euthanized per year. Bob Windsor, "Polar Bear Alert Program," *The Fur Harvester*, Winter 2013–14, 3–6.

55   Technical Workshop, *Polar Bears: Proceedings of the Technical Workshop of the IUCN Polar Bear Specialist Group*, Grand Canyon, Arizona, February 1983, 8–9. For more popular coverage see *Polar Bear Alert*, 1982. The *Globe and Mail* also did a piece on polar bear education in Churchill's elementary school: see "Churchill Pupils Are Intrigued by Nanook, but Parents Fear His Northward Migration," *Globe and Mail*, 15 October 1971. A 1985 survey of Churchill's residents reported that almost 90 per cent of respondents were satisfied with the Polar Bear Alert program. Struzik, *Arctic Icons*, 173.

56   As of 1980 the official stance of the Canadian government, presented in a bear safety pamphlet to employees working in bear country, was "Shoot to kill only as a last resort." According to the pamphlet, one was to give the inquisitive creature a chance by first trying to scare it off through non-lethal means. Thomas G. Smith, *Danger, Polar Bear!* (Ottawa: Energy, Mines and Resources Canada, 1980).

57   Carol MacKenzie, "Letter to the Editor," *Northport News* [Churchill], 28 October 1972.

58   Struzik, *Arctic Icons*, 91–93.

59   For example, the term "bear jail" was used by the science magazine *Omni* in 1985. George Nobbe, "Bear Jail," *Omni*, April 1985, 36.

60   "Churchill, Canada's Polar Bear Alert Program," Polar Bears

International, http://www.polar-
bearsinternational.org/media/
video/churchill-canadas-po-
lar-bear-alert-program (accessed
August 7, 2014). The popular media
has reflected this perspective and
suggests that the Polar Bear Alert
program and the capacity for Churchill's wildlife officers to humanly
address the presence of polar bears
will only grow in importance as
climate change reduces the bears'
access to seals and causes them
to seek food within Churchill. Ed
Struzik, "Polar Bear Wrangler Job
Getting Harder, Thanks To Climate
Change," *Huffington Post*, 22 November 2015.

61   Golden, "A Plethora of Polar
     Bears," 70–71.

62   Richard C. Davids, *Lords of the
     Arctic: A Journey Among the Polar
     Bears* (New York: Macmillan,
     1982), Appendix I.

63   Fred Bruemmer, "Churchill: Polar
     Bear Capital of the World," *Cana-
     dian Geographic*, January 1984, 26.

64   *Polar Bear Alert* (National Geo-
     graphic Society, 1982).

65   Richards, "Henry Hudson's Chang-
     ing Bay," 380–404; Fred Bruemmer,
     "Never Trust Nanook," *Interna-
     tional Wildlife*, July–August 1979,
     20–27.

66   Jennifer Price, *Flight Maps: Adven-
     tures with Nature in Modern Amer-
     ica* (New York: Basic Books, 1999),
     197. Modified nature, such as ski
     hills in the American Rockies, also
     attracted affluent tourists looking
     to escape their daily lives. On ski
     tourism, see Annie Gilbert Cole-
     man, *Ski Style: Sport and Culture in
     the Rockies* (Lawrence: University
     Press of Kansas, 2004), 147–213.

On the construction of experience
and the social complexities of
tourism in the twentieth century,
see Hal Rothman, *Devil's Bargains:
Tourism in the Twentieth-Century American West* (Lawrence:
Lawrence Press of Kansas, 1998);
and Ian McKay, *Quest of the Folk:
Antimodernism and Cultural Selection in Twentieth-Century Nova
Scotia* (Montreal: McGill-Queen's
University Press, 1994).

67   Churchill's polar bear viewing in-
     dustry repeated a situation played
     out in 1960s Africa, where photo-
     graphic safaris and films of African
     fauna situated animals as part of a
     recreational economy wherein they
     were valued by affluent tourists
     for their aesthetic qualities. Gregg
     Mitman, *Reel Nature: America's
     Romance with Wildlife in Film*
     (Cambridge, MA: Harvard Univer-
     sity Press, 1999), 194.

68   Marshall Macklin Monaghan
     Limited, *Churchill Tourism and
     Transportation Study* (Transport
     Canada and Manitoba Department
     of Highways and Transportation,
     1985), 9.14.

69   Lemelin, "Wildlife Tourism at the
     Edge of Chaos," 189–91.

70   Ibid., 192–93; Downs Matthews
     and Ian N. Higginson, "Dan Gu-
     ravich (1918–1997)," *Arctic* 51 (June
     1998): 181–82.

71   The Churchill Wildlife Man-
     agement Area is nearly 850,000
     hectares and protects the region's
     polar bears' summer resting area
     and maternity denning areas.

72   Lemelin, "Wildlife Tourism at the
     Edge of Chaos," 189.

73   The parallels between Tundra
     Buggies and the jeep of the African

safari are worth noting. Both vehicles transport visitors into a foreign environment that is conceptualized as the domain of the animals tourists are looking to see. The vehicles buffer the tourists from the animals and restrict the experience to one of sight, as opposed to touch, despite the close proximity of the impressive creatures, who become habituated to the presence of the travelling humans.

74 The true polar bear experience was thus restricted to the privileged, more affluent classes of society. This situation continues. An all-inclusive one-day bear watching tour for October 2014 aboard a Tundra Buggy, return flight to Winnipeg included, costs $1,500 according to Frontiers North Adventures. "Churchill Polar Bear Adventure," Frontiers North Adventures, http://www.frontiersnorth.com/adventures/churchill-polar-bear-adventure (accessed 21 July 2014).

75 Price, *Flight Maps*, 175.

76 Feazel, *White Bear*, 164.

77 Anne Fadiman, "The Great White Bears," *Life*, February 1984, 42–46. A similar photograph appeared in *Canadian Geographic*. Bruemmer, "Churchill: Polar Bear Capital of the World," 20.

78 Fadiman, "The Great White Bears," 42–46. The closeness of bears to people in Churchill was also demonstrated in *Popular Photography*, which noted that a picture of polar bears was shot from 7 feet away, and in the travel magazine *Travel Incorporating Holiday*. *Outdoor Canada* made a similar observation. Guravich, "King of the Arctic," *Popular Photography*, May 1984, 77; Wayne Lynch, "Making

Tracks to the Bears," *Travel Incorporating Holiday*, October 1983, 38; John Sylvester, "Polar Bear Safari," *Outdoor Canada*, April 1983, 31.

79 Marshall Macklin Monaghan Limited, *Churchill Tourism and Transportation Study*, 4.29.

80 Ibid., 4.12. The caution employed around the expansion of the bear-watching industry positions polar bear tourism as an early example of ecotourism. Definitions for ecotourism vary; however, the principal goals are to "foster sustainable use through resource conservation, cultural revival and economic development and diversification." David Newsome, Susan A. Moore, and Ross K. Dowling, *Natural Area Tourism: Ecology, Impacts and Management* (Toronto: Channel View Publications, 2002), 14.

81 Feazel, *White Bear*, 159.

82 Magdalena A. K. Muir and Lloyd N. Binder, "Traditional Knowledge and Northern Wildlife Management: The Arctic Circumpolar Route," in *Collecting and Safeguarding the Oral Tradition*, ed. John McIlwaine and Jean Whiffin (München: K. G. Saur, 2001), 137.

83 Struzik, *Arctic Icons*, 147.

84 "Ultimate Churchill Adventure," Natural Habitat Adventures, www.nathab.com/polar-bear-tours/ultimate-churchill/ (accessed 16 September 2014).

85 Foote and Wenzel, "Conservation Hunting Concepts," 124.

86 Stéphane Roussel and John Erik Fossum, "The Arctic Is Hot Again in America and Europe," *International Journal* (Autumn 2010): 799–808.

87 Climate change is acknowledged to be affecting Arctic tourism ventures in general. A 2010 article examining Arctic cooperation and Canadian foreign policy cites the increase in cruise ships and yachts to Greenland as but one example of how warmer temperatures are changing Arctic tourism. Michael Byers, "Cold Peace: Arctic Cooperation and Canadian Foreign Policy," *International Journal* (Autumn 2010): 902.

88 Some researchers, such as Linda Gormezano, an ecologist at the American Museum of Natural History, suggest that polar bears faced with six months on land could offset their shortened seal hunting season by consuming snow geese and their eggs as well as caribou. See Linda Gormezano and Robert Rockwell, "What to Eat Now?: Shifts in Polar Bear Diet During the Ice-Free Season in Western Hudson Bay," *Ecology and Evolution* (September 2013): 3509–23; D.T. Iles et al., "Terrestrial Predation by Polar Bears: Not Just a Wild Goose Chase," *Polar Biology* (September 2013): 1373–79.

89 The wealth of media coverage on polar bears and climate change is significant, making polar bears into arguably one of the most recognizable species in western media. Jon Mooallem's *Wild Ones* offers a decent overview of the Center for Biological Diversity's legal and public relations strategy in their effort to have the bear listed as endangered. Mooallem, *Wild Ones*, 13–101.

90 Amongst polar bear biologists there appears to be disagreement about the impact of climate change on the health of populations. Reg Sherren, "Polar Bears: Threatened Species or Political Pawn?," *CBC News, Technology and Science*, 2 September 2014, www.cbc.ca/news/technology/polar-bears-threatened-species-or-political-pawn-1.2753645 (accessed 24 September 2014). The polar bear's evolutionary history also complicates discussion surrounding the animal's future in a changing climate. In 2011 evolutionary research on the polar bear revealed that modern polar bears emerged from interbreeding between the extinct Irish brown bear and a prehistoric polar bear. The researchers postulate that abrupt climate changes in the last ice age brought the two species into contact and may be a "mechanism by which species deal with marginal habitats during periods of environmental deterioration." Ceiridwen J. Edwards et al., "Ancient Hybridization and an Irish Origin for the Modern Polar Bear Matriline," *Current Biology* 21 (9 August 2011): 1251–58.

91 Daniel Scott, Colin Michael Hall, and Stefan Gössling, *Tourism and Climate Change: Impacts, Adaptation and Mitigation* (New York: Routledge, 2012), 340.

92 Chotka, *Climate Change and the Tourist Economy of Churchill*, 14.

93 Ibid., 18.

94 Jackie Dawson, Emma Stewart, and Daniel Scott, "Climate Change and Polar Bear Viewing: A Case Study of Visitor Demand, Carbon Emissions and Mitigation in Churchill, Canada," in *Tourism and Change in Polar Regions: Climate, Environment and Experience*, ed. Jarkko Saarinen (New York: Routledge, 2010), 96.

95 As quoted in Mooallem, *Wild Ones*, 44.

Cetaceans in the City: Orca Captivity, Animal Rights, and Environmental Values in Vancouver

Jason Colby

In March 1967, "Walter the Whale" arrived in Vancouver, British Columbia. A six-year-old, 15-foot killer whale (*Orcinus orca*), "Walter" had been captured in Washington State's Puget Sound a month earlier by Seattle Marine Aquarium owner Ted Griffin, who agreed to display the animal at the upcoming Vancouver Boat, Trailer and Sport Show, held in the city's Pacific National Exhibition grounds. Hoping for Walter to make a good impression, Griffin cautioned would-be visitors that the whale might act a bit skittish. In addition to fatigue from the long journey by truck, he noted that killer whales were "quite gregarious" and that the young animal "probably misses the others."[1] He need not have worried about the public response. Displayed in a small pool at the boat show, Walter charmed and amazed curious spectators. Among them was a local fisherman, who reluctantly admitted to Griffin that he had shot a large number of "blackfish" – then a common term for orcas.[2] The high point of the visit came on 16 March, when Griffin arranged for a phone call between Walter and two pod-mates being held at the aquarium in Seattle. Broadcast by a Vancouver radio station, the whales' "conversation" drew even more attention to Walter and the boat show, which boasted a ten-day attendance of over 100,000.[3] The obvious public interest helped convinced the Vancouver Aquarium to buy the killer whale from Griffin for $20,000. Soon after, the staff discovered the young animal was female and renamed her "Skana" – the Indigenous Haida nation's term for killer whale. Visually striking and responsive to training, Skana quickly became the aquarium's top attraction and a key asset for the city's growing tourist industry.[4]

For the next thirty-four years, Skana and other captive killer whales played a powerful and controversial role in the shifting economy and environmental values of Vancouver and the surrounding region. On the one hand, the Vancouver Aquarium's orcas became iconic attractions for British Columbia's increasingly urban-based tourist industry.[5] By the early 1970s, it was not only hunting and fishing opportunities in the surrounding areas that drew visitors to Vancouver but also the chance to see trained performances by an animal that was rapidly coming to symbolize the broader Pacific Northwest. In the process, captive killer whales became virtual mascots of the city, with local reporters following the news of performances, accidents, births, and deaths at the aquarium much as journalists in San Diego covered Sea World following the acquisition of its first killer whale, also from Griffin, in late 1965.

On the other hand, the presence of captive killer whales at the Vancouver Aquarium, located in the city's beloved Stanley Park, intersected in complex ways with broader demographic and cultural trends. In the late 1960s and early 1970s, even as traditional maritime industries such as fishing declined, Vancouver emerged as the countercultural epicentre of western Canada. From the beginning, protests in the city focused on environmental as well as Cold War issues. The most famous example of this confluence was Greenpeace, a Vancouver-based protest group that emerged from a 1971 expedition to protest US nuclear testing in Alaska and later turned its attention to commercial whaling.[6] It was no coincidence that the world's first anti-whaling organization originated in a city with publicly displayed cetaceans. Not only did the aquarium hold a prominent place in Vancouver's growing international profile, but the presence and actions of Skana and other captive orcas directly impacted the thinking and politicization of scientists and activists who played key roles in Greenpeace's development. Indeed, the organization likely would not have turned its focus to whaling in the mid-1970s, and hence gained worldwide fame, without a series of momentous interactions between humans and captive orcas.

Not limited to Vancouver, this transformative interspecies encounter extended throughout the transborder region washed by the "Salish Sea" – a term encompassing the Strait of Juan de Fuca, Puget Sound, and the Strait of Georgia. By the early 1970s, the capture, display, and sale of orcas by Sealand of the Pacific in Victoria, British Columbia, and Griffin's aquarium in Seattle had raised heated public debate on both sides of the border. In Vancouver, however, in contrast to Puget Sound and southern Vancouver Island, it was captivity, not capture, that became the central question. There were two main reasons for this. First, unlike Sealand in Victoria and the Seattle Marine Aquarium, the Vancouver Aquarium did not directly capture killer whales in local waters after 1964. Second, the aquarium, like the adjacent but unaffiliated zoo, was located in Stanley Park. In addition to being Vancouver's celebrated and symbolic "nature" reserve, Stanley Park was public, and hence easily politicized, space. As a result, the question of orca captivity became closely tied to the environmental and countercultural currents sweeping the city by the late 1960s.

The story of Vancouver's orcas speaks to key questions in the fields of environmental, urban, and animal history. In recent years, environmental historians have increasingly turned their attention to questions of urban values and identity, particularly in the Pacific Northwest. Matthew Klingle, for example, places the fate of the region's wild salmon at the heart of his environmental history of Seattle.[7] Likewise, scholars have explored wildlife conservation policy on the national and international levels, including recent studies of the science, diplomacy, and culture of commercial whaling. In *The Sounding of the Whale* (2012), historian D. Graham Burnett emphasizes the striking shift in global environmental values in which whales – "an anomalous order of elusive, air-breathing marine mammals" – came by the early 1970s to serve as "nothing less than a way of thinking about our planet."[8] Other scholars have examined the phenomena of spectacle and performance in human–animal relations. In her *Spectacular Nature* (1997), Susan Davis analyzes the business culture of Sea World in San Diego and emphasizes the iconic role of the "Shamu" killer whale shows in the tourist culture of southern California. More provocatively, Susan Nance's recent study *Entertaining Elephants* (2013) explores the role of animal agency in shaping the structure, culture, and economics of the North American circus.[9]

The presence and actions of killer whales have not figured prominently in the urban and environmental historiography of North America, for seemingly obvious reasons. In contrast to domestic animals, for example, orcas do not live intimately with humans. Moreover, as in the case of other marine fauna, their displacement by urban growth has been less visible than that of terrestrial species. Partly for this reason, the cultural and political impact of their shifting relations with humans has received little attention from historians. In her sweeping interpretation of Canadian wildlife conservation measures, for example, Tina Loo does not discuss killer whales or any other marine species.[10] Likewise, historians of Vancouver have given little attention to the aquarium and its captive orcas. In his superb study of Stanley Park, for example, Sean Kheraj observes that the park originally stood as a "living metaphor for Vancouver's origins and progress" and later became a "temple of atonement for the environmental destruction that was necessary to build the city and the province," but he devotes little discussion to the role of the zoo and aquarium in that transition.[11] For his part, Frank Zelko, in his history of Greenpeace, offers anecdotal discussion of the aquarium's orcas, but his primary interest is the organization's anti-whaling campaign, not the urban politics of killer whale captivity.[12]

Yet the orcas of Stanley Park played a prominent role in many of the political and cultural trends scholars have highlighted. Their story maps closely, for example, onto what Loo has termed "an emerging urban sentimentality about predators."[13] Well into the 1960s, killer whales, much like wolves, were viewed as threats to both people and resources, particularly salmon. In fact, orcas were often labelled, first by their detractors and later by their admirers, as the "wolves of the sea." In this sense, Vancouver's encounter with captive killer whales provides a revealing register of the city's shifting relationship to the regional environment and its marine wildlife. At the same time, the killer whale debate exacerbated tensions between Vancouver's growing tourist economy and the emerging ethos of animal rights. It was a bit awkward, after all, that the city known for launching the "Save the Whales" campaign proved reluctant to set its own whales free. Although some Vancouverites expressed discomfort with orca captivity from the beginning, local businesses benefited tremendously from the drawing power of such an attraction. For its part, beginning in the mid-1970s, the Vancouver Aquarium publicly espoused anti-whaling and other

10.1 Skana being transferred to her pool at the Vancouver Aquarium, March 1967. Courtesy of Terry McLeod.

conservationist causes, in part to shield itself from criticism. Yet these efforts proved only temporarily successful. With the end of capture in the Pacific Northwest and the importation of orcas from Iceland, ecologically based arguments against captivity lost much of their force. As a result, by the late 1980s, animal rights activists had taken centre stage in the opposition to killer whale captivity. Their efforts were bolstered by a rising public distaste for trained animal performances – a form of public spectacle long associated with circuses, and more recently with the "Shamu" shows at San Diego's Sea World.[14] Such criticism continued to mount, despite the aquarium's shift to a more "natural" form of presentation. After gaining momentum through a successful campaign to shut down the Stanley Park Zoo in the early 1990s, the local animal rights movement mounted an effective challenge to orca captivity at the aquarium. By that time, it was clear that the saga of Vancouver's killer whales was part of the transformation of the city itself.

The arrival of Skana was hardly the first time residents of British Columbia had contemplated the meaning of whales. The coastal Indigenous peoples of the region had long incorporated cetaceans into their economies and belief systems, and orcas in particular held an important place in the folklore and clan structure of nations such as the Haida and Tlingit. One of the most prominent tales was that of "Natsilane," a young Tlingit who creates the first "blackfish," which in turn helps him drown his treacherous siblings before promising friendship with people.[15] Beginning in the 1840s, British Columbia became an important base for the commercial whaling industry, itself part of the extractive economy that characterized European settlement of the region. Whalers rarely targeted orcas, however, and the main postwar whaling port of Coal Harbour, on northern Vancouver Island, closed five months after Skana's March 1967 arrival to Vancouver.[16] Yet killer whales did draw the attention of local residents, many of whom considered "blackfish" a threat to the commercial and sport fishing industries.

In fact, the species was neither fish nor, strictly speaking, whale. The largest member of the dolphin family, *Orcinus orca* is the world's apex marine predator. Intelligent, adaptable, and intensely social within their matrilineal pods, killer whales have developed an astonishing array of feeding strategies throughout the ocean. In the Salish Sea, their population is sharply divided between two "ecotypes" or cultures: "transients," which live in small pods of between two and six animals and hunt seals and other marine mammals; and "residents," which live in larger pods of twenty to forty and feed primarily on salmon.[17] The resident killer whales are also generally separated into "northern" and "southern" populations, dividing approximately at Seymour Narrows, midway up Vancouver Island. Although whaling ships in Pacific Northwest waters sometimes encountered transients in their hunt for baleen whales, it was resident orcas that were most frequently targeted by local fishermen, who worried the "killers" would scare away, or simply devour, local salmon. Indeed, just as cougars and wolves were blamed for the scarcity of game and targeted by the government for elimination, orcas became a convenient scapegoat for declining salmon runs. And as in the case of land predators, this perception spurred government violence. In 1960, for example, the federal Department of Fisheries went so far as to install a machine gun on Seymour Narrows, north of Vancouver, to eliminate killer whales – after deciding that a mortar would be impractical.[18]

By the mid-1960s, however, as in many other North American cities, the environmental politics of Vancouver were in flux. In addition to the rising concern with industrial pollutants raised by publications such as Rachel Carson's *Silent Spring* (1962), a growing number of city dwellers were coming to view wildlife outside the framework of economic utility. Spurred by seminal works such as naturalist Farley Mowat's memoir *Never Cry Wolf* (1963), many urban Canadians re-evaluated the ecological role of previously vilified predators.[19] While this shift is often associated with the reduced importance of farming and ranching in the interior, it had its parallel on the West Coast, where the fishing economy was already in steep decline by the time local aquariums began acquiring their own "sea wolves" for display.[20]

Vancouver came by its first captive killer whale by accident. Since its 1956 founding as a public institution under the Stanley Park Board, the Vancouver Aquarium had grown steadily under the directorship of Chicago-born Murray Newman, who proved skilled at raising funds from local business leaders. Although the institution would later become famous for the exotic species Newman collected all over the world, it initially focused on regional fauna.[21] In the spring of 1964, in anticipation of the opening of the aquarium's new "Pacific Northwest Hall," Newman hired artist and part-time fisherman Samuel Burich to slay a killer whale and use its body as a model for a sculpture in the building's foyer. On 16 July, after months of waiting, Burich and his young assistant, Josef Bauer – another Vancouver fisherman – harpooned a juvenile orca in the nearby Gulf Islands. Despite being struck by the harpoon just behind the head and shot several times, the young animal survived. Initial news reports placed the event in a heroic light, with one *Vancouver Sun* reporter writing glowingly of the two brave Vancouverites doing "battle" with a killer whale.[22] In reality, Burich and Bauer were so touched by the orca's screams and the efforts of its pod-mates to keep it afloat that they found themselves shielding the animal when local fishermen arrived to help finish it off. Soon after, Newman decided to bring the young whale alive to Vancouver.

10.2 Skana performing at the Vancouver Aquarium with trainer Terry McLeod, 1968. Courtesy of Terry McLeod.

The inadvertent capture immediately raised spatial questions. Even a juvenile killer whale was too large for the aquarium's facilities, forcing Newman to find a holding area for his new prize. In fact, as the boat towing the whale approached the city, Newman's primary concern was not whether the public would object to the aquarium's harpooning a killer whale but rather where he could put the animal. After much cajoling, he convinced Burrard Drydock to provide space for a temporary pen in a flooded berth. Within days, however, the company's manager was complaining that the animal's presence was disrupting operations, not only by occupying a berth but also by distracting his workers and attracting thousands of sightseers.[23] On 24 July, the aquarium moved the whale to a shallow pen located at the Jericho Army Base, just west of the Kitsilano neighborhood. A range of local businesses and government agencies assisted in the ten-hour process: the dry dock allowed its berth to be towed away, Navy frogmen from the Esquimalt navy base in Victoria helped connect the pens, and the Vancouver police boats used their sirens to scare the reticent whale into its new enclosure. With all this equipment and time donated locally, Newman declared, the aquarium had a "debt" to the city and "couldn't sell the whale." Eager to nurse the animal back to health, however, the veterinary staff declared the site closed to the public.[24]

Yet excited locals could hardly wait to catch a glimpse of the fearsome creature. Among them was seventeen-year-old Mark Perry, a Vancouver resident whose stepfather worked in the BC fish-packing industry. "Killer whales and fishermen were like oil and water," Perry recalled. "The fishermen thought the killer whales ate all the salmon, and every time they had a chance to take a shot at one, I think they did." When he learned of the animal's move to Jericho Beach, however, Perry decided to have a look, even if it meant sneaking onto an army base. "It was low tide, so I stayed down by the water, out of sight of the MPs," he explained. "And I heard this explosive breath out in the water to my left – scared the heck out of me." Rather than flee, however, Perry decided to linger, mesmerized: "Every time it came up to breath, the fin was there – the dorsal fin. And, I thought, 'wow, that's amazing. This huge animal isn't trying to tear the place apart.' I couldn't believe how placid it was." Moved by his experience, Perry attempted to share it with his stepfather. "He thought it was all a waste of time. I couldn't convince him," recalled Perry. "But it sure changed my attitude."[25] Indeed, the chance encounter helped shape his life's path. Three years later, he would catch a glimpse of Skana at the Vancouver Boat Show, and a year after that he would be working as one of her trainers at the Vancouver Aquarium. For Perry, as for so many other Vancouverites, an encounter with a captive killer whale was the beginning of a transformation in their views of the region's environment and wildlife.

The young orca's capture immediately raised the profile and prestige of the aquarium. Newman himself was named Vancouver's Man of the Year, and soon after he dubbed the animal "Moby Doll"—mistakenly believing it was female. The killer whale's presence also stirred interest among researchers, including Patrick McGeer, head of the Kinsmen Laboratory for Neurological Research at the University of British Columbia (UBC) and one of Vancouver's MLAs in the BC Legislature (1962–86). McGeer continued these efforts after the young animal's death. Weakened by his wounds and insufficient feeding, and exposed to the warm, polluted, and desalinated water on the surface of Vancouver's English Bay, Moby Doll died in October 1964. Scientists such as McGeer and future killer whale expert Michael Bigg used the ensuing necropsy as another opportunity to examine the understudied species, with McGeer harvesting the brain as a unique specimen for his laboratory. For its part, the public in Vancouver, as it would many times over the following decades, mourned the death of a captive orca.[26]

For the next two and half years, Vancouver did not play much of a role in the unfolding story of people and orcas. Despite aggressive collection of other species in BC and throughout the world, Newman did not attempt another direct capture of a killer whale. In June 1965, he had a chance to acquire a second orca when fishermen near Namu, BC, accidentally netted a calf and young bull, but he lost interest when the calf escaped, and as a result it was Ted Griffin, owner of the Seattle Marine Aquarium, who stole the headlines. After paying the fishermen $8,000, Griffin transported the bull, now named "Namu," to Seattle, where it became an international sensation, particularly after Griffin began performing with the animal in the water. Even before Namu's death in the summer of 1966, Griffin was capturing killer whales in Puget Sound for sale to other aquariums. In the fall of 1965, Sea World bought a young female, which became the first "Shamu," and in February 1967, Griffin netted a resident pod in Puget Sound that included the future "Skana" – the orca that would put Vancouver and its aquarium back in the spotlight.[27]

By the time of Skana's arrival in March 1967, the city's political culture was changing. Over the previous year, the anti-war movement had grown more visible, due in part to an influx of US draft resisters.[28] In addition, many young Vancouverites, particularly in the Kitsilano neighbourhood, were espousing elements of the West Coast counterculture associated with California's Bay Area. Referring to San Francisco's famed hippie district, Mark Perry went so far as to dub Vancouver "Haight-Ashbury North." Young people were trying to "do their thing" in the face of "huge opposition from the mayor and the police," he recalled. "It was a tumultuous time."[29] In May 1967, less than two months after Skana's arrival, the first issue of the influential countercultural newspaper *Georgia Straight* appeared. Over the following years, American expatriates helped form the city's first environmentalist groups, including a Vancouver branch of the Sierra Club. And as historian Frank Zelko observes, "the site where Vancouver's alternative scene met the city's mainstream was Stanley Park," which became the site of regular "ecological protests" by 1969–70.[30] It was no coincidence that this same space witnessed the world's first public debate over killer whale captivity.

The central figure in the controversy was scientist Paul Spong. A native of New Zealand, Spong had been trained in psychology and neuroscience at UCLA, where he had immersed himself in the local counterculture and become fascinated with the work of John Lilly. A decade earlier, Lilly had won funding from the US Navy to establish research facilities in the Virgin Islands, where he conducted experiments on captive dolphins. By the 1960s, Lilly was a leading figure in the transformation of cetacean science, and his books *Man and Dolphin* (1961) and *The Mind of the Dolphin* (1967) made a deep impression on Spong.[31] As a result, when Spong learned of a position at UBC's Kinsmen Laboratory, which included a research contract with the Vancouver Aquarium, he leapt at the opportunity. Clean-shaven and bolstered by impressive credentials and a compelling proposal to study the aquarium's dolphins, he won the appointment. When Spong arrived with his wife Linda months later to begin his work, however, he made his allegiance to the counterculture clear. As his former research assistant Don White put it, "when Paul had come up [for the interview], he was very clean cut – short hair, wore a tie." When he arrived to take up the position, however, he looked "not dissimilar to Allen Ginsberg." In fact, according to White, Newman and his staff "were in shock" at Spong's hippie-like appearance and demeanour.[32]

Over the following year, Spong and White, then an honours psychology undergraduate student at UBC, conducted a series of tests on the aquarium's cetaceans. Aimed at assessing visual acuity, the tests initially focused on the facility's Pacific white-sided dolphins. In the spring of 1968, however, Newman instructed Spong to shift his research to Skana. The tests themselves were fairly simple, requiring Skana to distinguish between two lines whose distance from one another was adjusted. If she pushed the correct lever with her rostrum (snout), a light went on and she received a partial herring as a reward. Over the course of several weeks, Skana learned to respond accurately. During one session with White, however, she abruptly began giving entirely incorrect responses while vocalizing loudly. Interpreting her behaviour as an expression of boredom and frustration, White found himself profoundly affected. "For me, personally, that was transformative," he reflected. "I've got an organism in front of me [whose] behaviour I can explain by assuming it has similar thought processes to my own." Once he made that leap, White found himself asking, "What does it feel like to be in this tank?"[33]

Skana's behavior had an even more radical impact on Spong. Initially frustrated with the animal's intransigence, he, too, began contemplating the reasons behind her actions. One day in August 1968, as he sat pondering these questions with bare feet dangling in Skana's pool, he experienced a stunning display of Skana's subjectivity. After several benign passes, the young killer whale suddenly opened her mouth, lightly raking Spong's feet with her teeth and causing him to yell and yank his legs from the water. After recovering from his shock, Spong returned his feet to the water, only to have them raked once again. After a dozen passes, he finally managed to keep his feet still. Once he stopped responding, Skana ended her experiment.[34] For Spong, it was a revelatory moment, spiritually as well as intellectually. "I thought she did that deliberately to get rid of my attitude toward her," he later observed. "I considered that a great gift, as I've never felt fear around another whale again." In the process, he found himself wondering about the alien marine intelligence before him.[35]

The changes in Spong's thinking were closely tied to his immersion in the Vancouver counterculture. By the spring of 1968, he and Linda had moved to Kitsilano and were socializing with activists, musicians, and writers who regularly discussed issues such as the Vietnam War and social inequality. In fall 1968, the Spongs attended an anti-war speech on the UBC campus by American Yippie leader, which prompted a protest action at the faculty club.[36] Meanwhile, Spong was waging his own fight against the aquarium's power structure. Much of this centred on his interactions with an orca calf the aquarium had recently acquired from fishermen in Pender Harbour, north of Vancouver. Dubbed "Tung Jen" by Spong, the calf had been held in an isolation pool for months, where he seemed to grow despondent. Himself the father of a young son about Tung Jen's age, Spong became deeply concerned about the lonely calf's mental health. Convinced that both killer whales were suffering from social and acoustic deprivation, Spong brought noisemakers, musical instruments, and eventually live bands into the aquarium. Although Skana and Tung Jen seemed to respond eagerly, Spong's methods clashed with the aquarium's straight-laced approach. Murray Newman seemed worried that the counterculture was seeping into his staid institution. For head trainer Terry McLeod, however, the main issue was the safety of his animal charges. In particular, he was livid when he found wine glasses at the bottom of Skana's pool after one of Spong's nighttime gatherings.[37]

Soon after, Spong shifted to full rebellion. In April 1969, he delivered a lecture at UBC in which he emphasized the intelligence and social ties of killer whales as well as their need for acoustic stimulation. Arguing that the decision to keep Tung Jen in isolation had "severely damaged" the young animal psychologically, he concluded that "these whales should probably be freed, and that we should continue our studies with free or semicaptive *Orcinus orca* in its natural habitat."[38] Considering that many of Spong's aquarium and university colleagues were in attendance, it was an act of profound professional courage. It was also the last straw for Murray Newman, who cancelled Spong's contract with the aquarium. But the young scientist refused to go quietly. By June, he was mounting a sit-down protest calling for Skana's release, and he quickly gained the support of local activists. After suffering a mental breakdown, however, he checked into UBC's psychiatric ward, where a reporter from the *Georgia Straight* talked him into an ill-advised interview. "I was thinking of destroying the Vancouver Public Aquarium, and letting the whale go," he declared to the interviewer. "I was just beginning to get into Skana's space, just beginning to feel what the whale needed, what the whale wanted, WHAT THE WHALE WAS, just beginning to feel it, man. And they fired me."[39] Such ravings aside, Spong's sit-down protests deeply affected some aquarium staffers. "I'd go into work, and there were times when I felt, 'Jeez, I'm on the wrong side here,'" reflected Mark Perry. "I felt like I should be sitting with Paul."[40]

Over the following months, the public controversy over killer whale captivity at the aquarium seemed to abate. By the summer of 1970, Spong was devoting his energies to setting up a research outpost in Blackfish Sound at the northern end of Vancouver Island. Combining the counterculture's back-to-the-land impulse with Spong's desire to develop passive means of studying orcas, the venture would eventually lead to the founding of OrcaLab on Hanson Island. At the same time, the debate over the treatment of killer whales increasingly turned to the question of capture. In March 1970, Sealand in Victoria made headlines when it netted a small pod of orcas, including a young "albino" female.[41] The decision of Sealand owner Bob Wright to hold the remaining animals in the bay over the following months stirred public criticism as well as dissent from his employees, several of whom quit after one of the whales drowned. Meanwhile, in August 1970, the Seattle Marine Aquarium captured nearly the entire southern resident orca population off Whidbey Island in Puget Sound. Onlookers protested the removal of six calves for sale, and the public was further horrified when the bodies of several calves washed up on shore in the following months.[42] Amid these dramatic events, the Vancouver Aquarium's display of two captive orcas received little attention.

Yet Newman's aquarium faced public criticism on related issues. In August 1970, just as the countercultural Vancouver band "Fireweed" was travelling north to serenade wild killer whales near Spong's new outpost, the aquarium captured and transported six narwhals to Vancouver for display. The three calves died almost immediately, and the adults soon after. For many Vancouverites, it was the first time they questioned the aquarium's collection operations, as well as the costs of captivity to animal life. Among the most outspoken critics was Irving Stowe, author of *Georgia Straight*'s "Greenpeace Is Beautiful" column. In September, Stowe quoted Patrick McGeer as stating: "It's really a much better life for a narwhal in captivity because of the dangers to them in the Arctic." Denouncing such "doublethink," Stowe asked, "Do you feel godlike enough to decide that deathtrip captivity is a 'better life' for a whale than its normal environment?"[43] Stowe's question was significant on several levels. First, McGeer had close ties to the Vancouver Aquarium, having studied Moby Doll during his captivity and participated in the Arctic narwhal expedition. Second, Stowe himself would play a central role in founding the organization that took its name from his column. Although "Greenpeace" would spend its early years focused on nuclear testing, commercial whaling, and the harp seal hunt, Stowe's comments underscored the connection between cetacean captivity at the aquarium and the city's shifting environmental politics.

The initial formation of Greenpeace had little to do with the aquarium or Paul Spong. Rather, it emerged from the so-called "Don't Make a Wave Committee," which launched a protest voyage against US nuclear testing on Alaska's Amchitka Island. For transportation, organizers hired John Cormack, a struggling fisherman whose boat, the *Phyllis Cormack*, was temporarily renamed the *Greenpeace* – a transaction that highlighted the simultaneous decline of the fishing industry and rise of environmentalism. The quixotic voyage captured headlines around the world and generated great enthusiasm in Vancouver, leading to the official foundation of the Greenpeace Foundation in early 1972. At this early stage, however, the group remained focused on the existential and ecological threats emanating from the Cold War.[44]

Meanwhile, Spong was splitting his time between studying killer whales on Hanson Island and promoting social justice in Vancouver. In 1971, he played a prominent role in the debate over the Maplewood Mudflats. Located along the shores of North Vancouver, the area had long been a site of informal housing for marginalized people, including adherents to the counterculture such as Spong and his family. Although he vocally opposed city plans to clear the Mudflats, he was away in December 1971 when officials evicted residents and burned their homes. The thought of his wife and young son standing in the cold watching their home in flames further radicalized him and strengthened his tendency to look to cetaceans to inspire solutions for human problems.[45] Over the following years, he would repeatedly call on people to turn to killer whales as models for living in harmony with the environment and each other. In the process, he played a central role in popularizing the use of the term "orca" to underscore the shifting public view of the species.

The convergence of Greenpeace and the whaling question began with an impromptu chat between Spong and naturalist writer Farley Mowat. In November 1972, Mowat was visiting Vancouver to promote his new book, *A Whale for the Killing* (1972), an account of his failed attempt to save a trapped fin whale from the ignorance and cruelty of locals in a small Newfoundland village. Moved by Mowat's impassioned warning about the impact of commercial whaling, Spong resolved to jump into the fight. By December 1972, he and Linda were busily distributing "Save the Whale" pamphlets throughout the city, and in early June 1973, Spong organized a "Whale Celebration" in Stanley Park. The following autumn he met with Greenpeace leaders, convincing them to approve a fundraising initiative for an anti-whaling campaign. By the end of 1973, Vancouver had become the centre of an incipient movement to end commercial whaling.[46]

If Spong's "Whale Celebration" implicitly challenged the Vancouver Aquarium's cultural authority in Stanley Park, Greenpeace's anti-whaling campaign presented the aquarium with a public relations opportunity. Eager to associate his institution with conservation efforts, Newman allowed Spong to hold a press conference at the aquarium in February 1974 to announce his upcoming speaking tour in Japan, on the condition that he not raise the question of captivity. The event proved a transformative experience for Greenpeace leader Bob Hunter. As reporters looked on, Skana joyfully greeted Spong, then gently took Hunter's head in her mouth before releasing him. While the orca's intentions are impossible to determine, the encounter left a deep impression on Hunter's psyche and helped drive his messianic crusade against whaling in the coming years. Indeed, in her encounter with Hunter, as in her earlier influence on Spong, Skana had unknowingly helped shape the development of Greenpeace.[47]

The organization's anti-whaling expedition in turn brought new attention to Vancouver as a centre of environmental and animal rights activism. In the spring of 1975, as Spong engaged in a publicity and intelligence-gathering tour of Iceland, Norway, and Western Europe, Greenpeace prepared to launch its first anti-whaling expedition. Focusing its efforts on the Soviet whaling fleet rumoured to be operating off the coast of California, it received a range of endorsements in Vancouver, with the aquarium, the BC Federation of Labour, the Vancouver Police Department, Socialist Premier David Barrett, and timber company MacMillan Bloedel all voicing their support.[48] On 25 April 1975, the Greenpeace crew visited Skana one last time for a "farewell serenade." The following day, they departed from Jericho Beach, the site of the now-closed naval base. None in the group seemed to reflect that it was near the very spot that Moby Doll had died eleven years earlier, but they did carry with them their new Greenpeace banner, which proudly incorporated an Indigenous Kwakwaka'wakw image of a killer whale. Two months later, the expedition's confrontation with the Soviet whalers, occurring simultaneously with the annual meeting of the International Whaling Commission in London, brought Greenpeace massive international attention. After a triumphant visit to San Francisco, the crew returned to Vancouver where they were greeted by thousands.[49]

The expedition's media success had an immediate impact on the Pacific Northwest killer whale debate. In August 1975, just weeks after the Greenpeace team's return, Sealand captured a transient pod of six orcas in Pedder Bay near Victoria. Fresh from their confrontation with the Soviet fleet, Spong and his fellow Greenpeacers jumped into action, gaining the ear of the provincial government. Although maritime activities remained regulated by Ottawa, the BC government attempted to outlaw orca capture in provincial waters.[50] The following year, Washington State had a similar confrontation with the US government in response to a Sea World capture operation in Puget Sound. In this charged atmosphere, officials at the Vancouver Aquarium realized that future acquisition of killer whales would have to come from outside the Pacific Northwest. At the time, this did not seem a pressing matter. Skana and Tung Jen (now renamed "Hyak") were still drawing large numbers of visitors, while the continued public focus on commercial whaling facilitated the aquarium's efforts to claim a conservationist mission. Indeed, by the late 1970s, it seemed that most Vancouverites had accepted captive killer whales as part of their city's cultural landscape.

Yet the following decade brought new challenges to the aquarium. In October 1980, after thirteen years of captivity, Skana died suddenly of a vaginal infection. Newman immediately began exploring options to acquire more killer whales, but he knew times had changed. Because "the people of British Columbia and particularly those of the Victoria-Vancouver region had become familiar with killer whales through the aquarium and the media," he reflected, "I knew it would be unpopular for us to try to capture a live killer whale locally and felt a little frustrated about it." Instead, he announced plans to purchase killer whales from Iceland. Although the aquarium succeeded in importing two orcas (soon to be named "Finna" and "Bjossa") in December 1980, it faced fierce opposition from Greenpeace and other environmental and animal rights groups.[51] The criticism only grew over the following years as Newman used the acquisition of the whales to push for a substantial expansion of the aquarium. His logic was simple: as he later put it, "you can't remain small and keep killer whales."[52] But many in the public perceived a clash between the importance of Stanley Park as "natural" space, and the expansion of the aquarium's "artificial" whale shows.

These debates came on the cusp of a new era in Vancouver's environmental politics. The mid-1980s brought a surge of environmental and animal rights activism in the city, which continued to grow into the 1990s. At the heart of this shift was the city's changing economic and demographic profile. Although Vancouver remained an important hub for extractive industries such as timber, its culture was increasingly defined by young, middle-class residents more oriented toward the urban economy, and hence inclined to view the environment and wildlife more in terms of recreation and spiritual connection than extraction and livelihood. Vancouver's municipal government celebrated this new identity through its hosting of a world fair, EXPO '86, which emphasized the city's transition away from its extractive past and toward a modern future. Among the attractions city leaders sought to highlight was the Vancouver Aquarium and its killer whales. Many residents, however, found the aquarium's trained performances, as well as the nearby Stanley Park Zoo, offensive. Indeed, it was no coincidence that the following year brought the first of three public referenda on the future of the zoo.

At the centre of these efforts was Annelise Sorg. Born into an international banking family in Lima, Peru, Sorg had lived in Toronto and Ottawa before moving to Vancouver in 1983. A lifelong champion of animal rights, she quickly connected with local activists, including the Vancouver Humane Society. Hired as an interpreter during Vancouver's EXPO '86, Sorg had shepherded foreign dignitaries through the aquarium on VIP tours, an experience that left her incensed at what she considered the "demeaning" nature of the whale shows. The following year, she was appointed head of the Humane Society's Entertainment Committee. In addition to pushing successfully for a ban on circuses within city limits, she led the fight to close the Stanley Park Zoo.[53] Driven primarily by animal rights sentiment rather than environmental concerns, Sorg and her colleagues were well positioned to make their case. After all, by the late 1980s, there was no compelling *ecological* reason for the release of the aquarium's killer whales. By this time, most scientists agreed that the major threat to the local orca population was pollution, maritime traffic, and the depletion of salmon. Ecologically, the fate of three orcas – two of which were from Iceland – was of negligible importance. On the other hand, a growing number of Vancouverites were uncomfortable with the killer whale shows, which many believed denigrated an animal increasingly revered as a symbol of regional culture.

Some within the aquarium shared these sentiments. In 1984, the institution unveiled a sculpture entitled "Killer Whale, Chief of the Undersea World." Although its creator, Haida artist Bill Reid, later disavowed it, the sculpture became part of the aquarium's effort to join the regional celebration of the species.[54] Soon after, in an effort to mute criticism and distance itself from the circus-like atmosphere of Sea World, the aquarium ended its scheduled whale shows, instead encouraging visitors to observe the animals' "natural" behaviours.[55] At the same time, it made several moves to bolster its educational and scientific credentials, including hiring biologist John Ford, who would become a leading expert on killer whales.[56] Along with the end of orca capture in the region, this growing emphasis on research and education helped mute the environmentalist critique of the aquarium. Yet these changes were less suited to dispelling the claims of animal rights activists, who focused on the lives and emotional health of individual animals rather than the long-term fate of species and ecosystems. In fact, the aquarium likely made itself more vulnerable to such protests through its naming practices. In contrast to Sea World, for example, which tended to mask the individuality of its captive orcas with glitzy "Shamu" shows, the Vancouver Aquarium gave each animal a unique, and geographically evocative, name. While this decision likely helped emphasize the "foreign" origins of "Finna" and "Bjossa," it also enabled activists to refer to the animals by name, rather than simply as "the orcas." The implications of this became apparent following the death of Hyak in February 1991.[57] After performing a necropsy, the aquarium opted to dispose of its long-serving captive by cutting him into pieces and dropping them into the Strait of Georgia. When local tides washed several grisly pieces ashore, however, the aquarium was forced to admit they belonged to Hyak, prompting widespread outrage. Aquarium staffers and the broader public were further saddened when a calf sired by Hyak and delivered by Bjossa died shortly after birth.[58]

In the wake of these events, public misgivings toward the captivity of killer whales and other large mammals continued to grow. One indirect expression of this sentiment came in a 1993 referendum, in which city voters stunned the Park Board by choosing to shut down Stanley Park Zoo. Although the vote did not directly affect the aquarium and its captive orcas, it was becoming clear that a growing number of Vancouverites viewed animal captivity as incompatible with the civic and environmental meaning of Stanley Park. Indeed, subsequent analysis revealed that many believed they were voting to close the aquarium as well as the zoo. Such sentiment helped convinced Sorg and others that a campaign against killer whale captivity was feasible, despite the immense political influence of the aquarium.[59] And as they geared up for this next struggle, activists received an unexpected boost from the Hollywood movie *Free Willy*, which depicted a young boy helping a killer whale escape from an aquarium. Released in July 1993 amid the preparations for the zoo referendum, the popular film spurred private efforts to release the animal used to make the movie – an Iceland-caught male named Keiko then held in Mexico – and brought greater public attention to the issue of killer whale captivity.[60]

In the following years, the Vancouver Aquarium found itself drawn into an increasingly heated debate. Tension only grew when John Nightingale replaced the retiring Murray Newman. An aggressive operator with previous controversial stints at the Seattle Public Aquarium and New York Aquarium, Nightingale clashed with activists and aquarium staffers alike. Among the most contentious issues was his demand for the resumption of scheduled killer whale shows.[61] In the eyes of many aquarium employees, the institution could not ignore changes in public opinion. "For the first twenty years, Vancouverites loved the killer whales," recalled former aquarium employee Kathryn Cook. "It was just like a love affair." By the mid-1990s, however, there were frequent protests outside the aquarium entrance. They tended to be small affairs, she noted. "Annelise and her little crew of supporters would come." Yet Cook conceded that the small protests belied a larger groundswell of public sentiment. "If you were to poll Vancouver back in the 1990s," she speculated, "you would have found a strong number of people felt that killer whale captivity was wrong." Moreover, she noted, some staffers shared their misgivings. The death of another calf born to Bjossa in March 1995 proved particularly painful. As Cook recalled, both within the aquarium and through the city, "there was a real sense of sadness when the calf died." Throughout the 1990s, she observed, "people were wrestling with [the question] 'we love it, but is it right?' 'Is it still okay?' Inside and outside the aquarium, those conversations were taking place."[62]

Events in the late 1990s finally tipped the balance. In 1996, Sorg and other activists convinced the city to pass a municipal bylaw restricting the importation of whales and dolphins into Vancouver parks. That same year, the Park Board, now with members sympathetic to the activists, forbade the aquarium from holding any killer whale captured after 1996. The death of Finna in July 1997 further soured many. Although Nightingale pushed for a continued killer whale program, public opposition had grown too fierce, and in April 2001 the aquarium sold its last orca, Bjossa, to Sea World in San Diego, where she died six months later.[63]

The departure of Bjossa ended a significant chapter in the history of Vancouver and the broader Pacific Northwest. Beginning with the arrival of Moby Doll in July 1964, and especially following the purchase of

Skana in March 1967, the Vancouver Aquarium had become a famous and contentious site of killer whale display. The presence of orcas brought expansion and fame for the institution and its top officials and contributed to the rapid growth of Vancouver's tourist industry throughout the 1970s and 1980s. Yet the debate over killer whale captivity also played an underappreciated role in the city's shifting environmental politics. Informed by the growing counterculture of the late 1960s and 1970s, encounters between orcas and people at the aquarium helped radicalize key scientific figures such as Paul Spong and had a profound impact on the institutional development of Vancouver-based Greenpeace. Although the debate over killer whale captivity subsided in the late 1970s, its resurgence in the late 1980s and early 1990s came to reflect the city's shift from an outpost of extractive industry to a middle-class urban centre that valued the environment and wildlife for their recreational and symbolic meaning. By the time of Bjossa's departure in April 2001, a large number of Vancouverites viewed the captive orcas of Stanley Park as incompatible with the imagined values and identity of their city.

Yet the departure of the last killer whale did not end the captivity debate. The aquarium still held small cetaceans such as dolphins and belugas for display, and animal rights activists continued to press for their release. In 2005, activists exposed the aquarium's unauthorized importation of dolphins from Japan, and soon after, Nightingale announced an ambitious plan to develop a live-breeding program of dolphins and belugas, as part of a $60 million expansion of the aquarium into the old grounds of the Stanley Park Zoo. Over the following years, the protests continued, gaining a boost with the 2013 release of the documentary *Blackfish*, which criticized the history of killer whale captivity, particularly at Sea World.[64] As it had so often before, the aquarium argued that the protestors were only a "small group," dwarfed by the much larger number of willing patrons. What the aquarium could be less sure of, however, was broader public opinion in a city that increasingly considered cetacean captivity, in the words of the *Vancouver Courier*, "a relic that must end."[65]

Notes

1   "Whale of a Time Awaits Walter,"
    Saskatoon Star-Phoenix, 11 March
    1967.

2   Ted Griffin, *Namu: Quest for the
    Killer Whale* (Seattle: Gryphon
    West Press, 1982), 216–21. Al-
    though "blackfish" was an Indige-
    nous term for orcas, it had assumed
    a pejorative connotation among
    white residents in the region by the
    postwar period.

3   "Killer Whales 'Talk' Over Tele-
    phone," *St. Joseph News-Press*, 17
    March 1967.

4   "Walter Is Really Whale of a
    Girl," *Vancouver Sun*, 21 March
    1967; Murray Newman, *Life in a
    Fishbowl* (Vancouver: Douglas and
    McIntyre, 1994), 107–8.

5   On the development of the BC
    tourist industry see Michael
    Dawson, *Selling British Columbia:
    Tourism and Consumer Culture,
    1890–1970* (Vancouver: University
    of British Columbia Press, 2005).

6   On the origins of Greenpeace in
    Vancouver, see Frank Zelko, *Make
    It A Green Peace!: The Rise of Coun-
    tercultural Environmentalism* (New
    York: Oxford University Press,
    2013), chapter 3.

7   See, for example, Matthew Klingle,
    *Emerald City: An Environmental
    History of Seattle* (New Haven,
    CT: Yale University Press, 2007);
    and Jeffrey C. Sanders, *Seattle and
    the Roots of Urban Sustainability*
    (Pittsburgh: University of Pitts-
    burgh Press, 2010).

8   On conservation, see, for example,
    Tina Loo, *States of Nature: Con-
    serving Canada's Wildlife in the
    Twentieth Century* (Vancouver:
    University of British Columbia

    Press, 2006); and Kurkpatrick
    Dorsey, *The Dawn of Conserva-
    tion Diplomacy: U.S.-Canadian
    Wildlife Protection Treaties in the
    Progressive Era* (Seattle: Univer-
    sity of Washington Press, 1998).
    On whaling, see Kurkpatrick
    Dorsey, *Whales and Nations:
    Environmental Diplomacy on the
    High Seas* (Seattle: University
    of Washington, 2013); and D.
    Graham Burnett, *The Sounding
    of the Whale: Science and Ceta-
    ceans in the Twentieth Century*
    (Chicago: University of Chicago
    Press, 2012), 329.

9   Susan G. Davis, *Spectacular Na-
    ture: Corporate Culture and the
    Sea World Experience* (Berkeley:
    University of California Press,
    1997); and Susan Nance, *Enter-
    taining Elephants: Animal Agency
    and the Business of the American
    Circus* (Baltimore: Johns Hopkins
    University Press, 2013).

10 Loo, *States of Nature*.

11 Sean Kheraj, *Inventing Stanley
    Park: An Environmental History*
    (Vancouver: University of Brit-
    ish Columbia Press, 2013), 190.

12 Zelko, *Make It A Green Peace!*.

13 Loo, *States of Nature*, 10.

14 See Davis, *Spectacular Nature*;
    and Nance, *Entertaining Ele-
    phants*.

15 See Mary Giraudo Beck, *Heroes
    and Heroines: Tlingit-Haida
    Legend* (Anchorage: Alaska
    Northwest Press, 1989), 1–14. See
    also Robert Bringhurst, *A Story
    as Sharp as a Knife: The Classical
    Haida Mythtellers and Their
    World* (Vancouver: Douglas and
    McIntyre, 2011).

16 Robert Webb, *On the Northwest: Commercial Whaling in the Pacific Northwest, 1790–1967* (Vancouver: University of British Columbia Press, 1988); L. M. Nichol et al., *British Columbia Commercial Whaling Catch Data 1908 to 1967: A Detailed Description of the B.C. Historical Whaling Database* (Nanaimo: Pacific Biological Station, Fisheries and Oceans Canada, 2002).

17 For an introduction to the species, see John K. B. Ford, Graeme M. Ellis, and Kenneth C. Balcomb, *Killer Whales: The Natural History and Genealogy of Orcinus Orca in British Columbia and Washington State* (Seattle: University of Washington Press, 2000).

18 John K. B. Ford, "Killer Whales of the Pacific Northwest Coast," *Journal of the American Cetacean Society* 40, no. 1 (Spring 2011): 16.

19 Loo, *States of Nature*, 173–77.

20 On the history of the Salish Sea fisheries, see Lissa K. Wadewitz, *The Nature of Borders: Salmon, Boundaries, and Bandits of the Salish Sea* (Seattle: University of Washington Press, 2012).

21 Newman, *Life in a Fishbowl*, chapters 1–3.

22 "Two Battle Killer Whale in Strait," *Vancouver Sun*, 16 July 1964.

23 Murray Newman, "Close Encounters of an Unexpected Kind," Moby Doll Symposium, Saturna Island, 25 May 2013; "Killer Whale to Quit Dock for Jericho Beach Pen," *Vancouver Sun*, 18 July 1964.

24 "Moby Doll the Killer Whale Is Not For Sale," *Daily Free Press* (Nanaimo), 25 July 1964.

25 Author interview of Mark Perry, 15 May 2013.

26 "Death of Whale Claimed Needless," *Vancouver Sun*, 10 October 1964.

27 Two years later, a similar sensation hit Victoria. In April 1969, the newly created Sealand of the Pacific acquired its own orca, also from Griffin. The young bull "Haida," along with a rare "white" killer whale captured the following year, would draw unprecedented attention and tourist traffic to the growing provincial capital.

28 John Hagan, *Northern Passage: American Vietnam War Resisters in Canada* (Cambridge, MA: Harvard University Press, 2001).

29 Author interview of Mark Perry, 15 May 2013.

30 Zelko, *Make It A Green Peace!*, 30–39; quote from 57.

31 Burnett, *Sounding of the Whale*, chapter 6.

32 Rex Weyler, *Song of the Whale* (Garden City, NY: Anchor Press/Doubleday, 1986), chapter 1; author interview of Don White, 28 September 2013.

33 Author interview of Don White, 28 September 2013.

34 For the best account of Spong's interaction with Skana, see Weyler, *Song of the Whale*, chapter 1.

35 Paul Spong, "Adventures with Orcas," Saturna Island, 3 May 2014.

36 Rex Weyler, *Greenpeace: How a Group of Ecologists, Journalists, and Visionaries Changed the World* (Vancouver: Raincoast Books, 2004), 47–48.

37 Weyler, *Song of the Whale*, 46; author interview of Terry McLeod, 25 April 2015.

38   Weyler, *Song of the Whale*, 53.

39   "Dr. Spong Wails," *Georgia Straight*, 26 June–2 July 1969.

40   Author interview of Mark Perry, 15 May 2013.

41   "Killer Whale Captured," *Palm Beach Daily News*, 5 March 1970.

42   Jason Colby, "The Whale and the Region: Orca Capture and Environmentalism in the New Pacific Northwest," *Journal of the Canadian Historical Association* 24, no. 2 (2013): 425–54.

43   "Can An Enemy of the Whales Be a Friend of the People?," *Georgia Straight*, 23–30 September 1970.

44   Zelko, *Make It A Green Peace!*, chapter 4.

45   Weyler, *Song of the Whale*, 99–100.

46   On Greenpeace's fundraising, and particularly the "Whale Show" and December 1973 concert, see Zelko, *Make It A Green Peace!*, chapter 5.

47   Robert Hunter, *Warriors of the Rainbow: A Chronicle of the Greenpeace Movement from 1971 to 1979* (Amsterdam: Greenpeace International, 2011[1979]), 139–42.

48   Zelko, *Make It A Green Peace!*, chapter 7.

49   Ibid., chapter 9.

50   Weyler, *Greenpeace*, 344.

51   "A Whale of a Flight," *Ottawa Citizen*, 22 December 1980.

52   Newman, *Life in a Fishbowl*, 191–200, quote on 191.

53   Author interview with Annelise Sorg, 22 March 2014.

54   Reid interviewed in Douglas Hand, *Gone Whaling: A Search for Orcas in Northwest Waters* (Seattle: Sasquatch Books, 1994), 75–76.

55   Author interview of Elin Kelsey, 9 July 2013.

56   Over the next thirteen years, Ford would conduct acoustic research on the aquarium's captive orcas, as well as studies of wild killer whale populations.

57   "Star Killer Whale Dies at Vancouver Aquarium," *Spokesman Review*, 18 February 1991. Just four days later, at Sealand, a bull orca named Tilikum, acquired from Iceland, killed a trainer named Keltie Byrne, prompting owner Bob Wright to sell the animal to Sea World.

58   Author interview with Kathryn Cook, 8 May 2013.

59   Author interview with Annelise Sorg, 22 March 2014.

60   For a superb analysis of these events, see the documentary *A Whale of a Business*, *Frontline* (November 1997).

61   Author interview of Elin Kelsey, 9 July 2013.

62   Author interview of Kathryn Cook, 9 May 2013.

63   "Orcas to Get More Companionship," *Victoria Advocate*, 20 April 2001.

64   As recently as Sunday, 23 March 2014, activists mounted a "children's protest" against cetacean captivity at the Vancouver Aquarium, with many of the young participants citing *Blackfish* as their inspiration. For media coverage of this event, see http://www.cbc.ca/player/News/Canada/BC/ID/2444043795/.

65   Geoff Olson, "Captive Whales a Relic That Must End," *Vancouver Courier*, 27 March 2014.

Epilogue: Why Animals Matter in Urban History, or Why Cities Matter in Animal History

Sean Kheraj

In this collection on urban animals in Canada we see, in part, why animals matter in urban history and why cities matter in animal history. Non-human animals, as it turns out, played a significant role in the growth and development of urban environments in Canada and elsewhere around the world. They had the capacity to shape and influence history. Cities, built environments most associated with human endeavour and artificiality, are multi-species habitats. They are home to humans and nonhuman creatures alike. Urban histories attuned to animals open up new ways of thinking about cities and reveal the degree to which cities are hybrid environments, the products of both natural and cultural causation.[1] Similarly, animal histories that situate their analyses within the environmental context of cities can expand our understanding of human–animal relations.

What Animals Bring to Urban History

Throughout this collection, we find ample evidence of the ways in which animals shaped Canadian cities. Sherry Olson explicitly traces the impact of the horse on Montreal, perhaps the most consequential domestic animal in urban history. Joanna Dean follows by showing how human relations with urban horses were implicated in the history of tetanus, with subsequent influences on health in Canadian cities. And Carla Hustak explores the ways in which perceptions of risk associated with urban milk supplies and anxieties about race, motherhood, and health prompted the development of elaborate systems of inspection and management of bovine and human bodies. These are just some of the ways in which animals have shaped urban history in Canada.

Olson is convincing in her description of the enduring legacies of such animals as "phantom shadows" that can still be found in the layout of city streets and lots or the narrowness of roads, lanes, and alleys first established at a time before the ascendency of the automobile. They are the vestiges of an urban past when humans and domestic animals cohabited urban environments. Indeed, in many ways, cities were built with domestic animals in mind. Horses, cows, pigs, chickens, and even sheep could be found in some of the largest cities across the country. These animals played critical roles in the development and sustainability of urban environments, especially in the nineteenth and early twentieth centuries as urban populations exploded in cities like Montreal, Toronto, Winnipeg, and Vancouver. At a time when nearly all material consumer goods were made with animal and other organic products and when the primary source of energy for urban transportation was the horse (or other draft animals), domestic animals were absolutely vital to the functions of a growing city and central to the lives of ordinary Canadians.

My work focuses on the regulation of domestic animals in nineteenth-century Canadian cities to show the significance of these animals to urban growth and development. Municipal governments devoted much attention to the management and regulation of animals. Some of the first modern bylaws in Canada targeted domestic animals because they were sources of environmental pollution or "nuisance," obstacles to the movement of traffic, and potential health hazards. The autonomous behaviour of nonhuman animals and the environmental consequences of their bodies compelled municipal governments to develop extensive systems of regulations to control and manage urban environments. These regulations, however, did not seek to entirely exclude domestic animals from cities, at least until the early decades of the twentieth century. As I have argued elsewhere, the management of animals in nineteenth-century Canadian cities was intended to accommodate both human and nonhuman animals.[2] Although this accommodation ultimately served human needs and interests, municipal governments still had to consider the protection of the health and the well-being of animals because they were such valuable sources of food and labour. Concerns over domestic animals influenced a wide range of areas of municipal regulation, including public health, street and traffic management, nuisance abatement, garbage removal, public markets, and licensing. Animal management was one of the primary tasks of municipal governments and, to some extent, it shaped the development and expansion of municipal authority in Canada.

The time that municipal governments across the country devoted to thinking about animals and how to regulate their behaviour and their place in cities may seem extraordinary to us now. As early as 1810, the *Rules and Regulations of the Police for the City and Suburbs of Montreal* set out rudimentary limits on the keeping of animals and the management of their waste. Article 7 regulated the disposal of animal waste or other refuse. It prohibited the dumping of such waste into local rivers, streets, or squares, but it allowed for disposal "into the pond behind the Citadel," and in the St. Lawrence River during the winter.[3] Dead animals were a fact of everyday life in nineteenth-century cities, such that the police in Montreal specifically mandated their removal and burial in these early regulations. Residents were liable and could be fined for failing to remove any dead animal left above ground in any part of the city or in local rivers. In spite of this longstanding rule, dead animals on city streets were a persistent problem. In 1880, the Chief of Police for Montreal first reported statistics on the number of dead animals constables removed from the streets. He documented the removal of 6 sheep, 12 goats, 21 horses, 408 cats, and 718 dogs.[4]

These rules also attempted to establish control over urban livestock husbandry practices. While it was permissible to raise cattle, horses, pigs, and other domestic animals in nineteenth-century Montreal, the practice of free-range livestock husbandry was restricted. Free-roaming domestic animals were a common nuisance in early Canadian cities. They could obstruct traffic, injure people (and themselves), create health hazards, and cause property damage. Two articles in the 1810 police regulations for Montreal attempted to partially restrain such practices. The regulations forbade the free running of horses, pigs, and goats. They went one measure further when it came to pigs, an animal considered even more troublesome in cities. Article 14 established that "no person shall keep any hogs within the city or suburb so near to any square, street or lane, as to be offensive to the neighbours or passengers."[5] In spite of these restrictions, humans and their animals regularly violated such rules. Cities across the country thus developed pound systems to capture and impound stray cattle, horses, pigs, and many other animals found roaming the streets. In Montreal, the city police were responsible for impounding free-roaming animals. Between 1863 and 1873, the police captured more than 3,000 animals. Horses and cattle were the most common animals police impounded in this decade, while pigs, goats, sheep, and even geese found their way into police custody.[6]

By the end of the nineteenth century, municipalities continued to permit the keeping of animals in cities, but they placed greater restrictions on urban livestock husbandry. In Toronto, for example, the city council banned all free-range animal husbandry in 1876. The new bylaw amendment prohibited the free roaming of all domestic animals within the city limits. And in 1890, the public health bylaw severely curtailed the keeping of cattle, limiting each household to no more than two cows. While such practices persisted just outside the borders of the city in the periurban environment, such regulations began a process of extirpating livestock from cities.[7]

Even industries that utilized live animals and animal by-products began to feel the pressure to move out of the city by the early decades of the twentieth century. Take, for instance, Toronto's eastern neighbourhoods along Danforth Avenue. Prior to the construction of the Prince Edward Viaduct across the Don River Valley in late 1918, the eastern half of the city was largely cut off from the downtown core. As a result, it was sparsely settled and home to a handful of farms and many of Toronto's so-called noxious industries. Businesses found open air to spew foul smells and local streams and creeks to dispose of waste. It was here that John Harris relocated his family's animal rendering factory, W. Harris & Co., in 1894 (Fig. 1). Until 1922, this enormous 80-acre facility for the processing of animal waste materials operated at the intersection of Danforth and Coxwell. W. Harris & Co. produced a wide range of products used every day in nineteenth-century Canada, including glues, fertilizers, oils, grease, and tallow. Many of the thousands of bodies of horses, pigs, cows, and other animals that lived and worked in Toronto found their way to W. Harris & Co. on the city's east side in what we might see to today as a massive recycling facility.[8]

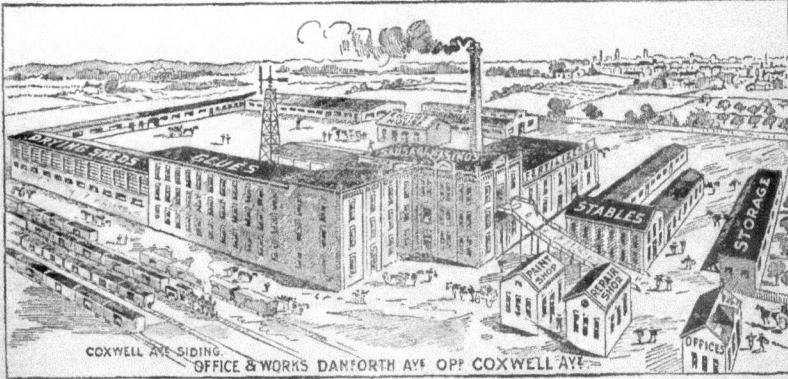

GLUES   W. HARRIS & CO.   Fertilizers

Manufacturers and Cleaners of

SAUSAGE CASINGS

DEALERS IN

Grease, Crackling, Hog and Horse Hair, Horns, Bones, Etc.

W. HARRIS & CO.   TELEPHONE 4386   Correspondence Solicited

DANFORTH AVENUE, TORONTO

11.1 Advertisement for W. Harris & Co., 1900. Originally published in the *Toronto City Directory, 1900*.

The trouble, of course, for the growing city of Toronto was that the Harris family's "dead horse factory," as it was sometimes called, made for an undesirable neighbour. The construction of the Prince Edward Viaduct and the eventual extension of street railway service to Danforth and Coxwell opened up new possibilities for suburban development. Property developers subdivided the area around the Harris factory and began to construct new housing even prior to the completion of the viaduct. Before 1918, the factory stood alone surrounded by empty, undeveloped fields, but within a short period of time, it was suddenly subsumed by a fast-growing streetcar suburb (Fig. 11.1).

The new neighbours quickly objected to the Harris factory, finding it less than appealing. Danforth Glebe Estates, one of the nearby development firms, led local residents and other developers in a lawsuit against W. Harris & Co. in 1918, objecting to foul stenches emitted from the factory. One witness at the hearing into the dispute alleged that the air was so bad,

"I had to scrape my tongue against my teeth to get the odor off." The complainants objected to the foul smells and accused the factory of driving away prospective home buyers. In their suit, they called for an injunction against the Harris factory and $200,000 in compensation for damages.[9] Within a couple of months, John Harris conceded and agreed to relocate the factory to Ashbridge's Bay at the mouth of the Don River and subdivide his land for development.[10]

A few years later, the massive animal rendering facilities were gone, replaced by dozens of detached and semi-detached houses that were connected to the city centre by the extension of electric street railway service to Danforth and Coxwell in 1921. A new residential neighbourhood emerged on the grounds of the former animal by-products factory just as Torontonians began to move away from the use of live domestic animals in the city for transportation and labour. The horse population of Toronto went into decline in the years after 1911, replaced by electric streetcars and automobiles. The history of this small neighbourhood reveals the legacy of that transition in the place of animals in the city. New "horseless" transportation options and the industrialization of dairies and animal slaughter displaced domestic animals from the urban environment in the early decades of the twentieth century. By the 1920s, horses, cows, and pigs were no longer as populous in Toronto as they had been just decades earlier. The residents of this new streetcar suburb on the east side sought further geographic segregation from the sensory evidence of the remaining traces of animals in the city.

These are just some of the many ways that animals shaped urban environments and urban history in Canada. Animals were active agents of change whose behaviours prompted and required various human responses. In fact, humans and animals co-developed cities into hybrid human–animal environments. Although the streets of Canadian cities may no longer be filled with horses and other domestic animals, the influence of nonhuman animal life persists.

What Cities Bring to Animal Studies

In another volume on the history of urban animals, Peter Atkins explores some of the reasons why the study of cities in the twentieth century ignored the role of animals. One reason, he suggests, "is that in the twentieth century the study of cities was anthropocentric, to the extent that the category 'urban' acquired a transcendentally humanist quality in which animals played only bit parts, to satisfy our hunger for companionship or for meat."[11] The reverse may be true in animal history. Critical historical scholarship on animals has only recently come to consider the role of cities (and the environment more broadly) in shaping human–animal relations.[12] Both humans and nonhuman animals coexist within particular environmental contexts. A web of ecological relationships that include other organisms and inorganic components of an ecosystem shapes the relations of humans and animals. This collection situates the study of human–animal relations within the specific historical and ecological contexts of urban environments in Canada.

Several chapters in this collection highlight the role that cities played in influencing human attitudes toward animals. We see this expressed in the presentation and display of animals in circuses, zoos, museums, and aquariums. This spectacle of animals was, in part, related to urbanization. Crowded populations of humans in cities sought new ways to connect with and think about animals. By the end of the nineteenth century, as Canadian urban centres began to experience their most intense period of population growth, various forms of animal display had become popularized across the country. The city was a place for many species. Zoos, circuses, museums, and aquaria in North America can be seen as products of an urban culture that brought the spectacle of large wild animals to towns and cities across Canada and the United States. Elephants, polar bears, penguins, lions, whales, and numerous other species of so-called exotic wild animals joined a collection of more quotidian creatures, including horses, cows, pigs, chickens, rats, mice, raccoons, and squirrels, telling a rather sad and complicated tale of human–animal relations. Christabelle Sethna finds one such example in the story of the death of Jumbo, a captive zoo and circus elephant. Will Knight shows how the museum became a medium to make fish knowable to urban audiences. And Jason Colby explains the changing relationship between people and cetaceans in Vancouver in the context of the city's aquarium.[13] We also see in Darcy Ingram's work the ways in which an urban context came to shape the animal welfare movement in Canada.[14] In all of these case studies, the city itself is implicated profoundly in the relationship between humans and animals. These authors ably show that to understand human–animal relations, historians must consider the environmental contexts in which those relationships occur and change over time.

We can also see how changing ecological conditions in urban environments had effects on the relationship between people and wild animals, especially those animals that took advantage of the opportunities cities provided for food and shelter. Kristoffer Archibald examines the ways in which an extraordinary wild animal, the polar bear, adapted to and engaged with urban ecosystems in Churchill, Manitoba, while George Colpitts captures a similar dynamic in his analysis of the interactions among domesticated dogs, wild animals, and rabies in western Canada. Throughout urban North America, wild opportunist species found cities to be desirable environments in which to thrive and reproduce. The relationship between people and these wild animals changed over time within the context of such ecological interactions. Like the wild polar bear and the unleashed dog, the ever-adaptable Norway rat, for instance, quickly became the scourge of cities across North America. In Alberta, the provincial government sought to purge the creature from its borders, employing a massive public education and extermination program in the mid-twentieth century.[15] In building environments for the mass settlement and congregation of humans, people also inadvertently created suitable habitat for a number of wild animals that adapted to urban conditions. We call these creatures synanthropes: rats, mice, raccoons, seagulls, pigeons, coyotes, and even squirrels.[16] They are the unintended consequences of urban development, the products of both natural and cultural causation that illuminate the hybridity of urban environments. The food waste we produce, the nooks and crannies of concrete infrastructure, and the urban heat island effect create conditions for co-evolution and serve as selective agents for particular wild animals that take advantage of these opportunities for food and shelter. As they have thrived under these conditions, their relationship with humans has changed over time.

As Etienne Benson has shown in the case of the urban squirrel in the United States, the emergence of prominent synanthropes in cities was a historical process. "The urbanization of the gray squirrel in the United States between the mid-nineteenth century and the early twentieth century was," as Benson argues, "an ecological and cultural process that changed the squirrels' ways of life, altered the urban landscape, and adjusted human understandings of nature, the city, and the boundaries of community."[17]

It was the product of culturally induced human labour interacting with the autonomous behaviours of animals. Squirrels appealed to a number of human sensibilities and, thus, people encouraged the growth of squirrel populations, especially in urban parks. In Vancouver, the city park board actively stocked Stanley Park with grey squirrels purchased from a Pennsylvania game company. Over time, squirrels adapted to urban conditions and found ideal shelter and food sources to support a burgeoning population over the course of the nineteenth and twentieth centuries, far beyond the purview of human control. In Stanley Park, grey squirrels established a self-sustaining population and cohabited the park with the native Douglas squirrel. In some cities, however, squirrel populations grew so large many people came to view them as undesirable pests rather than attractive urban amenities. Rachel Poliquin confronts similar issues in the case of the beavers in Stanley Park, animals which found the preserved natural spaces of this large urban park to be suitable habitat to construct dams and lodges, often against the wishes of park officials.[18]

The history of the urban raccoon tells a similar tale.[19] Raccoons have long been part of the ecology of Toronto and its region, but they were far less populous in the late nineteenth and early twentieth centuries than they are today. In 1913, J.H. Faull's *The Natural History of the Toronto Region* described the raccoon as "still not uncommon." As such, human responses toward raccoons in the early twentieth-century city differed greatly from those in the present. For instance, in the early hours of the morning on 21 May 1895, a playful raccoon escaped from its owner and attracted the attention of "a few hundred people" at the corner of Queen and Berkeley Streets, according to one newspaper account. Scrambling up a telephone pole, the liberated creature entertained the crowd of curious onlookers who stood anxious as a man carefully climbed the pole to recapture the raccoon in a bag, narrowly escaping a treacherous fall. Not only was this animal somebody's property (possibly a pet), but it was also remarkable enough to hold the interest of a large number of passersby as well as the man who was willing to risk his own safety to retrieve it.[20]

In Toronto, raccoons were once objects of entertainment, leisure, and fashion. In the late nineteenth and early twentieth centuries, they drew the attention of tourists who came to see them in the city's zoos. In 1907 at Riverdale Zoo, park workers built a separate structure just to house the zoo's raccoon collection. Trappers and ordinary hunters also prized the raccoon. For example, Daniel Mewhort and Thomas Armstrong, two rail-way workers, caught some media attention during the course of a local raccoon hunting excursion in West Toronto when Thomas accidentally shot Daniel, mistaking him for a raccoon. Local hunting reports also identified parts of North Toronto near the Don River Valley as a place "where 'coons are to be had." And for many Torontonians, raccoons could always be found at Eaton's and other department stores where their furs appeared as fashionable luxury goods.[21]

By the early twenty-first century, the raccoon population of Toronto had exploded, and with the population boom came adjustments to human responses toward the raccoon in the city. The enormous quantities of garbage and compost that Toronto residents produced were just a couple of the ecological conditions that facilitated the raccoon's adaptation to the city and its emergence as one of Toronto's predominant synanthropes. Toronto had become so ridden with raccoons that in 2006 local airline company Porter Airlines adopted a cartoon raccoon as its company mascot. As with many other municipalities in North America, the City of Toronto had to develop animal control and urban wildlife policies and programs to manage its raccoons and other wild animals that now thrived in urban environments. Educating the public became a key policy for managing conflicts between people and raccoons in the city.[22]

The relationship between people and raccoons in Toronto today is fraught and complicated. The animals are so common that they are no longer kept in local zoos and their fur is no longer used to manufacture luxury goods. They have become vermin in the eyes of many Toronto residents. Local media sometimes refer to the conflict between people and raccoons as the "War on Raccoons,"[23] indicating the substantial changes that had occurred in the relationship between people and raccoons in Toronto over the course of the twentieth century. While not always at "war," city residents continue to have an ambivalent relationship with raccoons in Toronto, one that found an odd expression in the form of a makeshift memorial for a dead raccoon nicknamed Conrad at the intersection of Yonge and Church Streets in the summer of 2015.[24] That relationship was shaped by the changing ecological conditions of the urban environment. As the city grew, people inadvertently created ample food and shelter for a burgeoning raccoon population. In the eyes of many Toronto residents, the raccoon transformed from a creature of entertainment, leisure, and luxury into a pest that is openly hated or admired grudgingly for its clever adaptability to the urban landscape. The process of that transformation cannot be understood outside of the broader ecological transformations of the urban environment of Toronto.

As this collection makes evident, urban history and animal history have much to offer each other. By thinking about animals in urban environments, we can find richer histories about the places that humans share with other creatures, the ones we exploit, the ones we admire, the ones we loathe, and the ones we ignore. Humans and nonhuman animals are, however, but two actors in an ecological relationship that includes many other organic and inorganic actors. I would like to suggest that this collection offers a compelling case for historians to situate humans and animals within the broader ecological contexts in which their interactions transpire and within the complex web of relationships that constitute an ecosystem. The field of animal history, which seeks to explore human–animal relations, does so in a limited manner when it excludes environmental considerations. This is where environmental history can expand scholarship in animal history. By examining human–animal relations within the urban context, this collection casts light on those broader ecological relationships and sets new directions for the field of animal history. This collection points toward the need for historians to emphasize that relations of humans and animals are shaped by a web of ecological relationships that include other organisms and inorganic components of an ecosystem.

New Directions in Urban History and Animal History

In bridging urban history and animal history, this collection sets forth new avenues for research in both fields of study. The essays in this collection clearly show how scholars can expand our understanding of urban development and change over time by moving beyond an exclusively anthropocentric perspective of cities. Humans and animals both played significant parts in urbanization, creating multi-species environments. There continues to be a need for further research in this area. While horses, cattle, pigs, and chickens were populous and influential in urban development, how did these animals interact within growing cities of the nineteenth and twentieth centuries? What effects did their interactions have on urban planning and the development of regulation and infrastructure? How did federal and provincial authorities interact with municipal governments in the regulation of animals in Canadian cities? How did municipal governments go about extirpating livestock husbandry from within their boundaries? What effects did this have on their regional hinterlands? What were the regional differences in approaches to dealing with urban animals across Canada from the Atlantic provinces to central Canada to the prairies and the Pacific coast? How did towns and cities confront animals in northern environments of the Subarctic and Arctic?

The history of animal diseases, especially zoonotic diseases (those which can pass from animals to humans), is another area that can expand scholarship in urban and animal history. As Dean, Hustak, and Colpitts show, tetanus, bovine tuberculosis, and rabies are just three examples of zoonotic diseases that emerged within the context of urban environments in the nineteenth and twentieth centuries with consequences for the development of public health. Research might also explore other diseases, such as equine influenza, glanders, and bovine spongiform encephalopathy, to see what other ways animal diseases may have influenced the development of public health policy in urban centres in Canada.

Archibald's polar bears and Colpitts' coyotes, wolves, and foxes reveal the tantalizing possibilities for further explorations of synanthropes in urban and animal history. Pigeons, seagulls, rats, squirrels, and raccoons are some of the most populous urban animals in Canada today, yet their histories have gone relatively unexplored. Canadian historians have devoted more attention to charismatic wildlife species, such as bison, caribou, deer, and moose. Given the daily experiences of so many millions of Canadians with urban animals, the interactions of humans and synanthropes will likely yield important new insights into human–animals relations. Given that the most common domestic animals in Canadian urban environments today are pets (mostly cats and dogs), historians also need to look at the environmental histories of pet keeping in Canada. This too would highlight important aspects of the most common daily interactions of people and animals.

Further research is needed in Canadian urban history on the place of Indian reserves and First Nations people in urban development. Here too we may find new insights into the historical relationships between humans and nonhuman animals. Some of Canada's largest urban environments developed adjacent to (and eventually encircled) large Indian reserves. In Vancouver, for instance, the federal government established reserves at Musqueam, Kitsilano, and Homulchesan (Capilano), now located in the most urbanized environments of western Canada. In the late nineteenth century, Squamish people living at Homulchesan began to raise introduced livestock animals, including horses and cattle, to serve the growing lumbering operations on Burrard Inlet. This is just one example of the complex relationships among Indigenous people, livestock animals, and emerging urban environments.

Finally, the essays in this collection point to new possibilities for research on the spectacle of animals in urban environments. Colby's analysis of cetaceans in the Vancouver Aquarium, Knight's look at the national fish museum, and Sethna's sad tale of Jumbo all speak to the ways in which animals in captivity have had a long and complicated urban history. Nearly all of the major metropolitan centres in Canada have hosted large zoos with diverse populations of exotic species, from toucans in Toronto to penguins in Vancouver and giraffes in Calgary. The display of zoo animals in Canadian cities was part of an international phenomenon of urban spectacle dating back to the late decades of the eighteenth century. What form this spectacle took in Canada and how it changed over time in response to both local demands and international influences has yet to be examined in a sustained historical study.

This collection generates new questions about human–animal relations within the context of urban environments. This should inspire new research and result in expanded knowledge of the complicated ways in which the ecological interactions among humans, animals, and environments have been shaped by mutually constitutive forces of natural and cultural change over time.

Notes

1   I draw from the arguments of Richard C. Hoffmann and his use of the interaction model from the school of social ecology in Vienna. This is outlined in the introduction to *An Environmental History of Medieval Europe* (Cambridge, UK: Cambridge University Press, 2014), 1–20. Hoffmann's model for environmental history provides scholars with a means to avoid what Martin Melosi calls "the nature/built environment nexus," a belief that there are two separate

environments, one natural and the other artificial. Instead, both Melosi and Hoffmann call upon environmental historians to think about nature and culture as mutually constitutive (but autonomous) realms. See Martin Melosi, "Humans, Cities, and Nature: How Do Cities Fit in the Material World," *Journal of Urban History* 36, no. 1 (2010): 3–21.

2   See Sean Kheraj, "Living and Working with Domestic Animals in Nineteenth-Century Toronto," in *Urban Explorations: Environmental Histories of the Toronto Region*, ed. L. Anders Sandberg, Stephen Bocking, Colin Coates, and Ken Cruikshank (Hamilton, ON: L.R. Wilson Institute for Canadian History, 2013), 120–40, and Sean Kheraj, "Animals and Urban Environments: Managing Domestic Animals in Nineteenth-Century Winnipeg," in *Eco-Cultural Networks and the British Empire: New Views on Environmental History*, ed. James Beattie, Edward Melillo, and Emily O'Gorman (London: Bloomsbury, 2015), 263–88.

3   *Rules and Regulations of Police for the City and Suburbs of Montreal* (Montreal: 1810), 14–16.

4   *Annual Report of the Chief of Police for the Year 1880* (Montreal: 1881), 14.

5   *Rules and Regulations of Police for the City and Suburbs of Montreal* (Montreal: 1810), 14.

6   See *Annual Report of the Chief of Police* for the years 1863 to 1873.

7   By-law 474, "A By-law to provide for the appointment of Pound-keepers, and to regulate the Pounds in the City of Toronto,"

25 September 1876; By-law 2477, "A By-Law relating to the Local Board of Health," 13 January 1890, *By-Laws of the City of Toronto, 1834 to 1890* (Toronto: Roswell & Hutchison, 1890).

8   Barbara Myrvold, *The Danforth in Pictures: A Brief History of the Danforth* (Toronto: Toronto Public Libraries, 1979), 16.

9   "Could 'Scrape' Off Smell," *Toronto Daily Star*, 27 March 1918, 5.

10   "Dispense with Odors by Utilizing Residue," *Toronto Daily Star*, 19 July 1918, 4.

11   Peter Atkins, "Introduction," in *Animal Cities: Beastly Urban Histories*, ed. Peter Atkins (Burlington, VT: Ashgate, 2012), 2.

12   Several recent publications in urban environmental history demonstrate a new focus on the role of cities in historical animal studies. See, for instance, Jennifer Mason, *Civilized Creatures: Urban Animals, Sentimental Culture, and American Literature, 1850–1900* (Baltimore: Johns Hopkins University Press, 2005); Clay McShane and Joel Tarr, *The Horse in the City: Living Machines in the Nineteenth Century* (Baltimore: Johns Hopkins University Press, 2007); Catherine McNeur, *Taming Manhattan: Environmental Battles in the Antebellum City* (Cambridge, MA: Harvard University Press, 2014).

13   I have written about similar issues and the ways in which urban experiences with animals can shape perceptions of wildlife in Sean Kheraj, "Demonstration Wildlife: Negotiating the Animal Landscape of Vancouver's Stanley Park, 1888–1996," *Environment and History* 18, no. 4 (2012): 497–527.

14 For more on Ingram's work see Darcy Ingram, "Beastly Measures: Animal Welfare, Civil Society, and State Policy in Victorian Canada," *Journal of Canadian Studies* 47, no. 1 (2013): 221–52.

15 See Lianne McTavish and Jingjing Zheng, "Rats in Alberta: Looking at Pest-Control Posters from the 1950s," *Canadian Historical Review* 92, no. 3 (2011): 515–46.

16 Dawn Day Biehler explores the history of urban synanthropes in nineteenth- and twentieth-century America in *Pests in the City: Flies, Bedbugs, Cockroaches, and Rats* (Seattle: University of Washington Press, 2013).

17 Etienne Benson, "The Urbanization of the Eastern Gray Squirrel in the United States," *Journal of American History* 100, no. 3 (2013): 692.

18 Sean Kheraj, *Inventing Stanley Park: An Environmental History* (Vancouver: University of British Columbia Press, 2013), 129.

19 See Lauren Corman, "Getting Their Hands Dirty: Raccoons, Freegans, and Urban 'Trash'," *Journal for Critical Animal Studies* 9, no. 3 (2011): 28–61.

20 J.H. Faull, *The Natural History of the Toronto Region* (Toronto: Canadian Institute, 1913), 210; "A New Coon in Town," *Toronto Daily Star*, 21 May 1895, 4.

21 "Coons for the Zoo," *Toronto Daily Star*, 28 September 1903, 1; "At Riverdale Park," *Toronto Daily Star*, 22 August 1907, 7; "Man Mistaken for a Coon," *Toronto Daily Star*, 1 September 1908, 1, 3; "Trappers in Ontario," *Toronto Daily Star*, 10 February 1906, 21.

22 "Introducing Mr. Porter," Porter Airlines, https://www.flyporter.com/about/News-Release-Details?id=ae2c07e5-0675-4e0f-8b59-f559c3b679f1&culture=en-CA (accessed 31 July 2015).

23 "Man Charged after Raccoons Attacked," *Toronto Star*, 2 June 2011, A1.

24 "#DeadRaccoonTO Honoured By Toronto with Sidewalk Vigil," CBC News, http://www.cbc.ca/news/trending/deadraccoon-to-honoured-by-toronto-with-sidewalk-vigil-1.3146036 (accessed 20 October 2015).

Contributors

KRISTOFFER ARCHIBALD studies modern environmental history and is particularly interested in changing interpretations of the natural environment. He has a doctorate in History from Concordia University and is a research associate at the Gorsebrook Research Institute in Halifax. His dissertation research focuses on how industrial pollution was perceived within the deindustrializing city of Sydney, Nova Scotia.

JASON COLBY is associate professor of history at the University of Victoria. He is currently completing a book on killer whale captivity and environmental politics in the 1960s and 1970s, entitled *Orca: How the Quest to Capture Killer Whales Transformed Our View of the Ocean's Greatest Predator* (forthcoming, Oxford University Press).

GEORGE COLPITTS teaches environmental history at the University of Calgary. His books include *Game in the Garden: A Human History of Wildlife in Western Canada to 1940* (2002) and *Pemmican Empire: Food, Trade, and the Last Bison Hunts in the North American Plains, 1780–1882* (2015).

JOANNA DEAN teaches animal history and environmental history at Carleton University as an associate professor. She is currently writing a book on Ottawa's street trees.

CARLA HUSTAK is an independent researcher in the history of gender and sexuality. She has a doctorate in History from the University of Toronto and held a Mellon Post-Doctoral Fellowship at the University of Illinois at Urbana-Champaign. She has published articles in various journals such as the *Journal of the History of Sexuality, the Transnational Journal of American Studies, Subjectivity*, and *Gender, Place and Culture: a feminist journal of geography*. She has a forthcoming book with Duke University Press tentatively titled, *Radical Intimacies: The Politics of Love in the Transatlantic Sex Reform Movement, 1900-1930*.

DARCY INGRAM is a Senior Fellow with the Centre on Governance in the Faculty of Social Sciences at the University of Ottawa. He is the author of *Wildlife, Conservation, and Conflict in Quebec, 1840-1914* (2013), and is currently working on governance issues in connection with the environmental and animal welfare/rights movements in Canada and beyond.

SEAN KHERAJ is an associate professor of Canadian and environmental history in the Department of History at York University. He is the author of *Inventing Stanley Park: An Environmental History* (UBC Press, 2013). He is also the director and editor-in-chief of the Network in Canadian History and Environment. His work can be found at http://seankheraj.com.

WILLIAM KNIGHT is curator of agriculture and fisheries with the Canada Science and Technology Museums Corporation in Ottawa. He wrote his doctoral dissertation on the Canadian Fisheries Museum, and is currently researching a book on the role of fish introductions and reactions to invasive species in North American fisheries management.

SHERRY OLSON is Professor of Geography at McGill University and a member of the Centre interuniversitaire d'Études québécoises (CIÉQ). She authored a book-length environmental history of Baltimore and co-authored with Patricia Thornton a social history titled *Peopling the North American City, Montreal 1840-1900* (MQUP, 2011). Recent papers address environmental challenges of city-building, the competition for street-space, and the problem of "pinning to the map" census families and their nineteenth-century moves.

RACHEL POLIQUIN is a freelance writer and curator engaged in all things orderly and disorderly in the natural world. She has a doctorate in early modern natural history from the University of British Columbia and a post-doctorate from the Massachusetts Institute of Technology in the cultures of taxidermy. She is author of *The Breathless Zoo: Taxidermy and the Cultures of Longing* (2012) and *Beaver* (2015) and writes for *The New York Times*. Her curatorial works include "Ravishing Beasts: The Strangely Alluring World of Taxidermy" for the Museum of Vancouver, and the permanent vertebrate exhibits for the Beaty Museum of Biodiversity.

CHRISTABELLE SETHNA is an historian and Associate Professor teaching in the Institute of Feminist and Gender Studies, University of Ottawa. She has published widely on the history of sex education, contraception and abortion in Canada, focusing on the transnational dimensions of this research and its impact on women's sexual and reproductive health. Her framework emerges out of postcolonial studies and the intersectionality of gender, race, class and sexuality. Her chapter in this volume represents the evolution of this framework to consider the relationship between non-human and human animals.

Jacket Artist

MARY ANNE BARKHOUSE was born in Vancouver, BC, and belongs to the Nimpkish band, Kwakiutl First Nation. Working with a variety of materials, Barkhouse examines environmental concerns and Indigenous culture through the use of animal imagery. Her work has exhibited widely across Canada and the United States and is in many major collections such as the National Gallery of Canada, with public art installations located throughout Ontario.

Index

Page numbers in bold refer to illustrations

A

personalization of, 303
as representations, 146, 286
ANT. *See* Actor Network Theory (ANT)
anthropomorphism, 35, 42, 91
anti-cruelty legislation, 96–97, 102–5
anti-whaling campaigns, 288, 300
Antitoxin Laboratory. *See* Connaught Laboratories
antitoxin production, 162, 163–65, 169–77
antivaccination movements, 167–69
antivivisection movements, 4, 95, 97, 168–69
aquariums, 116, 118–20, 128–29. *See also* Vancouver Aquarium
Archibald, Kristoffer, 17, 18, 316
Arctic foxes, 219, 230. *See also* foxes
Arnup, Katherine, 167
Arstingall, George, 36
arts and fashion, 3, 104
assemblage, 7, 8, 156, 157, 159
Atkins, Peter, 9, 191, 314–15
avian flu, 78
Avon company, 210
Ayrshire cows, 202–3

B

Baartman, Saartjie, 31–32
Ballantyne, A.A., 226, 227, 228, 230, 243
Ballentine, Mr. (of Hamilton), 197
Bands of Mercy, 92, 98
Banff Advisory Council, 235, 236–38, 239, 241, 242, 243
Banff National Park
animal controls, 231–35
bears in, 262
domestic animals in, 220–21, 235–40
rabies education, 228, 230
wildlife takes over, 240–42
Banton, J.F., 168
Baratay, Eric, 8
Barlett, Abraham, 32–33
Barnum and Bailey Circus, 34, 35–37, 38

Barnum, P.T., 33–34, 35–37, 39–40, 42
Barrett, Bob, 46–47
Barrett, David, 300
Bauer, Josef, 291
bears, 226–27, 241, 242, 244, 262. *See also* polar bears
Beauchamp, Joseph, 67
Beauchamp, Pierre family, 71–72
Beaver Lake, 144, **145**, 148, 150–53
beavers
characteristics of, 10, 17, **140**, 142–43, 145–46, 149–50
in Stanley Park, 139, 144, 147–48, 150–53
Behring, Emil Adolf von, 162
Belcher, S.D., 199
belugas, display of, 118, 305
Belzoni, Battista, 42, 45
Benson, Etienne, 9
Berger, John, 3
Bergh, Henry, 168
Berreville, Oliver, 211
Biehler, Dawn, 9
Biel, Alice Wondrak, 256, 262
Bigg, Michael, 293
birding, 259
birds, made into hats, 104
Bjossa (killer whale), 301, 304
blackfish. *See* killer whales
Blackfish (film), 305
Bliss, Michael, 167
Boer War, use of horses in, 76
Boston Aquarial Gardens, 118
Bourgeois, Louise, 3
Bourniot, Mrs. (of Ottawa), 194
bovine growth hormones, 190, 210
bovine tuberculosis, 244
Bowman, Charles, 66–67
Bradbury, Bettina, 15
Braidotti, Rosi, 6
breast milk, 189, 204–5, 209–10
breastfeeding, 189, 194, 203–5, 208

breeds and breeding
cows, 202
horses, 71, 76
Brick Top (serum horse), 175–76
British Army, tetanus prevention in, 165–66
British Columbia
cougar control, 15
whale capture opposition, 300
British Columbia Society for Prevention of Cruelty to Animals (BCSPCA), 100
Bronnum, Winston, 45
Brown, Adam, 100, 102–3, 105
Brown, Karen, 9
Bruce, Sir David, 165
Buckland, Frank, 117
Burdett-Coutts, Angela (Baroness), 93, 95
Burich, Samuel, 291
Burt, Jonathan, 4

C

Calgary, AB, anti-rabies campaigns, 227, 228, 230
Calgary Herald, on anti-rabies measures, 232, *233*, 234
calves, in vaccine production, 163–64, 166, 167, 168
Cambridge Bay, NT, 219
Canada. *See also* Canadian Fisheries Museum
animal anti-cruelty debates, 102–5
animal control programs, 226
antitoxin funding, 163, 166
beaver as symbol of, 146
dairy business reports, 198
fisheries department, 115–16, 117, 120–21, 126–27, 128–29, 132–33, 134, 291
historiographies of, 8–12, 14–19
milk quality reform, 198–200
rabies crisis, 219–20, 223, 224, 232
tourism promotion, 258, 268–69
Canada Day, 47

Canadian Anti Vivisection League, 169
Canadian Fisheries Museum, 116, 123–24, 126, 127–28, 129–32, 133–34
Canadian Fisherman, on fisheries museum, 133
Canadian Geographic, on Churchill polar bears, 271
Canadian Horse and His Diseases, The, 158–59
Canadian Society for Prevention of Cruelty to Animals (CSPCA), 90, 93–96, 97–98, 101
Canadian Wildlife Service, 269
capitalist treatments, of human and cow's milk, 190, 209–11
Careless, J.M.S, 14
Carle, Antonio, 160
Carnegie Corporation, 198
Carson, Rachel, 192, 291
Carter, Sam, 219
carters
housing and stables, 68, 70
Montreal strike, 15, 66
social and economic opportunities, 58–61, 71–74
Castonguay, Stéphane, 15
cat owners, on licensing and leashes, 237–38
catarrh of horses, 78
cats, control programs, 220, 221, 225, 232, 234, 237–398, **240**
Center for Biological Diversity, on polar bears, 274
cetaceans, 7, 290–91, 293–94, 295–98, 305
Check List of the Fishes of the Dominion of Canada and Newfoundland, 131
Chicago Exposition (1893), 123, 126, 128
chickens, studies of, 9
children. *See also* infant health
in animal welfare narratives, 92–93
health and illnesses, 157–58, 192, 228
humane education programs for, 93, 95
milk consumption by, 201–2, 204
protection of, 99, 100

environmental history perspectives, 11–12, 15–16, 18
Era of Biologicals, The (Thom), 174
Erickson, Bruce, 5
Eskimo Museum, 274
Esquimalt Navy frogmen, 292
Ethnological Congress (circus show), 36–37, 38
eugenics, cow breeding as, 202–3, 209
Evans, D. (of Hamilton), 196
evolutionary theory and animal welfare movement, 91

F

Fahrni, Magda, 16
farms
    dairy, 199–203, 210–11
    dogs on, 230–31
    in serum production, 163–65, 166–67, 168, 169–77
fashions with animals, 3, 104, 318
Feazel, Charles, 272
feminism in Victorian Canada, 87–89, 102, 107–8
Ferguson, Duncan, 198, 199
ferries, horse-driven, 62
fetishes, animal specimens as, 40
Fiamengo, Janice, 5
Field, BC, rabies crisis, 220, 232, 236, 240
Finna (killer whale), 301, 304
firefighting, horse-driven, 62
Fireweed (Vancouver band), 298
First Nations. *See* Indigenous peoples
First World War
    horses used in, 76, 163
    tetanus measures, 165–66, 169, 174, 175–76
fish culture and hatcheries, 116–18, 119–24, 129
fish exhibitions, 115, 116, 118–20, 128–29
fish taxidermy, 124–26
fisheries. *See also* Canadian Fisheries Museum

exhibitions and museums, 116, 117, 120–22, 128–29, 134, 148
    killer whales as threat to, 290–91, 293
FitzGerald, John Gerald, 162–63, 166, 172, 175
Flach, E.H., 43
food study historians, 15–16
Ford, Harrison, 49
Ford, John, 303
Fort Churchill, MB, founding of, 258, 259
Fort Fitzgerald, AB, rabies crisis, 219
Fort Vermilion, AB, rabies crisis, 219, 222–23, 228, 230–31
fox hunt historians, 15
foxes, 219, 222, 226–27, 228, 230, 244
France
    fish culture, 116
    horsemanship culture, 58
Franklin, Dwight, 125
freakery, 30, 49, 55
Free Willy (film), 303–4
Fudge, Erica, 8
fur trade and furs, 149, 258, 259, 318
Fur Trade in Canada, The (Innis), 10

G

game hunting, 30, 40–41
Garland-Thompson, Rosemarie, 33
Gatineau-Ottawa rabies controls, 225
Gaynor, Andrea, 9
gender in animal welfare movement, 87–91
General Motors, 211
genetic modification of cows, 210
Geological Survey of Canada museum, 131
Georgia Straight, 294, 297, 298
Gilson, Geoffrey, 16
glanders, 77, 79–80
Gooderham, Colonel A.E., 163
Gordon Point, MB, 270
Gorgeous Beasts (Landes), 149
Gosse, Philip Henry, 118

Grand Trunk Railway (GTR), 30, 37, 65, 66

Grande Menagerie animal tour, 31

Great Moments in Pharmacy (painting series), 174

Greene, Ann Norton, 58, 67

Greenpeace, 286, 298–99, 299–300, 301

Grey Owl, 146

Grier, Katherine C., 8

Griffin, Ted, 285, 286, 294

Grisdale, J.H., 199, 202–3

growth hormones, 190, 210

GTR. *See* Grand Trunk Railway (GTR)

Guattari, Felix, 7, 156

guinea pigs, as research animals, 163, 182n30

Guravich, Dan, 270

Gwynne, Julia, 100

H

Hackett, Paul, 16

Haida, and killer whales, 286, 290

Halifax fishery exhibit, 128

Halkett, Andrew, 116, 127–28, 129–30, 131, 133–34

Hamilton Dairy, 201

Hamilton, ON, milk and dairy reform, 191, **195**, 196–97, 206, 207, 208

Hamilton Society for Prevention of Cruelty to Animals, 100

Hansen, Bert, 174

Hanson Island, BC, 297, 299

Haraway, Donna, 5, 8

Harris, Cole, 16

Harris, John, 312–14

Haslam, Andrew, 104

hay, **63**, 66, 70, 72, 75

Heap, Margaret, 15

Henry, W.J., 126, 127

Herman (transgenic dairy bull), 210

Herns, Frank, 199

High Modernism, in rabies control, 227

Hippocrates, accounts of tetanus by, 156–57

Hird, Myra, 5

Holstein-Friesland cows, 202

Holt, L.E., 206–7

Hornaday, William T., 124–25

Horne's Zoological Arena, 145, 146

horse boats, 62

horse diseases, 77–78, 79–80, 158–59

horse manure, 66–67, 159, 161–62

horsemanship culture, 58, **64**

horsepower, 63–64, 68

horses. *See also* workhorses
  in antitoxin production, 17, 163–65, 170–77
  breeding of, 71, 76
  health and illnesses of, 76–80, 158–59, 160–61
  as members of working class, 4
  modern urban, 57, 81

horsey trades, 58–66, 71–73

Hovorka, Alice, 9

Howells, Philip, 9

Hribal, Jason, 4, 8

Hudson's Bay Company, 146, 258, 259

human identity, 5–6, 7

human slavery, as parallel to animal capture, 30, 32

humane societies, 90–91, 93, 98–101. *See also* Toronto Humane Society (THS)

Hunter, Bob, 300

hunting. *See also* trapping
  exotic game, 30, 40–41
  polar bear, 258, 259
  raccoon, 317–18
  sanctioned, 226–27, 231, 234–35, 241–42, 257

Hustak, Carla, 17, 18, 310

Hyak/Tung Jen (killer whale), 296, 300, 301, 303

hydrophobia. *See* rabies

I

Sydenham, Charles Poulett Thomson, Lord, 157
Sydney Herald, on tetanus horses, 170
synanthropes, 316–19, 320
synurbanization, 13

T

Talon (tetanus victim), 158
Tambo (circus boy), 37
Tarr, Joel, 58, 67, 162
Tarry, Doug, 44–45, 46, 48
taxidermy
    of fish, 120, 124–26, 131–32
    of Jumbo, 40, 42
Taylor, Joseph, 115
tetanus, 155–61, 163, 169–78
Thom, Robert A., 174
Thomas, Keith, 4
Thompson, Frances M.L., 58
Thornton, Patricia, 16
THS. *See* Toronto Humane Society (THS)
Tisdale, David, 102–3, 104, 105
Tlingit and killer whales, 290
Tom Thumb (elephant), 38
Toronto Humane Society (THS), **88**, 91, 99–100, 102, 105–6
Toronto Industrial Exhibition displays, 117–18, 119, 120, 132–33
Toronto, ON
    animals in, 15, 161, 225, 312, 314, 317–19
    anti-vaccination protests, 167, 168
    dairy regulations, 191, 193, 197, 207
Toronto Star
    animal stories, 12
    antitoxin and vaccination stories, 169, 171, 175
tourism
    economic value, 17, 286, 288
    and Indigenous influences, 273–74
    rabies control and, 225, 232, 233–34, 238

wildlife experiences, 255, 256, 258–59, 262, 268–72, 274–75
toxicity, in milk, 192
trade
    in horses, 76, 77
    in wildlife, 30, 31, 49, 145–46, 148, 294, 298
transnationalism
    of animal exchanges, 8–9
    of dairy industry, 202
    of milk quality reform, 190, 198, 208
transspecies urban theory, 14
trap-shooting prohibition debates, 102, 104
trapping, 149, 222, 226–27, 237–38, 265, 266
treatment of animals. *See also* animal welfare movements
    parallels with slavery, 32
trophy hunting, 30, 40–41
trout, in aquarium display, 119
tuberculin testing, 200
Tucker Jones, Ryan, 8
Tufts University, donations of animal specimens to, 40, 42
Tundra Buggies, **269**, 270, 271
Tung Jen/Hyak (killer whale), 296, 300, 301, 303
Turner, James, 4

U

Underground Railway, 37
United States
    animal welfare movement, 87
    dog vaccinations, 224
    killer whale captures, 300–301
    milk quality reform, 190, 198–99, 208
    serum production, 167, 168, 174, 176
    species at risk classifications, 274
    tetanus fatality rates, 159
    wildlife depopulation programs, 226
University of British Columbia killer whale research, 295–97

University of Toronto
   antitoxin production, 169, 171–72
   immunology science at, 162
urban design, influence of animals in, 17, 57, 67–71, 80–81, 310–14
urban reforms
   public health, 190–92, 194, 204–5, 206–9
   sanitary, 191, 193–97, 209, 225
urban spaces. *See also* polar bears; urban design
   animal-human accommodations in, 1–2, 8–9, 12–16, 90, 149, 243, 257, 287
   disease threats in, 228, 230, 244
US Army Air Corps, 258

V

vaccine farms, 166–67
vaccines and vaccinations
   dual role of horses, 80
   public concerns about, 167–69
   rabies, 222, 224, 225, 232
   sled dog program, 226
Valenze, Deborah, 211
Vancouver Aquarium
   anti-whaling endorsements, 288–89, 299–300
   killer whales in, 285–86, 287, 291, 293–94, 295–97, 298, 301–5
Vancouver, BC
   anti-whaling support, 300
   countercultural activities in, 286, 294, 296
   EXPO '86, 301–2
   fishery exhibits, 134
   founding of, 141
   killer whale holding, 292–93
   whale and dolphin bylaw, 304
Vancouver Boat, Trailer, and Sport Show, 285, 293
Vancouver Exhibition
   fishery exhibit, 128–29
   request for beavers, 148

Vancouver, George, 141
Vancouver Humane Society, 302
Velten, Helen, 9
Verneuil, Aristide, 160–61
veterinary medicine
   rabies control, 227, 230, 231
   studies and profession, 74, 75, 76–77, 80
Victoria Bridge construction, 63
Victoria Memorial Museum, 130–31, 133
Victorian Order of Nurses, 208
vivisection historians, 15
von Behring, Emil Adolf, 162

W

W. Harris & Co., 312–14
Walter the Whale. *See* Skana
Ward, Henry, 40
wardens
   Rocky Mountain parks, 231, 232, 234, 235–42, 243
   Stanley Park, 150, 151, 153
wars, and disease risks, 76, 157, 163
Washington State, opposition to whale captures, 300
waste
   dead animal disposal, 311
   manure, 66–67, 159, 161–62
Wawa, ON monument, 45
Weil, Kari, 6
Wells, K.F., 220
Wentworth Dairy, 193, **194**
West Nile virus, 244
Whale for the Killing, A (Mowat), 299
whale shows, 118, 285–86, 287, 289, 301–2, 304
whales. *See also* killer whales
   as agents of history, 8
   skeletons in museums, 132, 134
   symbolism of, 287, 299, 300
whaling industry, 290, 299. *See also* anti-whaling campaigns
Whalley, M.E., 205–6